Cambridge studies in medieval life and thought

JOHN OF WALES

Cambridge studies in medieval life and thought
Fourth series

General Editor:
J. C. HOLT
Professor of Medieval History and
Master of Fitzwilliam College, University of Cambridge

Advisory Editors:
C. N. L. BROOKE
Dixie Professor of Ecclesiastical History and
Fellow of Gonville and Caius College,
University of Cambridge

D. E. LUSCOMBE
Professor of Medieval History, University of Sheffield

The series Cambridge Studies in Medieval Life and Thought was inaugurated by G. G. Coulton in 1920. Professor J. C. Holt now acts as General Editor of a Fourth Series, with Professor C. N. L. Brooke and Professor D. E. Luscombe as Advisory Editors. The series aims to bring together outstanding work by medieval scholars over a wide range of human endeavour extending from political economy to the history of ideas.

JOHN OF WALES

A Study of the Works and Ideas of a Thirteenth-Century Friar

JENNY SWANSON

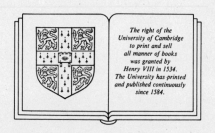

The right of the
University of Cambridge
to print and sell
all manner of books
was granted by
Henry VIII in 1534.
The University has printed
and published continuously
since 1584.

CAMBRIDGE UNIVERSITY PRESS

CAMBRIDGE

NEW YORK   NEW ROCHELLE   MELBOURNE   SYDNEY

Published by the Press Syndicate of the University of Cambridge
The Pitt Building, Trumpington Street, Cambridge CB2 1RP
32 East 57th Street, New York, NY 10022, USA
10 Stamford Road, Oakleigh, Melbourne 3166, Australia

First published 1989

Printed in Great Britain at the University Press, Cambridge

British Library cataloguing in publication data
Swanson, Jenny
John of Wales: a study of the works and ideas of a thirteenth-century friar
1. Franciscans. John of Wales
I. Title
271'.3'024

Library of Congress cataloguing in publication data
Swanson, Jenny, 1958–
John of Wales: a study of the works and ideas of a thirteenth-century friar/
Jenny Swanson.
p.   cm. – (Cambridge studies in medieval life and thought: 4th ser., 10)
Bibliography.
Includes Index.
ISBN 0 521 33074 2
1. John, of Wales, 13th cent. I. Title. II. Series.
BR 754. J64S93 1988
271'.3'024–dc19   88–18660

ISBN 0 521 33074 2

For David d'Avray, who began it all,
Beryl Smalley, who gave valuable help along the way,
and my husband Alistair.
Without them this book could never
have been written.

CONTENTS

Contents

ACKNOWLEDGEMENTS

My deepest thanks go to David d'Avray, who first cured me of my undergraduate notion that medieval history was dull, and has been a tower of strength ever since. He directed me to Beryl Smalley, who proved to be the perfect supervisor for the thesis upon which this book is based: I miss her more than I can say. After her death, Christopher Brooke and David Luscombe provided generous moral support and helped me in a number of ways, not least in the preparation of this book. I am grateful to the British Academy, which funded the manuscript study in Europe which formed the basis of chapter 8, and to the Warburg Institute in London, whose timely award of a short-term Frances Yates Fellowship provided me with congenial surroundings in which to complete the preparation of this text.

ABBREVIATIONS

AFH	*Archivum Franciscanum Historicum*
AFP	*Archivum Fratrum Praedicatorum*
AHDLMA	*Archives d'histoire doctrinale et littéraire du Mayen Age.*
Ars Praed.	*Ars Praedicandi*
BBM	Antonius Sanderus, *Bibliotheca Belgica Manuscripta* (1641)
BL	British Library
BN	Bibliothèque Nationale
Brev. de Sap.	*Breviloquium de Sapientia sive Philosophia Sanctorum*
Brev. de Virt.	*Breviloquium de Virtutibus Antiquorum Principum et Philosophorum*
Collat. in Ioh.	*Collationes in Evangelium S. Iohannis*
Collat. super Matt.	*Collationes super Matthaeum*
Communiloq.	*Communiloquium sive Summa Collationum*
Compendiloq.	*Compendiloquium de Vitis Illustrium Philosophorum et de Dictis Moralibus Eorundem*
De Poen. Inf.	*De Poenis Inferni*
De Poenit.	*De Poenitentia*
EHR	*English Historical Review*
Exp. in Ioh.	*Expositio in Evangelium Iohannis*
Exp. Reg. OFM	*Expositio Regulae Ordinis Fratrum Minorum*
Legiloq.	*Legiloquium* or *Tractatus de Decem Preceptis*
Moniloq.	*Moniloquium*
Ord. Vit. R.	*Ordinarium seu Alphabetum Vitae Religiosae*
Post. in Apoc.	*Postilla in Apocalypsim*
Serm. de Evang.	*Sermones de Evangeliis Dominicalibus et Quadragesimales*
Serm. de Temp.	*Sermones de Tempore*

Abbreviations

Summa Iust.	*Summa Iustitiae* or *Tractatus de Septem Viciis*
Super Orat. Dom.	*Expositio super Orationem Dominicam*
Tract. Exemp.	*Tractatus Exemplorum*
TRHS	*Transactions of the Royal Historical Society*

INTRODUCTION

The appearance and growth of the Orders of friars, and the rise of the universities, are central features of the thirteenth century. The close link between friars and universities has long been recognised. The Franciscan and Dominican Orders, founded early in the century, quickly established the aim of providing informed preaching to the population as a whole. Informed preaching had as its prerequisite informed teaching: the friars moved rapidly into the university sphere, and soon established themselves at the heart of it. Franciscans and Dominicans alike organised their own schools and teachers, but their members played a major part in wider university life.

It is against this background that we must set the British Franciscan scholar John of Wales, who arrived in Paris from Oxford by early 1270, if not before. He was already an established scholar, having been lector to the Oxford Franciscans a decade previously. He must have been acquainted with fellow-Franciscans like Roger Bacon, John Pecham and Bonaventure. Bacon, who joined the Oxford Franciscans in *c.* 1257, had been John of Wales' junior at the Oxford convent for many years, and some of his Paris visits may have overlapped with John's. Pecham and Bonaventure were already resident in Paris when John of Wales arrived. John appears to have been close to Pecham, who as Archbishop of Canterbury later summoned him from France to act as his emissary to Llewellyn of Wales. John would probably have attended Paris sermons (and perhaps lectures) by both these fellow-Franciscans, and perhaps also by Dominicans such as Thomas Aquinas. They in turn may have attended his own sermons. This group of men walked the same streets at the same time, used the same buildings and facilities and had many of the same interests. Yet today the other men are well known, their importance long established, while until recently John had largely fallen into obscurity.

This can be accounted for by the nature of his works. While St Thomas Aquinas and St Bonaventure mainly produced scholastic theology, biblical commentaries and, in the case of Aquinas, commentaries on philosophical texts, John of Wales put his knowledge to a different purpose. Although he wrote his quota of biblical commentaries (some of which circulated for centuries under a mistaken attribution to Bonaventure), he devoted most of his time and energy to the production of a stream of encyclopaedic preaching aids. Both encyclopaedias and preaching aids proved of immense value during the thirteenth to fifteenth centuries, and both they and their writers merited very high regard at this time. John of Wales was himself both well known and highly respected in late thirteenth-century Paris and subsequently. His preaching aids fell into neglect when such products were no longer used in their own right for their intended purpose. They then became matter for history, and the high regard in which they were once held has tended to be overlooked.

Yet preaching was of major importance in the later Middle Ages. The growth in the production of preaching aids, whether encyclopaedic or not, is closely bound up with the thirteenth-century explosion in preaching. And this in turn is tightly bound to the increase in the number of learned men, caused by the establishment of the universities. The Fourth Lateran Council of 1215 had shown awareness of a greater need for preachers. The friars and the universities between them provided a means to meet this need,. but an educated mind and a copy of the Bible were not in themselves sufficient tools to supply the necessary informative preaching and pastoral care. The variety of preaching aids available from the later thirteenth century reflects the breadth of the need: handbooks on sin, on penance, on vices and virtues; collections of *exempla* or illustrative tales with which to enliven sermons, biblical concordances, skeleton sermons and technical treatises on the art of preaching all flourished. There were also assorted encyclopaedias, some of which – like Vincent of Beauvais' *Speculum Maius* – were intended by their authors to have a potential use as a preaching aid. Encyclopaedias were welcomed by preachers as a valuable source of varied material with which to inform and illustrate their sermons.

John of Wales benefited from the developments in encyclopaedic organisation made by scholars like the Dominican Vincent of Beauvais. Like Vincent, he showed a wide range of reading and a fondness for accurate reference to his original source. But his perennial motive for writing was to provide tools for preachers, and particularly young preachers. This influenced the way in which his preaching aids were set out. Where many such aids, as for example the *Manipulus Florum* of Thomas of Ireland, used an alphabetic organisation by topic, and where Vincent of Beauvais' *Speculum Maius* used a historical framework, John tended to use as his basis groups of divisions which would be very familiar to preachers, and easy for them to work through. The virtues, the vices, the Ten Commandments, the divisions of philosophy, the groups and sub-groups which make up human society – each of these was utilised as the framework of one of John's texts.

I have concentrated on John's four earliest preaching aids: the *Breviloquium de Virtutibus*, *Communiloquium*, *Compendiloquium* and *Breviloquium de Sapientia Sanctorum*, which appear to have been written as a group in Oxford and Paris sometime between 1265 and 1275. One cannot always draw a clear line between encyclopaedias and preaching aids, but these four works by John were primarily intended as preaching aids, and it is in this context that I have examined them. In addition, John's *Communiloquium* is a rich source of material about his own interests and attitudes, when examined in the light of thirteenth-century society. For this reason, *Communiloquium* has been given the central role in this book.

Chapter 1

THE CAREER OF JOHN OF WALES

John of Wales was an important Franciscan scholar active in the mid-to late thirteenth century. Until recently, we knew relatively little of his career, and although more intensive study of his works has enabled us to fill the gaps, we are still far from knowing the whole story. In this chapter I seek to detail all we know of John's career, and then to discuss the dating of some of his works.[1]

First John's birth: as is often the case with medieval scholars, we know nothing of this. In John's case, Pantin estimated that it fell between 1210 and 1230.[2] The appellation 'John of Wales' suggests that John was born a Welshman, and there is other evidence to support this. We know from a Cambridge MS that John belonged to the Franciscan custody of Worcester, which included North Wales.[3] That John had some knowledge of Wales and the Welsh is also indicated by his spell as ambassador to Llewellyn in the 1280s.[4]

A list of eminent entrants to the Franciscan Order describes John as a Bachelor of Theology from Oxford,[5] so he was one of the many young scholars whom the Franciscans attracted during the early to mid-thirteenth century. We cannot date John's first arrival in Oxford, or his move into the Franciscan Order, but we can deduce that both occurred sometime before 1258. John is not mentioned by Eccleston, whose chronicle finished in 1258 and included the first five Franciscan lectors at Oxford,[6] but we know from the continuation of Eccleston's list that John was the sixth lector. We can therefore assume that John's lectorship post-dated 1258: Little dates the lectorship to 1259–62.[7] John must have completed his first degree and joined the Order some years before this.

After the fairly firm date (1259–62) of John's lectorship, his career again becomes obscure. Pantin believed that John went to Paris

---

[1] This is intended as a supplement to the information in A. B. Emden, 1957, p. 1960.
[2] W. A. Pantin, 1961, pp. 297–319.   [3] Cambridge, Jesus College, MS 67.
[4] D. L. Douie, 1952, pp. 238 and 247.   [5] J. S. Brewer, 1858, I.542.
[6] A. G. Little, 1951, pp. 51–3.   [7] A. G. Little, 1926, p. 845.

around 1270 or a little later.[8] We have a collection of Paris sermons which includes a sermon of John's dated to 29 June 1270,[9] indicating that John was in Paris by the middle of that year. It does not help us to know when he arrived or how long he stayed. However, there is some evidence that John was already in Paris well before this date. I shall discuss this evidence later, in the context of John's works.

We have several pieces of information about John in the years from 1281 to 1285, which shows that he was in Paris for much, but not all, of this time. In the years 1281–3, John was Regent Master of Theology at Paris, according to his title in a contemporary collection of sermons. We have three of his sermons from these years, preached on 11 November 1281, 19 April 1283 and 1 May 1283.[10] Glorieux tells us that from 1281 until 1283 there were two Franciscan regents in theology,[11] so John would have shared his responsibilities. Acting as regent was not John's only activity in these Paris years. In 1282 he travelled to Wales as Archbishop Pecham's ambassador to Llewellyn – he made two trips in the late autumn of 1282. We do not know when John crossed the Channel or how long he stayed.[12] From 1283 to 1285 John was part of the commission appointed to examine the works of Peter John Olivi.[13] It is thought that he died in April 1285,[14] before the commission had completed its function. He was certainly buried in Paris.[15]

We thus have a reasonable amount of information about the last years of John's life, and only a couple of dates before that. There are many things about John which these pieces of information do not reveal – for example, when he first went to Paris, and how firmly he was fixed there before 1281. We ask ourselves when he first went to Oxford, when he joined the Franciscan Order, and where his works fit into his career. Careful study of the surviving texts has provided some useful information about the dates, and also the 'birthplaces', of some of the works.

Very many texts have been attributed to John through the centuries, often wrongly. In the same way, some of John's genuine works have been erroneously attributed to others. Some twenty

---

[8] W. A. Pantin, 1961, p. 297.   [9] Paris, BN, MS lat 15034, ff. 127, 129d.

[10] Paris, BN, MS lat 14947, ff. 187, 144c and 166b respectively.

[11] P. Glorieux, 1933, p. 275.

[12] D. L. Douie, 1952, pp. 238 and 247. Edward issued John with a safe conduct on 25 October 1282. This first mission of John's was not completely successful. He made a second journey to Snowdon in November.

[13] P. Glorieux, 1933, p. 260.   [14] A. G. Little, 1926, p. 845.

[15] A. G. Little, 1917, p. 175.

works are still accepted as his by modern scholars.[16] These range
from homiletic works like the vast *Communiloquium*, through biblical commentaries, to sermon series and single sermons. We are
fortunate that John was always very particular about providing
accurate references for the sources of any of his works. This raises the
possibility of dating some of the works, at least roughly, through
John's references to works of fixed date or limited circulation, and
also of placing the works in some kind of sequence through internal
cross-references. A first attempt at this was made by W. A. Pantin,
who observed that four of the works – the *Breviloquium de Virtutibus
Antiquorum Principum et Philosophorum, Communiloquium, Compendiloquium* and *Breviloquium de Sapientia Sanctorum* – had been
written in that order, according to the cross-references.[17] Pantin also
cited a MS of the *Breviloquium de Virtutibus* which stated in the *explicit*
that the work was written at the instance of the Bishop of
Maguelonne,[18] and he deduced from this that the work was written
after John's arrival in Paris in about 1270. The MS is fourteenth
century in date, and we know of no other MS with the same
statement attached to it, although some 140 MSS of the *Breviloquium*
survive, some of which are earlier. We should therefore be prepared
to treat the statement with some caution. A careful study of John's
sources for the *Communiloquium*, the second work in this sequence,
suggests that it was not produced primarily in Paris during the
1270s, and this implies that its predecessor, the *Breviloquium de
Virtutibus*, was not produced then either.

We have already established that dates for John's life are few, and
in some cases shaky. Most fall within the last five years of his life,
when he seems to have been involved in a number of different
activities. We have little information on his activities in the decades
prior to 1280, but we might reasonably suppose that these activities
included the bulk of his writing. If he did not begin the *Breviloquium
de Virtutibus*, one of his earliest works, until 1270 or later, then the
decade from 1270 to 1280 must have been very full indeed. We must
remember that John left a very substantial quantity of writings.[19]

[16] See Appendix 1.
[17] W. A. Pantin, 1961, p. 298.
[18] Oxford, Oriel College, MS 183, f. 161v. The explicit runs: *Explicit breviloquium de
virtutibus antiquorum principum et philosophorum quod venerabilis pater magister frater
Iohannes Walensis compilavit ad honorem Dei et utilitatem ecclesie sue sancte ad instanciam
episcopi Maglonensis*. As Pantin points out, the Bishop of Maguelonne from 1263 to
1296 was Berengar of Fredol (W. A. Pantin, 1961, p. 296).
[19] See Appendix 1.

How early could John have begun to write? For the *Breviloquium de Virtutibus*, the *Communiloquium* and the *Compendiloquium*, *termini a quo* are provided by references to other works dating from the middle of the thirteenth century. All three cite a 'Commentator on Ethics' who is Robert Grosseteste.[20] Grosseteste produced the first complete Latin version of the *Nichomachean Ethics*, together with a translation of Greek commentaries by Eustratius and others.[21] Daniel Callus tells us that the finished work was not circulated before 1245/6, or more probably 1246/7.[22] The *Communiloquium* further cites the *Summa Aurea* of Henry de Suza, which was completed in 1253.[23] This firmly establishes these works as dating from the early 1250s at the very soonest.

Can we get any closer than that? As it happens, we can. One useful piece of information concerns Seneca. Roger Bacon wrote his *Opus Maius* between the early 1260s and 1268, and its third part was much longer than he had originally intended, because of his discovery of 'rare books' by Seneca – the *De Ira, De Brevitate Vitae, De Providentia, De Constantia, De Consolatione ad Marciam* and *De Consolatione ad Helviam*.[24] All three of the above-mentioned works by John make reference to at least one of these Senecan works, with *Communiloquium* and *Compendiloquium* citing them ten and seventeen times respectively. It seems unlikely that Bacon would have deemed them so rare and exciting if John had been able to obtain and use them in Oxford in the 1250s. We are now talking about 1260 as the *terminus post quem* for this trio of John's works.

This confirms what we might already have suspected from the little we know of John's life, but it does not help us to date the works with respect to John's translation to Paris. We can derive further help from the history of Aristotle's *Politics*. The first Latin version of this work was produced in about 1260, by William of Moerbeke.[25] It was taken up in Paris and used by both Albertus Magnus and Thomas Aquinas, but it is unlikely that its circulation was at all wide until Aquinas prepared his Commentary, probably between 1269 and

---

[20] E.g., *Communiloq.* 1.6.6.
[21] B. G. Dod, 1982, pp. 49 and 61.
[22] D. Callus, 1963, p. 64. J. McEvoy, 1982, p. 475, confirms that Grosseteste was occupied with the composition from 1236 to 1246. R. W. Southern, 1986, agrees.
[23] *New Catholic Encyclopedia*, s.n. for Henry de Suza.
[24] Bacon announced his 'discovery' of Seneca's *Dialogues* in 1266: see R. H. Rouse, 1979, p. 149.
[25] M. Grabmann, 1946, p. 112.

1272.[26] It seems probable that if John had been writing in Paris around 1270 or later, he would have had access to a copy of the work. As a senior scholar and a Franciscan he would have had the appropriate contacts, and it is a work which would have interested him considerably.

The *Politics* is also a work which would have had much bearing upon John's *Communiloquium*, and particularly on the very substantial section on 'Politics and the state' which opens the work. *Communiloquium* quotes some 122 works from some 45 authors dating from before AD 450, and some 82 works from 56 authors of later date. There are 1,600 non-biblical references in the whole work, including 14 to Aristotle's *Ethics*, 9 to other Aristotelian works, and 9 to the *Commentary on Ethics*.[27] There is no reference to Aristotle's *Politics*. The most likely explanation is that John simply was not acquainted with it. This helps us to narrow down the date of the *Communiloquium*. If it was written in Paris, it must surely have been completed by *c.* 1270, while if it was an Oxford production it could have been somewhat later. Since we know that John reached Paris by mid-1270, *Communiloquium* should have been substantially completed by that date in either case.

If John had gone to Paris while *Communiloquium* was not begun or still in progress, and if his answer to the question 'And what are you working on now?' had included the information that he was preparing a work with a strong element of politics and of education for rulership, the new *Politics* must surely have been mentioned, once Aquinas' Commentary became available. And it seems most unlikely that John, knowing of the *Politics*, could have resisted the temptation to use it. It is possible that the work was still so little known in the early 1270s that John was able to complete the *Communiloquium* in Paris during those years without hearing of it or being able to obtain access to a copy, but this is very dubious. Moreover, it would require the 1270s to have been a time of truly feverish activity for John as an author, in contrast to an apparent barrenness in the years before 1270.

We know that John did gain access to the *Politics*, because he

[26] J. A. Weisheipl, 1974, pp. 380–1. Aquinas' Commentary only covered books 1–3.6. Commentary on the later books was provided by Peter of Auvergne, probably between 1274 and 1290. For reception and interpretation of Aristotle's *Politics*, see J. Dunbabin, 1965; C. Martin, 1951.

[27] See source-lists for chapters 4, 5, and 6 below: pp. 102–5, and 138–4 and 164–6 respectively.

quotes it in *Compendiloquium*,[28] which we know to be of later date than the *Communiloquium*, and which is much less concerned with politics. This suggests that we can draw a line between *Communiloquium* and *Compendiloquium*, marking a change in the availability of material and a date *c*. 1269–72. Some of John's references suggest that for *Communiloquium* he was partly dependent on Parisian sources available from the mid-1260s, while others of his references are characteristic of Oxford. *Communiloquium* was therefore written all in Paris, or partly in Paris, or in Oxford with help from Parisian contacts.[29] The *Breviloquium de Virtutibus*, which preceded the *Communiloquium*, should have been written in the early to mid-1260s, possibly in Oxford, unless John went to Paris well before 1270. We should not rule out the possibility of a short visit to Paris by John, perhaps soon after his Oxford lectorship.[30] Such a visit could have provided an opportunity to meet the Bishop of Maguelonne and to receive from him encouragement to write the *Breviloquium de Virtutibus*. If *Compendiloquium* were written after 1269, then so was its successor, the *Breviloquium de Sapientia*.

On the evidence of the *Politics,* we are able to provide approximate dates for at least four of John's works. Although the four are a coherent group, often copied and published as such, we can, as indicated above, clearly distinguish a break between *Communiloquium* and *Compendiloquium*. Another of John's sources, the *Noctes Atticae* of Aulus Gellius, can be used to confirm this break in composition.

It was not until the fifteenth century that whole texts of this work became common. Until then, copies of books 1–7 were rare all over the continent, and the text of books 9–20 was also rare in England. Book 8 was and is lost. The transmission of Aulus Gellius has been thoroughly studied,[31] and I wish to examine John's place in this transmission in a later chapter. For the moment it is enough to say that in thirteenth-century England both early and late parts of the *Noctes Atticae* were very rare. It has been said that Richard of Bury, Bishop of Durham 1333–45, was the only English author to quote the *Noctes Atticae* more than once or twice between 1200 and 1400.[32]

[28] *Compendiloq.* 1.2.
[29] For detailed discussion of this problem, see below, pp. 24–37.
[30] I.e., 1262 or later.
[31] E.g., A. C. de la Mare, P. K. Marshall & R. H. Rouse, 1976, pp. 219–25. Also P. K. Marshall, J. Martin & R. H. Rouse, 1980, pp. 353–95.
[32] P. K. Marshall, J. Martin & R. H. Rouse, 1980, p. 383.

In fact this statement is incorrect, as John of Wales quotes the work at least seventy times.[33] There are ten quotations from this text in *Communiloquium*, and all come from books 1–7. There is no special change in topic or emphasis between the earlier and the later parts of the *Noctes Atticae*, so we may believe that at the time John had access to books 1–7 only. *Compendiloquium*, on the other hand, quotes the *Noctes Atticae* 57 times, ranging widely through both the earlier and the later parts. Therefore by the time he wrote the *Compendiloquium* John had access to a full text of Aulus Gellius. Such a full text came to Paris in 1272, when the books of Richard Fournival were transferred to the Sorbonne,[34] and it seems probable that this was the text that John used in his preparation of *Compendiloquium*. This would place *Compendiloquium* and *Breviloquium de Sapientia Sanctorum* firmly in Paris in the 1270s.

We have so far discussed the sequence and dating of only four of John's works. We have some information, though rather less, about the others. For example, John's *Legiloquium*, in which he discusses the Ten Commandments, makes four references to the *Communiloquium*.[35] From our earlier argument, it follows that the *Legiloquium* was not written before *c.* 1270, and probably not until some time after John's move to Paris. This probability is supported by the fact that *Legiloquium* also quotes the later books of the *Noctes Atticae*.[36]

The *Legiloquium* further makes three references to a *Tractatus de Vita Philosophorum*.[37] John first refers to this in connection with a comment about how much the 'Gentiles' (a term he uses to denote pagans) hated vice and went to great efforts to support the state. The extent of this, he says, is shown in the histories and deeds of princes and in the books of the gentile philosophers, of which enough has been said in this and other collections such as the *Tractatus de Vita Philosophorum*.[38] There are several reasons for believing that this may be a reference to John's own *Compendiloquium*. The alternative title for this work is *De Vita et Dictis Notabilibus, atque Exemplis Imitabilibus Illustrium Philosophorum*, and it was written to show that the

---

[33] Other Oxford friars also made use of Aulus Gellius in the early fourteenth century. Beryl Smalley, 1960, p. 232, says that Gellius was a 'favourite book' for them.

[34] P. K. Marshall, J. Martin & R. H. Rouse, 1980, p. 379.

[35] Oxford, Bodleian, MS Lincoln College, 67e, ff. 143r, 150v. I shall refer to this manuscript as L.

[36] L, ff. 148r, 152r.   [37] L, ff. 143r, 143v, 145v.

[38] L, f. 143r: 'de quibus dictum est in parte et aliis collectionibus sicut in tractatu de vita philosophorum satis'.

philosophers had just these virtues of hating vice and supporting the state. That the Gentiles had these virtues to a high degree was a personal obsession of John's. The other two references to this *Tractatus* are also in the context of the virtues of the ancient philosophers. John does not give specific references, but the two philosophers whom he cites in these *exempla* do appear in *Compendiloquium*.

John was usually very specific in naming his sources: if he did not know the name of the author of a tract, and it lacked a specific title, he would describe it as 'a certain tract'[39] and give some comment on its contents. If he referred to a work like his own *Communiloquium*, he only gave the name and did not mention that he wrote it. So this *Tractatus de Vita Philosophorum* could very well be his. We may adduce a slightly different argument here, other than that John wrote such a work with such a title and such contents, and made his references in a characteristically anonymous and modest way. If John believed, as he says in the *Legiloquium*, that this *Tractatus de Vita Philosophorum* wrote 'satis' about the Gentile philosophers and their particular virtues, there would have been no point in his writing his own *Compendiloquium* thereafter. So there would seem to be good reason to believe that John's *Legiloquium* post-dated *Compendiloquium* as well as *Communiloquium*. This would mean that it was written some time after *c.* 1271/2, which date is also suggested by the sources used for the work. One last piece of evidence on the possible predecessors of *Legiloquium*: as Miss Smalley pointed out, the *Legiloquium* refers to John's *Moniloquium*.[40] This, then, would also predate the *Legiloquium*.

The *Moniloquium* seems to belong to John's Paris years, as it cites the *Breviloquium de Virtutibus*,[41] the *Communiloquium*,[42] the *Compendiloquium*[43] and the *Ordinarium Vitae Religiosae*.[44] This helps us to place the *Ordinarium* in sequence. It has a relatively narrow selection of sources and makes no reference to any other work of John's, so we can get no help there. In a sense it complements the *Communiloquium*, for it discusses the behaviour of the various classes of religious in the same way as *Communiloquium* primarily deals with the secular

---

[39] E.g., L, f. 153v: 'Sicut ait quidam sapiens in suo tractatu', etc.
[40] B. Smalley, 1960, p. 52.
[41] London, BL, MS Harley 632: e.g., f. 296v.
[42] London, BL, MS Harley 632: e.g., f. 301r.
[43] London, BL, MS Harley 632: e.g., f. 299r.
[44] London, BL, MS Harley 632: e.g., f. 301r.

groups in society. *Communiloquium* does contain a short section on the behaviour of the religious, but it makes no reference to the much more detailed *Ordinarium*. One hesitates to make too much of an argument from absence, but it is probably viable in the circumstances. As we know that John regularly cross-referenced his works, we may plausibly suggest that the *Ordinarium* had not been composed when *Communiloquium* was written. This would place the *Ordinarium Vitae Religiosae* some time after the late 1260s. The *Exposition of the Franciscan Rule,* which quotes the *Ordinarium,*[45] must post-date it.

The cross-references in the *Moniloquium* should also help us to place John's *Summa Iustitiae*. *Moniloquium* cites four of John's earlier works in a number of places where they give information on topics which are also discussed in the *Summa Iustitiae*, which gives a much fuller discussion of the vices than John found room for in the *Moniloquium*. Again this suggests that the *Moniloquium* predates the *Summa Iustitiae*, as John would surely have cited the latter otherwise.

Do we know anything of the dating and sequence of others of John's works? We can make a start on the sequence of his biblical commentaries, for John's *Collations on St Matthew* make three references to his *Commentary and Collations on St John.*[46] Miss Smalley tells us that the *Commentary on Matthew* appears to belong to Oxford, on the grounds that it contains a quotation from Clement of Lanthony, who was popular among the Oxford Franciscans but little known on the continent.[47] Our knowledge of John's career indicates that the earlier *Commentary on John* should also belong to Oxford. Miss Smalley's investigations indicate that this is borne out by the contents and format of the *Commentary on John*. Moreover, this commentary uses work produced by Bonaventure between 1254 and 1257. Most probably it, and the *Commentary on Matthew*, were written around the late 1250s and early 1260s, at about the time when John of Wales was lector to the Oxford Franciscans. We should probably place these biblical commentaries earlier than the *Breviloquium de Virtutibus* and *Communiloquium*, which seem to belong to the mid- to late 1260s. A lector would be expected to produce biblical works rather than collections of classical *exempla,* however moralistic their purpose.

Turning now to sermons, we have four surviving single speci-

---

[45] P. Glorieux, 1934, p. 553.
[46] Baldwinus ab Amsterdam OFM Cap., 1970, p. 82.
[47] B. Smalley, 1981, p. 244, n. 153.

mens of known date, from 29 June 1270, 11 November 1281, 19 April 1283 and 1 May 1283. All were given in Paris.[48] The sermon from 1270 presumably falls between *Communiloquium* and *Compendiloquium* in date, and the sermon from April 1283 tells us that John did not remain in England many months after his brief spell as ambassador to Wales in the autumn of 1282. We would have expected him to return to his responsibilities as regent in Paris, and indeed we know he was there from June to September 1283, while the examination of Peter John Olivi was being conducted.[49]

This is the current state of our knowledge of John's career and of my understanding of the chronology and sequence of his works. The works which have been investigated have yielded up their clues, and have helped to provide a fuller picture of what our Franciscan scholar was doing during those blank years in his career, the 1260s and 1270s. The relationships between John's works can usefully be summarised in chart form (see fig. 1). I have arranged the works in approximate sequence of date, the earliest at the top of the page, the latest at the bottom. Where a firm date is known, it is marked. Where two works appear at the same level, this indicates that we do not know their relationship to each other in terms of sequence.

I here summarise my conclusions about the sequence of John's works:

1 The *Commentary and Collations on John* predate the *Commentary on Matthew,* and both post-date 1257. The suggestion is that they belong to John's Oxford lectorship, *c.* 1259–62.
2 *Breviloquium de Virtutibus* is quoted in *Communiloquium*, and both seem to predate 1270 while post-dating 1260.
3 We have a sermon from 1270, given in Paris.
4 *Communiloquium* is quoted in *Compendiloquium*, which in turn is quoted in *Breviloquium de Sapientia.* These latter two seem from their sources to postdate 1272, and belong firmly to John's Paris period.
5 *Legiloquium* refers to *Communiloquium, Compendiloquium* and *Moniloquium*, and also seems to be later than 1272.
6 *Ordinarium Vitae Religiosae* is not quoted in *Communiloquium* and probably post-dates it. It is quoted in *Moniloquium*, which must have been written later still.
7 *Moniloquium* also quoted *Compendiloquium* and its predecessors

[48] For details of the sermons, see J. B. Schneyer, 1969, Vol. 3.
[49] P. Glorieux, 1934, p. 260.

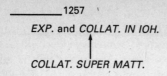

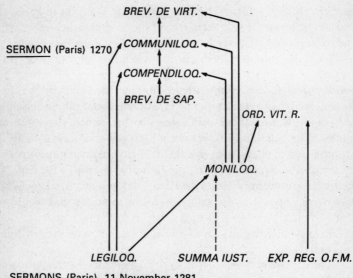

Fig. 1. Interrelations and chronology of John's works.

the *Breviloquium de Virtutibus* and the *Communiloquium*, so it can have been written no earlier than the early 1270s.

8 *Summa Iustitiae* is not mentioned in *Moniloquium*, so should post-date it, because of the nature of its contents.

9 The *Ordinarium Vitae Religiosae* is cited in the *Exposition of the Franciscan Rule,* so this exposition must join the *Summa Iustitiae* as one of the later works in the sequence.

10 We have Paris sermons from 1281 and 1283.

Chapter 2

THE WORKS OF JOHN OF WALES:
SOURCES AND TECHNIQUE

John of Wales' pastoral handbooks are remarkable in many ways, and in particular for the wide variety of texts which he employed to educate his readers. His fascination with the ancient world appears to have led him to seek out an extraordinary range of sources, some of them extremely rare in his time. His use of more than fifty classical authors (and nearly 100 classical texts) establishes him as a major classicising writer for the thirteenth and fourteenth centuries, and he seems to have been an important link between the classical interests of Robert Grosseteste (d. 1253) and the wider classicising tendencies of the group of fourteenth-century English friars so vividly described by Beryl Smalley.[1]

John was well placed to be a beneficiary of the developments in the organisation of written material which were made by the friars who prepared the *Registrum Librorum Angliae*.[2] The contents of this library list were mainly patristic, so it cannot be used to account for John's wide classical learning, but it is a clear indication that English Franciscans were making advances in method, and in co-operation, from which John could well have benefited. Similarly, the Lyons Index of Robert Grosseteste,[3] a topic index to both patristic and classical works, shows that before John of Wales joined them the Oxford Franciscans were already making a contribution to the development of reference tools. Such tools and systems were essential precursors of the very precise and detailed use which John of Wales makes of his source material.

John's use of source-material is one of the most distinctive features of his works – to some scholars, particularly those in search of philosophical arguments and original theology, perhaps excessively distinctive. Some modern writers have believed that John's works

[1] B. Smalley, 1960.
[2] R. A. B. Mynors, 1957, pp. 199–217.
[3] S. Harrison Thomson, 1934, pp. 139–44.

consist solely of one long chain of quotations, and see this as cause for condemnation.[4] Again, it has been observed that John does name source after source with accuracy, but it has been held that he was to a considerable extent dependent on florilegia and other secondary sources.[5] Both A. G. Little and W. A. Pantin gave some discussion of John's sources:[6] these discussions are a beginning, but they are far from complete and in places even misleading. Much closer examination of John's sources is required before we can properly reach any conclusions.

Disparaging remarks have been made about John's 'long chains of quotations'. The existence of these chains of quotations has to be recognised. John, like most of his medieval predecessors, contemporaries and successors, had a respect for authority and a tendency to amalgamate previous work with his own. But there are better reasons than this for the vast quantities of quotation in most of John's works. John was a writer of preachers' handbooks. He wrote them on a variety of topics, but they were designed to help preachers, particularly the young ones.[7] The handbooks aimed to cover all sorts of topics, giving an authoritative view, a number of named authorities in support of this view, a series of *exempla* and appropriate extracts for use in preaching, and suggestions for further reading. This last is of special importance. It is clear from John's style that he does intend his works to point the interested in the right directions to learn more. Though John's works are very substantial, their compass is vast, and so many topics receive only elementary coverage. This would be enough for the average priest, who perhaps lacked the resources of a library or the capacity to do much research into suitable authorities for his sermons. Others, surely, would have wanted to use John as an introduction and a set of useful pointers. Or at least John hoped some people would use his works in this way, and so the pointers were provided.

John was not unusual in using many sources as he wrote his works, particularly in his special field of preaching aids. He was, however, somewhat unusual for his time in giving detailed references to the works he quotes. He gives not only the name of the author and work, but also the book number, if there were more than

---

[4] A. Charma, 1866, p. 8; also A. G. Little, 1917, p. 191.
[5] A. G. Little, 1917, p. 191.
[6] *Ibid.*, pp. 186–91; W. A. Pantin, 1961, pp. 305–6.
[7] For the purpose of his works, see his own introductions. John's particular interest in *young* preachers was pointed out by Baldwinus ab Amsterdam, OFM Cap., 1970, pp. 71–96.

one, the chapter numbers, if chapters existed, or a general indication of the whereabouts of the quotation in the work, if no divisions were provided. The immediate implication of these detailed references is that John had the actual works before him – or had done preliminary research in them and taken careful notes. Few of his predecessors provided references detailed enough to have been copied by John, and certainly not covering the vast range that he does.

The suggestion that most of John's references were obtained directly from the originals is borne out by three further points. First, he did sometimes quote at second or even third hand, and tells us so with scrupulous attention to details. Secondly, most of his references are completely accurate: he both pinpoints the origin and whereabouts of his quotations correctly, and gives a very faithful rendering of the original text. Thirdly, the frequent comment 'et ibi bene de hoc',[8] tacked on to a reference, implies that John knew more of the text than the portion quoted. These comments are one of the ways in which John seems to invite the reader to delve deeper. He also often names a work, or a section of it, as being relevant to a particular point, without using any quotation or *exemplum* from the work in his own text. Again this indicates independent knowledge of individual texts, and shows that John was trying to provide a guide to further reading.

What kinds of sources did John use, and in what quantities? A general impression of the numbers of quotations can easily be obtained by browsing through the pages of any of his works. A careful count of the references, grouped by author and work, gives a much more accurate impression. As examples one might take John's *Breviloquium de Virtutibus Antiquorum Principum et Philosophorum* and his *Communiloquium*. In the *Breviloquium de Virtutibus*, probably the earliest of John's preaching aids and one of the shortest, John cites 52 works by 35 authors (excluding the Bible). Many of these authors are classical, while those who are not are generally used as a quarry for tales of the ancient world. This is in keeping with the subject under discussion. It is interesting to compare these figures with those for *Communiloquium*, a very much larger book, which aims to discuss all the different groups in society. Here John's non-biblical sources number over 200 works by over 100 authors. Again there is a strong classical bias, particularly in the earlier parts of the work, which deal with secular society. In both these works biblical references are considerably less numerous than non-biblical.

---

[8] Which might be translated as 'and more here on this' or 'see further'.

It is also instructive to compare the 'Top Twelve' non-biblical authors for each of these two works.

BREV. DE·VIRT.		*COMMUNILOQ.*	
Valerius Maximus	65	Augustine	237
Augustine	29	Gregory the Great	210
Seneca	25	Seneca	170
Cicero	24	Jerome	123
Celius Balbus	19	Valerius Maximus	122
Vegetius	13	Cicero	103
John of Salisbury	8	John of Salisbury	67
Helinand	7	Hugh of Saint-Victor	52
Macrobius	7	St Bernard	50
Jerome	5	Ambrose	34
William of Conches	4	*Vitae Patrum*	34
Robert Grosseteste	4	John Chrysostom	31
Hugh of Saint-Victor	4		

In the *Breviloquium*, all other authors rate only one or two references, while in the *Communiloquium* few of the authors outside the 'Top Twelve' receive more than eleven references.

The sources for the *Breviloquium* appear at first to have a much stronger classical bias than those for *Communiloquium*, but this is misleading. In *Communiloquium*, Augustine, Jerome and Ambrose are most often used as a source of classical *exempla*. The same is true of John of Salisbury's *Policraticus*. The high place taken by Hugh of Saint-Victor is because he provides the base text for John's analysis of the ecclesiastical world.

More detailed analyses of the sources of John's individual works are provided separately in the appropriate chapters. Here I give only a general discussion of the range of John's sources.

First his patristic sources. As one might expect, he makes much use of the big names of earlier centuries. We saw from the sample lists that Augustine is most prominent among these. Indeed, Augustine holds first place in the *Communiloquium*, *Legiloquium* and *Breviloquium de Sapientia*, second place in the *Breviloquium de Virtutibus*, third in the *Compendiloquium*, and fourth in the *Ordinarium Vitae Religiosae*. One can correctly deduce from these facts that John had in many ways a very Augustinian outlook, but Augustine was also one of John's favourite quarries of classical lore and *exempla*. John's quotations from Augustine derive from a wide range of works, mostly genuine, some now regarded as spurious. John names 63 works by Augustine, besides making numerous references to the *Epistolae* and to the various sermons. The work most frequently referred to is the *De Civitate Dei*, which John refers to on more than 200 occasions. The *Epistolae* and *Confessions* follow, with around 60 references each. The sermons rate somewhere above 40, and the *Super Iohannem* more than 25. No other work is quoted more than 20 times in the group of texts examined,[9] and many only once or twice.

Other favourite writers include Jerome (again a source of information on antiquity), Gregory the Great and St Bernard. Popular to a lesser extent were St Ambrose, Hugh of Saint-Victor and John Chrysostom, Cassian and the *Vitae Patrum*. All these appear in one or more of the 'Top Twelve' lists. In each case John quotes from a significant number of the author's works. John also refers to Pope Alexander III, Albertus Magnus, Anselm of Canterbury and Anselm of Laon, Bede, Cassiodorus, Chrysippus, Clement, Dionysius the Areopagite, Eusebius, Gregory Nazianzen, Haimo, Innocent III, Isidore, Orosius, Origen, Petrus Alphonsi, Peter Comestor, Peter Damian, Peter Lombard, Rabanus and Tertullian. None of these authors rates a great number of references. The most popular with John was perhaps Anselm of Canterbury, with thirty or more citations, followed by Cassiodorus with over twenty, Eusebius with about fifteen, Isidore and Origen with a dozen or so, Peter Comestor's *Historia Scholastica* with ten and Tertullian with six. It should be remembered that these figures are for a group of works rather than for any one text.

One can see from this elementary breakdown that John knew and used a considerable range of patristic and later Christian authors – exactly what one would expect of a scholar who was to hold a theology chair in Paris. If we were to analyse the sources for his specifically theological works, such as his Bible commentaries, we would expect to find many more citations of biblical scholars and patristic writers, and fewer from the wide range of other sources which he used in his preaching aids. Particularly interesting among these others are some of his classical sources, for many of these were still rare in John's time.

The first requirement for any discussion of John's classical sources is a basic checklist. The list reflects the wide range of material which

[9] E.g., *Breviloquium de Virtitubus, Breviloquium de Sapientia, Communiloquium, Legiloquium, Ordinarium Vitae Religiosae.*

was available to the alert and interested scholar, and is testimony to the fact that John was such a scholar. The classical authors to whom John refers in his preaching aids are tabulated below.

Aesop	*Fables*
Apuleius	*De Deo Socratis*
Aristotle	*De Anima*
	De Animalibus
	De Caelo et Mundo
	De Meteoris
	De Somno et Vigilia
	Liber Naturalium
	Metaphysics
	Nicomachean Ethics
	Physics
	Politics
pseudo-Aristotle	*De Vegetabilibus*
Boethius	*De Arithmetica*
	De Consolatione Philosophiae
Cato	
Chalcidius	*Commentary on Timaeus*
Cicero	*Academica Posteriora*
	De Amicitia
	De Divinatione
	De Legibus
	De Natura Deorum
	De Officiis
	De Oratore ad Marcum Brutum
	De Paradoxis
	De Rhetorica
	De Senectute
	Hortensian Dialogues
	Philippics
	Tusculan Questions
Claudian	
Hesychius	
Herodotus	
Horace	
Josephus	
Juvenal	
Expositor on Juvenal	

Livy
Lucan
Macrobius
Marcellianus
Ovid
Petronius
Plato
Pliny
Ptolemy   *Almagest*
Quintilian
Quintus Curtius
Sallust
Satyrus   *Bioi*
Seneca   *De Beata Vita*
                                  De Beneficiis
                                  De Brevitate Vitae
                                  De Clementia
                                  De Constantia Sapientis
                                  De Ira
                                  De Naturalibus Quaestionibus
                                  De Providentia
                                  De Remediis Fortuitorum
                                  De Tranquillitate Animi
                                  De Virtutibus
                                  Epistulae
                                  Liber Declamationum
pseudo-Seneca   *Proverbiae*
Silius Italicus
Solinus
Suda
Suetonius
Sulpicius Severus
Terence
Thaurus
Theophrastus
Trogus Pompeius
Valerius Maximus
Varro
Vegetius
Virgil

It would be an enormous task to check every single quotation by every single author, as they number many thousands. But some checks have been made in the case of each author. John did not have first-hand access to every author and work on the above list: several of them were known only through intermediaries. John is usually quite open about it, giving quotations of this sort in a characteristic form. For example, '. . . prout ait Salustius libro secundo recitans verba Scipionis',[10] '. . . et maxime secundum illud Ennii prout recitat Tullius ubi supra',[11] '. . . Augustinus epistola quinta recitans verba Salustii . . . et inducit ibi versus Iuvenalis'.[12] In one case we even get a third-hand quotation: in *Communiloquium* 1.1.1., John says: '. . . prout recitat Augustinus de civitate dei ca. xix recitans diffinitionem reipublice datam a Scipione et recitatam a Tulio'.[13]

Where John's use of an intermediate source is not admitted in this form, it is usually clear from the juxtaposition of a general reference to a classical author with a specific reference to the work which is the source: for example, the *Contra Iovinianum* of Jerome, the *Noctes Atticae* of Aulus Gellius or the *Policraticus* of John of Salisbury. Only occasionally have we no positive indication one way or another.

From such indications, and a number of textual comparisons, it is possible to identify a small group of classical authors whom John refers to at second hand. However this does not invariably mean that he *only* knew them indirectly: for instance, in the third of the quotations given above, John refers to Juvenal through one of Augustine's letters, while we know from elsewhere in the texts that John had seen and used at least some of Juvenal in the original.[14] Writers whom John quotes at second hand include:

Aesop	through Aulus Gellius, Augustine, Jerome and Apuleius
Cato	through Augustine
Cicero, *De Republica*	through Augustine
Ennius	through Cicero and Augustine
Ethicus	through Jerome
Frontinus	

[10] 'As Salustius wrote in book two, repeating the words of Scipio.'
[11] 'And much follows on this in Ennius, as Cicero says above' (*Communiloq.* 1.1.6).
[12] 'Augustine, letter five, quoting the words of Sallust . . . and he brings in there a verse of Juvenal.'
[13] 'As Augustine says in *De Civitate Dei* chapter nineteen, repeating the definition of the republic given by Scipio and quoted by Cicero'.
[14] See individual source-lists in subsequent chapters.

Horace	
Juvenal	through Augustine
Livy	through the *Policraticus*
Lucan	
Ovid	
Petronius	
Plato	through the *Policraticus*
Pliny, *Nat. Hist.*	through the *Policraticus*
Quintilian	through Aulus Gellius and the *Policraticus*
Sallust	through Augustine
Satyrus	through Jerome
Scipio	through Sallust and Augustine
Silius Italicus	
Terence	
Thaurus[15]	through Aulus Gellius
Theophrastus[16]	through Jerome
Varro	through Augustine, Aulus Gellius
Velleius	
Virgil	through Augustine, Hugh of Saint-Victor, Seneca

Some of these authors were not available in the original: for example, Thaurus' *Commentarium super Gorgias* and Theophrastus' *Liber de Nupciis* do not seem to have survived into the medieval world. John therefore had no option but to quote them indirectly. Several works that did survive do not seem to be quoted except at second hand, but John does make direct quotations from Cicero and Juvenal, Plato, Pliny, Sallust and possibly others.

The number of times John quotes any given work or author varies widely. John's particular favourite of the classical authors is Seneca, who tops the list for *Compendiloquium*, comes second for the *Ordinarium Vitae Religiosae*, third in *Communiloquium* and *Breviloquium de Virtutibus*, fourth in the *Breviloquium de Sapientia* and ninth in the *Legiloquium*. John makes over 370 references to Seneca in these works. He makes frequent use of the later letters of Seneca, and of the 'rare' Senecan works which so excited Bacon in the 1260s.[17]

John also gives very frequent references to Cicero and Valerius Maximus, with over two hundred citations each, and to Aulus

---

[15] *Commentarium super Gorgias.*   [16] *Liber de Nupciis.*   [17] See pp. 29–32.

Gellius, with over seventy. Macrobius, Vegetius, Boethius and Aristotle are also popular. For most of the other classical authors used, the number of references varies from one to about a dozen.

The appearance of Aulus Gellius' *Noctes Atticae* among the classical sources is of particular interest. It was not until the fifteenth century that whole texts of this work became common. Until then, copies of books 1–7 were rare all over the continent, and the text of books 9–20 was also rare in England. Book 8 was and is lost. John quotes the *Noctes Atticae* at least seventy times. There are ten quotations from the text in *Communiloquium*, all from books 1–7. There is no special change in topic or emphasis between the earlier and the later parts of the *Noctes Atticae*, so we may reasonably believe that at the time John had access to books 1–7 only. We see a different situation in his *Compendiloquium*, for there he quotes the *Noctes Atticae* 57 times, ranging widely through both the earlier and the later parts. By the time he wrote *Compendiloquium*, John must have had access to a full text of Aulus Gellius. The number and scale of his quotations make it impossible for him to have used an intermediary in *Compendiloquium*.

John's use of Aulus Gellius is both interesting and important. The real significance lies in the fact that he was able to choose to do so: he had access to the author, and we must ask where and how. There are a number of possible answers, partly dependent on where we believe John was when he wrote *Communiloquium* and *Compendiloquium*. W. A. Pantin and others have held that John arrived in Paris *c.* 1270, and subsequently began to produce his 'loquia'.[18] But *Communiloquium* bears strong indications that it was written in the mid- to late 1260s. If John first went to Paris *c.* 1270, then *Communiloquium* should be an Oxford production. If, however, he went to Paris well before 1270 (and we know nothing about his activities in the 1260s) then *Communiloquium* could have been written in Paris.

Let us first consider the situation in England. This has been assessed by Marshall, Martin and Rouse,[19] who tell us that the early books of Gellius were first known in two florilegia: S, written at Salisbury Cathedral *c.* 1100 and containing extracts from Valerius Maximus and *Noctes Atticae* 1–7,[20] and φ, containing extracts from

[18] W. A. Pantin, 1961, p. 298.
[19] P. K. Marshall, J. Martin & R. H. Rouse, 1980, pp. 353–95. The authors have failed to take account of John of Wales' use of Gellius, observing that 'Richard of Bury, Bishop of Durham 1333–45, is the only English author to quote the Attic Nights more than once or twice between 1200 and 1400.'
[20] *Ibid.*, p. 369.

both the earlier and the later books of *Noctes Atticae*.[21] The twelfth-century writers William of Malmesbury and John of Salisbury both used φ, and there is apparently no evidence that either of them knew of a full text of Gellius in England. Gerald of Wales also quoted Gellius in the late twelfth century: in his references to the early books he seems to have used one of the florilegia already mentioned, and there is no evidence that he knew any more of the early books.[22] It is Ralph of Diss (1120/30–1202) whose works suggest the existence of a full text of Gellius in England, as his *Abbreviationes Chronicorum* makes numerous references to Gellius.[23]

We therefore have six possible sources of Aulus Gellius references in England, apart from a full text. Can we show that John of Wales used any of these as an intermediary in his *Communiloquium*? The answer to this question would seem to be no. The Gellius references in *Communiloquium* are as follows:

COMMUNILOQ.	NOCTES ATTICAE
2.4.1	1.17.1–3
5.8.1	2.1.1–3
1.1.3	2.12.1
5.1.3	4.19.1–2
1.4.3	5.1
5.1.3	5.3
5.1.8	7.10.2–5
1.9.5	7.14.1–4, 5, 14ff.

A comparison of these with the quotations in the Valerius/Gellius anthology S rules out the latter as a possible source, as it does not contain the relevant sections; φ can also be ruled out, as it seems to have quoted from books 9–16, 1, 2, 3 and 5, and we can see that John's quotations include some from books 4 and 7. William of Malmesbury and John of Salisbury both relied on φ, so it is unlikely that either of them could have provided John's quotations. Gerald of Wales also depended on this florilegium, and in any case has only three references to the earlier books, compared to John's seven. Ralph of Diss (de Diceto) does quote from three of the same Gellius chapters as John, but even if his wording was the same, this would provide only a partial solution.

We would seem to have eliminated the obvious English inter-

[21] *Ibid.*, p. 370.   [22] *Ibid.*, p. 373.   [23] *Ibid.*, p. 374.

mediaries. Moreover, John's manner of reference suggests that he did have access to a whole text. For example, he describes the source of one quotation as *Noctes Atticae* 3, saying 'et Agellius plenius ubi supra li.iii. ante finem ubi ait puer . . .', which suggests that he knew both the origin of the chapter and its context.[24]

John could have found a complete MS of books 1–7 of Gellius in England. An obvious candidate would be Cambridge, Clare College, MS 26. This MS is English, dates from the early thirteenth century, and seems to have come from a monastic or episcopal scriptorium in southern England.[25] It contains a complete text of books 1–7 of Gellius, sharing with many fifteenth-century MSS the reversal of books 6 and 7. This characteristic appears to rule it out as John's source, for in his references to books 6 and 7 we find no reversal. Neither Clare MS 26 nor any descendant is likely to have been John's source. But from where did the Clare MS derive?

Marshall, Martin and Rouse suggest that it originated in St Albans, partly because Richard of Bury gives five long quotations from the early Gellius books and reverses books 6 and 7. Richard obtained 34 volumes from the St Albans library just before he took up the bishopric at Durham. Possibly these books included the Clare Gellius. Certainly in 1391 Durham had all the *Noctes Atticae* in two parts – and Christ Church, Canterbury is the only other library in England known to have had either portion before the Renaissance.[26] A copy of books 9–20 was brought to Canterbury by Becket after his exile.[27] If the Gellius used by Richard of Bury had, as the above implies, reversal of books 6 and 7, this would also be an unsatisfactory solution to the problem of an English source for John, who has not reversed books 6 and 7. In fact, we cannot pinpoint any particular source at the moment. We know too little about the existence of full MSS of even books 1–7 of Gellius, let alone of books 9–20. We know there were some MSS of books 1–7 in the early fourteenth century, as Bury had one and Durham had one, and C at least survived. There are indications that these three were in fact one and the same, or at least closely related, though there may have been others in the family, now lost. But what of the full text to which Ralph of Diss apparently had access? We know nothing of where it

---

[24] In fact the quotation is from book 4, the error in the 1475 edition being due either to scribe or to typesetter.

[25] P. K. Marshall, J. Martin & R. H. Rouse, 1980, pp. 353–4.

[26] *Ibid.*, p. 384.

[27] A. C. de la Mare, P. K. Marshall & R. H. Rouse, 1976, p. 223.

came from or went to: it or a copy might well have survived into the thirteenth century to be used by John. All we can say is that it is not impossible that John could have found and used a full text of books 1–7 of Gellius in England, but that if he did we cannot trace it.

. If we now turn our attention to Paris, we have a new range of options to consider. We can confidently state that John's *Compendiloquium* was written in Paris. In this work he makes 57 references to *Noctes Atticae*, drawn from throughout the text. This indicates that his access to the text had expanded since the *Communiloquium* was composed. We might argue that it was John's arrival in Paris that opened up new access to Aulus Gellius, or alternatively that he was already there during the composition of *Communiloquium*. In this case we might deduce either that a full text of *Noctes Atticae* arrived in Paris after *Communiloquium* was completed, or that one was there all along, but that John did not know about it.

It is clear that copies of both the early and the late Gellius books were available in Northern France by the thirteenth century, although few continental writers quote the *Noctes Atticae* enough to suggest that they were using a whole text.[28] However, the Gellius quotations in the margins of Bern, Burgerbibliothek, MS 276, which originates from the Loire region, indicate the existence there of a MS of the whole of the *Noctes* in the mid-thirteenth century. Marshall, Martin and Rouse suggest Orleans as the most likely site, supporting this with two pieces of evidence: (1) the *Florilegium Gallicum*, compiled in the mid-twelfth century and probably at Orleans, gives brief quotations from all of Gellius; and (2) extracts from the whole of Gellius appear in the *Manipulus Florum* of Thomas of Ireland, written at the Sorbonne before 1306. We are told that Thomas obtained his extracts both from florilegia and from books in the Sorbonne library, and that as the *Noctes Atticae* were not quoted in the florilegia he used – the *Flores Paradysi* and the *Liber Exceptionum ex Libris Viginti Trium Auctorum* – his source for the quotations must have been the Gellius MS which came to the Sorbonne in 1272 with the books of Richard de Fournival.

But at least one of Thomas' Gellius quotations seems to derive directly from John of Wales' *Communiloquium*, and there is a strong possibility that more of Thomas' quotations were taken from John. The *Manipulus Florum* refers to *Agellius li. vii* as a source for the

---

[28] P. K. Marshall, J. Martin & R. H. Rouse, 1980, p. 378.

heading *correctio da.*[29] The Aulus Gellius quotation is from book 7, chapter 14. It abbreviates sections 1–4 and then jumps directly to section 14. Exactly the same phrases and parts of these sections are run together in *Communiloquium.*[30] *Manipulus Florum* has nothing of the original which is not in *Communiloquium*, while *Communiloquium*, which was written some decades earlier, continues where the *Manipulus Florum* breaks off. If Thomas of Ireland did use a whole text of *Noctes Atticae*, it was not the source of all his Gellius quotations.

This is an interesting sidelight on the sources of the *Manipulus Florum*, and an indicator that the works of John of Wales may have encouraged increased use of Gellius quotations, but it does not alter the fact that a Gellius MS did reach the Sorbonne by the early 1270s, and that this MS was probably a full copy of both earlier and later books. This might provide a quick and easy answer to our search for John's source of Gellius quotations. We have John writing his *Compendiloquium* in Paris around the early 1270s and making use of a full Gellius text, and we have a full Gellius text in the Sorbonne library at the same period. Very possibly John used the Sorbonne text. But, even if he did, we have only half an answer. We deduced that when *Communiloquium* was written, John knew only *Noctes Atticae* 1–7. This means that the Fournival Gellius should have not been his source when writing *Communiloquium*, and that *Communiloquium* must have been written before John had access to this complete copy of the text. So if *Communiloquium* was written in Paris, it was written before the Fournival text became available in 1272, suggesting that John's arrival in Paris must have dated to the 1260s. As an alternative, we would have to suppose that *Communiloquium* was after all written in England, and that it was there that John gained access to a text of the first seven books of the *Noctes Atticae*.

At this stage, and using the evidence of John's use of Gellius, we cannot decide the issue either way. Books 1–7 of *Noctes Atticae* may well have been available in Paris in the 1260s, but we have no confirmation. And equally we suspect that there were some copies of books 1–7 in England, apart from Clare MS 26, but we cannot pinpoint a particular one. John's use of a full text of *Noctes Atticae* 1–7 in *Communiloquium* does not tell us where the work was written, but

---

[29] *Ibid.*, p. 391.   [30] *Communiloq.* 1.9.5.

it does help us to know when. Whether written in Oxford or Paris, *Communiloquium* seems to belong to the 1260s.

The *Noctes Atticae* of Aulus Gellius is only one of the classical sources used by John. Another author who is of interest is Seneca. It is no surprise that John, a medieval writer with moralising tendencies, makes frequent use of Seneca. He refers to almost the whole range of the prose works, and also to the spurious works which circulated under Seneca's name in the Middle Ages. John makes a number of references to the *De Beneficiis, De Clementia*, and *De Naturalibus Quaestionibus*, and seems to know eight of the ten dialogues (the exceptions are the *De Otio* and *Ad Polybium de Consolatione*). He also refers to the *Proverbiae, De Virtutibus, De Remediis Fortuitorum* and *Liber Declamationum*,[31] and makes use of the full range of the *Epistulae*. John's knowledge of the *Epistulae* and of the *Dialogues* is unusually wide.

For many centuries Seneca's *Epistulae* circulated in two parts, letters 1–88 and 89–124. The first group was by far the more common, the second remaining rare into the twelfth century – and beyond, in some areas. Many libraries of the twelfth century possessed only letters 1–88,[32] but copies of letters 89–124 had reached England by the thirteenth century, if not earlier.[33] Reynolds tells us that more than twenty twelfth-century writers, including some of the most prominent, quote from the *Epistulae* but that only four seem to know letters 89–124. These four are William of Malmesbury, Robert of Cricklade, Petrus Cantor and Peter of Blois.[34]

That letters 89–124 were available in at least part of England by the twelfth century is indicated by their use by Robert of Cricklade and William of Malmesbury, and by their appearance in an English florilegium of the twelfth century, the *Florilegium Morale Oxoniense*.[35] We do not know exactly when this work was written, though it seems to have ties with Worcester and the surrounding area[36] – as do William of Malmesbury and Robert of Cricklade. William certainly had a text to hand, because he quotes copiously and accurately.[37] London, British Library, MS Harley 2659, written

[31] All spurious.
[32] L. D. Reynolds, 1965, p. 107.
[33] *Ibid.*, p. 110.
[34] *Ibid.*, pp. 116–20.
[35] Oxford, Bodleian, MS Bodley 633; ed. by Ph. Delhaye and C. H. Talbot, Analecta Mediaevalia Namurcensia, 5–6 (Namur–Lille, 1955–6).
[36] L. D. Reynolds, 1965, p. 122; also Ph. Delhaye, 1952, pp. 203–24.
[37] L. D. Reynolds, 1965, p. 122.

at the Benedictine Abbey of St Peter's in Gloucester just after the mid-twelfth century, contains both parts of the letters. It is clear that both were available in the Severn area by the twelfth century, and that some writers had noticed and were making use of them.

We have little evidence of this use extending to thirteenth-century Oxford. Roger Bacon shows knowledge of both parts in his *Opus Maius*, but makes a distinction between the two.[38] Robert Holcot was delighted to 'discover' the 36 later letters in the early fourteenth century.[39] John of Wales, however, quotes copiously from Seneca's *Epistulae*, and refers to the later series as well as the earlier one. For example, his *Communiloquium* makes 94 references to the letters, 10 being to letters 89–124. *Compendiloquium* makes 68 references to the letters, 21 being to letters 89–124. We have no problem explaining how he used them in *Compendiloquium*, written in Paris and after 1270, in a time and place where the letters were readily available and being used by scholars like Roger Bacon. But we must ask about *Communiloquium*, apparently written before 1270, and possibly at least partly in Oxford, and also about the *Commentary and Collations on John*, written *c.* 1259–62 in Oxford.[40] This latter contains three quotations from Seneca's later letters.

There are essentially three possibilities here: John wrote these works in Oxford, or he wrote them in Paris, or he wrote them partly in each place – more particularly, he may have gathered his material in both places. If he wrote them in Oxford, he must either have obtained access to a complete copy of the *Epistulae* in England, have had one sent by an acquaintance in Paris (perhaps someone like Bacon), or have lacked access to a whole text but used an intermediary. Are we in a position to whittle down these possibilities? We must start by considering the possibilities in Oxford.

Oxford, and in particular the Franciscans there, seem to have lacked access to the later Seneca letters in the early to mid-thirteenth century, for the Lyons Index of Grosseteste, a subject index of books available to him, refers only to letters 1–89.[41] However, it is perfectly possible that John, with a strong interest in classical texts, which must have dated from quite early in his life, should have been able to make enquiries and come to hear about a full text of Seneca's *Epistulae*, or a text of the rarer and later letters. At least one copy of such a text, and probably more, was available in the Gloucester/ Worcester area. And it is perhaps no coincidence that John is John of

[38] *Ibid.*, p. 122.
[39] *Ibid.*, p. 122.
[40] See above, pp. 12–14.
[41] R. W. Hunt, 1963, pp. 121–45.

Wales, believed to have originated on the Welsh border, and that he enrolled in the custody of Worcester and was presumably once a schoolboy in the area. He must have had contacts there who could turn up such a text for him if he could not do it in person.

This must be a possible explanation of John's access to a full text of the *Epistulae*. It seems unlikely that he obtained a text from Paris. Although Bacon shares John's use of the later letters, and two must have met or known of each other, John does not share Bacon's view of the letters as being two separate books;[42] this suggests that they were not using the same text. If John had sent to Paris for a text, we cannot guess who provided it. And if John were to send out emissaries in search of rare texts, or specifically Senecan ones, he was just as likely to enquire in the area between Oxford and Worcester as in Paris – indeed, probably more so.

We cannot entirely rule out the possibility that John found the text for himself in Paris. We know he was in Oxford until around 1262, and that he had arrived in Paris by June 1270. The date or dates when he crossed the Channel are unknown. *Communiloquium* appears to have been written before 1269/70, and at least partly in Oxford, but it could also be partly a Paris production. This could explain its ten references to letters 89–124, which were readily available in Paris by the 1260s, but it does not explain the references in the *Commentary and Collations on John*, which are surely earlier Oxford productions.[43]

This could perhaps be explained if John used an intermediate source. So far, investigation has ruled out this solution. An obvious possibility for the intermediary would be the *Florilegium Morale Oxoniense*. This contains 18 quotations from letters 89–124, but none of the ten quotations in *Communiloquium* is included, and neither of the two in the *Commentary and Collations on John*. It is difficult to think of another intermediary which would fit the bill, because accurate references are an essential part of John's work. Certainly by the time he wrote *Communiloquium* John's references to the *Epistulae* included the letter number at the very least. Few of John's predecessors could live up to this and provide the information necessary if John were to make detailed references without recourse to a whole text. In *Communiloquium*, John makes his references to the *Epistulae* in a wholly characteristic fashion, showing good knowledge of their contents. He shows the capacity to paraphrase a letter and to bring

[42] L. D. Reynolds, 1965, p. 122.
[43] For background on Oxford University, see J. I. Catto, 1984.

out the parts which are particularly relevant to his point; he also shows the capacity to jump knowingly from letter to letter to put appropriate sentences together. He uses the later letters as a source for Virgil, [44] and tells us that he is getting Virgil at second hand. This openness about using secondary sources from time to time is also characteristic of John of Wales.

Thus we have no problem with John's use of Seneca's later letters in *Compendiloquium* and subsequent works, as these were written in Paris, where the later letters were readily available by the 1270s. The references in the *Commentary and Collations on John* and the *Communiloquium* are more problematic. It is possible that the references in the *Commentary and Collations* could have come from an intermediate source, as the text refers only to Seneca and makes no mention of the work or part of a work which was used as the source. [45] However, it has not been possible to find the relevant quotations in any earlier work as yet.

Possible intermediates have also been checked for the ten quotations from the later letters which appear in *Communiloquium*, but no suitable earlier text has been found. The *Communiloquium* contains material which is distinctively Parisian, and material which is characteristic of its period in Oxford, most probably because the idea was conceived in Oxford, and much of the material prepared there, while some of the collection of material and final composition would have been carried out after John's transfer to Paris. The ten references to Seneca's later letters may have been found in England, as whole texts of Seneca's *Epistulae* do seem to have been available there, or they may have come from a text in Paris. We cannot at the moment decide between the two, though detailed comparison between John and early Seneca texts might help us. John's references in *Communiloquium* are all numbered, but the numbers do not match those in the modern text, being in general two or three too high for their correct placing. This suggests that John's text of Seneca was numbered incorrectly according to modern understanding, and this might help in the identification of John's particular source.

So far examination has been made of John's use of the *Noctes Atticae* of Aulus Gellius and of the later letters of Seneca, which were both unusual texts in John's period. Their availability depended to some extent upon whether a writer worked in England or in France, but in neither case has it been possible to fix on one country as

---

[44] *Communiloq.* 3.2.6., citing Seneca, Epistula 108.24.
[45] The quotations are from Seneca's Epistulae 108 and 110.

distinctly more likely than the other where John of Wales is concerned. Help may be sought from others of John's sources.

In addition to all of Seneca's letters, John appears to have used most of his *Dialogues*. His references to these in *Breviloquium de Virtutibus, Communiloquium* and *Compendiloquium* are tabulated below.

	BREV. DE VIRT.	COMMUNILOQ.	COMPENDILOQ.
Ad Elbiam	–	1	4
De Beata Vita	–	1	1
De Brevitate Vitae	–	1	2
De Consolatione	–	–	4
De Constantia Sap.	1	4	3
De Ira	9	13	7
De Providentia	1	5	1
De Tranquillitate Animi	–	5	5

It is only necessary to refer to these three of John's works, because almost all other works of fixed sequence belong after *Compendiloquium* and were certainly produced in Paris. It was in Paris that Roger Bacon 'discovered' Seneca's *Dialogues*, as he announced in 1266.[46] The discovery so excited him that he considerably extended his *Opus Maius* in order to include lengthy extracts. We know that medieval scholars frequently 'discovered' works which were not as new and exciting to everyone as they themselves believed, but no one has disputed the importance or genuine quality of Bacon's discovery of Seneca's *Dialogues*. What are the implications for *Breviloquium de Virtutibus* and *Communiloquium* if we continue to accept the originality of Bacon's discovery *c.* 1266 (or possibly as early as 1265, as he may have found the works some time before he made his announcement)? It has been argued that John's *Communiloquium* was substantially completed before Aquinas' return to Paris *c.* 1269 and before production of his commentary on Aristotle's *Politics*. John could have been in Paris during the mid-1260s – we have no evidence to the contrary. If he were, we can see a simple explanation of his use of the Senecan *Dialogues*. As a former Oxford scholar, and as a friar working in Paris, John would have moved in the same circles as Roger Bacon. We know that they were both interested in rare classical texts, and it is possible that Bacon promptly shared his exciting discovery with his Oxford acquaintance. If

[46] R. H. Rouse, 1979, p. 149.

we accept this, we must accept that *Communiloquium*, and possibly *Breviloquium de Virtutibus*, are at least partly Paris productions, and that John was established in Paris for some time before his first recorded appearance in June 1270.

As a refinement on this, we might suggest the possibility that John of Wales actually anticipated Bacon with the Senecan *Dialogues* and was already using them before 1266. This would broaden the time-span in which *Breviloquium de Virtutibus* and *Communiloquium* could have been written. Certainly John does not seem to be the kind of man who would boast of any rare finds that he made. He does not parade his use of any of his rare sources, but simply quotes them as appropriate.

If we do not accept John's presence in Paris in the 1260s, we must postulate that Bacon's 'discovery' did not justify his excitement – that is, that the texts were available to a scholar in Oxford. This is possible, but unlikely. Our other possibility, as always, is that John was not using complete texts in *Breviloquium de Virtutibus* and *Communiloquium*, but was making use of intermediaries.

But close examination of John's numerous quotations from the *Dialogues* indicates that he had direct access to the texts. He does not quote mere snippets, but paragraphs and groups of paragraphs, and he shows good awareness of the whereabouts of his quotations in the text. We may well conclude from this that, like Bacon, John came across the *Dialogues* in Paris in the mid- to late 1260s. We cannot say which of the two was the first to spot and use them, though the *Opus Maius* probably went into circulation before the *Communiloquium* and possibly before the *Breviloquium de Virtutibus*.

If John was working in Paris by 1265/6, it would help to explain his access to some other rare works: for example, the Latin version of Plato's *Phaedo* and some of Cicero – the *Academica Posteriora*, *De Divinatione*, *De Legibus*, *De Natura Deorum*, *De Oratore ad Marcum Brutum* and *Hortensius*. John also knew Cicero's *De Amicitia*, *De Officiis*, *De Paradoxis*, *De Rhetorica*, *Philippics* and *Tusculanae Quaestiones*, but these were much more common.

The Latin *Phaedo* certainly reached Paris by the 1270s, as there was a copy among the Fournival books which went to the Sorbonne library in 1272.[47] Richard Rouse suggests that the *Phaedo* would have been available in the 1260s, although it was not then officially part of the collection,[48] and he points out that Roger Bacon and John of Wales were the first schoolmen to know the text.[49] If Bacon could

[47] *Ibid.*   [48] *Ibid.*   [49] *Ibid.*

use it in the 1260s, then so presumably could John. There is certainly a lengthy quotation from it in *Breviloquium*, in a form which indicates that John was using the text directly.[50]

We can see that John of Wales and Bacon had access to, and were using, many of the same books when most of their contemporaries showed little interest. It would be interesting to know what kind of relationship the two shared – though it is probably impossible to find this out.

To return to John of Wales and Cicero, the table below enumerates John's references to Cicero's more unusual texts.

	BREV. DE VIRT.	COMMUNILOQ.	COMPENDILOQ.
Academica Posteriora	–	–	I
De Divinatione	–	I	5
De Legibus	–	I	–
De Natura Deorum	–	3	4

The quotations are few, but more numerous than most thirteenth-century authors were able to produce. Cicero's *Academica Posteriora* and *De Finibus Bonorum et Malorum* were very rare in the thirteenth century.[51] John of Salisbury's *Policraticus* contains four echoes of the *Academica*, but in each case the passage derives from Augustine's *Contra Academicos*.[52] The Dominican encyclopaedist Vincent of Beauvais knew the *Academica* and quoted it under its own name.[53] Vincent and Roger Bacon both also knew the *De Finibus*, quoting it four and two times respectively.[54] Vincent of Beauvais completed the *Speculum Historiale* by 1244,[55] so the works must have been available in Paris by that time. The reference to the *Academica Posteriora* in *Compendiloquium* is merely an echo, and the work is not specifically named.[56]

We have now discussed John's use of unusual works by three different classical authors. These, taken with the other classical

---

[50] *Brev. de Virt.* 3.5. See also *Compendiloq.* 3.3.14.

[51] R. H. and M. A. Rouse, 1978, pp. 333–70.

[52] *Ibid.*, pp. 333–70.

[53] Vincent of Beauvais, *Speculum Historiale* 6.29 quotes Cicero, *Posterior Academics* 5.18. For Vincent, who was the greatest encyclopaedist of the thirteenth century, see M. Lemoine, 1966; W. J. Aerts *et al.*, 1986.

[54] R. H. and M. A. Rouse, 1978, pp. 333–70.

[55] *Ibid.*

[56] The identification was made by Luke Wadding in his edition in 1655.

works which he quotes, indicate an unusually wide range and a deep interest in antiquity and its writers. We have seen that John not only found and made use of virtually ignored texts, but also quarried his texts for authors otherwise beyond his reach. His 'second-hand' quotations are exclusively from classical authors. He does not seem to have used any florilegia – all his quotations can be accounted for otherwise. Florilegia were certainly available in Oxford and in Paris, so John's lack of use may indicate a deliberate policy of avoidance. This would fit well with his obvious penchant for accuracy and detailed references, and his apparent interest in obtaining access to original texts. Where florilegia gave references, they tended to be of a general kind only, so they would not have fitted with John's determination to refer closely to texts. Indeed, John's frequent incitements to the reader to look further in the works quoted do indicate that he was most concerned that the originals should be used. John's own works do not fit well into the category of florilegia.

John's abundant and accurate quotations are not confined to the patristic and classical authors listed and discussed above. As the source-lists at the ends of later chapters show, he refers to a whole range of other works and authors. For example, he uses a number of canon law collections. He mentions the *Summa* of Hostiensis or Henry de Suza, the *Extravagantes de Ius Iurandum*, Gratian's *Decretum* and the *Summa de Casibus* of Raymond de Pennaforte. John also refers to earlier medieval encyclopaedias, including the *De Naturis Rerum* of Alexander Nequam and the *Speculum Maius* of Vincent of Beauvais.

John shows a considerable fondness for the Arabs. He uses them even in his biblical commentaries.[57] In his preaching aids he makes particular use of Algazel, Alphorabius (Al-Farabi), Avicenna, Gundissalinus and the translations of Constantinus Africanus. John's Oxford background is shown by his use of works by Grosseteste, for example his Latin version of the *Suda*[58] and his translation of and commentary on the pseudo-Dionysian corpus.

So John had access to, and used, a great number and range of sources. The material which he drew from these sources was carefully controlled and accurately presented in a logical sequence. This was a tremendous feat, and we are bound to wonder how it was

[57] For discussion of the commentaries on the Gospels, see B. Smalley, 1985, pp. 213–26.

[58] For details of this translation, see S. Harrison Thomson, 1940, pp. 63–4; also R. Southern, 1986.

accomplished. The *Communiloquium*, for example, contains over
1,500 extracts from other works. How did John organise and control
such a huge amount of material?

Our first conclusion must be that John did not, in general, copy his
chosen extracts into his own text directly from the original copies.
This would have been an impossibly unwieldy system, even if John
had already studied all the volumes available, mentally noted which
extracts he wanted, and made sure that each work would be available
whenever he wanted to use it. It seems likely that John would have
used some written method of extraction and organisation when he
approached his tasks.

A modern writer, setting out to produce a volume of over 1,500
coherently linked extracts, would have immediate recourse to a
card-index, or a word-processor with a good memory, organising
his material alphabetically or by topic, or perhaps by a combination
of the two. John's own approach was probably not so very different.
He was certainly capable of creating a series of divisions and
subdivisions into which he could place *exempla*: the skeleton divisions of his own works are proof enough of that. In many ways the
medieval way of thinking was ideally constructed for this kind of
analysis: the virtues, the vices, the ages of man were all standard sub-
divisions. To these John presumably added new categories: 'virtues
of philosophers', perhaps, and the names of individuals like Plato
and Socrates (all these appear as categories in the *Compendiloquium*).
The latter categories might well have had sub-divisions like 'early
life', 'profound sayings', 'mode of death', as these again are sections
which John uses in his texts. It seems natural that the collection and
organisation of extracts should be a fairly continuous process, and
that when John was writing a given section of a given work he would
examine his personal store of carefully copied *exempla* and select
those which seemed suitable – or make a search in the original
volumes if he had nothing to hand.

If we accept this, then we must accept that John was indeed using a
topic index, just as we might do today. There is nothing implausible
in this, as concordances of various types were becoming established
by John's period.[59] W. A. Pantin suggested that John used a system
of alphabetical tables as a preliminary to writing and might well also
have used Grosseteste's subject-index and annotated volumes of the
fathers.[60]

---

[59] M. B. Parkes, 1976.   [60] W. A. Pantin, 1961, p. 307.

John might indeed have used these aids, not only as a guide to suitable sources of *exempla* on certain topics, but also as an example of what could be done in terms of searching a body of material. Grosseteste's indexes and texts, which became part of the library of the Oxford Franciscans, could certainly have provided a starting-point for John's researches. The Index names 150 texts or authors, mainly patristic or later Christian. John refers to 61 of these, often by the same titles, in the course of his first four *loquia*. As some of the works cannot now be traced under the particular titles they used,[61] we must suppose that they were occupants of the Franciscan library at Oxford, and that John used them there.

If John did use the Grosseteste Index, it was only a part of his armoury. He refers to a mere two-fifths of its contents, and his own range of material was very much wider than the 61 works which it lists. Moreover, texts like John's *Breviloquium de Virtutibus* used almost no patristic material. What else might John have used? One possibility is the *Registrum Librorum Angliae* which had been put together by the English Franciscans in the mid-thirteenth century. This would have supplied John with the names of works by likely authors, together with their whereabouts. He could then easily have travelled to the appropriate libraries, or have had texts copied for or lent to him.[62] What then? He surely did not simply compile alphabetical tables to the classics, for this presupposes that he was confident of finding full copies whenever he wanted them, something which he should not have counted upon. It seems more probable that he collected actual copies of extracts, carefully and accurately made and with their origin noted as fully as possible, these individual extracts being grouped and stored probably on a subject basis, as this was how John worked when it came to compilation.

Such a system has a predecessor in Grosseteste. We have mention of a group of parchment 'slips' written by Grosseteste and later kept in the library of the Oxford Franciscans.[63] These were presumably a close equivalent to our file cards. John no doubt was aware of their existence, and would have been well able to recognise the potential of such a system in his own work.

There are signs in John's texts which do indicate that he was using

[61] E.g., the work cited in the *Tabula* as the *De Bono Virginali* of Augustine: see R. W. Hunt, 1963, p. 142.

[62] For the *Registrum Librorum Angliae*, see R. A. B. Mynors, 1957, pp. 199–217.

[63] R. W. Hunt, 1963, p. 127.

a system of written extracts grouped by topic.[64] Such a system leads to a particular type of error which is difficult to explain otherwise: for example, the faithful reproduction of an *exemplum*, followed by an incorrect reference which actually belongs to a different *exemplum* on the same subject. The mistake is an easy one to make – many a modern scholar has made just this kind of error in compiling footnotes. John gives us a clear example in his *Compendiloquium* where he tells a tale about Plato and gives a specific reference to Augustine's *Confessions*, near the end of book 7. There is a story about Plato in exactly that place, but not the one which John quotes. That tale appears, word for word, in a quite different place in the same text (book 7, chapter 9, rather than chapter 20, the last one in the book).

John could not have made such an error in copying from the original text, for he would easily have been able to see that he was not at the end of the book. Nor could he have been relying on memory, as the text is reproduced too faithfully, and a memory good enough to do this would be unlikely to have forgotten the accompanying reference. The most probable explanation is that the two *exempla* were close together on the same sheet marked *Plato*, and that after he had copied the chosen example, John's eye slipped and he copied in the other reference. We might note that the second Plato story does not appear in any of the MSS or texts by John which I have yet examined, thus supporting the suggestion that John collected more material than he chose to use in the end.

An organised system of slips would also explain such points as the characteristically Oxford quotations found in the *Communiloquium*, when some of its material was certainly found in Paris. On his transfer across the Channel, John would simply have packed up his collection of *exempla* and extracts and taken it with him. New material found in Paris would have made a substantial expansion possible.

A further question arises: how did John *collect* the material which he handled so carefully? Was the collection an unaided effort, or did he have one or more assistant friars commissioned to search volumes and libraries on his behalf? We may doubt whether the collection of material was done single-handed; it would have been a massive task. We know that the use of research assistants was well established

---

[64] For an example indicating that John had adopted such a method, see the discussion below, pp. 121n, 122.

among the friars in Paris.[65] It seems likely that there, if not during his earlier years in Oxford, John was able to share the burden of routine collection with some other Franciscans. However, there is no evidence to suggest that the composition of the texts was done by teamwork. The works attributed to John of Wales show none of the inconsistencies which have pointed to teamwork in the volumes attributed to Hugh of Saint-Cher.[66] Quite the reverse: all John's works follow a characteristic and distinctive pattern, and the style of composition and the attitudes expressed are internally consistent. The comments in the works also show a good knowledge of the wider contents of the original texts which John quotes. We may be sure that much of the work was done by John quite independently, particularly among the classical texts which he found so absorbing.

[65] R. E. Lerner, 1985, pp. 157–89.   [66] *Ibid.*

Chapter 3

THE *BREVILOQUIUM DE VIRTUTIBUS ANTIQUORUM PRINCIPUM ET PHILOSOPHORUM*

The virtues were always a popular topic with medieval writers, in the thirteenth century as much as in any other, and the period *c.* 1250–1300 was one in which many friars were producing volumes of advice to princes.[1] The subject of philosophers was becoming more popular in the thirteenth century, in association with the spread of Aristotelianism in the universities. John's *Breviloquium* is related to the general group of works on the virtues, and to the *Fürstenspiegel*, or volumes of advice to princes, but his combination of the two is unusual for his century, as is his inclusion of the philosophers. His *Breviloquium de Virtutibus* seems to stand at the intersection of three topics which were considered interesting and important in the period when it was written. Its presence at this intersection reflects John's deep-rooted personal interest in three areas: virtue, the great deeds of ancient men, and philosophy and philosophers. The fact that these interests were shared by many others, though not always as a threesome, must have contributed to the success of the work.[2]

As its title suggests, John's *Breviloquium de Virtutibus Antiquorum Principum et Philosophorum* is a collection of *exempla* illustrating the virtuous behaviour of ancient princes and philosophers. These *exempla* were designed for the instruction of rulers. This *Breviloquium* is one of the earliest of John's works, and certainly the first in the sequence of *loquia*,[3] so it is valuable as a source of information on John's early views and interests.

The *Breviloquium de Virtutibus* is a relatively short work – some 15,000 words – so it is intriguing that its introductory and final sections seem to bear so little relation to each other. If one separates them from the main text, it is difficult to accept that they are the

---

[1] J-P. Genet, 1977, p. xii. [2] For the extent of this success, see below, chap. 8.
[3] See above, p. 1.

beginning and end of one work. This is one of several indications of apparent casualness of composition to be found in this *Breviloquium*, and it may be as well to discuss them before examining the ideas in the main text.

John's conception of his *Breviloquium* is nicely expressed in his opening passage. He begins with a quotation from Proverbs 20: 'Mercy and truth guard the king'; or rather, he continues, the four cardinal virtues – Prudence, Temperance, Fortitude and Justice – are like pillars which support the throne.[4] Therefore he presents some model and persuasive tales for the use of those in authority and the instruction of rulers ('narrationes exemplares et persuasorie ad utilitatem presidentium et instructionem in thronis residentium'). The examples come from the deeds of rulers and wise men and the world of philosophers, for the examples of the saints are sufficiently shown in their deeds and in the tales of holy scripture.[5] John is partly motivated by the belief that the good example of the saints is already well known, while that of men from the ancient world is not. This is a theme which runs throughout his works. At a time when the use of classical *exempla* was still disputed, and when many friars were positively rejecting the practice, John was entirely in favour of it.[6]

After his brief introduction, John plunges into the main text, a division and analysis of the virtues, with numerous stories to illustrate their various aspects. For some time he adheres to the pattern of prefacing each aspect of a virtue with a remark about its use to rulers, and of giving between *exempla* some brief comments on how a ruler should behave. There comes a point, however, where the introductory remark more often emphasises that the virtue 'flourished in antiquity'.[7] Though the examples still come from the lives of ancient men, or in some cases women, the references to what one might term contemporary princehood become much less frequent. In most of the fourth and fifth sections, princes have vanished altogether. Why?

One might be tempted to argue that John had run out of ideas about princes, or lost interest in them, but this is not so. The

---

[4] Unless otherwise stated, quotations come from the 1496 edition of the *Breviloquium de Virtutibus*, in *Margarita Doctorum*, printed in Venice by G. Arrivabenis. I have collated this with two Oxford MSS: Oxford, Bodleian, MS Hatton 105, and Oxford, Bodleian, MS Bodley 58.

[5] John returns to the deeds of the saints in his *Breviloquium de Sapientia Sanctorum* (see below, chapter 7).

[6] J-P. Genet, 1977, p. xiii, cites examples of friars opposed to the use of classics.

[7] Around the opening of section 3.

Communiloquium, written after this *Breviloquium*, has a long section on princes which refers back to this earlier work. The *Communiloquium* lists twenty aspects of appropriate princely behaviour and discusses them in some detail,[8] also providing an analysis of the prince's role in the state.[9] Lack of interest or of opinion does not in itself explain any changes of emphasis in this *Breviloquium*.

The nature of the change is clear from the final section of the treatise. This section, headed *De ordinatione virtutum* ('on the ranking of the virtues'), opens with the observation that if the ancients could be so virtuous in the doing of good works, the faithful ought to be able to achieve a good deal more. This is a preoccupation of John's, appearing again and again in others of his works. If in this *Breviloquium* he had redefined the point with particular reference to medieval rulers, or indeed had simply ended on it, it would relate quite neatly to his opening remarks. But this is not the case. The remaining part of the work, deriving primarily from book 5 of Augustine's *De Civitate Dei*, discusses the relationship of the virtues to pleasure (*voluptas*) and roundly condemns the stance of the Epicureans, who would subordinate the former to the latter. John becomes quite excited about this and recapitulates Augustine's arguments at some length. Eventually the work ends on a devout note, moving through a discussion of the virtues as a pathway to glory and ending with an 'Amen'.

One can follow the train of thought as the treatise progresses. From using examples of ancient virtue to stimulate contemporary rulers, John moves on to emphasise the virtues of the ancients in their own right, and hence to the conclusion that all Christians could take a leaf out of their book. He abandons *exempla* and considers the attitudes of the ancients, and particularly their philosophers, to virtue – hence the discussion of Epicureanism. He then proceeds through a synthesis of Augustine's views to comment on what the virtues should signify to any Christian. A change in emphasis, though a coherent and understandable one, has certainly taken place.

Can we see why or how this happened? There are various possibilities. First, the work might have been written hastily and never revised, so that John slipped off the point without realising it, and never regained his train of thought. Secondly, it might have been written over a long period – that is, it might have been set aside and not taken up again until John's thoughts had altered and he could

---

[8] *Communiloq.* 1.3.   [9] *Communiloq.* 1.2.

not recapture his former mood. If we are seriously to consider either of these possibilities, we should note that the virtues which head the four central sections of the work are in a different sequence to that given in the introduction,[10] and that two of the stories told in the first half of the work reappear in the second. Such inconsistencies and repetitions are far from unknown in medieval compilations. Pantin points to their existence in John's work as evidence of haste in preparation.[11] In the case of a short work like the *Breviloquium de Virtutibus*, however, one might plausibly reverse the argument and suggest that they are a sign of a gap in composition.

There seems to be no clear way to select either of the above alternatives as correct. As a third possibility, one might consider an intrinsic rift between the schematic layout of the *Breviloquium* and the way in which it was actually written: between the formal structure which John selected and the ideas he really wanted to put forward. From the essential difference between the promise of the introduction and the schematic division on the one hand, and the actual development of the work on the other, it may be possible to say something about the way in which the *Breviloquium* was composed. The dichotomy suggests that John, having obtained a brief list of virtues and their sub-divisions, did not write a quick foreword and simply pigeonhole an array of examples in order to create his text, but worked through from beginning to end to produce an 'organic' structure with its own natural development.

This possibility is supported by the fact that there is a subtle chain of connections between neighbouring *exempla*, so that one is connected to the next by the name of a person or place or a shading of the virtue under discussion. For example, Julius Caesar's *clementia* in weeping over the head of his dead enemy, Pompey, is followed by the story of Pompey's own *clementia* in restoring a kingdom to a defeated Armenian king.[12] What seems to have happened is this: as John worked through his set sequence of chapters, organising and grouping *exempla* in the text, his own personal fascination with the ancients and their virtue began to increase in importance, so that the work developed a rather different ending from that one might expect from the earlier chapters.

---

[10] Introduction: Prudence, Temperance, Fortitude, Justice. Text: Justice, Prudence, Temperance, Fortitude.
[11] W. A. Pantin, 1961, p. 307.　　　　　[12] *Brev. de Virt.* 3.2.

The fact that John apparently exercised careful selection in deciding which *exempla* to use, coupled with the probability that the development and writing of the work cost him much thought, makes the *Breviloquium de Virtutibus* worthy of examination. However, because the work is brief and in some respects overshadowed by successors like the *Communiloquium*, it tends to offer only tantalising glimpses of what becomes, with further study, a much fuller picture.

Let us now look more closely at the contents of the *Breviloquium de Virtutibus*. Its skeleton is provided by the analysis of the virtues given below.

IUSTITIA:	*De iustitia in possidendo*
	De iustitia in statuendo leges iustas
	De observatione legum
	De providentia circa rempublicam
	De iustitia erga inimicos
	De partibus iustitie
PRUDENTIA:	*Memoria*
	Intelligentia
	Providentia
	De reliquis prudentie partibus:
	Ratio
	Intellectus
	Circumspectio
	Providentia
	Cautio
TEMPERANTIA:	*Continentia*:
	Cohibitio gule
	Cohibitio luxurie
	Cohibitio cupiditatis et avaritie
	Cohibitio ambitionis et superbie
	Clementia
	Modestia
FORTITUDO:	*Magnificentia*
	Fidentia
	Pacientia
	Perseverantia

A number of analyses of the virtues survived from the ancient world to be used by medieval writers. John's analysis and definitions are an unusual combination from Cicero and Macrobius.[13]

Having explained the nature of the *Breviloquium de Virtutibus*, John proceeds directly to his collection of stories and comments. It is clear from the very title of the work that he was interested in rulers and philosophers, and the text shows that he knew a considerable amount about the ancient world. He tells his stories for a moral purpose; he is not acting as a historian and makes no attempt to criticise his material.[14] It is no surprise to the modern reader that many of his stories are patently untrue, but this should not lessen their value as indications of what interested John. Indeed many of his *exempla* remain impressive in their own right – it takes some force of mind to remember that they belong to what we might term an alternative reality, and that many of the ancients would have had difficulty in recognising the picture of their world presented by John.

I have said that John's interest in the ancient world had an essentially moral purpose, but he indicates in at least two places that he is interested in ancient religion and rituals in their own right. The first occasion relates to a description of the lawcode of the Spartan Lycurgus.[15] John gives some information about the oracle at Delphi, whence the lawcode was said to derive, and then digresses to observe that Apollo was also worshipped on the island of Delos, where there was a temple and a holy place (*locus divinationis*). This latter information does not come straight from John's source for the lawcode – Justin's *Epitome* of Trogus Pompeius – which fails to mention it, but rather from Grosseteste's commentary on Aristotle's *Ethics*, as John correctly points out. Grosseteste post-dates Justin by many centuries, so the *Epitome* provides no hints that the Grosseteste commentary contains any relevant information. It must be John himself who made the connection and thought it worthy of inclusion in his *Breviloquium*.

The second example of a particular interest in ritual is John's moralisation of the Roman Triumph.[16] This was originally an Etruscan ritual of primarily religious significance, although its purpose had become clouded by the middle Republic.[17] So there is a

---

[13] This was pointed out by R. Tuve, 1963, pp. 68–72. John uses Macrobius, *In Somnium Scipionis* 1.8, for his definitions, and Cicero, *De Inventione* 2.53–4, for the parts of the virtues. Normally a medieval writer used only one or the other.

[14] On *exempla*, see C. Bremond, J. Le Goff & J-C. Schmitt, 1982; also P. Von Moos, 1984, pp. 207–61.

[15] *Brev. de Virt.* 1.2.

[16] *Brev. de Virt.* 2.3. See p. 50–51.

[17] R. M. Ogilvie, 1976, pp. 38–40.

certain delight in finding it used to illustrate the Roman capacity for victory without vanity. This again is one of the comparatively rare occasions when John refers to more than one source for a single *exemplum*. [18]

We turn now to others of John's attitudes, and to the question of what the *Breviloquium de Virtutibus* can contribute to our understanding of them. The *Breviloquium* purports to have been written for rulers, so they are the natural jumping-off point. John makes few open remarks about princes, but most of what he does say appears in the first two parts of the *Breviloquium*. His comments and *exempla* span two main areas: the personal behaviour and characteristics of a prince, and his relationship to the state and people. We know from John's *Communiloquium* that he recognised the definition 'respublica est respopuli', at least on paper. It is clear that he was deeply interested in the *respublica* – indeed, in the first section of the *Breviloquium de Virtutibus* we learn as much about the state as about rulers as a special class.

That John's section on justice is biased towards the state and politics is clear from the chapter headings. John opens by telling the reader that justice is the noblest of virtues, [19] and that in it is all *virtus*. [20] Kingdoms without justice are *magna latrocinia*, and *latrocinia* or groups of brigands are *parva regna*. Just laws need to be established so that they may be followed. [21] John then explains the origins of the Lycurgan lawcode of ancient Sparta and lists the twelve Lycurgan laws. It is interesting that they are the only illustration given in the section on just law. We can see why a friar like John would find them attractive, although they are infinitely remote from the legal system of his own day. They include the recommendation of frugality to all, communal living without luxury, restriction of money and precious metals, a simple life for the young, and no dowries for girls. They also provide for the taking-up of all land in common and the giving of equal portions to each citizen. Though John does not discuss this, the system seems to have worked so that a property reverted to the state on the death of its 'owner' and was then reallotted, so that effectively a man had not ownership but a lifetime's use in exchange for his services to the state. [22] This could have been of great interest to

---

[18] In this case, to Hugh of Saint-Victor, Jerome and Ovid.

[19] *Brev. de Virt.* 1.1.

[20] Based on the fifth book of Aristotle's *Ethics*. In general I have not given detailed references to John's sources, as these are readily available in the original text, to which I do make detailed reference.

[21] *Brev. de Virt.* 1.2.   [22] See in general W. G. Forrest, 1968.

a friar, while the wrangle about possessions continued.[23] It would be valuable to know how far John was aware of this aspect of the system.

John gives his source for these Lycurgan laws as Trogus Pompeius, whom he knew through Justin's *Epitome*, and he would seem to have used this latter work directly. John of Salisbury does give an abbreviated version of the code in his *Policraticus* but does not name his source. John of Wales' version differs from Justin's in that he has transformed a continuous text into a series of separate, numbered laws and has removed certain subsidiary clauses, but the two versions are so similar that there is unlikely to have been an intermediary between them.[24]

From the observation that laws should be just, John moves on to point out that they should be obeyed by all.[25] He tells us that in antiquity the laws were guarded with wondrous severity, and gives instances of ancient lawmakers who set an example in obeying their own laws, like Karundo, who forgot his own law that no one should wear a sword in the council house and, when reminded of it, righted the wrong by falling on the sword in question. John points out that many rulers do not obey the laws which they set up for their subjects, and draws an analogy with the spider's web, which restricts the weak but allows bigger and stronger animals to pass through.[26] This *exemplum* is shared with John of Salisbury, but again it is our later John who gives the fuller version and names the source.[27] Though John refers frequently to the *Policraticus* of John of Salisbury, he does not seem to have used it as a secret short cut to classical *exempla,* as has been implied by Pantin.[28]

In his next chapter, *De providentia circa rempublicam,* John tells the stories of Marcus Regulus and of the Athenian king Codrus, to show that one should be ready to surrender one's own life for the state.[29] He quotes a precept of Plato's, that those who act for their own benefit, forgetting the common good, should be killed, and then comments on the wrongness of private wealth, which was claimed by Augustine as a cause of the decline of the Roman Empire. Note, says John, how poor ancient consuls were – like Lucius Valerius, whose tomb had to be paid for by public subscription. This example

---

[23] M. D. Lambert, 1961.
[24] This is clear from comparison of *Brev. de Virt.* and Justin's *Epitome* 3.2 and 3.
[25] *Brev. de Virt.* 1.3.
[26] *Brev. de Virt.* 1.4.
[27] Valerius Maximus.
[28] W. A. Pantin, 1961, p. 306.
[29] *Brev. de Virt.* 1.5.

is followed by a number of other tales of men who rejected wealth or bore its loss without complaint.

John also tells an *exemplum* about a Roman emperor whom he names as Helyo. When the state wanted to make him emperor he asked that his son should become Augustus, for he deserved to rule, not because of birth but on merit, and he who rules because he is born a king, rather than because he deserves to rule, is useless. We cannot say how far John was in agreement with these sentiments, but his decision to use the *exemplum* must reflect interest. John goes on to tell us that one should economise on nothing where the health of the state is concerned. He gives numerous examples of how a father should not spare his son, nor a son his father. Finally he gives the *exemplum* of the two *sapientes* cast adrift on a yacht which can only support one. What are they to do? John tells us that the less wise should give place to the more wise, who would be of greater use to the state. He prudently avoids the question of how to decide which man deserves which title. There are two important points here: that value to the state is seen as a valid criterion for judging precedence, and that wise men are expected to contribute to the state.

Chapter 5, *De iustitia inter inimicos,* gives examples of honourable behaviour towards enemies. In one *exemplum*, we hear that one night the Roman general Fabricius received a visit from Pirrus' doctor, who offered to poison his master. Fabricius, refusing the offer, ordered the doctor to be chained and returned to Pirrus to confess. Other examples describe similar situations.

The following chapter, *De partibus iustitie*, discusses two aspects of justice – *securitas* and *liberalitas*.[30] The acts of the ancients show that both flourished among them. John cites Alexander as one of a list of generous ancients. He then gives an alternative division of justice – into *innocentia, amicitia, concordia, pietas, religio, affectus* and *humilitas* – and repeats that the deeds of the ancients show that these all flourished among them.[31] John further confirms his interest in the state and in suitable rulership by telling a story from the Roman geographer Solinus, about a certain island race whose choice of king was based not upon noble birth, but upon universal suffrage. The people chose from those of mature years, tested by time and shown to be clement and having no children, lest the kingship should become hereditary.

Further on in the chapter, John gives an analysis of *amicitia*, with

---

[30] *Brev. de Virt.* 1.6.
[31] This time John cites Macrobius rather than Cicero.

examples of how the ancients handled it. He also tells us that the prince ought to discipline his soldiers, but as a father would punish his sons rather than a master his servants. John's fondness for the paternal relationship also appears in the *Communiloquium*.[32]

This completes John's comments on the first of the virtues. He next discusses *prudentia*, opening the section with the remark that three qualities brought victory to the Romans – *scientia, exercitatio* and *fides*.[33] John observes that Roman emperors and generals were not illiterate, and quotes the old adage 'Rex illiteratus quasi asinus coronatus' ('an illiterate king is like a crowned ass'). Ancient princes all had tutors: for example, Trajan had Plutarch, Nero Seneca, and Alexander Aristotle. A weak king endangers his people and their cities. Ancient rulers exercised prudence and were studious: for example, Ptolemy Philadelphus, who, when told that he had 20,000 books, replied that he wanted 50,000 and the emperor Theodosius, who liked to spend the nights reading and thinking rather than sleeping. We can see that John admires both personal education and a wider patronage of learning. He tells us that the prince ought not to be wise only in human affairs and laws, but also in divine law. This leads him to the conclusion that if by chance a ruler is illiterate, the advice of *litterati* is necessary for him to rule.

John next turns to the *prudentia* of philosophers.[34] His illustrations include Archimedes the philosopher, who, during an attack on Syracuse, continued teaching geometry as he was gradually hacked to pieces, and even politely asked the soldiers not to disturb his diagrams in the dust. John says this is an example of someone prudently preserving knowledge, which he esteemed above all temporal things. He also tells of philosophy students who threw away their money as useless, because one cannot buy knowledge.

John now discusses *memoria*.[35] Cicero, he says, tells us that *prudentia* is the quality of being able to distinguish good from evil. It has three parts: *memoria*, which repeats those things which are past, *intelligentia*, by which the spirit recognises things as they are, and *providentia*, through which the spirit sees something which might happen. All these qualities, says John, flourished among ancient princes, as they ought to among all. He mentions three characteristics which led to Rome's victory over her neighbours, giving as an example of *memoria* a detailed description of the ritual of the Roman Triumph, his third factor contributing to Roman success. The

---

[32] See the analysis of *Communiloquium* in chaps. 4, 5 and 6.
[33] *Brev. de Virt.* 2.1.   [34] *Brev. de Virt.* 2.2.   [35] *Brev. de Virt.* 2.3.

victorious leader, wearing the *tunica Iovis*, sat in a chariot and was led
as far as the Capitol by white horses. Lest he forget himself through
these honours, he had to undergo three vexations on that same day.
First, he was accompanied by a slave, to give hope to all of low rank
aspiring to such honours. Secondly, the slave took care that he
should not become proud, whispering to him not to become puffed
up over the honour, but to remember that he was a man. Thirdly, for
that day anyone could say anything they liked to the man, whether
to impugn his victory or whatever, and no revenge could be taken.
John plainly found this rather unusual example of the quality of
memoria attractive, as he gives much detail.

John's fifth chapter deals with *intelligentia*. This, says John, is a
quality which princes ought to possess with respect to the dangers
surrounding them, and particularly the danger of adulation. After
giving definitions of adulation, John gives us examples of ancient
leaders who would not put up with it, like Augustus Caesar and
Alexander. John shares with other medieval writers a great fondness
for Alexander stories.[36] He also uses this chapter to tell us that rulers
ought to be aware of the transitory nature of power and high place.
Yet again Alexander appears as an example.

We come next to *providentia* or foresight.[37] This quality was
displayed in antiquity, as it should be in all kingdoms. John tells the
reader about Xerxes' lack of foresight in starting a war against the
Greeks, drawing the moral that well-disciplined men are more
important than sheer numbers, as in the case of the 300 Spartans.[38] A
multitude is as nothing without *providentia*. Ancient princes also
possessed foresight in consideration of death: Alexander had a
golden tomb prepared for himself in advance. John tells the story of
the sword of Damocles to show Dionysius' understanding of the
threats to his position, and reveals that Aristotle, on the point of
death, was still able to give sound advice to his pupils.

The final chapter of this part of *Breviloquium de Virtutibus* covers
various parts of *prudentia*.[39] John gives Macrobius' division into
ratio, the aspect of the mind which distinguishes good from evil,
chooses virtue and loves God; *intellectus*, the part of the spirit which
perceives the invisible; *circumspectio*, or caution against vices; *providentia*, or consideration for future events; and *cautio*, the capacity to

[36] See G. Cary, 1956; D. J. A. Ross, 1985; P. Noble *et al.*, 1982; L. Engels *et al.*, 1978.
[37] *Brev. de Virt.* 2.5.
[38] This is clearly a reference to the battle of Thermopylae.
[39] *Brev. de Virt.* 2.6.

distinguish between the virtues and the vices. John says that *cautio* is particularly necessary because there are vicés which seem to be virtues, and illustrates the point with the story of the Trojan horse.

Part Three of this *Breviloquium* deals with the virtue of *temperantia*. This is a necessity for rulers, says John, and has three parts: *continentia, clementia* and *modestia. Continentia* itself is fourfold, embracing restraint of appetite, sexual indulgence, covetousness and greed, ambition and pride.[40] John gives a charming collection of classical *exempla* to illustrate each aspect. With respect to appetite: Alexander only nibbled dry bread on a walking trip with his friends; the Roman general Marcus Scaurus was trapped up an apple-tree all day and never touched the fruit; and Augustus Caesar lived on small amounts of common food – bread and a few tiny fish, bits of dried beef and green figs. Regarding restraint of *voluptas* and *luxuria*, John tells us how Alexander was presented with a beautiful maiden, but with great self-control returned her to her betrothed without even looking at her. Restraint from avarice also flourished among the ancients, for they wished to rule not for financial gain, but for the glory and health of the state. Roman generals proved this point by consistently refusing bribes and perks. John also tells us how these four branches of *continentia* flourished among the philosophers. Diogenes, for example, used to carry a wooden cup, until one day he saw a small boy cupping his hands to drink and threw his cup away, crying 'Nature provides its own drinking vessel.'

Clementia, or temperance in exercising power and leniency towards inferiors, is also fourfold.[41] The forms were

1 Bearing willingly the evil of others (*In conspatiendo affectualiter alienis malis*)
2 Returning good to those doing ill (*In remittendo perfectibiliter malum facientibus*)
3 Giving freely to the poor (*In dando largiter ingratis et indignis*)
4 Humbly abasing himself (*In condescendendoque humiliter suis*)

All these flourished in antiquity. Seneca tells us that *clementia* well befits a king. John tells us how Julius Caesar wept over the head of his dead enemy Pompey, and how Pompey himself had showed clemency towards an Armenian king whom he had defeated, by replacing his diadem and confirming his continued rule of the kingdom.

Modestia, the subject of chapter 3, is passed over almost without

---

[40] *Brev. de Virt.* 3.1.   [41] *Brev. de Virt.* 3.2.

comment. John is anxious to begin his fourth section, *De fortitudine*.

Fortitude of mind and body flourished in antiquity, says John. It is again a fourfold virtue, the parts being *magnificentia, fidentia, pacientia* and *perseverantia*.[42] Under the heading of *magnificentia*, we get examples of differing circumstances in which the virtue can be shown.[43] In one instance it was shown by a captive prince whose people were ill-treated by their Roman conquerors. The prince explained the distinction between a *bona pax*, which would last in perpetuity, and a *mala pax*, which would not, and persuaded the Romans to arrange a peace benevolently. *Magnificentia* can be seen not only in great deeds, but also in profiting from advice. An example of failure to do this is given by John: Aristotle sent a pupil of his on an errand to Alexander, warning him that he should speak pleasingly to the king, but that it was safer to remain silent in the king's hearing. The pupil was shocked by Alexander's adoption of Persian customs and rebuked him. In consequence he lost his life.

In the chapter on *fidentia*, or loyalty, we hear how Alexander was once ill, and the doctors wanted him to take a particular medicine, but he preferred to take another offered by his friend Philippus, because he had been warned that Philippus was treacherous, and he wanted to show his faith in his friend.[44] Plato too showed faith in a friend in a similar manner.

Patientia, being fourfold in its own right, receives considerably more space.[45] The four aspects are listed as putting up with insults, enduring pain with no sign, forgiving injuries, and showing moderation in punishing misdeeds. We learn how Julius Caesar put up with rude and joking songs sung about him, and with aspersions cast on his origins, and how someone once addressed Augustus Caesar 'O tyrant', and he responded simply by saying: 'If I were, you would not dare to say so.' Also, we are told of how the philosophers endured people speaking ill of them, and of Socrates' patience when Alcibiades asked an impertinent question about how he endured his bad-tempered wife. Patience in enduring pain was shown by Alexander, when as a boy he burnt his arm while performing a sacrifice, by Pompey, by the philosopher Zeno and by Leonidas, the man who led the Spartans at Thermopylae. The forgiving of injuries is illustrated with Philip of Macedon's reception of a rude embassy from Athens, and with Alexander's reception of a would-be assassin, who was complimented on his courage in making the attempt

---

[42] *Brev. de Virt.*, introduction to part 4.

[44] *Brev. de Virt.* 4.2.

[43] *Brev. de Virt.* 4.1.

[45] *Brev. de Virt.* 4.3.

and sent back to his master unharmed. Moderation in punishment, the last aspect of patience, is again described as having flourished in antiquity. John records Seneca's opposition to anger and Plato's refusal to punish a slave in anger.

Finally John deals with *perseverantia*.[46] We are told of the good behaviour of Stoic philosophers caught on a ship in a storm, and the fortitude of a woman of antiquity, who tossed her daughters into a river to save them from rape. The ancients, says John, were unusually brave in accepting the death of their children and the loss of their possessions.

John has now completed his discussion of the individual virtues. Part 5 of this *Breviloquium* bears the heading *De ordinatione virtutum* ('On the ordering of the virtues') and takes a more general view of virtue. John tells the reader that if those ancients, who were not illuminated by faith, ordered by charity or supported by hope, were so virtuous in doing good things and sustained so much for the love of honour and temporal good, how much more honest a life should be achieved by the faithful, who have the advantage of these virtues! This seems to be one of the driving arguments of this *Breviloquium*, and, indeed, of all John's works. He repeats it again and again with abundant examples of ancient behaviour and customs. The desire to justify this opinion, to persuade others of its truth and to spur them on to greater efforts in their own lives seems to have been both an important factor in John's decision to write books, and a major force in the shaping of his works and his choice of topics and material.

John goes on to say that Augustine discussed the ordering of the virtues in *De Civitate Dei*, and that some philosophers believed that the summit of human good lay in the virtues. Others, however, achieved a poor balance between virtue and *voluptas*. Augustine told us that these philosophers were accustomed to paint a picture of *voluptas* in a kingly chair, as if a delicate queen sat there with the virtues ranged round her like attendants, watching her commands and doing what she ordered.[47] There is nothing more shameful and deformed than this picture, repeats John, and nothing less able to bear good fruit. Among the Epicureans, virtue is regarded as the minister of pleasure. But to order the virtues thus is to disorder them and to abuse them, for virtue is the pathway to *gloria* or the art of living virtuously. John now gives various definitions of the functions of the virtues in life, again taken from Augustine. For example,

---

[46] *Brev. de Virt.* 4.4.   [47] Augustine, *De Civitate Dei* 5.20.

temperance has the task of restraining libido, fortitude of tolerating adversity, justice of punishing iniquity, and prudence of overcoming evil.

The faithful spirit ought fervently to wish to drink at the fountain of God, says John. If Plato's pagan pupil could feel so great a desire for the future life that, after reading his teacher's book on the immortal soul, he threw himself from a wall and thus left this life, so that he might be translated to a life which he believed to be better, how much more should the faithful desire the eternal life promised to them. They ought not to kill themselves after the example of the badly erring pupil, but they ought to desire this eternal life. The virtues, John assures us, teach the eternal wisdom of God. He then gives a number of biblical comments and closes with an 'Amen'.

So the *Breviloquium* ends not with discussion of the relevance of the virtues to rulers, but with discussion of the paramount importance of virtue in its own right, and of its relevance to Christians in their search for God. Virtue was important in John's world. What role does it play in *Breviloquium*? Perhaps its most significant function is the provision of a developed structure, of a sequence of topics within which John can deploy his ancient *exempla* and his comments to rulers. By using this structure, John not only makes his work easier to follow, but is able to show that all aspects of all virtues can be successfully and effectively illustrated using ancient *exempla*. It is odd, perhaps, that John confines his discussion to the classical virtues and their divisions. The Christian triad of faith, hope and charity receives only a bare mention in the epilogue, when John tells the reader that the ancients performed their virtuous deeds without the benefit of acquaintance with these virtues. John makes no attempt to equate any of his pagan virtues with the Christian ones, or to condemn the ancients for their lack of faith, hope or charity. His picture of the virtuous ancients is consistent and perhaps rather one-sided, for their vices are not discussed, or even acknowledged in passing. And although John uses much of Augustine's material, he totally ignores those parts of Augustine's works which were in any way unfavourable to the ancients – with the exception of the condemnation of the Epicureans. John seems dedicated to the attempt to persuade his readers that the ancients were peculiarly virtuous as a class.

Should John's *Breviloquium de Virtutibus* be considered as part of the general category of *Fürstenspiegel* or 'Mirrors of Princes'? And, if so, where does it belong in the development of the genre? Neither

Berges[48] nor Kleineke[49] discussed the *Breviloquium de Virtutibus* in his studies of *Fürstenspiegel*, despite the acceptance by both of a very broad definition of the term.[50]

A tighter definition of *Fürstenspiegel*, and one more useful for our purpose, has been offered by Jean-Philippe Genet.[51] He argues that the true 'Mirror of Princes' developed in the second half of the thirteenth century, in association with the Capetian court, and singles out a group of eight works belonging to this period, from authors including Guibert de Tournai, Vincent of Beauvais, Guillaume Perrault, Bartholomaeus Vincentinus, Egidius of Colonna and Thomas Aquinas.[52] All these men were friars, and Genet identifies this as one of the main characteristics of the group. The 'Mirrors of Princes' by these authors span the years 1259–1300, and we might profitably ask how they compare with the *Breviloquium de Virtutibus* of our friar, John of Wales, written probably in the mid- to late 1260s.

Genet identifies three distinctive features in these *Fürstenspiegel* written by friars in Northern France. First, they are all concerned with pedagogic problems, and their tone is didactic rather than political.[53] Secondly, they show a fundamental concern with ethics and morals, coupled with a near-total disappearance of references to antiquity, the surviving references being few and at second hand.[54] Thirdly, they gradually develop a sound Aristotelian base, in reasonable harmony with Augustinian tradition.[55] How do these features relate to the *Breviloquium de Virtutibus*?

John's *Breviloquium* is not highly charged politically, but 'pedagogic' may not be an appropriate description. Its instruction is rather understated, and teaching is by example rather than by argument. With respect to the second characteristic, John does show a concern for ethics and morals, but most Franciscans did, and the theme seems to run through all of John's works. The most important difference between John's *Breviloquium de Virtutibus* and the *Fürstenspiegel* of this group of friars must surely be the latter's rejection of classical authors and *exempla*. John must be regarded as at the opposite extreme on this point; he could hardly use more classical *exempla*, and nearly all seem to come directly from original sources.[56] The

---

[48] W. Berges, 1938.   [49] W. Kleineke, 1937.

[50] Kleineke does mention the *Communiloquium*, so perhaps he and Berges deliberately excluded the *Breviloquium de Virtutibus* from the category.

[51] J-P. Genet, 1977, p. xii.   [52] *Ibid.*, pp. xii–xiii.

[53] *Ibid.*, p. xiii.   [54] *Ibid.*, p. xiii.

[55] *Ibid.*, p. xiv.   [56] See chap. 2 for detailed discussion of this point.

works of the French moralists seem to indicate a deliberate rejection of classical *exempla* at least by one specific section of the friars' movement. If there was such a rejection, John of Wales had no part in it. Indeed, so much of John's writing follows the *Breviloquium de Virtutibus* in hammering home the value of classical *exempla* and the virtues of ancient writers, rulers and philosophers that we might plausibly suggest that he is making a positive stand in defence of the use of classical literature.

On the question of Aristotelian/Augustinian blending, John certainly has elements in common with his French contemporaries. There is a little of this blending in *Breviloquium*, and more in the *Communiloquium*, which he wrote soon afterwards. As a final point, most of the *Fürstenspiegel* listed by Genet were aimed at individual rulers, would-be rulers, or members of royal or noble households, whereas John's work was intended to be of general application.

It would therefore seem correct to say that John's *Breviloquium de Virtutibus* did not take its inspiration from the *Fürstenspiegel* of his fellow-friars in Northern France, and that this work should not be considered as part of that group. In so far as *Breviloquium de Virtutibus* does have characteristics in common with the group, these are characteristics found in the writings of friars on a variety of subjects, and particularly in the writings of Franciscans. This is especially true of concern for moral teaching.

Is there an alternative source of inspiration for the princely aspect of *Breviloquium de Virtutibus*? If we accept that it was probably written in Oxford, and that it falls outside the French tradition of the period, an obvious candidate is the *Policraticus* of John of Salisbury. John of Wales certainly knew this work, as he quotes it eight times in *Breviloquium de Virtutibus* and more frequently in *Communiloquium*, where it is mainly used in the section on the *Respublica*.[57] In *Breviloquium*, John of Wales' main message to rulers is that they should be virtuous in every way, that they should recognise and obey the law and that they should not be autocratic. There is nothing here to conflict with *Policraticus*, and this latter work also used a number of classical *exempla* and showed an appreciation of classical authors. If *Breviloquium de Virtutibus* is to be considered a *Fürstenspiegel* at all – and it certainly is one, to the extent that it deals with model princely behaviour – it belongs to a humanistic English branch of the tradition.

---

[57] See the source-lists at the end of chaps. 3, 4, 5 and 6.

John claims that *Breviloquium de Virtutibus* is intended for the instruction of rulers, and, indeed, he treats of virtue as demonstrated by rulers of old, thus giving credence to the claim. Though John was interested in rulers, we may doubt whether they were the topic of chief importance in this work. By the end of the *Breviloquium*, virtue, and particularly ancient virtue, would seem to have won outright. Certainly John himself did not feel that the *Breviloquium* dealt fully with the question of princes, for he had much more to say about them in the first part of his *Communiloquium*.

At the beginning of this chapter, I isolated three main themes which come together in this *Breviloquium*: virtue, princes, and philosophers. We have been able to see that John expresses admiration of ancient virtue and of the virtuous behaviour of philosophers, a conviction that virtue is important to all Christians, and a concern that Christian princes, like their subjects, should strive for virtue with all their might. These are all themes to which John returns at greater length in later works: to princes and their role in *Communiloquium*, to philosophers in *Compendiloquium*, to virtue in his *Moniloquium*, to the excellence and relevance of ancient examples repeatedly. Therefore we shall return to these themes. Three further points deserve some attention here, as they foreshadow discussion in later works.

On the relationship of the state and the law, John tells us that a state requires just law and that everyone, including rulers, must obey the law.[58] He tells us that a ruler should be prepared to surrender his life for the state,[59] a father his son or a son his father,[60] and that if two wise men have only one chance at life between them, the wiser, being more useful to the state, should be the survivor.[61] This shows that John possessed a definite concept of the state and ranked it as important. The question of the withdrawn philosopher, and of the value of the active life over the contemplative, attracted much discussion in the thirteenth century.[62] We can already see which side John was on. His philosophers are expected to take part in the world.

Philosophers seem to play three roles in John's *Breviloquium*: they appear as examples of frugal living, as in the story of how Diogenes abandoned even his wooden cup and drank from his hands;[63] they appear as archetypal wise men, issuers of profound advice and maxims; they also appear as the tutors or advisers of ancient rulers, as

---

[58] *Brev. de Virt*. 1. See p. 48.
[59] *Brev. de Virt*. See p. 49.
[60] *Brev. de Virt*. 1. See p. 49.
[61] *Brev. de Virt*. 1.4.
[62] For discussion, see below, pp. 72–3.
[63] *Brev. de Virt*. 3.1.

in the classic partnerships of Alexander and Aristotle, Seneca and Nero. They are never 'other-worldly', or wrapped up in themselves to the exclusion of others: they are phlegmatic ascetics with at least one foot placed firmly on the ground.

As a subsidiary to John's admiration for the ascetic philosophers, we might consider his treatment of the question of wealth. Throughout the *Breviloquium*, John displays a profound suspicion of wealth and material possessions. If one has wealth, one should be generous with it: John cites the example of Alexander, who gave a city to someone who asked him for a denarius.[64] However, it is clearly better not to have wealth, as in the case of the consul Lucius Valerius, who was so poor that his tomb had to be paid for by public subscription.[65] On more than one occasion John sets up desire to serve the state and desire for wealth as alternative motives for action, as in his comment that the ancients did not wish to rule for financial gain, but for the glory and health of the state.[66] John does seem to recognise desire for wealth and precious goods as a natural human instinct, because he speaks approvingly of the various ancients who refused bribes[67] or bore patiently with the theft or destruction of their property.[68] Suspicion of wealth and property was deeply ingrained in all Franciscans, so in this John is again quite characteristic of his Order.

We now turn to the question of John's sources for the *Breviloquium de Virtutibus*. Even at this early stage in his career, John exhibits a characteristic desire for accuracy in quoting and referring to his sources. He gives the name of the author and, usually, the work, and book and chapter numbers where they were available to him. Apart from various books of the Bible, John refers to works by 36 authors. If the works are divided into two groups – 'ancient' works, written before *c.* AD 450, and 'medieval' works, written after this date – the quotations can be classified as follows:

　186 quotations from 35 works by 18 ancient authors,
　60 quotations from 19 works by 18 medieval authors,
　30 quotations from the Bible.

This chronological division of the sources, rather than the more conventional division into classical, patristic and so on, provides a more accurate reflection of the proportion of John's references which are concerned with examples from the classical world. Authors like

---

[64] *Brev. de Virt.* 1.6.　　[65] *Brev. de Virt.* 1.4.　　[66] *Brev. de Virt.* 3.1.
[67] *Brev. de Virt.* 3.1.　　[68] *Brev. de Virt.* 1.4 and 4.4.

Augustine and Jerome, who are normally classified as 'patristic', are most commonly used as a quarry for ancient *exempla*, rather than as a source of theological comment. There are, of course, exceptions: *Policraticus* in particular is used as a source of classical tales, despite its medieval dating, and Augustine and Jerome do appear as fathers of Christian thought on some occasions. However, using this basic division, we can see that the bias in the sources lies strongly in favour of the ancient world. John's 'Top Twelve' authors in this text are as follows:

Valerius Maximus	65 references
Augustine	29
Seneca	25
Cicero	24
Celius Balbus	19
Vegetius	13
John of Salisbury	8
Helinandus	7
Macrobius	7
Jerome	5
Moralium Dogma Philosophorum	4
Robert Grosseteste	4
Hugh of Saint-Victor	4

No other author rates more than one or two references.

John's use of Seneca's later letters and his *Dialogues* and of Plato's *Phaedo* is particularly interesting (these texts were rare), and combines with what we know of the sequence of his works to suggest a date in the early to mid-1260s for the composition of *Breviloquium de Virtutibus*. A full list of the sources appears at the end of this chapter.

In *Breviloquium de Virtutibus*, John has made an attempt to merge the structures of two traditional genres – the *De Virtutibus* and the 'Mirror of Princes' – to provide a showcase for his great interest in the impressive deeds of the ancients, and for his conviction that they were a valid and influential model for medieval Christians. He succeeded in combining different traditions of moralistic writing to produce something fresh and unusual, and so it would be wrong to condemn him as uninventive and pedestrian, at least as far as the *Breviloquium de Virtutibus* is concerned. It would be equally wrong to believe that he was uninfluential. His contemporary audience was far from finding his work unsatisfactory, for it was an extraordinary success. John's popularity is discussed in detail in the final chapter of this book. Briefly, we can say here that some 150 copies of this *Breviloquium* survive in Latin, that the work was owned and used by several hundred people all across Europe from its publication until the late sixteenth century, and that it inspired at least ten separate translations and abridgements, in five different languages. Few works of the thirteenth century could compete with such a record, even in the field of preaching literature, where there was a large potential audience of users.

SOURCE LIST FOR THE *BREVILOQUIUM DE VIRTUTIBUS ANTIQUORUM PRINCIPUM ET PHILOSOPHORUM*

I. SOURCES FROM BEFORE AD 450

Ambrose	*De Virginitate*	2 references
Aristotle	*Ethics*[69]	2
Augustine	*De Beata Vita*	1
	De Civitate Dei	20
	De Spiritu et Anima[70]	1
	De Verbis Domini Sermones	1
	Epistolae	5
	Super Genesi ad Litteram	1
Cicero	*De Amicitia*	2
	De Inventione[71]	8
	De Officiis	10
	Tusculanae Quaestiones	2
Florus	*Epitome*[72]	1
Jerome	*Contra Iovinianum*	1
	Epistolae	3
Juvenal	*Satires*[73]	3
Ovid		1
Plato	*Phaedo*	1
Quintus Curtius	*Historia Alexandri Magni*	1
Seneca	*De Beneficiis*	3
	De Clementia	2
	De Constantia Sapientis	1
	De Ira	9

[69] In the translation of Robert Grosseteste.   [70] Spurious.
[71] Cited as *De Rhetorica*, 1 and 2.
[72] John gives the title as *Historia Romanorum*.
[73] Cited sometimes as Juvenal, sometimes as 'Egregius versificator'.

	De Naturalibus Quaestionibus	1
	De Providentia	1
	Epistulae[74]	9
Solinus	Collectanea Rerum Memorabilium[75]	2
Sozomen	Historia Tripartita[76]	1
Trogus Pompeius[77]	Historia	2
Valerius Maximus	Factorum ac Dictorum Memorabilium Libri ix	65
Vegetius	De Re Militari	13
Virgil	Aeneid	1

2. SOURCES FROM AFTER AD 450

pseudo-Ambrose	De Moribus Brachmanorum	1
Bernard of Clairvaux	De Consideratione	1
	Sermones de Adventu	1
Boethius	De Consolatione Philosophiae	1
Celius Balbus	De Nugis Philosophorum	19
Expositor	Super Boetium De Consolatione[78]	1
Gregory the Great	Moralia	1
Helinand	Chronicle	7
Hugh of Saint-Victor	De Sacramentis	2
John of Damascus	De Orthodoxa Fide	2
John of Salisbury	Policraticus	8
Papias	Vocabularium	1
Petrus Alphonsus	Disciplina Clericalis[79]	1
Peter Comestor	Historia Scholastica	1
Robert Grosseteste	Commentary on Ethics	4
Anon.	Secreta Secretorum[80]	2
Anon.	Vita Iohannis Elemosinarii	1
Anon.	Moralium Dogma Philosophorum	4

(There are two references to a 'Poeta Natos'; this is probably a corruption of 'Naso', which many medieval writers preferred to our modern 'Ovid'.)

---

[74] Quoting from the later letters in addition to the more common letters 1–88.
[75] John does not give the title.
[76] Usually referred to without the author's name.
[77] John uses Justin's *Epitome*, although he always refers to Trogus Pompeius.
[78] This is probably William of Conches.
[79] Cited as 'Petrus Alphonsi, tractatus suus'.
[80] Cited as 'Epistola Aristotelis ad Alexandrum', or as Aristotle, *De Regno*.

Chapter 4

COMMUNILOQUIUM, PART 1: JOHN OF WALES ON THE STATE AND ITS MEMBERS

The *Communiloquium* is the second in John's series of *loquia*, having been written after his *Breviloquium de Virtutibus* and before his *Compendiloquium*.[1] It was substantially completed before Aquinas wrote his commentary on Aristotle's *Politics c.* 1269/72;[2] at least, *Communiloquium* makes no reference to this highly relevant work. However, it does make use of rare sources which were available in Paris by the mid-1260s, so it must have been completed some time after 1266, as its predecessor, the *Breviloquium de Virtutibus*, also has a few passing references to some of these sources. There is no evidence that these sources also became available in Oxford before 1270, by which time *Communiloquium* must have been practically completed, so we can conclude that *Communiloquium* was partly produced in Paris and that John was already in France before his first recorded appearance there in June 1270. I say 'partly produced' in Paris because many of the sources used in *Communiloquium* are character-istic of Oxford and are not known to have been available in Paris in the 1260s or early 1270s. So it is possible that John found the inspiration for *Communiloquium* in Oxford and had already prepared the outline and gathered together some of the material before he transferred to Paris some time in the mid- to late 1260s. *Communiloquium*, then, was produced between *c.* 1265 and 1269/70.

Communiloquium is a vast handbook for preachers, crammed with extracts from a wide variety of sources. Preachers' handbooks were a popular type of work in the thirteenth century, and we have several written in the same form as *Communiloquium*, where different groups in society are addressed according to their status.[3] Why was it written? John provides a ready answer, for he expresses his purpose clearly in his prologue. The evangelical preacher, he says, ought to be able to instruct all people and to admonish them effectively, not

---

[1] See above, pp. 6–10. [2] See above, pp. 7–9.
[3] Both Humbert de Romans and Guibert de Tournai produced collections on similar themes.

only in declamatory preaching, but also in friendly conversation.[4] And he ought to admonish them according to their age and status and circumstances, as the apostles taught the people of God. John again shows an interest which appeared in the *Breviloquium de Virtutibus*, by adding 'and not only the apostles and learned fathers taught men according to such distinctions, but also the Gentile philosophers'. We hear much from the Gentile philosophers and other pagan writers in this work, as in most others from John's pen, for he was fascinated by the life of the Greeks and Romans.

John next tells the reader that the preacher should have the right words and material to influence his listeners and to be useful to them. Because not many preachers have the time to inspect numerous volumes, he has gathered together certain generalisations (*generalia*) for the instruction of men according to their varying status. John points out that he is not setting a precedent in using the works of pagan philosophers, but is, rather, following the examples of Jerome and Augustine.

So the work was written to help preachers who lacked the time, facilities or knowledge to go directly to the sources, and in particular to provide a wide range of suitable *exempla* for use with different audiences. Books of this nature performed a valuable function in the Middle Ages. They have sometimes been condemned as hotch-potches of *exempla*, with no originality. Indeed a Parisian professor once described another of John's works as a 'prime example of the intellectual sterility of the age'.[5] We are no longer so harsh in our assessment of the later half of the thirteenth century, and this should apply to our assessment of John and his works. Close examination of *Communiloquium* shows that it is not unoriginal, impersonal or a hotchpotch, and that it tells us a good deal about John and his own ideas.

As the prologue indicates, *Communiloquium* is intended to help preachers to instruct all sorts of people. It therefore serves a double purpose: it provides what John believed to be appropriate informa-tion and material for preachers, and it also provides what he believed to be the correct basic instruction for all the different groups in society. So the work has value as one scholar's view of the world, and it gives us John's point of view on a large range of issues.

If we are to use the work as a source of John's ideas, it is important

---

[4] I have used the edition printed at Augsburg by A. Sorg in 1475, the earliest edition of the longer and fuller recension of the work. This edition lacks foliation; hence I refer to John's divisions and headings.   [5] A. Charma, 1866, p. 127.

to say a word about method. Very few of the comments in *Communiloquium* come originally from John of Wales. But a thoughtful reading of the text soon shows that, as the headings of the chapters follow one another in a logical fashion to produce a coherent skeleton, so the extracts under a particular heading combine to make a linked series of comments with clear linguistic or conceptual connections. Indeed, if John did not list his sources so rigorously, it would often be difficult to detect the breaks between extracts, or to tell that there was not a single author at work. Behind the extracts selected lies a distinctive image and a definite train of thought. The selection and arrangement of the extracts must have been done with considerable care.

To attempt to reach one man's mind through the words of others may seem futile. But in that case I would suggest a simile between John preparing a section of *Communiloquium* and a person selecting an outfit of clothes. The individual may not have designed or made all the garments and accessories involved, but the combination of items and the way in which they are worn conveys a distinctive impression of the wearer – and is meant to do so.

In the course of *Communiloquium*, John divides and re-divides humanity according to a variety of classifications. The work has seven main parts: the first discusses the state and the functional groups within it; the second takes the theme of personal relationships, and the third groups of natural or artificial origin – for example, men and women (natural) and spinsters and widows (artificial); the fourth part covers the ranks of the clergy, the fifth scholars, the sixth members of religious orders, and the seventh the dying.

These parts vary considerably in length, the first being the longest. It has ten sections, which we may conveniently divide into three groups: the first dealing with the state as an entity in its own right, the second with the *princeps* or ruler, and the third with the rest of the state. John's analysis follows a sequence common in other medieval writers – that given by a comparison with the body, working from head to foot. It is characteristic of John's generation that much space should be devoted to the *princeps*; but John is unusual in having written so much about the state. The *Communiloquium* claims to be a source of admonitions to all sorts of men, for the use of preachers. What John does not mention is that one cannot preach *to* the state from a pulpit or in general conversation: one must preach *about* the state to those who are involved in it.

It will be clear from what John wrote that he had a distinct and positive concept of the state, and that he was able to distinguish between what his beloved ancients did in their states and what should have been or was being done in his own time. He may, as Pantin suggested, have caught his language and way of thought from classicising or classical writers,[6] but there is more to it than that. John was an intelligent Franciscan of high reputation writing a book for practical purposes, and the work shows no signs of degenerating into a collection of favourite stories with no serious application. John seems really to have cared about the state and to have seen it as a viable concept for thirteenth-century people; otherwise he would not have discussed it at length in a work such as *Communiloquium*.

We should pause here and ask what John meant by the term *respublica*, which I have translated as 'state'. This is the term which he uses most frequently, although he sometimes speaks of the need to do particular things for the benefit of the *communitas*. The physiological simile upon which he bases the section indicates that he sees the *respublica* as all the people, whatever their rank. As all belong to the state, so all have a duty to the state. Even the *princeps* comes within the state, so no man or group of men is outside or above the state. John's discussion of the *princeps*, the next section of *Communiloquium*, makes clear that no man is above the law either. We can see that John uses the term *respublica* in at least two senses, one abstract and one concrete. In concrete terms the state is all the people and also a political and administrative unit. There is also the concept of the state as an abstraction to which people owe a certain loyalty, moreover a direct loyalty, not channelled through any individual. The *respublica* is represented neither by the *princeps* nor by anyone else.

It is easy to find a parallel to this attitude in the ancient city-states and in the Roman republican ideals of Cicero, but it is clear that John means to apply the concept to his own times. One cannot fail to consider the issue of the community of the realm, a concept which had caused much trouble in England in John's own lifetime. The late F. M. Powicke pointed out that in the early to mid-thirteenth century there was a clear development of a concept of the realm which was wholly tied to the king, but somehow also included all the population and land of a kingdom, together with a more spiritual

---

[6] W. A. Pantin, 1961, p. 312.

element which is rather difficult to define.[7] The reforming barons claimed that both they and King Henry III owed a duty to this 'realm', of which each was an integral part.

John's concept of the state must be related to this: he was an Oxford friar, not an ivory tower academic, and he had lived through the troubles of the 1250s and 1260s. Indeed, if our dating of *Communiloquium* is correct, he was writing immediately after, or even during, the difficulties of 1265/6. This would make his comments on state and prince highly topical, and we can surely absolve him of writing without thought for his own beliefs and the rights and wrongs of the matter.[8] His concept of the *respublica* seems to go further than anything we can distinguish of baronial attitudes, perhaps partly because of his training in thought and his classical education, but partly also because he was not a baron, and the right of that particular group to a share in the state was not a priority for him. He talks about loyalty to a genuine abstraction which is neither church nor king, yet is politically and socially viable as a unit. Perhaps the nearest we can come to understanding his meaning is to say that he did not use the term *respublica* for 'state' in a way that we would talk of the state today, when discussing state machinery or the power of the state, but rather as we would talk of our country when in a patriotic mood.

The direction of John's thought about the state is indicated by the chapter headings of this section of *Communiloquium*:[9]

1 What is the state?
2 From whom and how the state is established
3 That the state ought to be regulated by law
4 That the state ought to be built upon justice
5 That the state ought to be fortified by unanimous harmony
6 That the state ought to be enhanced by faith
7 That the state ought to be directed by wholesome advice
8 That the state ought to be decorated by good customs
9 That the state ought to be regulated by good intentions
10 That the state may be destroyed by defects in the aforementioned
11 How much the ancients did and undertook for the good of the state
12 That Christian doctrine does not oppose the state.

[7] F. M. Powicke, 1947, II. 469–70.
[8] The involvement of churchmen on the side of the reforming barons is shown by J. R. Maddicott, 1983, pp. 588–603.
[9] The chapter headings vary slightly from edition to edition and between various MSS. The edition of 1475 is used here.

As always, John's skeleton of thought is amply clothed in quotations from other writers, in accordance with the specific purpose of the work. Yet his attitudes show through clearly. He begins with a series of progressive definitions.[10] First he uses the well-worn physiological simile whereby the state (*respublica*) is likened to a body, the ruler (*princeps*) filling the place of the head, the officials (*prepositi*) and judges (*iudices*) the eyes and the ears, the council (*senatus*) the heart, the soldiers (*milites*) the hands and the workers (*laborantes*) the feet. John cites the pseudo-Plutarchan *Institutio Traiani* as his source for this.[11] Subsequent definitions come from Augustine's *De Civitate Dei*. The state (*respublica*) is the people, the community, the citizens (*respopuli, res communis, res civitatis*); moreover, it is the *respopuli* justly and well ruled, whether by one king or a few excellent men or by the whole people.[12] John goes on to give a few *exempla* on the theme of how the different sections of the community should pull together as participants in the state. He clearly has an eye for attractive and appealing similes: in this case he uses the example of the harmony which can be achieved when different musical instruments make an effort to play together, and extends his earlier parallel to remind the reader that *all* the limbs and parts of the body make a contribution to its activity. The cumulative effect is considerable.

Justice and law are preoccupations of John, and he refers to them time and time again under various headings. In particular, he tells us that the state should be regulated by laws and that these should be established for the good of the state as a whole.[13] John uses book I of Cicero's *Rhetorica* to give authority to the view that judges ought to set down laws for the good of the state, rather than to serve their own interests. He then turns to Cicero's *De Legibus* and *De Natura Deorum* and to Gratian's *Decretum* for a discussion of the purposes of law. Law, says John, is necessary for the stability of the state, in that it promotes the good and prohibits the bad. From Seneca John takes the information that after the age of tyrants the ancient kingdoms were brought within the grasp of the law: for example, when Solon established equal rights (*equo iure*) in Athens, and Lycurgus instituted law in Sparta.[14] John is interested in Solon: he tells us that this man's laws were inscribed on wooden tablets so that they might last for ever; he also recommends Aulus Gellius and Trogus Pompeius as

---

[10] *Communiloq.* I.I.I.
[12] *Communiloq.* I.I.2.
[14] Seneca, *Epistulae* 10.4.

[11] A. Momigliano, 1955; S. Desideri, 1958.
[13] *Communiloq.* I.I.3.

sources of further information. All laws ought to emanate from the divine law, says John, citing Proverbs 8: 'Through me kings rule'. He tells us that laws should be kept by the powerful as by the lesser folk, lest they become like the spider's web, which traps the weaker animals, but allows the stronger to pass through.

John next discusses the need for justice in the state.[15] Velleius said that there is nothing more harmful to the state than injustice, and Augustine declared that a kingdom far from justice is mere brigandage. Justice is necessary to all, and particularly to those who sell and buy, hire, invest or make contracts, for these things cannot proceed without justice. Even those who live by crime cannot manage without justice and groups of brigands have their own codes which they observe among themselves. The importance of justice should be properly recognised, says John, as by the Gentiles, who dedicated a temple to justice.

In the next chapter, John points out that the state should be fortified by unanimous concord.[16] According to the Commentator on *Ethics* (John is using Grosseteste's commentary), there is nothing more useful to the state than unity (*concordia*), an example being the unity of the Greeks against Xerxes and the degree to which they were strengthened by it. John goes on to argue that the state should also be assisted by fidelity (*fidelitas*), which is the root of justice and therefore of stability.[17] Faith (*fides*) was held in great reverence among the ancients: Cato tells us that it had its own temple, close to that of Jove on the Capitol. John seems willing to recognise a capacity for piety among pagan ancients.

The state should be directed by good advice, and John observes that there is good advice where there are many counsellors.[18] He supports this claim with the example of Solon, who profited the Athenians when it came to the Persian wars, because the war was successfully conducted through the advice of the senate which he had set up. John continues his ancient examples in the following chapter, which deals at length with how the state should be embellished by good customs.[19] John presents the reader with a paraphrase of Augustine on how the strength of Rome lay in her ancient customs, before progressing to a chapter on the need for the state to be regulated by good intentions.[20] Again John shows strong feelings, presenting a number of attractive and powerful examples. Good intentions are required of all the limbs of the state rather than of any

---

[15] *Communiloq.* 1.1.4. [16] *Communiloq.* 1.1.5. [17] *Communiloq.* 1.1.6.
[18] *Communiloq.* 1.1.7. [19] *Communiloq.* 1.1.8. [20] *Communiloq.* 1.1.9.

single one. All should favour the common good of the state, nor should anyone wish to injure the others. In this way the state will be stable.

To inconvenience others in order to improve one's own position is greatly against nature. Cicero tells us that the nobility of the ancient world, loving the state, intended good to others just as to themselves. We may wonder whether this is a sly dig at contemporary nobility, who are discussed in detail later in John's *Communiloquium*. Here John goes on to quote Cicero and Seneca in order to show that they considered nothing human as alien to them; this may lend support to the suggestion that John is indeed thinking of contemporary nobles, and not entirely approvingly. The chapter proceeds to discuss how individuals can put the welfare of the state above their own concerns, as when Cicero claimed that it mattered greatly to him that the *respublica* should be the same after his death as it was when he was alive.

The ancients awarded divine honours to some, to encourage others to undertake tasks for the state. From such unanimous desires and intentions of the people in the state is it helped and preserved. A ship will progress regularly while it is blown steadily by the winds, and similarly a battle-line advances and is made strong as long as it is held together by unity; and thus in all communities. John ends by saying that the fullest desire for unity in a community is found in the church; therefore only the ecclesiastical state (*ecclesiastica respublica*) is perfect. The state can be destroyed by deficiency in the qualities already mentioned, just as a picture fades with age and loses its colour and form if no one takes the trouble to renovate it.[21] John follows Augustine in giving the example of the decline of the Roman Republic, and lists a number of things harmful to the state: ignorance, laziness and lustful passion, civil war, love of power and greed. Therefore, says John, those who wish to be loyal to the state should ensure that it is ruled by proper laws and ordered by justice, and they should beware of the reverse.

John then turns to a favourite theme and devotes a lengthy chapter to the matter of how much the ancients were prepared to undertake for the good of the state.[22] They showed great concern for it, undertaking dreadful and dangerous tasks on its behalf and freely giving their lives and those of their friends and relatives. John refers to his own *Breviloquium de Virtutibus* as a further source on this and

[21] *Communiloq.* I.I.IO.   [22] *Communiloq.* I.I.II.

gives many examples, including Seneca's remark that the Roman people gave up much for the state, so that the state was rich while they were poor in their own homes. He tells Seneca's story of the woman who, when told that her son had fallen in battle, responded by asking about the fate of the state, saying, 'If the state is healthy, I do not mourn my son.' The ancient did such things from love of their homeland (*patria*) and not from desire for human praise. The philosophers believed that men ought to live for the sake of others, and if they knew this and could do it well, Christians should be able to do much better. Again we see the re-emergence of one of the themes which dominated the *Breviloquium de Virtutibus*.

On the organisation of the state John quotes Avicenna.[23] Everyone should contribute something useful to the state, and laziness should be condemned. Those who will not co-operate should be expelled from the state, and inheritances should be withheld from those who contribute nothing useful. There should be no wrestlers or gamblers, because they give nothing to the state and take from the fruits of others. Such activities as are counter-productive should also be banned: for example, theft and fornication. In a state ordered thus, anyone would be able to live in peace and productively and to possess what was his.

The final chapter on the state denies the accusation that Gospel teaching opposes the state, a charge which John says was made in Augustine's time.[24] He runs quickly through Augustine's defence that if a Christian is endeavouring to be virtuous he can do no harm to anyone, least of all the state, which had plenty of problems even before the coming of Christianity.

These, in brief, are John's views on the state as expressed in *Communiloquium*. He has a distinct concept of the *respublica* and he means it to operate in the contemporary world – hence his exhortation to Christians to do more for the state than the admirable ancients did. As John's examples were chosen to show that the ancients were prepared to put the state above everything – personal comfort, life and limb, family and friends – he must have been thinking of something approaching total dedication to the state from the contemporary faithful. He sees sacrifice for and loyalty to the state as real virtues, so loyalty to the state must have been a genuine issue with him. The classic illustration of his attitude is the *exemplum* which he used earlier, in his *Breviloquium de Virtutibus*, about the

---

[23] John gives the reference as *Philosophia* lib. 10, cap. 4.
[24] *Communiloq.* I.1.12.

dilemma of two wise men (*sapientes*) shipwrecked on a raft which will only hold one. What are they to do? John tells us that the less wise should give place to the more wise, *because this one is of more use to the state*!

John thus emphasises his belief that *everyone* has a duty to be involved in the state, and to give their best or their all for its support and preservation. The question of involvement in the state, and of its desirability, was one which was answered differently in the ancient and the early medieval world, and was vigorously disputed in the thirteenth century, when the ancient ideal re-emerged with the works of Aristotle. To put it very simply, Aristotle presented the view that a community or state is natural,[25] that the congregation and functioning of men within a state is also natural, and that each individual should actively contribute to the state for the common good. In the ancient world, withdrawal was seen as a fault. In the early medieval world, on the other hand, the prevalent view was that of the church, which held that involvement in worldly matters was dangerous, and that it was perfectly acceptable for the individual to withdraw from such involvement, for his or her own individual good.

With the revival of learning in the later eleventh century, the ideal of active involvement was rediscovered, and by the thirteenth century it again held sway in some sections of society. For example, the Italian communes of the mid-thirteenth century accepted the ideal of service to the community. The legist Odofredo of Bologna wrote in his gloss to the Peace of Constance that the good citizen must defend the rights of his *patria* and serve in the government.[26] In Paris, Averroist commentaries observed that the philosopher should not withdraw from the world, but should practise all the virtues, including good citizenship.[27]

John of Wales was no Italian and no Averroist. Indeed, he served on the commission which investigated the works of Peter John Olivi, which must indicate that his orthodoxy was fully accepted. Yet he takes the line that philosophers could and should be involved in the state and government. He might well have agreed with a nearly contemporary commentator on Aristotle's *Ethics*, who justifies the philosopher as a good citizen, before going on to debate the superiority of the contemplative life over the life of those administer-

[25] Natural in the teleological sense: that is to say, part of Nature's grand design.
[26] G. Post, 1976, p. 402.
[27] F. Gautier, 1948, pp. 292–3.

ing for the common good.[28] His argument essentially runs as
follows: philosophers are virtuous, therefore they should be a part of
the community rather than expelled from it. The state is responsible
for creating peace to assure *felicitas civilis* (civil harmony); this is
inferior to *felicitas contemplativa* (contemplative harmony) which
only the philosophers can achieve, but the former is the means to the
latter. Furthermore, as happiness includes the good of the soul in
addition to that of the body, the truly happy man is not only a
philosopher but also a political animal. He should be a good citizen,
helping and also needing others. The author goes on to argue against
the claim that the *vita civilis et activa* (civil and active life) is actually
better than the *vita contemplativa* (contemplative life). The former
does indeed aim at the good of the whole community rather than the
individual. However, what is good for the single man rather than the
state is better and more worthy, though not more useful.

John of Wales is not prepared to discuss the issue in quite these
terms, although he is adamant that involvement is a proper duty for
all. As he progresses to discussing the roles of the various government officials, we see him point out the dangers to the individual
soul of power and authority, but he adds that it is right to do one's
duty by the state and become involved. He therefore seems to accept
all three of the basic Aristotelian tenets outlined above, while
remaining aware of the Christian view that worldly involvement is
risky. This moderate standpoint may have been one of the reasons
for his enduring popularity over the next 250 years.

The abstract element of the *respublica* is of interest to historians,
and was clearly important to John, but it was not his only priority.
Having dealt with the *respublica*, he goes on to discuss the roles of the
various groups within it, producing a delightful mixture of moral
and practical advice. He begins with the *princeps*, whom he sees as
sufficiently important to merit twice the space allotted to the
respublica. It may be said of the *princeps*, as it was of the *respublica*, that
the average preacher was unlikely ever to find one in his audience.
Therefore John's ideas on the *princeps* were probably for the ears of
subjects, as his ideas on the state were surely intended for its
members.

Part 1, distinction 2 of the *Communiloquium* bears the heading 'Of
information for the prince in the state', and contains three chapters.
John begins by carefully justifying the equation between the *princeps*

---

[28] G. Post, 1976, pp. 403–8. The commentary is anonymous and incomplete and Post
believes it was composed before 1277.

in the state and the head in the natural body.[29] He uses a variety of authorities to show that the *princeps* occupies a special place, that he has particular duties towards the *respublica* and that it in turn owes him particular allegiance. He further points out that it is natural that someone should lead, and gives the example of an elephant herd, where the biggest elephant is selected for this duty.

All this establishes the *princeps* as someone rather special. But John is anxious that this should not go to his head, and as the discussion progresses it becomes clear that there are distinct limitations on the *princeps*. John tells us that desire for power is a disadvantage in a ruler, and that virtue and high rank do not inevitably go together.[30] High office can make bad men worse, and an evil man can corrupt any office he holds. John mentions the dangers of greed and ambition, and adds that power should not be sought from these motives, but rather undertaken from the desire to benefit the state. He goes on to discuss the limits of temporal power, in a selection of extracts from Gregory's *Moralia*. As an example he cites Canute's failure to command the tide.[31] He also mentions the many men of antiquity who positively fled power or only accepted it under compulsion, for the good of the *respublica*. John balances the corrupting potential of power and the personal danger faced by individuals in positions of authority against the need to serve the state, and concludes that it is right to set aside personal feelings and do one's duty.

Positions of authority should be accepted in the proper spirit, says John, with the intention of obeying God and the church in the proper fashion and according to the law.[32] He goes on to discuss the sources of the authority to institute a ruler, and produces four methods which he considers valid if the church gives its consent, including succession through the father and election by the soldiers or populace. John offers Moses as an example of selection by divine authority, and points out that many ancient rulers and consuls were chosen by the army or the people. He also tells Solinus' story of a certain island where the king was elected and had to be childless to prevent hereditary succession. The chapter ends with a collection of biblical texts on divine authority for kingship.

Communiloquium 1.3 contains twenty chapters of varying length, on the personal virtues of princes. The prince undertakes anxiety and

---

[29] *Communiloq.* 1.2.1.   [30] *Communiloq.* 1.2.2.

[31] John does not name the king who figured in this tale, but there is no doubt whom he means.

[32] *Communiloq.* 1.2.3.

hard work. He ought not to undertake his position from love of rule
or pleasure or punishment. He should assent to the church and take
up the princehood with fear and trembling, with a humble heart and
good intentions, and he should use his power for the glory of God
and the good of the people, putting down evil and requiring good.[33]
To carry out such office properly involves much work and worry,
says John, citing the sword of Damocles as an indication of the
discomforts of a ruler. This brings him naturally to the question of
threats to rulers and protection for them. John tells how Plato, after
he saw the guards around Dionysius, asked what evil he had done
that he needed them. Finally John returns to emphasise that those
who are given leading rank should be virtuous and powerful men,
that blood in itself is not enough, and that in any case all men in
authority must behave in the proper manner and obey the laws.

John states that the prince should be humble in himself and
obedient and respectful to God and the church.[34] He should be
perfectly pure and should rule rightly and with mercy, clemency and
perfect justice, being generous to all and extremely patient in his
words and deeds. Most of these points are picked up and elaborated
in later sections. Here the need for respect for church and churchmen
is emphasised by reference to Gregory and to various biblical books.
God gave authority to the priests; therefore they should be respected
and not ignored. The rewards for proper respect for the church are
illustrated by Constantine's dream of the cross in the sky, and how
he heeded the dream and was victorious. John says faithful rulers
everywhere ought to imitate his resultant humility and piety.

The *princeps* ought not to be stained by sordid guilt. He should
lead a clean and chaste life and beware of luxury and greed.[35] John
follows Jerome in singling out women as a threat, observing that the
love of women sapped the strength of Samson, made a jest of the
wisdom of Solomon and corrupted the purity of David. For John,
there can be no lasting power or stable rule where love of pleasure
reigns in the *princeps*. He points out that the power of Rome was
exhausted under Nero, whose appetite devoured everything. This
would seem to provide a practical reason for limiting indulgence, as
does the example of the disaster which overcame Hannibal's troops
as they relaxed after an over-generous banquet, and the advice from
Valerius that a prince should be sober at all times, so that he may use
his reason in cases requiring sudden decisions. The chapter is

[33] *Communiloq.* 1.3.1.   [34] *Communiloq.* 1.3.2.   [35] *Communiloq.* 1.3.3.

rounded off with numerous examples of great men who practised abstention with respect to food, women and money.

John emphasises that the prince, besides being free from sin, should be positively virtuous.[36] Particularly, he ought to set a good example to encourage others in their duties, and he should not order anything that he cannot do himself. Julius Caesar and Lycurgus are cited as examples of men who obeyed this last precept.

John elaborates the virtues of mercy, piety and clemency,[37] drawing largely on Seneca's *De Clementia*, and recommending that the reader turn to this work for fuller details. John quotes Seneca to show that, just as medicine is useful to the sick but abhorrent to the healthy, thus through clemency, however well-deserved the penalty, the innocent tend the guilty. This might be taken in two ways: that it is easy to despise clemency when one does not need it oneself, or that to receive clemency when punishment is deserved somehow heals the guilty of their crime, as medicine heals sickness. We cannot tell which of these interpretations John would have preferred, if either, but we can see that he feels very strongly about the desirability of clemency, which comes up for discussion several times in *Communiloquium*. We get the distinct impression that John felt that punishments were often too severe, and that milder treatment would bring better results.

Again through Seneca, we learn that no clemency is too great to become a prince, and that, while fierceness is acceptable on a battlefield, at home one should strive for tranquillity and try not to be angered by injuries and offences. We are told of a number of great men of old who practised clemency, like Pompey, who restored to the Armenian king the kingdom which he had just lost. As an example of ancient piety we have 'pius Aeneas' from Virgil.

From clemency and mercy we travel naturally to justice and the law.[38] John says that a state needs justice and that the *princeps* should dispense it fairly, observing the laws and seeing that others observe them, judging cases properly and awarding reasonable sentences. There is much honour in the making of lawcodes, as is clear from Apollo's inability to decide whether Lycurgus was a god or a man. It is important that lawmakers and rulers should submit to the laws like anyone else, and princes ought to pay attention to the poor, examining their cases and dealing with them to their satisfaction.

John now justifies the need for the prince to be illuminated by

---

[36] *Communiloq.* 1.3.4.   [37] *Communiloq.* 1.3.5.   [38] *Communiloq.* 1.3.6.

knowledge.[39] His first reason is that the prince will then be able to institute laws conforming to the divine law. This is illustrated with the example of the king in Deuteronomy 17:18 who wrote his laws with the help of the priests. To this end ancient princes, even Gentiles, were instructed in *humana scientia*. John mentions the tale of Ptolemy's commission of the Septuagint as illustration, then discusses the classic partnerships of Alexander and Aristotle, Nero and Seneca, Trajan and Plutarch. The more recent partnership of Alcuin and Charlemagne also rates a paragraph. Ancient princes who were not wise themselves took care to have good advisers, says John, and he emphasises that study and wisdom are intended to benefit all the people, and are not only for the good of the individual ruler.

Because it is the part of a prince to be good and charming to all, John says that he ought to be generous in giving. Meanness in rulers is presented as a serious fault – a prince should perform acts of giving frequently and cheerfully. The point that giving reflects the status of the giver is rammed home with a reference to Alexander's willingness to give away cities, followed by a story of how Antigonus was once asked for a talent and refused on the grounds that it was too much for the seeker to ask, but equally refused to donate a denarius on the grounds that it was less than a king ought to give. That the prince ought to be approachable and good-tempered is illustrated by a number of examples,[40] including the tale of how Julius Caesar earned the love of his soldiers by moving among them, and the description of how Alexander surrendered his seat by the fire to an old soldier who was feeling the cold. Many of the stories relate particularly to relationships with soldiers or veterans. Examples of hospitality include Solomon's generosity towards the Queen of Sheba and the way in which Aeneas and his men were received by Dido, and later by Evander. John makes a point of reminding the reader that over-generous feasting does no good to anyone.

A prince should be patient and imperturbable, so that he may dispense justice in tranquillity and work with steady application.[41] He should beware of anger, because it clouds the soul's ability to see the truth, and because an angry man does not function according to God's justice. The prince should first conquer anger, the enemy within which confuses the kingdom of the spirit, and then turn against invaders, the enemies of the external kingdom. Many princes were most patient when they were at their most powerful. John offers

[39] *Communiloq.* 1.3.7.   [40] *Communiloq.* 1.3.9.   [41] *Communiloq.* 1.3.11.

abundant examples: Augustus' toleration of Pollio's rendering of historical events,[42] Tiberius' and Domitian's stance in favour of free speech, King Antigonus' readiness to forgive the rude remarks which he heard his soldiers make. Philosophers such as Aristippus and Xenophon, Socrates and Diogenes also appear as examples of how to endure verbal abuse, before John turns to the terrible things which men can do when led astray by wrath. Curiously, the Persians provide most of his examples: Darius and Cambyses, Xerxes and Cyrus all figure in acts of cruelty, alongside Lysimachus and Harpalus, one-time companions of Alexander.

Chapter 13 of *Communiloquium* is headed 'De informatione Aristotelis ad Alexandrum'. As John tells us, it consists of a number of extracts from the *Secreta Secretorum*, which he describes as 'the letter which is said to be from Aristotle to Alexander', and which, he says, 'contains much relating to princes'.[43] The portions selected combine to make a picture very like that which John is presenting in this whole section of *Communiloquium*: one should rule well and kindly, behave generously, establish good laws and abide by them, refrain from bestial passion, respect lawmakers and religious and wise men and seek advice from them, look to the future, and so on. John occasionally backs up a point from the letter with a reference to some other authority: for example, John of Salisbury.

The next four chapters (numbered 13–16 in the edition of 1475)[44] are concerned with aspects of war, the headings being 'That the prince should not wage unjust war', 'That in war the prince should beware of offending God', 'That the prince should be cautious in war' and 'That the prince should be consistent in his discipline'. Princes should be instructed on times of war, says John, because Ecclesiastes established that there was a time for war and a time for peace. A prince should undertake war for just causes.[45] Such a war, if properly conducted, is not a sin. A plethora of biblical references is used to illustrate the importance of having God and the church on your side if you wish to be victorious in war.[46] John then emphasises the value of knowing something of the art of war, and gives the example of how Alexander, in choosing troops for a dangerous campaign, picked out the veterans in preference to the strong youths

---

[42] This was less than complimentary to Augustus and his family.
[43] M. Th. d'Alverny, 1983, pp. 132–40.
[44] This edition has two chapters numbered thirteen. Errors in the numbering are quite common throughout the text.
[45] *Communiloq.* 1.3.13.   [46] *Communiloq.* 1.3.14.

of the kingdom.[47] He goes on to discuss the importance of discipline
for troops and leader alike.[48] Lack of proper discipline is described as
a hindrance to victory: for example, the Romans advanced themselves so far in discipline that they were able to conquer the world.
Discipline makes up for lack of numbers, as was shown by the 300
Spartans who held back Xerxes, and by the defeat of the superior
force at the Battle of Salamis.

We are now told that for good relationships with others, and
particularly with soldiers, one must behave in a friendly and caring
manner.[49] John quotes Cicero, Valerius and Seneca on the points
that you cannot buy true loyalty with money, and that the way to the
hearts of one's soldiers is to show true concern for them. As
examples of proper interest in others, John cites Themistocles'
knowledge of the names of all his citizens and the ability of a certain
Metriades to speak the languages of all the 120 peoples over which he
ruled. Then, still on the military theme, he observes that victory
derives from the heavens, so that a prince ought to be truly faithful
and piously to ask God to lead him in war and be his true protector.
John gives the example of Theodosius' defeat of Eugenius and
Arbogastres. For these reasons, he says, presumably referring to the
power to provide victory, a prince ought to honour the church of
God and its ministers. This seems a very practical way of looking at
the matter.

These eighteen chapters present a tall order, perhaps, but the final
two chapters bring together all the previous information and show
that John meant his exhortations seriously and saw the entire section
on the prince as a distinct entity. He uses a number of *exempla* to put
across the message that the only true kings are those who rule
properly and lead the right kind of life.[50] Those who do not behave
correctly are not truly kings, but rather tyrants. John explains the
difference between kings and tyrants further.[51] The man who is
instituted by law and by divine and human authority, *and* who is also
virtuous and rules himself as has been described earlier, is the man
who is called a *princeps*. He who behaves in the contrary fashion is
truly a tyrant.

Thus there are two complementary qualities which make a true
ruler: correct institution and correct behaviour. John cites *Policraticus*
for the view that it is not a crime to kill a tyrant.[52] Having established
that a tyrant lacks the backing of the law, John goes on to warn

[47] *Communiloq.* 1.3.15. [48] *Communiloq.* 1.3.16. [49] *Communiloq.* 1.3.17.
[50] *Communiloq.* 1.3.19. [51] *Communiloq.* 1.3.20. [52] *Communiloq.* 1.3.20.

legitimately established princes of the dangers of slipping into tyranny through wrongful behaviour. As examples of such behaviour he lists the subjection of the people to unjust laws, the aggravation of these with taxes and punishments which are not fair, failure to defend them from invading enemies and the appointment of unjust officials at their head. He ends by reminding the reader that the reward of a good ruler is a place in the kingdom of heaven, while that of an unjust ruler is eternal damnation.

What are the essential points made in the section on the *princeps*? John presents a number of extracts in support of the view that rule by one man is natural. He emphasises that one is entitled to be called a *princeps* only if one has been instituted in an authorised manner – John is not too particular as to which manner, but seems to prefer a combination of establishment and recognition by the church and by the people – and subsequently behaves in an appropriate fashion. He describes various aspects of appropriate behaviour, from purely personal morality to respect for and obedience to the law, respect for the church and proper attention to the needs and rights of the common people. He seems to see the law in particular as a significant limitation on what the ruler can and cannot do. He observes that being a ruler should not be a soft option; the task should be undertaken wholeheartedly for the good of the *respublica*. Throughout this section of advice for princes, John tends to justify his recommendations in practical terms: a high standard of morality increases one's capacity to rule well, while a low one correspondingly diminishes it; educated people may give good advice and should therefore be listened to; a prince should keep on the right side of the church because God will help him to victory in battle; soldiers will fight better if they know and respect their leader; experience and discipline are more important than youth in an army; and so on.

We observed in the last chapter, after discussing definitions of *Fürstenspiegel* and the particular characteristics of those written by friars in the second half of the thirteenth century, that John of Wales' *Breviloquium de Virtutibus* can only be loosely described as a *Fürstenspiegel*, and has little in common with the contemporary works of the friars of Northern France. What of *Communiloquium*'s discussion of the *princeps*? Looking back at the characteristics which Genet has seen as shared by later thirteenth-century *Fürstenspiegel*,[53] we see that their concern with ethics was shared by John. However, the friars

---

[53] J-P. Genet, 1977, Introduction.

did not limit such concern to princes or to written works: it was deep-rooted in them and they would have applied it everywhere. Genet also isolated a didactic tone. We can see a didactic element in John's writing on the prince, but it is the same tone as one finds throughout *Communiloquium*, a tone inevitable in a work which claims to be a set of admonitions for use in conversation and preaching. One difference is this: *Communiloquium* is distinguished by its use of classical sources and *exempla*, while the *Fürstenspiegel* of other contemporary friars were distinguished by their reluctance to use such sources. Another difference is that, although there is an element of practical justification in what John writes, the work is not practical in the same way as these other contemporary *Fürstenspiegel*, which contain detailed instruction on how to educate one's family, both boys and girls, how to found a city, and so on.[54] Such a difference makes good sense when we remember the intended audience. Unlike the writers of *Fürstenspiegel*, John was writing for the general population.

In *Communiloquium*, as in the *Breviloquium de Virtutibus*, John's writing on the *princeps* should not be classified with the works of contemporary friars, although it would seem reasonable to classify it in the *Fürstenspiegel* genre, for which a wider definition is used. The *princeps* was clearly important to John of Wales. Good leadership was a major issue for him as much as for the friars writing for the Capetian court, but his audience was very different. Because of this we should perhaps reverse the usual question asked of a *Fürstenspiegel*, and examine what it tells ordinary people about the *princeps*, rather than what it advises the *princeps* to do on his own account. This must give added interest to the last two chapters, on the consequences of failing in princely behaviour. While comments on such issues as how to win the loyalty of one's men remain matters for the attention of princes, many of the passages pertaining to personal and official behaviour may be seen as a kind of checklist of qualities needed to retain the status of a recognised prince, for the attention of subjects as much as of rulers.

When we look closely at the final chapters of this section, we see that their message is clear. The prince or king, even if he is properly instituted, has limitations on his power. He cannot do as he pleases without possibly losing his legitimacy, and if he does lose his legitimacy, John says, there is no sin in taking his life. The overall

[54] L. K. Born, 1928, pp. 470–504.

message is not of a kind that Henry III would have wanted to hear in the average English pulpit.

Tyranny and tyrannicide are topics raised a century earlier by John of Salisbury in *Policraticus*, and our John acknowledges this by citing *Policraticus* as his authority for the view that a tyrant may be killed without sin. John of Salisbury's attitude towards tyrannicide must be pieced together from a number of scattered remarks which contain 'many reservations, qualifications and outright contradictions'.[55] John of Salisbury, like John of Wales, claims that a prince obeys the law, while a tyrant does not, and observes that a tyrant may once have been a legitimate ruler.

John of Salisbury uses the term 'law' very generally.[56] On tyrannicide, he on the one hand claims that a tyrant may be, and even should be, killed, but on the other remarks that the use of poison is unlawful, that any tyrannicide should be effected without loss of religion or honour, that tyrants should not be overthrown at once, but rebuked with patient reproof, that God punishes the wicked in the end in any case, and that the safest and most useful way of destroying tyrants is to pray to God for salvation. John of Salisbury's attitude to tyrannicide is therefore rather more cautious than some people have suggested. He did not propose tyrannicide as a plan of action, but rather discussed it as a warning to Henry II that God might punish him, and possibly through a human instrument, if he failed to rule within the law.[57]

When we compare John of Wales' comments with those from *Policraticus*, he at once appears more uncompromising. His debt to *Policraticus* is confined to the two points that a prince holds to the law while a tyrant rules arbitrarily, and that it is no crime to kill a tyrant. *Communiloquium* makes no mention of John of Salisbury's qualifications, though our John quotes this text often and we know he was well acquainted with the whole of it. He seems to have made a decision to leave out the qualifying comments, producing a stronger message which must reflect a firmer convicton that tyrannicide was a possibility, and was likely to prove a useful and relevant threat.

Was John thinking about the baronial troubles of the 1250s and 1260s when he wrote, and did they help to form his ideas? The answer to both these questions must be a qualified 'yes', for John was no literary ostrich with his head buried in the sands of past tradition.

---

[55] R. H. & M. A. Rouse, 1967, pp. 693–709.
[56] *Ibid.*
[57] I follow here the account given by Rouse (*ibid.*). See also J. van Laarhoven, 1984.

He seems to have lived in Oxford through the years of the Baronial Rebellion. He must have known what was happening, heard it discussed, held his own opinions. We know that a number of Franciscans were involved with the baronial cause:[58] very possibly John would have been acquainted with them. John's *Communiloquium* does not fit into the mainstream of French *Fürstenspiegel*. It is essentially an English production, and it seems logical that John should be following his own line for his own reasons. Therefore we may consider what he says to have genuine topical significance, rather than being a string of idle platitudes. John was writing a functional handbook which was definitely intended for use in the real world, and there is no sign that he was turning his back on reality. Thus, when he emphasises the need for many good counsellors, the importance of the king's taking their advice and the regrettable vulnerability of the *princeps* to the flattery of unsuitable persons mistakenly admitted to the court, we should pay heed to the echoes of the *Song of Lewes*[59] and of the baronial programme generally. The *Song of Lewes*, which is in Latin and therefore was not intended for popular consumption, is believed to have been written by a Franciscan friar in late 1264, after the Battle of Lewes. The latter part, which explains the aims of the barons and expounds the 'true' theory of kingship, includes the need for the community to have some say in the choice of the king's councillors, lest he be misled by unworthy candidates, and the importance of councillors' having knowledge of the country, its people and its customs (implying that they should not be foreigners). This is very similar to some of John's comments. The same applies to his warnings against unjust laws, taxes and representatives, and his insistence that royal power is not absolute. If John had been required to take sides in the baronial dispute, he might well have felt himself justified in supporting the barons. Certainly he does not make any attempt to argue against them, or for the complete authority of the king. This would be consistent with the attitude of other friars of the time. There were both Franciscans and Dominicans in the delegation which visited the king on 12 May 1264, to speak on behalf of the baronial party.[60] Among the items requested on this occasion was the withdrawal of the king's evil councillors and his adherence to the counsel of faithful Englishmen.

John's assessment of the king's authority again reflects his capacity to bring together and to reconcile differing threads of opinion to

[58] J. R. Maddicott, 1983, pp. 588–603. [59] Kingsford, ed., 1890.
[60] J. R. Maddicott, 1983, pp. 588–603.

produce a compromise which he can maintain without self-contradiction. Many scholars found difficulty in reconciling theocratic kingship with the right of resistance – Walter Ullmann cited John of Salisbury and Thomas Aquinas as examples of men who had problems over this.[61] The difficulty was not confined to scholars either. The renewed troubles between king and barons in mid-thirteenth-century England reflect continued tension over the role and limitations of the king.

The confusion over the status of the king in England is reflected in the comments of the 'Bractonian' *De Legibus*. On the one hand this claims that the king has no equal and no superior, and that no one may question the legality of his acts, while on the other it claims that the king is under the law, that he has a superior in his curia, that the will of the king alone cannot make law unless the assent and agreement of the barons are obtained.[62]

John of Wales therefore does well to achieve consistency in his attitudes. His recognition that both church and people could have a role to play in the making of kings acquires a new importance in this context. As a friar, John naturally sees the involvement of the church as a proper part of the establishment of a Christian king. However, he is far from believing that this gives the king limitless power. John is seen to accept fully the 'feudal' attitude that the king did not have sole power to make law, that he was of, rather than above, the community, and that he was subject to, rather than outside the law. He also successfully presents the concept of a form of contract between church, king and people. The recognition of the church gave the king his start, but to maintain his own legitimacy he had to perform certain tasks in certain ways. Failure to do this was more powerful than the previous recognition of the church and stripped him of his legal authority, leaving him a mere tyrant. At no point does John seem to contradict himself. This confirms that he had definite views of his own on kingship, and that he must have had some sympathy with the struggles of the barons. The whole tone of his discussion and comments also indicates that John was writing against a background of English problems and the contemporary English situation. Though he may have found some of his *exempla* in Paris, his inspiration lay on the English side of the channel.

John's discussion of groups other than the *princeps* serves to

[61] W. Ullmann, 1974, p. 131.
[62] A useful summary is given in *ibid.*, p. 176. See also F. Schulz, 1945, pp. 136ff.; G. Post, 1968; S. Thorne, 1977.

illustrate his essentially practical attitude to life. He is genuinely anxious that the preacher should be able to tell the various groups things that will be helpful to them as individuals and as members of the state, and to express these things interestingly and attractively.

Having discussed the role of the *princeps* or head (*caput*), John goes on to the ears, eyes and tongue, which he identifies with the provincial officials (*praesides provinciarum*), judges and lawyers respectively. He begins with two chapters on the officials (*praepositi*), warning them that they should not covet their office, for the same reasons as he has already applied to the *princeps*. They should not undertake office from ambition or the love of worldly gain or transitory honours, but from obedience to their superior *princeps* and concern for the good of the state. They should be capable, just and God-fearing, able to judge truly, to hate greed and to reject bribes. Moreover, they should not take advantage of or despoil their subjects.[63] They should imitate the good prince in their rule, being wary of secular pomp and careful not to extort money from the people unjustly.[64] John says that whether the listeners are provincial rulers or the ruling men of a town or the bailiffs of a village, the same advice should apply,[65] so he seems to be aiming his remarks at those who exert authority at all levels, high and low. The *ballivi villarum* should be as careful with their authority as any prince. John again uses mainly classical *exempla* to illustrate proper behaviour, and many of his protagonists are Roman senators.

John next discusses judges and other groups involved in the working of the law. Judges, he says, may be described as the eyes of the state.[66] Like the eyes in the natural body, they distinguish between what is useful and what is harmful, and therefore they are set high in the state, as the eyes are in the body. A judge must be just, wise and knowledgeable, brave and reliable. He should exercise justice diligently and not judge issues hurriedly or without proper evidence. He should be careful not to sentence the poor unjustly, and beware of those who seek to pervert justice. People are not always truthful, and to believe them too hurriedly may lead to perversion of justice, as when the Pharaoh believed his wife's accusation against Joseph and threw him into prison. Judges should not be swayed by hate or fear, love or desire for reward. John goes on to emphasise how diligent and careful the ancients were in discussing cases, and how reliable and thoughtful in deciding the dubious ones, giving the

---

[63] *Communiloq.* I.4.1.
[64] *Communiloq.* I.4.2.
[65] *Communiloq.* I.4, Introduction.
[66] *Communiloq.* I.4.3.

usual appropriate examples. Again there is particular emphasis on proper justice for poor folk (*pauperes*), indicating perhaps that John felt the *pauperes* of England were not receiving their due where justice was concerned.

The next chapter appears to be a plea for circumstances to be taken into consideration.[67] John gives several examples from Valerius of people who were found not guilty of some crime because they had been driven to it, or because they had freely admitted what they had done and showed true repentance. In John's opinion, the ancients were more inclined to absolve than to condemn, and he goes on to quote Augustine's *De Civitate Dei* on the Athenian Areopagus, giving the derivation of its name from its function as a homicide court, and explaining that if six of the twelve judges found a defendant not guilty then he went free, and that this was the standard practice where there was an equal split in the verdict. And if the pagans could do this well, then so should the faithful. So again we see John's belief in clemency, and again he gives the impression that the current system is unduly harsh, and therefore less than satisfactory.

In the fifth distinction of this section, John goes on to admonish other groups of people who may be involved in court cases. He warns orators, whether they be *advocati* or *legisti*,[68] that they occupy the place and function of the tongue in the state and should take care that cases are dealt with for the good of the state, as the tongue expresses what is necessary and useful to the natural body.[69] John follows Cicero in saying that such people should use all their knowledge for the good of the state and never do it any harm. They should be careful not to impugn the innocent, to defend wrongful cases or to justify wrong-doing with convincing reasons.

John advises all participants in trials against seeking what is not theirs, proceeding through falsehood, corrupting the judge or oppressing those who are poorer, because to enrich oneself in such ways is the road to damnation.[70] John then turns to witnesses. They should not offer false testimony or deny the truth, and in particular they should not lie for money. A false witness is a noxious thing, and such people will come to a sticky end – John provides a number of illustrative examples. He then explains that God will protect the

---

[67] *Communiloq.* 1.4.4.
[68] From the context, it is clear that John here uses a form of the medieval Latin term *legista*, meaning 'legist', according to Niermayer, *Mediae Latinitatis Lexicon Minus* (Leiden, 1976), p. 595.
[69] *Communiloq.* 1.5.1.
[70] *Communiloq.* 1.5.2–3.

innocent, so that they have no need to lie in court. If someone is on trial who has committed a crime, he should not increase his sins by lying and perjury or by the use of false witnesses, but should acknowledge his guilt and show true penitence. He should patiently accept punishment or death, recognising that it is better for himself to end his life in penitence than to live on in evil, and he should beg forgiveness from God and have confidence in the true saviour. This might not be very comforting to the guilty party, but it does still offer the hope of salvation, and it is certainly consistent with others of John's attitudes.

John informs the plaintiffs who act against the accused that they too should beware of perjury and should not summon people to court if they know the case against them to be false.[71] He gives a firm warning on the evils of false accusers, and makes brief suggestions on the behaviour of *intercessores* (mediators): they should behave with piety and compassion, not favouring the guilty or the criminal, while yet appreciating their situation and their penitence if they have any.[72] Throughout the distinction John shows a sensible attitude and considerable interest in the proceedings of trials and the processes of justice and punishment. He shows substantial concern for the need to make justice available to the poor, and strong support for clemency and the consideration of circumstances in awarding sentences. These are probably the most characteristic elements in his discussion of the processes of justice.

Distinction 6 offers advice to the 'senate'. John explains that by this term he means the collected counsellors, who hold the place of the heart in the state. The Senate in Rome took its name from *senectus* or old age, because the senators were chosen by Romulus from among the older men, and the senators' task was to help the city with advice. Similarly, the Athenian Areopagus advised the city and superintended its laws and institutions. As far as the authority of ancient councils went, Cicero comments that even the military affairs of Athens were entrusted to its council.[73] John then goes on to specify how counsellors ought to behave.[74] They ought to lead a good and holy life, free from vice and virtuous in the ways already described, and they should be experienced in hard work. They should speak the truth to those who consult them, whether it be prince or city or state, even if it does not please the listener. They should be careful to avoid flattery and falsehood, because these do

[71] *Communiloq.* 1.5.4. [72] *Communiloq.* 1.5.5–6.
[73] *Communiloq.* 1.6.1. [74] *Communiloq.* 1.6.2.

not promote the giving of good advice.[75] Counsellors should be clear-sighted and experienced in many types of work, and therefore they should be chosen for their mature minds.[76] They ought also to be stable characters, such as will not be swayed by fear or love or greed.[77] Those who put temporal good above the good of the state are bad counsellors and unreliable when it comes to giving advice.

John tells the reader that advice should be examined and carefully discussed before decisions are made, because of the importance of good counsel.[78] Prudence promotes good counsel; haste and wrath oppose it, and nothing should be advised if it is unjust. Aristotle's *Ethics* tells us that man is naturally advice-seeking, and Proverbs repeatedly exhorts people to listen to advice. John explains that if a prince picks wise counsellors and listens to them he will receive good advice, and gives a plethora of classical and biblical examples.[79] The prince, he adds, ought to be great in council.[80] He should listen carefully to the wise, but he should himself be more excellent in counsel, fairer and more opposed to injustice, more clement and more hating of cruelty, and more generous in giving gifts, for his heart should be more magnificent in every way than the hearts of his inferiors. Here John brings in Alexander as an example. Why should the *princeps* excel in all these ways? Because he is the representative and image of God on earth, and therefore he should be more like God than other people.[81] The final chapter of this section tells us of the need for secret discussion in some circumstances. John quotes Valerius and Vegetius on the value of taking private counsel in difficult or dangerous affairs and of not giving away information in response to sensitive questions.[82] Throughout this section, John was probably thinking of Henry III and his troubled relationship with the English parliament. The whole issue of counsellors, their selection and role, was very topical at the time when *Communiloquium* was being written.

John's advice to the *princeps* is not confined to the section which is officially devoted to him, but continues in Distinction 7, which discusses the treasury and ministers of the prince. The prince should only choose and associate himself with companions and ministers who are of value to him and to the state, and should see that they are

[75] *Communiloq.* 1.6.3.   [76] *Communiloq.* 1.6.4.   [77] *Communiloq.* 1.6.5.
[78] *Communiloq.* 1.6.6.   [79] *Communiloq.* 1.6.7.   [80] *Communiloq.* 1.6.8.
[81] *Communiloq.* 1.6.8. 'Ipse enim est vicarius et ymago dei in terris. Ideo deo conformior debet esse.'
[82] *Communiloq.* 1.6.9.

free from vice and not opposed to God. For if they are thus, it is not safe to live among them.[83] The prince should see that they are virtuous as previously described, industrious, honest in their behaviour and experienced in their duties.[84] He should strive that they should be such men, and if they do not wish to be thus then the prince should expel them from the palace as enemies of God.[85]

John then explains why treasurers are likened to the stomach, whether they represent the prince or the community or the state. The stomach receives the food necessary to the body and distributes it to the limbs, and thus aid for debts is poured into the treasury of the prince or state and poured out for the use of that same prince or state.[86] That which the prince receives from the people he should spend well for the good of the people, and the people ought not to complain passionately about him, as the limbs should not have complained about the stomach in the fable of Aesop. John now quotes the Song of Songs 7.2: 'Your stomach is like a stook of wheat.' The wheat, says John, has been gathered in a stook so that it may be used for the good of the community. Thus it was with the Romans, whose treasury was well filled while they were as paupers in their own homes. John cites Valerius for the point that the Romans defrayed the expenses of funerals or marriages from the common treasury. Then he declares that the stomach which takes in much and does not give anything back for the use of the limbs is a noxious thing. Thus the prince who receives much from the people and does not give it out or spend it for their advantage is a *pestifer*, generating much bad humour and introducing much serious distress and many bad customs into the body of the state.[87] One gets the clear impression that taxation was a sore point with John.

Distinction 8 concentrates on the seven curial vices, which John of Wales derives from the *Policraticus*, and devotes considerable space to the perils of life at court. He warns all the previously mentioned groups who are courtiers to beware of the vices of such a community, and particularly to beware of these seven, of which the first is desire for rank and glory.[88] John quotes from Cicero the fact that

---

[83] *Communiloq.* 1.7.1.

[84] John several times saves space by saying that a particular class should be virtuous 'as previously described'. He seems to be referring to his description of the moral behaviour of the *princeps*.

[85] *Communiloq.* 1.7.1.

[86] *Communiloq.* 1.7.2. John takes this fable from John of Salisbury's *Policraticus*: see C. C. J. Webb, 1909, II.66–72.

[87] *Communiloq.* 1.7.2.   [88] *Communiloq.* 1.8.1.

those who desire glory are more easily compelled to unjust deeds. For this reason, ancient nobles did not wish to benefit from the state except when it needed their services. John lists a number of examples of ancient men who took on power when necessary but surrendered it when they had done their bit.

The second vice in a community of courtiers is defined as flattery and adulation, because people coax their superiors and thus obtain honours.[89] John feels very strongly about flattery. *Policraticus*, he says, tells us that a flatterer is the enemy of all virtues. The ancients, knowing what an undesirable group flatterers were, did not permit them to speak with princes – indeed, according to Valerius they used rather to kill them. John gives some examples of ancient flatterers before quoting Ezekiel and Gregory's *Moralia* on the similarity between a flatterer and a scorpion. Flatterers are the agents of the devil; they flourish in courts and seduce others through their cunning lies, and it is very important to close one's ears to them. John thinks, however, that one should take no chances, and he approvingly tells a story from Trogus Pompeius, of an envoy who was refused access to a Greek king because he wished to flatter him according to the Persian custom.

The third curial vice is the taking of bribes.[90] Seneca likened many courtiers to fierce dogs who are gentled by the throwing of food. They are harsh and severe before they see the reward, which softens them. The reverse was true of the Roman nobility, says John, who tells a number of tales of those who rejected rewards and were properly suspicious of generous presents. If the pagans could do so well, he says, how much more ought the faithful to refuse gifts other than those which the law permits them to receive. And indeed those holding office should receive gifts from no one, for any reason.

This leads naturally into a chapter on the wrong of selling office, the fourth of the curial vices.[91] John quotes Sallust and Juvenal on how this got out of hand in Rome, and makes general comments on how such things snowball: when all start using rewards, charity is shut out. John makes a comparison with the Hydra, who grew three new heads to fill the gap if one was cut off. He also points out that if one man is satisfied to offer reward in exchange for office, and another is greedy enough to accept it, they will always seek one another out.

Next John considers the fifth curial vice, the simulation of friend-

[89] *Communiloq.* 1.8.2.   [90] *Communiloq.* 1.8.3.   [91] *Communiloq.* 1.8.4.

ship.[92] Courtiers pretend to be friends and poison the experience of friendship, which is properly defined as a companionship of the mind. The accepting of bribes shows that a relationship is a not a true friendship. John quotes Aristotle's *Ethics* on the three types of friendship, the first two dissoluble, the third permanent, and supports the definition with comments from Cicero's *De Amicitia* and Ovid's *De Ponto*. John of Wales' use of Aristotle's *Ethics*, which was not available in John of Salisbury's day, indicates that his discussion of the curial vices is not simply a slavish digest of the *Policraticus*.

The sixth curial vice, which John again takes very seriously, is cunning and sharp practice: pillaging the people, instituting unjust laws, favouring those offering bad advice, and following various other paths of wickedness. John likens the prince who does such things to a wolf devouring sheep, to a raging lion and to an angry bear, and his ministers likewise. He then quotes extensively from both biblical and non-biblical sources, to establish the cruel nature of the wolf, noting, however, in fairness to the species, that she-wolves will suckle abandoned children. He finishes by saying how inexcusable it is that those who are rich none the less take advantage of the poor.

John then turns to the seventh curial vice, that of being eaten up with leisure and pleasure.[93] Courtiers indulge in these vices and even make a particular study of them. John makes specific reference to the perversion of turning night into day, waking and sleeping at the wrong times, and also to the perils of feasting and drinking. He closes the distinction by emphasising that courtiers should make an effort to follow the model of the Roman Senate.

This ends John's advice to those involved in government, for the two remaining distinctions discuss military affairs and the various classes of workers. A number of points may be made at this stage. As people with authority, all the individuals in the groups discussed are expected to compete with the prince in the virtue stakes, while he in turn is expected to supervise and control them. No one is supposed to turn his position to personal advantage, although John recognises that it would be easy and tempting to do so. Also, and perhaps more significantly, each individual is expected to show devotion to the interests of the state and of the ordinary people. It is noteworthy that, for every group, John persists in holding up the example of the Greeks and Romans as a particularly good model. This, and his

[92] *Communiloq.* 1.8.5.   [93] *Communiloq.* 1.8.7.

emphasis on devotion to the *respublica*, are distinctive elements of John's work which he could not have lifted wholesale from his medieval predecessors.

Let us now look at what John has to say about soldiers (*milites*).[94] He goes into considerable detail and again reveals a practical attitude. He opens by observing that the *milites* are represented as the hands of the state.[95] The hands in the natural body are to repel the hurtful, to strike at danger, to obtain necessities and to defend all the other limbs, and the *milites* should perform these functions in the state. And, just as the limbs are particularly set to protect the head, so the *milites* in the state should particularly defend the *princeps*. In his next chapter, John speaks of the setting-up of an army, taking as an example the organisation of Rome by Romulus.[96] Having founded his city, Romulus chose a thousand fighters, who were called *milites* on account of their number, or perhaps because each was one chosen from a thousand. In any case they were picked out and named by Romulus, and hence *miles* was an honourable title. John goes on to quote Vegetius on the choosing of a *miles*, who should be outstanding in body and soul, take his duty seriously and, inevitably, lead a virtuous life. One should be very selective in choosing a *miles* – John reminds the reader again of the care exercised by the ancients in this respect.

The next chapter discusses the nature of the oath of allegiance, and makes clear that, in this section at least, John is thinking of the medieval knight.[97] He observes that the *miles* takes an oath to God and Christ, the Holy Spirit and the majesty (*maiestas*) of the prince, that he will protect the human race and strive to do anything his *princeps* wishes. When he takes his vow he receives the girdle and privileges of a *miles*; the title and office of a *miles* cannot be had without it. The chapter is filled out with examples, from Cicero's *De Officiis*, of noble Romans who took oaths as soldiers. John claims that these examples show the worthiness of a *miles* and the obligation of the knightly oath, whose form is that, first having faith in God, the knight will strive that the *princeps* and the state shall be unharmed. There is, says John, great danger for a knight if he does not pay heed to his vow. He then deals with the role of the church in the making of a knight, reminding the reader that on the day that anyone is decorated with the girdle of a *miles*, he should attend

94 *Communiloq.* 1.9.1–8.   95 *Communiloq.* 1.9.1.
96 *Communiloq.* 1.9.2.   97 *Communiloq.* 1.9.3.

church solemnly and lay his sword upon the altar and bind himself to God with it.

Although the examples in this chapter are from the Roman world, it is certainly the medieval knight who is under discussion here, and a contemporary one at that. There is no mention anywhere in the distinction of mercenary soldiers, or of payment of any kind for service. It might seem incongruous that John still took his examples from the Roman army, a highly professional paid force, but it is no more so than the recommendation that medieval rulers should model themselves on great men of the Roman Republic. John was always willing to take a good example where he found it, and he was convinced that much in the Roman army merited the attention of his contemporaries.

He certainly expected a considerable degree of dedication and preparedness from contemporary knights, as we can see in the next chapter, which deals with the virtues of the *milites*.[98] John quotes Bernard of Clairvaux, writing for the Knights Templar, on how knights should be strenuous and industrious, circumspect and quick to move when necessary.[99] It is, says John, the duty of the prince to teach the knights correct behaviour, and he quotes Sallust for the example of Pompey and how he drilled his men in all the necessary skills and made them strong and competent. Knights, says John, should not be effeminate or delicate or nervous. They should have the abilities already mentioned above, be ready to tackle the enemy and able to tolerate hard work, poor food and poor conditions. Many knights today, he says, indulge in laziness and pleasure and have become effeminate and inexperienced as soldiers. The Roman soldiers, according to Lucan, wore the customary toga. Today many pay more attention to the decoration of their clothes and weapons than to their usefulness in war and ability to stand up to work, when really the knights ought to shine more brilliantly than their weapons and clothing. This is a pointed and topical reference to the tendency of armour and accoutrements to become more bulky and showy, and less practical, as the thirteenth century progressed.[100] As always, John has an illustrative example from the ancient world – he tells us that Hannibal once crushed an eastern king who displayed himself

---

[98] *Communiloq.* 1.9.4.
[99] Bernard of Clairvaux, *Epistola ad milites*, in *Opera S. Bernhardi*, ed. J. Leclercq *et al.* (Rome, 1957–).
[100] See, e.g., N. Denholm-Young, 1946, p. 63; also J. F. Verbruggen, 1977, pp. 23–8.

decorated in gold and silver. Then he shows thoughtfulness on the subject by adding that such decorated armour is not blameworthy if its purpose is not vanity and ostentation but the frightening away of the enemy, as when the flashing of shields was used to disconcert the enemy in I Maccabees.

The next chapter deals with military discipline.[101] The ancients, says John, were amazingly severe in carrying through military discipline, and their soldiers were remarkably obedient to their princes and consuls; nor was any time wasted on pleasurable pursuits. Note Rome's military success against the Parthians, who had a most luxurious lifestyle, and the way Roman power faltered under Nero, whose appetite devoured everything. In good periods the Roman soldiers not only led a restrained life but also refrained from pillage: for example, Julius Caesar ordered that his soldiers should despoil neither men nor the temples of the gods. John gives many other examples of harsh discipline and praiseworthy restraint in the ancient world.

John now mentions the right of soldiers to wage war if they are faithful and led by a legitimately established prince, before going on to discuss how they ought to defend the church and fight for the good of the Catholic population, because *milites* accept their sword at the altar.[102] They should note that among ancient soldiers it was the custom to dedicate the spoils of war to the gods. If ancient pagans could do so well, Christian soldiers ought to do much more to defend and honour their church. Finally John describes a variety of militias.[103] There are four types. First come ordinary men; secondly the Christian army (*militia christiana*), who should be virtuous and faithful in order to conquer the devil; thirdly comes the army under oath (*militia votiva*), in which man fights against the enemies of his faith (as an example of such militia John gives the Knights Templar and other cross-bearing knights); fourthly he lists the virtuous or church army (*militia virtuosa sive ecclesiastica*), in which the preachers and prelates of the church fight against their enemies and against heresy and errors. All these militias should attend to the advice given, and if those in the first group ought to have the described virtues, how much more does this apply to the other groups! And the evangelical preacher should be sure to tell them so.

John now leaves the 'hands' of the state and turns to the working people or 'feet'.[104] The feet, he says, may conveniently be designated

101 *Communiloq.* 1.9.5. 102 *Communiloq.* 1.9.6–7.
103 *Communiloq.* 1.9.8. 104 *Communiloq.* 1.10.1.

as the *populus inferior*. The feet are of great service to the body and
therefore they ought to be protected, guarded and organised with
great care. As the *populus inferior* supports the body of the state, the
same may be said of them. John reminds us that all the groups in the
state ought to work faithfully at their duties. He then lists the seven
mechanical arts as given in Hugh of Saint-Victor's *Didascalion*; these
form the basis for the rest of his discussion.[105]

John begins with some general admonitions to working people.[106]
They should, of course, be free from sin – John specifies fraud and
theft, lying and sensual gratification – and they should work in a
regular fashion, for it is much better to work than to live in idleness
or to beg. In working, they should pray to God, and they should
freely release their tenth to the church. If they do these things they
will be such as are truly accepted by God. As an example John tells
the tale of how an ordinary peasant succeeded in exorcising a demon
when an abbot could not, because he led such an industrious and
God-fearing life.

John now tells the evangelical preacher that he should not only
instruct workers in general, but also each worker as part of his
particular craft.[107] Thus, when he sees woolworkers he should warn
them to make for themselves spiritual clothing. Similarly, when he
sees armourers he should warn them of the need for spiritual
armour. Sailors should be told to prepare for themselves the ship of
penitence, and farmworkers to till carefully the fields of the heart.
The principle is clear – the preacher should use the simple things of
everyday life to clarify spiritual needs.

Having given brief comments on how to address four of his seven
working groups, John goes on to present individual chapters on the
admonition of hunters, doctors and *lusores* or players. There are, says
John, three types of hunting – game-hunting, fowling and fishing.[108] There are many ways of going about hunting, and people
should be reminded which are permitted and which are not. Fishing
is allowed even for clerics and monks, but game-hunting and
fowling are not permitted to all people or at all times. John reminds
the reader that we know of no saints who were hunters, but that we
do have examples of saintly fishermen. Hunting may be forbidden
on account of the season, or on account of the person: for example, it
is not allowed to a bishop. Hunting is allowed to laymen for skins
and meat, though not for pleasure. And it is allowed to clerics if they

[105] *Communiloq.* 1.10.2. [106] *Communiloq.* 1.10.3.
[107] *Communiloq.* 1.10.4. [108] *Communiloq.* 1.10.5.

use a net and proceed without noise and clamour and dogs. It is the task of the preacher to portray the various forms of hunting, the imprudence of the chase, the time wasted in useless occupation, the slightness of the fruits as many soldiers and runners loudly pursue a little beast, perhaps a young hare. There are, however, hunts to exterminate dangerous animals like wolves and foxes, and these are permissible. John gives some examples of ancient reactions to hunting, and ends with the story of how King Edgar of England once called out his hunt on a Sunday, and of how he was reprimanded by the priest and forbidden to do it again.

This chapter presents a true churchman's view of the hunt, in that it condemns hunting for pleasure and takes pains to explain the distinctions regarding what is permitted to the different ranks of the clergy.[109] The chapter is characteristic of John in that it has a distinctly practical bias. Purposeful hunting, whether to exterminate the dangerous or to provide the necessities of life, is acceptable, provided it is carried out with due regard to season, which John mentions more than once as a limiting factor. Although the preacher is told in several places that he ought to explain to the people what they are allowed to do and what they are not, John neither details nor even mentions the forest laws which would have been the major limiting factor on most people's activities.[110] He may have assumed that the preacher would be acquainted with them already, but then he was writing primarily from a moral standpoint rather than a legal one. Both hunting and hawking were common objects of clerical disapproval, following the pattern set by Gratian's *Decretum*.[111] A *sententia* wrongly attributed to Jerome observed that there were no holy men among hunters, but several among fishermen, and this seems to have helped to consolidate clerical attitudes to the subject.[112]

John's next chapter turns to doctors.[113] The preacher should warn them to guard themselves against the diseases of the spirit, and not to attempt to cure others before they have been instructed in medical science. This is in many ways a sensible piece of advice, and not surprising from a university man, who could be expected to accept

---

[109] For the contrast between the nobles' view of hunting and that presented in canon law and the comments of various ecclesiastics, see M. Thiébaux, 1967, pp. 260–74.

[110] For the forest laws in England, see Ch. Petit-Dutaillis and G. Lefebvre, 1930, pp. 187–208.

[111] M. Thiébaux, 1967.

[112] *Ibid.*   [113] *Communiloq.* 1.10.6.

the value of training. The advice seems to reflect contemporary attempts to restrict the activities of the unqualified. Similar comments were made in at least one Oxford sermon of the 1290s: on 14 June 1293 John Westerfield OP gave a sermon in which he discussed the behaviour suitable to different groups of scholars.[114] He told doctors to avoid rash treatment in critical cases, lest they kill the patient unwittingly. He also said that it was one thing to practise medicine and another to receive authorisation to do so. Doctors in 'this university' were quite well controlled, but still many followed the course only for a year or two and then returned home, to set up a practice immediately. Concern about unqualified doctors was not confined to Oxford – in 1311 the Paris faculty of medicine attempted to stop unqualified persons practising their profession, by putting into force a statute which had apparently been established for some years. We know of at least one couple who were excommunicated under it the following year.[115]

Finally we come to the *lusores*, the players or gamblers.[116] The preacher should warn those who work in a 'theatre' to beware of unsuitable and lascivious gamers. John quotes Chrysostom's *Commentary on Matthew* to the effect that the devil, and not God, invented gambling. John makes an exception, however, for a sociable and honest game (*ludus socialis et honestiis*) for recreation and the solace of the body.[117] Even the philosophers played such games: Seneca says that Socrates did not blush to play games with the boys, and that Cato also liked to relax his spirit after the stress of public life. Fertile fields become exhausted if cropped without a pause, and similarly the spirit may break through continuous labour. You can, of course, have too much of a good thing: sleep is necessary, but continuous sleep constitutes death, and so it is with honest play. Therefore the establishers of laws instituted festive days when men could come together to enjoy themselves in public.

This seems like a clear case of classical influence. But John certainly means to apply his advice to contemporary times, for he adds that men of the church ought to be sober and temperate in enjoying any games. This inhibits a delightful picture of himself letting off steam after a hard day's studying or composition, but we may infer that this was a possibility, as he has implied that churchmen may join a game and, within limits, may take pleasure in doing

[114] B. Smalley, 1981, p. 186.
[115] Beryl Rowland, 1981, pp. 9–10.
[116] *Communiloq.* 1.10.7.
[117] Thomas Aquinas advocated recreation in his *De Studio*.

so. John closes his chapter with a particular warning against involvement with games of chance, whether as a participant or as an onlooker, and almost inevitably concludes that many ancients opposed such practices strenuously.

We may wonder exactly what John would have classified as a *ludus socialis et honestiis*. His only open objection is to gambling and games of chance: we know that games with dice were endemic in medieval Europe, probably partly because the equipment was both cheap and easy to carry around. Preachers were constantly complaining about dice games and other forms of gambling, apparently with little effect.[118] John would no doubt have shared the thirteenth-century acceptance of chess as a game with some moral status. Although it was regarded with some suspicion in earlier centuries, the churchmen of John's century were more tolerant.[119] The popularity of chess seems to have been such that by the early fourteenth century one writer could warn that it should not be played before noon on a Sunday.[120] Other boardgames were known in thirteenth-century England – for example, a form of backgammon[121] – and it seems likely that simpler games such as Nine Men's Morris would have had wide currency. John would probably have found such games acceptable, and also the various ballgames and sports which were current among the younger and more active members of society. Even a cleric could indulge in such games without harm.

In the last chapter of this first part of *Communiloquium*, John returns to those who have care of the state.[122] He tells them that the workers in the occupations just discussed are as the feet of the state and support it; therefore it should be the task of the magistrates to guard and protect and cherish them, the magistrates having been instituted because the few always take advantage of the many or the ordinary people. John repeats that *all* the groups within the state have their own functions and should concentrate on filling them to perfection, rather than trying to usurp the function of any other of the groups. Then he closes by recommending the reader to examine the second part of the *Communiloquium*, where he will find admonitions to some different groups.

Our survey of the first part of *Communiloquium* shows us that John based his work on a detailed and well-articulated plan, and that he was capable of sticking to this plan and of fleshing it out with a wide

[118] M. W. Labarge, 1980, p. 177. [119] *Ibid.*, p. 176.
[120] *Ibid.* [121] *Ibid.*
[122] *Communiloq.* 1.10.8.

range of appropriate *exempla* to express opinions on a vast range of issues. John truly admired the great ancients and believed that they had much to teach contemporary Christians, but his bias in favour of ancient sources rarely leads to his expressing unrealistic attitudes. The opinions which we can discern in his work, and the society of which he gives a picture, are firmly planted in the thirteenth century. There is, therefore, an interesting dichotomy in *Communiloquium*, in that John takes ancient and well-established patterns and *exempla* and uses them to build up a comprehensive contemporary system. He shows considerable flexibility in his capacity to divide and systematise humanity. In this first part of *Communiloquium* he has relied primarily upon the old simile of state as body, supplemented by such groupings as the seven mechanical arts as listed by Hugh of Saint-Victor.[123] This caused John to leave out of the discussion three substantial groups – the ecclesiastics, the merchant class and women – but these groups are all discussed fully later in the work.

In the course of Part 1 of *Communiloquium*, John reveals a number of interesting opinions. First, he consistently shows his belief in the wonders and virtues of the ancient world and their suitability as *exempla*. His discussion of the *respublica* strengthens the impression we gained from the *Breviloquium de Virtutibus* that John fully accepted and greatly favoured the concept of the community of the realm. He seems to take very seriously the principle that all could, and should, make a positive contribution to the state. He shows an awareness of the then current disputes on the value of the active life as opposed to the contemplative, and reaches the conclusion that it is the duty of each individual to become involved for the good of the community as a whole.

John places great emphasis on justice and the law, and again this interest had already begun to emerge in the *Breviloquium de Virtutibus*. John is clear that the source of law is not the king so much as the judges. Here again he reflects the contemporary situation, for the mid- to late thirteenth century was the great period of justice-made law in England. John's awareness that all law does not emanate from the king is associated with his conviction that the king is not above or beyond the law. John tackles the questions of the proper institution, duties and behaviour of a ruler, and also expresses an opinion on the issue of tyranny and tyrannicide. This issue was discussed in the previous century by John of Salisbury, and in John's

---

[123] Hugh of Saint-Victor, *Didascalion*, 6.

own century by the 'Bractonian' *De Legibus* in England and by Thomas Aquinas in Paris.[124]

The *De Legibus* took the line that tyrannicide was God's preroga- tive, and Aquinas expressed doubt about the advisability of tyranni- cide, on the grounds that, although it might not necessarily be wrong, it could lead to replacement by another and more successful tyrant who had learned from the experiences of his predecessor.[125] John was bolder in his simple declaration that there was no sin in killing a tyrant. His attitude was probably influenced by the situation in England in the years before and during *Communiloquium*'s com- position. Certainly John's whole attitude to kingship reflects English rather than continental circumstances.

John devotes most of his space in this part to those men with most power in the state. The corrupting potential of power and the degree of harm which one powerful man can cause provide a natural explanation for this priority. John is concerned about the behaviour of the powerful, because of the influence which they have over others, but he is equally concerned about the rights of the majority or lesser folk against the minority or great ones. This is as non-baronial as it is non-classical, but it is perhaps not uncharacteristic of a friar.

As *Communiloquium* progresses, John shows that his views on the ordinary people are quite as strong as those on kingship and rule. In this first part, he follows discussion of state and king with discussion of other men of authority. Characteristically, he shows more interest in some topics than in others. Judges, trials and the processes of the law come in for particular attention. John shows awareness of some of the weaknesses of the contemporary system, and gives every indication that he feels the present system is too harsh, and perhaps less favourable to the poorer people than to the better-off. John is critical of high taxation, and anxious that rulers should take proper advice before making important decisions. He shows a common- sense attitude and a good awareness of how the system worked in his own time.

John's discussion of the seven curial vices, in distinction 8, seems perhaps slightly laboured at times, but John found plenty to say on the subject, and was thoroughly disparaging about life at court. He discusses military matters from a number of viewpoints, giving precedence to the making of a knight and his subsequent role, but

[124] J. Dunbabin, 1965, pp. 65–85.
[125] *Ibid.*, p. 77.

finding time to condemn current trends in decorated and unwieldy armour, on the grounds that they are vain and impractical. John also gives a thorough discussion of proper behaviour on the battlefield.

When it comes to the more ordinary people, John shows a touching concern that the preacher should be able to reach them, to put his message across and to touch their hearts with careful use of words. John's discussion of hunting suggests that he took a strong personal interest in the rights and wrongs of the matter. His discussion of medicine is simple and sensible and reflects current concern over the activities of the unqualified and unlicensed, and his attitude to play is original and refreshing. In summary, this part of *Communiloquium* contains much of use and interest to the medieval preacher, and likewise much for the modern historian.

Before leaving the first part of *Communiloquium*, we should take a look at John's sources. His selection provides an interesting contrast to that used later in the work, and hence shows his capacity to select what is appropriate to any particular topic.

I shall use the same system of analysis developed for the *Breviloquium de Virtutibus*. Dividing John's sources into those 'ancient' works written before AD 450, and the 'medieval' works written after this date, we can classify his citations as follows. The first part of *Communiloquium* contains 460 citations from 82 works by 41 ancient authors, and 177 citations from 39 works by 26 medieval authors. If we exclude biblical citations, we have totals of 637 citations from 121 works by 67 authors, and if we add in the biblical citations we reach a total of 845 citations overall. The efforts involved in collecting, selecting and arranging this volume of material must have been enormous. The biblical citations are generally much shorter than the others, perhaps because the reader was assumed to have both a better knowledge of the Bible than of other works, and also more certain access to a copy of it. The non-biblical citations vary from a phrase or short sentence to long paragraphs. John intersperses his selected citations with brief comments of his own.

From the figures above, we can see that there is a definite classical bias in John's sources. When we remember that John's favourite medieval source for this section, the *Policraticus*, was used on 56 occasions, almost entirely as a quarry for classical lore, the bias becomes even more pronounced. We see the same bias if we examine the 'Top Ten' authors quoted in this section. The list runs as follows:

Augustine	88 citations
Seneca	71
Valerius Maximus	67
Cicero	65
John of Salisbury	56
Gregory the Great	50
Vegetius	19
Jerome	18
Aristotle	16
Ambrose	15
TOTAL	465

(out of a total 637 non-biblical citations)

We can see that a substantial proportion of the total number of citations comes from this relatively small group of authors.

SOURCE LIST FOR THE *COMMUNILOQUIUM*, PART I

I. SOURCES FROM BEFORE AD 450

Ambrose	*De Officiis*	7 references
	Hexameron	6
	Sermo de Passione	1
	Theodosius ut Ante	1
Apuleius	*De Deo Socratis*	1
Aristotle	*De Animalibus*	5
	De Caelo et Mundo	1
	Ethics	8
	Metaphysics	1
	Physics	1
Augustine	*Ad Chrisosti*	1
	Confessions	8
	Contra Faustum	1
	De Beati Iohannis Decollatione	1
	De Civitate Dei	46
	De Doctrina Christiana	5
	De Excidio Urbis	1
	De Lapsu Mundi	1
	Epistolae	16
	Sermons	5
	Super Iohannem	3

Aulus Gellius	Noctes Atticae	5
Cato[126]		1
Chrysippus		2
Chrysostom	De Instructione Iudicum	1
	Super Iohannem	5
	Super Matthaeum[127]	
Cicero	De Amicitia	3
	De Divinatione	2
	De Legibus	1
	De Natura Deorum	3
	De Officiis	48
	De Republica[128]	1
	De Rhetorica[129]	3
	De Senectute	1
	Philippics	1
	Tusculanae Quaestiones	3
Claudian	Verses	3
pseudo-Cyprian	De Duodecim Abusionibus	4
Ennius		2
Eusebius	Historia Ecclesiastica	5
Florus	Epitome	6
Frontinus	Strategemata	1
Hegesippus	On the Jewish War	8
Hermogenes[130]		2
Hesychius[131]		1
Jerome	Contra Iovinianum	2
	De Coniugio	1
	Epistolae	13
	Originalis[132]	2
Josephus	Concionados ad Iudeos[133]	1
Juvenal	Satires	5
Lucan	Pharsalia	1
Macrobius	Saturnalia	3
Natos (poeta)[134]		1

[126] Through Augustine.
[127] This is the genuine Chrysostom commentary, rather than the Opus Imperfectum, which also circulated under Chrysostom's name.
[128] Through Augustine.   [129] I.e. De Inventione.
[130] Probably through some rhetorical treatise. I have not identified the intermediary.
[131] Probably through Rabanus Maurus on the Old Testament.
[132] John's title. Quotations as yet untraced.   [133] Through Hegesippus.
[134] Probably a corruption of Naso, an alternative name for Ovid.

John of Wales

Ovid	De Arte Amandi	1
	De Ponto	1
Papias	Rhetorica	6
Petronius		1
Pliny	Natural History[135]	2
Sallust		6
Seneca	Ad Elbiam	1
	De Beata Vita	1
	De Beneficiis	8
	De Clementia	10
	De Constantia Sapientis	2
	De Ira	7
	De Naturalibus Quaestionibus	3
	De Tranquillitate Animi	2
	Epistulae	34
pseudo-Seneca	De Virtutibus	1
	Proverbia	2
Sillus Italicus		1
Solinus	Collectanea Rerum Memorabilium[136]	5
Suetonius	Liber de Vita Caesarum	5
Thaurus	Commentary on Plato's Gorgias[137]	1
Theodosian Code		1
Trogus Pompeius	(Justin's Epitome)	7
Valerius Maximus	Factorum ac Dictorum Memorabilium Libri ix	67
Vegetius	De Re Militari	19
Velleius		1
Virgil	Aeneid	5

2. SOURCES FROM AFTER AD 450

Alexander Nequam	De Natura Rerum	3
Algazel	Philosophia[138]	1
Avicenna	Liber Philosophie[139]	2

[135] Through *Policraticus*.
[136] Also known as the *De Mirabilibus Mundi*.
[137] Through Aulus Gellius.
[138] John's title.   [139] John's title.

Bernard of Clairvaux	*Ad Eugenium*	2
	De Gradibus Humilitatis	1
	Exhortation to the Knights Templar	2
	Sermones de Adventu	1
	Super Cantica	2
Boethius	*De Consolatione Philosophiae*	7
Cassian	*Collations*	2
Cassiodorus	*De Distinctione Scripturarum*[140]	1
	Historia Tripartita	1
Constantinus[141]		1
Erhardus[142]		1
Glosa		1
Gratian	*Decretum*	2
Gregory the Great	*Dialogues*	2
	Moralia	30
	Pastoralia	2
	Registrum Epistolarum	3
	Sentencia[143]	1
	Super Evangelia	5
	Super Ezechielem	4
Hugh of Saint-Victor	*Didascalion*	9
Isidore	*De Summo Bono*	3
	Etymologia	1
John of Damascus	*Tractatus*[144]	2
John of Salisbury	*Policraticus*	56
John of Wales	*Breviloquium de Virtutibus*	7
Petrus Alphonsi	*De Disciplina Clericalis*	1
Peter Comestor	*Historia Scholastica*	1
pseudo-Plutarch	*Institutio Traiani*	3
Robert Grosseteste	Commentary on *Ethics*	7

---

[140] I.e. *Institutiones Divinarum et Humanarum Lectionum*.
[141] Probably Constantinus Africanus, although I have been unable to trace the phrase.
[142] Probably a mistake for Einhardus – the topic is Charlemagne.
[143] John's title. It is not clear what he was actually referring to.
[144] The *De Fide Orthodoxa*, probably.

John of Wales

Anon.	*Moralium Dogma*	
	Philosophorum	2
Anonymous and as yet untraced:		
	Cronicis Brevibus	1
	Vita Beati Basilii	1
	Vita Iohannis Elemosinarii	1
	Tractatus de Viciis	1

Chapter 5

COMMUNILOQUIUM, PARTS 2 AND 3: JOHN OF WALES ON SECULAR SOCIETY

In the second part of *Communiloquium*, John discusses the bonds of society by focussing on different relationships: masters and servants, parents and children, and so on. In the third he re-divides the population a number of times according to the differences in their status, and admonishes the groups accordingly. He classifies his differences into two groups, *naturalia* (natural) – for example, men and women, young and old – and *contingentia* (contingent) – for example, spinsters and widows – before listing those he intends to discuss. First he takes the two sexes, then the different stages of life from infancy to old age. Thirdly, he turns to different conditions – noble and ignoble – and, fourthly, to differing amounts of natural gift, whether spiritual or corporeal. Fifthly, he lists the differences pertaining to the quality of life – that is, between sinners and penitents – and, sixthly, differences in position – that is, between spinsters, married women and widows. His seventh division is based upon poverty and wealth, and his eighth encompasses such pairs of opposites as adversity and prosperity, sickness and health.

The range of these groupings is considerable. Not only are they independent of those used to analyse the state, but the categories are not mutually exclusive. John would therefore seem able to recognise the individual as the centre of a nexus of differing obligations: to the state, to family and friends, to fellow-citizens, and so on.

It would be valuable to know how the various bonds were ranked in terms of priority – a question modern sociologists often ask about members of modern societies. Unfortunately John does not give us many clues in this respect, although he appears to place responsibility to the state above every other type of bond or obligation, with the obvious exception of duty to God and the church, which he does not really discuss in this section.

John begins with a series of admonitions on the theme of personal relationships. The persons who constitute the limbs of the *respublica*, he says, are held together by many bonds and should be admonished as to how these bonds should function.[1] He explains that he will deal first with legal bonds – namely, those between *dominus* and *servus* and vice versa – secondly, with natural bonds – namely those between parents and children and between siblings – thirdly, with bonds of affection – those between married people. Fourthly, John lists spiritual bonds – those between Christians in the body of Christ – fifthly, the bonds between citizens, and specifically neighbours; sixthly, the bonds of friendship; seventhly, the bonds between *socii* or acquaintances; and, finally, the matter of behaviour towards enemies. John again demonstrates his flexibility of outlook by redistributing his bonds into four main groups and giving each a motive force: bonds between Christians, directed by gratitude and charity; civil bonds, directed by living together; those of friendship, directed by those who are friends, and capable of enduring despite absence; and those of *socii*, directed by companionship and conversation. Those living in a state ought to classify themselves in these ways, and the preacher ought to tell them that they should be thus.

The establishment of distinct groups for the purpose of advising people according to their needs and conditions was a characteristic of the thirteenth century, and particularly of its preaching aids and sermons. In this John has much in common with men like Jacques de Vitry, Humbert de Romans and Guibert de Tournai, who all produced major *ad status* collections in the thirteenth century. We must ask how far John drew upon these three, and how far he was following a similar line in his *Communiloquium*.

The earliest of these three was Jacques de Vitry, who was born in the mid- to late twelfth century and died in 1240.[2] His *ad status* collection, which can be dated to between 1227/9 and 1240,[3] covers a wide range of secular categories. Like John, Jacques de Vitry uses the idea of society as a body of complementary limbs, and he also greatly expands the old threefold division into *clerici*, *milites* and *laici*: groups like the prelates, the religious, the knights, the burghers, the virgins and married women are all discussed individually.[4]

Humbert de Romans (late twelfth century to 1277), and Guibert de Tournai (*c.* 1213–84), the one a Dominican and the other a Franciscan, were closely contemporary with John. Guibert de Tournai drew heavily upon the *Sermones Vulgares* of Jacques de Vitry,[5] so these two inevitably had much in common, in their

[1] *Communiloq.* 2.1, Introduction. [2] A. Forni, 1980, p. 34. [3] *Ibid.*, p. 37.
[4] *Ibid.*, 1980, p. 46. [5] D. L. d'Avray and M. Tausche, 1980, p. 85.

analysis of society as in their discussion of individual groups. Humbert de Romans, however, seems to have worked quite independently of the other two. His *ad status* work appears in the second volume of his *De Eruditione Praedicatorum*, which contains comments applicable to 100 different groups. The first section is headed *Ad omnes homines*, and the second *Ad omnem populum Christianum*. The next 59 deal with various classes of churchmen, monks, canons, friars and all types of religious. In section 62 we come to *Omnes scholares*. Sections 63–70 deal with different classes of scholar and student, and 71–100 with other secular groups, including various classes of town-dweller: *laici* in *castris, villis* and *burgis*, nobles both faithful and badly behaved, those at court, the poor, youths, travellers, the sick and various classes of women. Humbert has a much narrower range of secular divisions than John of Wales, and his volume is heavily biassed in favour of the religious world,[6] while John's *Communiloquium* is weighted in quite the other direction. John does not appear to have used any of these continental *ad status* collections as a direct model for his own.

To see how John addresses his various secular groups, we must return to his text. He opens the section with a discussion of servitude.[7] The nature of the bond between *princeps* and *servus* has already been described, says John, but each ought to understand that the reason for ruling is sin. He recommends the reader to turn to Augustine's *De Civitate Dei* 19, 'ubi multum de hoc', but briefly describes why sin is the first cause of servitude: we can read in the Scriptures that the word *servus* was coined by Noah on account of the sin of his son. The name is therefore deserved by wrong, not by nature, and so a prince or leader should not be elevated overmuch by lordship, when he is lord not through a natural condition but through an unnatural one. Men ought to obey properly instituted princes; and Gregory's *Registrum* tells us that all men are born equal, but through varying merits do not retain equal status, so that some are ruled by others. The rulers should, however, show restraint: John tells a story from Seneca's *Epistulae* of how Seneca once advised the emperor that it would be a good idea if he dined together with his slaves rather than dining by himself while a crowd stood around unable to speak or even to move their lips. This latter custom, according to Seneca, was conducive to pride. A lord should

---

[6] I have taken this list of headings from Humbert de Romans, *De Eruditione Praedicatorum* 2.1.78 (*Maxima Bibliotheca Veterum Patrum*, tom. 25 (Lyons, 1677)).

[7] *Communiloq.* 2.1.1.

remember that in another time chance might have made him a *servus*. He should also remember that a *servus* may be free in spirit. John tells masters that they should not frighten their *servi*, nor treat them harshly. *Servi* cannot be permitted to live without discipline, but the discipline should be moderate and regulated by justice and reason. As an example of charity towards inferiors John suggests Christ washing the feet of his disciples. He then reaffirms that he does not deny that *servi* should reverently serve their masters: render unto Caesar what is Caesar's, and so on. There is nothing in this chapter to cause masters to preen themselves on their natural superiority. John seems almost to deny that there is such a thing – he certainly does so in his chapter on the nobility.[8] Again we see John's characteristic concern with clemency, and the implication that society is unnecessarily harsh, particularly to the poor people.

On the topic of servants, John recommends the preacher to tell the people that sin is the cause of servitude, so that they may hate sin.[9] They should remember that their minds are free, and not be cast down by their condition. John seems to take for granted that servitude is an unpopular condition. However, he goes on to tell *servi* of the fidelity with which they ought to serve their lords.[10] *Servi* and others who are subjects (soldiers, for example) are warned to show perfect obedience towards their lord or *princeps*, and to love him with a perfect affection, esteem him, care for his health, obey him promptly and guard his life and honour with concern. The ancients esteemed and obeyed their kings, as Virgil showed in *Aeneid* 1. John now quotes the *Summa Aurea* of the thirteenth-century Italian canonist Henry de Suza (also known as Hostiensis) *de feudis* (on feudal service). *Fidelitas* includes the giving of constructive and trusty advice and help, the protection of the lord through sickness and health, capture and all manner of wounds, and the ready doing not only of the easy tasks which the lord requires, but also of the difficult ones. John gives the form of the oath which he says is today taken by all: 'this I swear on the holy Gospels, that from this hour . . . until the last day of my life, I will be faithful to you, my lord, against all men except the emperor or king', and elaborates with Henry de Suza on what this amounts to in practice. He then turns to the *Extravagantes de Ius Iurandum* for the fact that prelates take an oath to the Pope when they are consecrated, and gives the form of that oath. Because of this, he says, clerics, like laymen, mostly hold to

---

[8] *Communiloq.* 3.3. [9] *Communiloq.* 2.1.2. [10] *Communiloq.* 2.1.3.

some form of loyalty. They should keep their faith, and the Lord will reward them. Note the example of ancient men, like Caesar's men, who were so devoted that they could not be separated from him, or the slave of Papinias, who, according to Valerius, switched clothes with his master when assassins threatened, and took a death which was not meant for him. John gives a number of other examples.

Finally he discusses the worthlessness and punishment of unfaithful *servi*, beginning with some examples of the true worthlessness of *servi* who kill their masters and usurp their wives, or otherwise betray trust, of how terrible such behaviour was thought in the ancient world, and of how truly the faithful should therefore serve their lords.[11] As an example John draws a parallel with the behaviour of bees guarding their leader, as described in book 4 of Virgil's *Georgics*.

In this distinction we see John using the *dominus–servus* terminology to cover a variety of relationships – from the ancient slave and master to the feudal bond or the subjection of a soldier to his leader – in much the same way as he earlier used *miles* for a Greek or Roman soldier as readily as for a medieval knight. He is very clear on the point that the existence of *servus* and *dominus* is an unnatural situation, and he suggests that the presence of any individual in one particular class is a matter of chance rather than one of inevitable right. This is a very long way from the Aristotelian view. John did not have access to Aristotle's *Politics*, so we cannot say that he has deliberately rejected Aristotle's attitude. However, what he says here suggests that he would not have approved of or been impressed by such a view, or at least would have found it very difficult to justify. On this point, John is decidedly Augustinian in outlook.

In the second distinction, John turns to relationships within the family. He begins by telling fathers how they should bring their children up under discipline.[12] Aristotle's *Ethics* and Ecclesiastes are used to support the point that a father is responsible for teaching his children so that they may grow up knowing right from wrong. Ancient nobles, says John, arranged teaching for their children, as in the case of Philip and Alexander of Macedon. He tells a story from *Policraticus* about the Emperor Augustus' belief that children should learn useful skills, and follows this with a description (from Cicero) of the hardships undergone by Spartan youth. He repeats Seneca's view that physical hardship encourages a strong body, and recom-

[11] *Communiloq.* 2.1.4.   [12] *Communiloq.* 2.2.1.

mends the reader to turn to the fifth part of *Communiloquium* for details on the education of boys.

John suggests Valerius Maximus as a source of much information about the proper severity of a father in correcting his sons. For example, Manilius Torquato ordered his son out of the house for a financial offence and, when his son hanged himself in remorse, still refused to go to the funeral. John follows this example with stories of parents who treated bad sons with moderation, and examples of parents who were positively indulgent. He then gives his own opinions: severity in correcting children is to be commended in a father, but not to excess. There should also be moderate praise when the child obeys the rules and keeps out of sin. If a father fails to correct a child's faults he will be punished by God for his negligence. In support of this latter point John cites Gregory's *Dialogues* and the pseudo-Boethian *De Disciplina Scholarium*. Finally, he observes that parents should not set a bad example – he particularly mentions gambling – and that they should pass on inheritances in good condition. This chapter provides yet another example of John expressing a clear opinion. He tells us that some fathers behave in one way, and others in another, and then describes what the proper course should be. John's stance in favour of moderation of punishment is in keeping with what we have already seen of his attitudes, and his recommendation of praise where praise is due has a quite modern ring to it. I shall discuss his attitude to childhood more fully later, as he tells us in more detail of the early stages of development and the proper way to approach the teaching of the young.[13]

John now turns to the love of children for their parents.[14] The proper behaviour towards parents is summarised as loving them with true affection, obeying them, honouring them, sustaining them and supplying necessities if they become indigent. John again recommends Valerius Maximus as a good source of examples to show that loving one's parents is the first law of nature. He gives a number of examples, including a daughter who fed her mother on milk from her own breasts, and concludes that the Romans generally displayed great respect for their parents. The preacher should use the kind of examples given to encourage children to respect their parents. The chapter closes with a horror story taken from Augustine, of some brothers and sisters who spoke ill of their mother and were punished with a dreadful palsy of the limbs. On

---

[13] See below pp. 126–9, 151–3   [14] *Communiloq.* 2.2.2.

this account, says John, children should beware of such behaviour.

In his third distinction, John turns to the bonds between siblings. He begins by telling us that siblings should hold each other in affection because they have the same parents and therefore the same origins.[15] He tells of a Roman general who refused a Triumph because he had lost his brother in the battle, and of another Roman who undertook a long and dangerous journey in order to free his brother from captivity. Brothers should beware lest the inheritance of property should lead to dissent between them. John gives several examples of how this can happen and of the sorrow it brings, again indicating that he has his feet planted firmly on the ground and is aware of the problems to be encountered in contemporary society. He goes on to give an example of ancient altruism with respect to inheritances, telling a story from Trogus Pompeius of how Xerxes left his kingdom to the first of his sons born during his reign, although he had already had one by the same woman. However, the brothers agreed to share the inheritance and ruled happily together. If pagans could behave so well in dividing an inheritance, says John, a Christian who has disinherited his brothers unjustly or is fighting them for the inheritance deserves to be rebuked.

So far we have seen John discuss the more intimate of the blood relationships from a variety of angles, and we can see that he ranks the blood relationship highly. Now he broadens his scope somewhat and gives us a chapter on how the *paterfamilias* ought to rule his *familia*.[16] The *pater* ought to admonish and discipline not only his natural sons but also the sons of his *familia*, this being the origin of his title of *paterfamilias*. He should give attention to all in the household, because he will have to render account to God for them. He should persuade them to beware of pride, drunkenness, fornication, wrath, excess, perjury and cupidity, which is the root of all evil.

The next chapter deals with the love between *consanguineos*, those related by blood.[17] Men are warned that they should have affection for those bound to them by bonds of nature or affinity. There are four ways in which men may be termed brothers: through nature, as with Jacob and Esau; by race, as with all Jews; by affinity, as with Abraham and Lot; and by affection. In this last category all Christians are said to be brothers. Love, says John, ought to be extended to all who are bound by affection. The saviour, says John, did not forbid natural love between parents and relatives, but rather

---

[15] *Communiloq.* 2.3.1.   [16] *Communiloq.* 2.3.2.   [17] *Communiloq.* 2.3.3.

that carnal love by which divine love is impeded. The ancients were loving (*affectuosi*), like Abraham and Lot, and therefore marriage was instituted to accommodate strangers (*extraneos*) between whom love and affection are extended, and where natural love does not serve adequately. John advises the reader to see Augustine's *De Civitate Dei* 15.16 for more information on this topic, before he turns more specifically to marriage, the subject of his fourth distinction.[18]

The legitimately joined man and woman represent the union of Christ and the church. According to Augustine, an alliance between a man and a woman is legitimate when each consents equally to the other. People thus inclined towards marriage ought to be instructed, so that it may be legitimately contracted between unrelated people. John refers briefly to I Corinthians 7 on marriage, and goes on to say that marriage is honourable – hence Christ was present at the marriage at Cana in Galilee (John 2). People ought to see that each is suited to the *conditio* of the other, lest marriage be followed by continual regret. John follows Valerius Maximus in a discussion of the dilemma faced by Themistocles regarding the advisability of marrying his daughter to a man who was poor but of good habits, and makes the point that the woman should not be richer than the man, because it creates arguments over who should provide for what. Because of this, says John, Lycurgus' laws included the provision that young women should marry without dowries. He implies that a man should think very carefully before marrying at all, as a wife will impede the study of philosophy and come between a man and his books, chattering and gossiping, asking questions about where a man has been, whom he has spoken to and so on. If the woman in question is beautiful, good-tempered, healthy, wealthy and of good family, then he should take her, as such a combination is rare. But he should bear in mind the disadvantages. John gives his source for this curious discussion of marriage as the *Liber de Nupciis* of Theophrastus. In fact the discussion comes from Jerome's *Contra Iovinianum*.[19] John enumerates many other reasons for a wife being an unpleasant creature to have in the house, elaborating a cruel stereotype of the nagging and materialistic woman. This was a very well-worn theme in much of medieval literature, and John makes no attempt to correct it before proceeding to his discussion of the need for modesty and chastity in women.

True chastity, says John, is attributed to those who have had the

---

[18] For general discussion of this topic, see J. Leyerle (ed.), 1973.
[19] Jerome, *Contra Iovinianum* 2.

opportunity to sin but do not take advantage of it. It is difficult to guard what many love, therefore the beautiful have more problems than the plain. John returns from the topic of chastity to still more discussion of the disadvantages of having a wife, including the comment that faithful servants will run a household better than the woman who is mistress of it. The general impression left by the whole chapter is that John cared little for marriage or women, and this impression is not really altered by his claim that 'these things are not repeated here to detract from marriage, but rather as ammunition for those who wish to avoid it, for many are the nuisances of marriage'.

Next, John deals with the problem of a wife who is ill-humoured.[20] Those who are committed to such a woman are told to provide compassionate support if their wife should turn out to be bad-tempered. She must be guarded and disciplined and her bad qualities subdued. John explains that the Romans forbade the use of wine to their women, because it affected their behaviour adversely. Mutual support and burden-sharing ought to be found in marriage, says John, but he adds that women are properly subjected to men.

He now discusses the need for mutual affection and faith between spouses, with suitable examples of devotion culled from Valerius.[21] John begins with examples of how greatly the ancients loved their partners, and how much they suffered when a husband or wife died. He makes the inevitable point that, if ancient people could love each other so deeply, faithful Christians should be able to love each other much more.[22] In his section on mutual faith between married people, John's storytelling takes a new turn, with descriptions of some peculiar foreign customs, such as the marriage of many women to one man, described by Solinus.[23] He then turns to examples of faith from the animal kingdom, telling the reader that oxen and horses love their companions.

John goes on to discuss the grave sin of adultery. God made one couple, and the woman was made from the man, and he ordered them to be a pair and have one body and one soul. If you separate the one body and divide the one spirit it is adultery, and not only adultery but also a major theft, because the wife and not the husband has *potestas* (power) over his body. John again uses an animal *exemplum* in his explanation of how everyone should hate adultery. An adulterous stork tried to escape detection by washing away the

---

[20] *Communiloq.* 2.4.2.   [21] *Communiloq.* 2.4.3–4.
[22] *Communiloq.* 2.4.3.   [23] *Communiloq.* 2.4.2.

smell before returning to its mate, but was caught out – perhaps one ought to say sniffed out – and deplumed by a crowd of angry fellows. If even irrational animals can hate adultery thus, says John, men should do better.

He now turns to the need for the married to perform religious works, to be faithful as discussed already and to look forward to the production of offspring, which is one of the functions of marriage.[24] John recommends the husband to love his wife without impetuous passion, and to beware lest he be brought 'headlong into coitus', as there is nothing more shocking than to love one's wife like an adulterer. He also observes that once the woman's stomach swells the couple should beware lest they lose the child – in context surely a recommendation of abstinence. This is a strong indication that John intended this whole section to be serious practical advice rather than abstract moralising.

The last chapter of this section deals with the permanence of marriage.[25] John praises women who do not remarry after they are widowed, mentions the existence of the Vestal Virgins in Rome, and recommends the reader to turn to the third part of *Communiloquium* for information on chastity.

John devotes a considerable space to marriage, and covers the topic thoroughly, if in a fairly elementary fashion. His views may usefully be compared with those in the marriage sermons of Jacques de Vitry, Humbert de Romans and Guibert de Tournai.[26] Comparison with these marriage sermons suggests that John's attitude to marriage is really very ordinary. He covers such commonplaces as the meaning of marriage, the need for it to be legitimately contracted, the honourable status of marriage, the need for husband and wife to be mutually supportive – but with the husband as senior partner – and the mutual love which should exist between two married people. He warns of the evils of adultery, and of the danger of taking too much pleasure in marital relations, and discusses the need to look forward to having children, and the wrongness of separation. His comments are perfectly proper, but his discussion is very general, and he gives very little technical detail. For example, he does not cover the varying circumstances in which a couple might wish to separate; nor does he give any real discussion of questions such as the times at which man and wife should abstain from sexual

[24] *Communiloq.* 2.4.5.
[25] *Communiloq.* 2.4.6.
[26] For these, see D. L. d'Avray and M. Tausche, 1980, pp. 71–119.

relations. Matters of this nature were covered in some detail by Jacques de Vitry and Guibert de Tournai.[27]

John's comments on marriage have much in common with those of the other thirteenth-century *ad status* collections, but we have no reason to believe that he was using any of them as a source. He shares not only general attitudes, but also some *exempla*. However, he provides detailed references to the sources he is using, and these do not include other *ad status* collections. For example, John's *exemplum* about the adulterous stork is similar to one told by Jacques de Vitry,[28] but John gives his sources as the *De Natura Rerum* of Alexander Nequam. Many of the comments shared by John and other collections can be traced, again with John's help, to Jerome's *Contra Iovinianum*.

John's section on marriage can therefore be seen as a very basic run-through of all the principal points which should be clear in the minds of ordinary preachers. He ends his section by saying that the preacher should tell the people all these things on the appropriate occasions, swaying them from the wrong course and guiding them towards the correct one.[29] The nature of John's discussion is therefore in keeping with his intention of providing an elementary handbook. Although the discussion is somewhat superficial, it is not totally lacking a personal stamp: one would still be able to tell that it was John's work if it was extracted from *Communiloquium*. First, John makes characteristic use of both classical and animal *exempla*. In his comments on adultery and marriage, he does not follow the other thirteenth-century *ad status* collections in using the animal kingdom as a source of examples of loose living: his animals are examples of loyalty, affection and hatred of adultery, and a challenge to Christians to do even as well, let alone better. John does not seem to have thought very highly of Christian behaviour in his own period, as animals and pagans invariably seem to do as well as any Christian. John's constant plea that Christians *should be able to do better* seems almost pathetic at times.

The typical John flavour also appears in his only remark about abstention from intercourse, where he recommends the couple to beware in the later months of pregnancy, lest they lose their child. It is entirely characteristic of John to provide a practical reason for avoiding one course of action, or for choosing another. Guibert de Tournai also mentions the duty to abstain from intercourse during

[27] *Ibid.*, pp. 87–101.   [28] *Ibid.*, p. 90.
[29] *Communiloq.* 2.4.6.

pregnancy, but he does not put forward any such practical reason.[30]

John's discussion contains other traces of individuality. His inclusion of arguments to help those who seek to avoid the nuisance of matrimony is interesting, and so is his concern about the problems of differing levels of wealth in a marriage, and his apparent approval of Lycurgus' law against dowries. Most men in medieval Europe would have had no objection to marrying a woman of some wealth, even if it was greater than the man's own.[31] John's inclusion of warnings about possible problems suggests that he had seen such disparate marriages run into difficulty.

John's discussion of the married state is followed by a discussion of the spiritual bonds between the faithful.[32] The faithful, John says, were created by one father and hence are truly brothers. Also they are the limbs of a single body, bound by the cords of *caritas* and enlivened by a single spirit. John uses Seneca, Chrysostom and Gregory to support his biblical texts on how Christians should treat each other as brothers, protect one another and drive out any ill feeling which comes between them.[33] Christians should beware lest they are destroyed by the enemy – namely, the devil – who may seek to dissipate their fraternal union.[34] Christians should be united by affection always, and never set apart by discord. And they should support each other in misfortune, like the limbs of a body.[35] If one is suffering, says John, all suffer with it. Similarly Christians ought to help one another and to offer assistance to the poor. They should shore each other up like the stones in a building, for they are like a living edifice. John follows these comments with examples of Christian behaviour, telling how the early saints laboured for the well-being of those around them.[36] They exposed themselves to death for the sake of their brothers, and even sold themselves to infidels that they might convert them and lead them to the faith. John tells several stories of how both pagans and Manichees were converted through the devoted service of Christians. The preacher, he says, should discuss this and other related matters in preaching to the faithful.

The next distinction of *Communiloquium* deals with the bonds regulating the citizenry. Citizens (*civiles*) should be warned that they

---

[30] D. L. d'Avray and M. Tausche, 1980, p. 100.

[31] Indeed marriage to a wealthy widow was considered by popular opinion to be one of the best ways to rise in the world.

[32] *Communiloq.* 2.5. [33] *Communiloq.* 2.5.1. [34] *Communiloq.* 2.5.2.

[35] *Communiloq.* 2.5.3. [36] *Communiloq.* 2.5.4.

should live together peacefully and for mutual benefit, and beware of evil.[37] They should be regulated by laws and rejoice in the Lord, living according to his ritual and heeding his advice. They are urged to love their neighbour as they love themselves, neighbours being defined by John as those close not through the blood relationship, but by reason of association. Those living together in towns are warned not to injure their neighbours, either by harming their persons or by spoiling their possessions, by open or concealed theft or by any other wickedness. Nor should they speak ill of people.

The people should help themselves.[38] They should support the poor, free the oppressed and console the desolate, and perform other such works of mercy, as Job did to his neighbours.[39] It is much better to have a good relationship with a neighbour than to conduct a wicked feud. John closes the chapter with a lengthy *exemplum* from the *Vitae Patrum* of an ordinary man who had been a good neighbour all his life and was welcomed by God in consequence.

John goes on to issue stern warnings against fraudulent merchants and usurers, the latter stealing not openly but in a roundabout manner.[40] He cites *De Civitate Dei* for the point that everyone wishes to buy cheap and to sell dear. Because of this there is much cheating in trade, through hidden faults and defective goods, the showing of things which are not what they seem, the reduction of measures, the mixing-in of useless items and many other such tricks. John quotes Leviticus 19 and Proverbs 20 on God's appreciation of good weights and measures, and points out that it is dangerous to be involved in trade on account of all the wickedness going about. He concludes that one should not knowingly deceive one's neighbours and that the preacher should warn those in trade to beware of the sins associated with their business.

John continues in a similar vein when he discusses the dangers of having usurers in the neighbourhood.[41] He quotes a number of biblical texts on the evils of usury, and says that people should help the poor freely. This was one of the most consistently held viewpoints of the church, and it is no surprise to find it here. However, John is clearly avoiding the vigorous debate on the topic which had been running since the beginning of the Crusades. He seems to be following the Second Lateran Council (1139) and the *Glosa Ordinaria*, in condemning all usury. Peter Lombard, William of Auxerre, Raymond of Pennaforte and Albertus Magnus had also

[37] *Communiloq.* 2.6.1. [38] *Communiloq.* 2.6.2. [39] Job 29.
[40] *Communiloq.* 2.6.3. [41] *Communiloq.* 2.6.4.

taken this view, while other theologians followed the line adopted by Ambrose centuries before, and claimed that Christians could rightfully exact usury from their enemies. In the context of the Crusade, this was taken to refer to Moslems, and Christian usury flourished in consequence. The issue of Jewish rights to collect interest also caused lively dispute.[42] For John's particular purpose, the simple statement was probably best: his prospective audiences could not all be expected to cope with the finer points of an acrimonious debate which had been running throughout the thirteenth century. For a full discussion of usury, John recommended the interested reader to turn to the *Summa de Viciis* and to the *De Officiis* of St Ambrose.

Throughout the last distinction, John shows a good grasp of the kinds of problems associated with the towns – feuds and quarrels with neighbours, poverty, fraudulent trading and the operation of money-lenders. Although warnings against such things were almost commonplace in any sermonising on towns and town living, they were quite certainly real problems, and therefore deserving of inclusion in *Communiloquium*.[43] John as always performs an additional educational function by providing not only suitable *exempla* to catch the attention of an audience, but also authoritative support for the views put forward, culling his comments from the fathers, the Bible and eminent writers of the ancient world.

The next three distinctions cover the topics of friendship, association and enmity respectively. John expects a greal deal from friendship. He begins by condemning simulated friendship, reminding the reader that he has already discussed this fully in the first part of *Communiloquium*, when dealing with the seven curial vices.[44] He recommends Jerome's forty-fifth letter as further reading, and defines true friendship as unanimous agreement about honest matters.[45] John repeats Cicero's opinion that the greatest thing in friendship is that the superior should be equal to the inferior. A friend is like an equal spirit. Christ was such a friend, because when he was superior to all he yet remained in the midst of his disciples. Friendship (*amicitia*) is named from love (*amor*), which is the prince of all the connections of friendship. John quotes Cicero again for the

---

[42] For a useful summary of medieval attitudes to usury, see B. Nelson, 1969, pp. 3–28; also J. T. Noonan, 1957; J. Gilchrist, 1969, pp. 62–70 and 104–15.

[43] See e.g. D. L. d'Avray, 1979.

[44] *Communiloq.* 2.7.1.

[45] Following Cicero's *De Amicitia*.

point that the law of friendship should be to love the friend neither less nor more than oneself, and Augustine's *Confessions* for how Augustine mourned for the death of a friend and observed how it diminished his life. There should be generosity and much communication in friendship, which is based on truth and respect and always seeks the good. John adds that a good man will do nothing against the state or against his oath, even for the sake of a friend. Once more he is following Cicero, who is one of the main sources for this section of *Communiloquium*. This comment on the relative importance of ties to friends and to the state reminds us of something which we have already noted about John – he appears to place the state above all personal ties in his order of priorities.

John turns to Valerius for examples of true friendship: the man who sought death when his friend died, the man who revealed himself to the enemy for the sake of his friend, the man who presented himself to the tyrant Dionysius in place of his friend, whom the tyrant wanted to kill. In the final chapter of the distinction, John warns against false friendships, and follows Boethius' *De Consolatione Philosophiae* in describing real friendship as the most precious form of riches.

Distinction 8 bears the heading *De colligatione sociali in convictu* ('On the social bonds between those living together'). It first discusses how a man ought to act towards his associates. As friends are admonished that they should be bound together by true friendship, allies are admonished that they should be bound by shared association. John gives some definitions of a *socius* from the *Magnae Derivationes* of Huguccio: he may be someone in the same group of soldiers or in the same lodging, a helper in a time of danger, a colleague in office or a companion on a journey, a comrade at table or in council. In whatever way they are brought together, says John, men ought to be sociable, because man is not a solitary animal, but a political and communicative one, according to the *Commentary on Ethics*.[46] As a further source, John recommends Seneca's *De Beneficiis*.

Bad society ought to be shunned.[47] John tells the weak that they

---

[46] The commentator on *Ethics* to whom John refers is Robert Grosseteste. The comment 'homo est animal non solitarium sed politicum et communicativum' was a favourite with John, who used it in *Coll. in Ioh.* 11.50 (printed in *Opera Bonaventurae* I, Rome 1588) and in his *Coll. in Matthew* on Matthew 12,35 (Magdalen College, MS 27. f.48). I am grateful to Miss Smalley for pointing out these quotations to me.

[47] *Communiloq.* 2.8.2.

should avoid the company of the corrupt, lest they should feel the urge to imitate them. Just as taking in bad air continually will damage the body, so continually hearing perverse words damages the spirit, and even good customs are perverted by depraved conversation. Good company, conversely, is to be sought after, because of the favourable effects which it can have on one and the support and help which it can provide, and because man was a social animal first of all the animals.[48] Certain factors dissolve associations – for example, greed and *luxuria* – and the preacher is exhorted to teach the distinction between good and bad society.[49]

Of particular interest in this distinction are John's definitions of man as a political and communicative animal, and as a social one. As his source for the first statement he invariably cites Grosseteste's *Commentary on Ethics*. Grosseteste does make a similar statement in his translation of *Ethics* 9.9.1169b 15–20, which reads: 'Inconveniens autem forte et hoc, solitarium facere beatum . . . Politicum enim est homo et convivere aptus natus, et felici utique hoc existit. Que enim natura bona, habet.'[50] Only minor rearrangement of this comment is required to reach John's phrase, but the fact that John consistently uses his own wording shows clearly that he had some kind of written index of quotations, paraphrases and *exempla* from which he was working, in preference to the original text of Grosseteste.

John sandwiches his comment that 'homo est animal sociale primo de animalibus' between two extracts from Seneca's *Epistulae* (90.3 and 95.53), but although these Seneca extracts deal with the topic of man in society, they do not provide a direct source for John's remark. The 1260s and 1270s seem to have been a period when such definitions of man were being put forward, particularly among the friars. Thomas Aquinas, as is well known, used the phrase 'animal politicum et sociale' in describing man.[51] Aquinas may have derived this from Macrobius, *In Somnium Scipionis* i.8.: 'sunt politicae hominis, quia sociale animal est'.[52] Alternatively, he might have obtained the phrase *animal politicum* directly from Aristotle's *Ethics*, which he knew.[53] Certainly Aquinas' definition is very close to John's, and suggests that the two men were thinking along very

[48] *Communiloq.* 2.8.3.
[49] *Communiloq.* 2.8.4.
[50] R. A. Gautier, ed., 1972.
[51] Aquinas made this remark sixteen times in the *Summa Theologiae*: see *Summa Theologiae* (Marietti, 1948), Index volume.
[52] W. Ullmann, 1974, p. 245.
[53] R. A. Markus, 1970, p. 219.

similar lines. John's phrase *non solitarium* and Aquinas' *sociale* surely represent alternative Latin translations of the same Greek concept in Aristotle's *Ethics*. The fact that John of Wales conflates his original two phrases, 'homo est animal polyticum, non solitarium et communicativum' and 'homo est animal sociale' (used in his biblical commentaries and *Communiloquium*) to the phrase 'politicum enim est animal natura est homo et sociale' (used in his *Compendiloquium*, written in Paris after 1270), may reflect standardisation of the phrase to the version given, and no doubt popularised by, Aquinas. Alternatively, he could also have derived the term *sociale* from Aristotle's *Ethics* 1.7.

John's ninth and last distinction of this part of *Communiloquium* continues the progression already established, and deals with the proper behaviour towards enemies. John begins by pointing out that it is praiseworthy to live well amongst evil.[54] It is not enough for the faithful to live as described among those with whom they have ties. They ought also to live well amongst those who oppose them. They should do this patiently and kindly, and thus convert their enemies and lead them back to a life of justice and truth.[55] John gives examples from Seneca of men who treated their enemies with friendship and won friendship in return, and tells us that even a lion or an elephant may be gentled by kindness.

We may pause here, before pressing on to consider the third part of *Communiloquium*. This second section makes several contributions to our understanding of John, and of the range and type of ideas which he was seeking to express. It shares what we might call the distinctive John flavour, with its subtle massing of extracts and comments from many authors, for the purpose of putting across a range of basic principles so that the preacher can express them interestingly and authoritatively to his audience. The ancient bias in the sources is retained, as of 243 citations 27 are from medieval authors, 79 from the Bible and 137 from ancient works. Augustine, Seneca and Valerius Maximus are significant favourites. We might note that John makes only one reference to the *Policraticus*, which he cited 54 times during the previous section of *Communiloquium*. This reflects the change of theme between the two sections of John's work, away from the political and courtly sphere towards the everyday social sphere.

Much of the message expressed in this section was commonplace

---

[54] *Communiloq.* 2.9.1. [55] *Communiloq.* 2.9.2.

for the period, and no doubt John intended that it should be so. But the section remains of interest. We see John as a man deeply impressed by vows, oaths and loyalties, his discussion of the feudal oath reflecting the seriousness with which he covered the knightly oath in an earlier chapter. John also shows interest in family relationships. Throughout his works the paternal relationship is an approved theme. In this section John is able to put forward different types of parental relationship and pick one as preferable. His comments on the destruction of family affection by quarrels over inheritances ring true, although his tale of how Persian princes amicably shared a kingdom is an optimistic one. Throughout the section, John succeeds in his plan of addressing groups bonded together in different ways, and his control of his material is impressive.

On now to part 3, which was designed to complement the first two sections and fill out our picture of secular society. During the course of this part, John returns to several of the themes already touched upon, thus helping us to flesh out our summary of his ideas. The lengths of the distinctions, and of individual chapters, vary considerably and may to some extent reflect variations in the strength of John's own interests, though one should be wary of reading too much into this. It is certainly noticeable that where admonitions to women are concerned, sections tend to be much longer and to contain many more examples and references to further reading. John may have felt that women were particularly in need of instruction, or he may have felt that they were more likely than some to be found in a preacher's audience. Some groups seem to have been added in to preserve the intrinsic balance between the divisions and hence rate only a couple of lines of generalisation under a chapter heading. One should be wary of relying too much on assessment of likely audience from chapter length, for the lengthy section on the prince, with which the volume opened, can have borne no relation to the probability of the average preacher having such a great man in his audience.

John's first distinction covers the appropriate behaviour for the two sexes. Not unexpectedly, men are dealt with first. They are warned to behave as men, and to be men in deed as well as in fact. The word *vir* (man) is described as a derivative of *virtus* or strength, and John follows Augustine in giving the function of this quality as the conquering of desire. A man should have good habits, says John. He should strive to be manly, because it is dreadful to be a man by sex but effeminate in behaviour. Too much of various indulgences – John lists sweet tastes and soft touches – has a gentling and feminising effect, and therefore such things should be avoided.

This is all that John has to say directly to men as a class, but he devotes the next four chapters to the admonishment of women. He opens with a diatribe on the need for sobriety, a point which he has already touched on earlier in the work.[56] Women are told that they must lead a virtuous life and be subject to their men. They should be quiet rather than chatty, and they should be neither lazy, absent-minded nor curious. They should not dress ostentatiously or be vain. Particularly they should be modest in eating and drinking, and take care to remain sober for the sake of modesty. Too much food leads to an increase in desire, and too much wine opens the door to all manner of sins. These are all themes which John has mentioned already in connection with the female sex, and which he will return to again. For the moment he concludes that women ought to be trained from infancy in perfect chastity and sobriety, and particularly through the example of their mothers.

John goes into detail about the correct attitude of women towards chastity, which he describes as a virtue which becomes them greatly.[57] Immodesty, he says, is neither praised by men in the present time nor rewarded by God in the future, while modesty is the reverse. Valerius is listed as a source of examples of modesty in women, and of women who went to great lengths to protect their chastity. John tells the story of Lucretia and Tarquin, and mentions a number of cases where unchaste women were punished by death. He goes on to quote from Augustine's *De Civitate Dei* that *pudicicia* (modesty) is a virtue of the mind and cannot be taken away against one's will. In the case of Lucretia, Tarquin forced himself on her, and therefore her *pudicicia* remained intact, for two bodies cannot become as one if the limbs are intertwined while the spirits are not. Because of this, people should not kill themselves either because they have been violated or because they fear that they may be. After speaking against any taking of life, John makes an exception for certain women, described by Augustine, who threw themselves into a river at a time of persecution. Because they did this on divine orders, they were rightly celebrated as martyrs.[58] John tells us that

---

[56] *Communiloq.* 3.1.2. The question of the danger to women from drink was discussed in *Communiloq.* 2.4.2.

[57] *Communiloq.* 3.1.3.

[58] For discussion of attitudes to suicide, see p. 159.

the ancients were very concerned about chastity, and uses Solinus to show that similar concern is demonstrated in India. Finally he tells women that they should not so much as kiss a man without good cause.

John follows up his earlier comments to women by elaborating on how they should avoid the characteristically feminine sins of chattiness, restlessness, laziness and over-interest in dress and adornment. John follows Jerome in a specific condemnation of make-up and elaborate hair-styles on the grounds that they interfere with the work of God. Finally he recommends the reader to see his later section on the different types of modesty becoming to maidens, married women and widows.

In his second distinction John turns to the different phases of a man's life,[59] which he divides up as follows: *infancia,* the first seven years; *puericia,* from seven to fourteen years; *adolescentia,* the years between fourteen and twenty-eight; *iuventus* or *virilitas,* the period extending until forty or fifty; *senium* or *senectus,* which lasts to the age of sixty or seventy; and finally the age which John describes as *etas decrepita,* which he says has no particular limits in numbers of years. John tells us that he has taken this list of divisions of life from Papias. He suggests that the reader turn to Augustine or Cicero if he wishes to learn more about these two later stages of life, and then turns to discussion of his first group, the infants.

John's chapter on infancy is naturally directed towards their parents, as he clearly realises that under-sevens would be unlikely to gain much from preaching.[60] He begins by reminding the reader that he has already discussed the proper behaviour of parents. They should educate their children, as Aristotle educated the son of Philip of Macedon, so that they may get some use from books. John agrees with Jerome that a wet-nurse should not be drunken or wanton or garrulous, then goes on to the importance and lasting quality of early impressions, and the impressionability of the first years. He cites Anselm as the source of a comparison with seals: if one wishes hard wax to retain a particular impression, the impression must be made while the wax is soft. Because children are impressionable, they should be denied wine, and attention should be paid to their diet. They should be baptised, guided into the faith and taught to have good habits and to pray to God. John seems to recognise the influence of the nurse on a child, because he repeats Jerome's

[59] On the divisions of life, see B. Rowland, 1975, pp. 17–29.
[60] *Communiloq.* 3.2.1.

comment that the nurse should not be a chatterbox. The early years are so impressionable that a child can be led very easily into good habits. Words are like milk or nourishment if they are good, but like poison if they are bad, and this is why people are warned against chattering nurses. John goes on to say that children must be punished for their sins, which Augustine tells us are numerous. As he says in his *Confessions*, 'so small a child, so great a sinner'. However, adds John, until the age of seven the parents are to be held responsible for the sins of the child. Parents are also advised to teach their children the skills suitable to their station: noble parents should teach their children that they should be noble in their deeds, and if parents have to live by their skills, then the children should be taught these skills, so that they may live justly.

As we saw in the previous section of *Communiloquium*, John does not believe in severe punishment, but says that a child should be punished moderately for its sins, but also praised when it does well.[61] This was an unusual attitude for the period, and indeed for the whole era from Greek civilisation until the eighteenth century. One scholar of childhood tells us that of over 200 statements of advice on child-rearing during this lengthy period, all but three approved of beating children, and most made no recommendations towards moderation.[62] The three who opposed beating totally were Plutarch and two Italians. None of these seems to have been read by John, so they cannot be used to explain John's attitude. We do, however, know of three other churchmen who advocated moderation in punishing children. The first of these was John Chrysostom, who wrote in his *Address on Vainglory* that a child should not be beaten too much, but should sometimes be won with gentleness and promises.[63] The second was Anselm of Canterbury, whom John quotes for the simile between a young child and soft sealing-wax. This simile first appeared, in a slightly different form, in the *Address on Vainglory* mentioned above. Anselm had a considerable reputation for compassion towards the young,[64] and he once advised an abbot to beat children gently, saying: 'Are they not human? Are they not flesh and blood like you?'[65] As Anselm is quoted by John more than once in *Communiloquium*'s discussions of the young, we may

---

[61] *Communiloq.* 2.2.1.
[62] Lloyd de Mause, 1976, p. 40.
[63] John Chrysostom, *Address on Vainglory*, trans. in M. L. W. Laistner, 1951, pp. 95, 99–100, 113: see R. B. Lyman, Jr, 1976, p. 87.
[64] M. M. McLaughlin, 1976, p. 167.
[65] Southern, ed., 1972, p. 38.

deduce that he was an important influence on John, or perhaps rather that John's inborn compassion, so often revealed, caused him to appreciate what Anselm had to say. There were few other writers who could provide quotations and *exempla* which favoured moderation in the treatment of children: one other example in the thirteenth century is Vincent of Beauvais.[66]

John's insistence on condemning chattering nurses, though less uncommon, is still interesting. We would like to know why he objected – presumably he recognised that nurses were very often ignorant and superstitious and would not benefit their charges much through their conversation.

John's recognition that there is a distinct stage of early childhood, and his accurate identification of some of its distinguishing features, is intriguing. Few medieval writers discuss the subject, although Bartholomaeus Anglicus gives a lifelike picture of small boys in his *De Proprietatibus Rerum*.[67] Also interesting is John's claim that a child under the age of seven is not responsible for its own misdeeds. This was a concept which was only beginning to be recognised in English law in the mid-1280s, as far as we know from records of court cases. The first recorded instance of a case dismissed on such grounds was in 1287, when a boy of nine was acquitted of homicide on the grounds that he was under age.[68] A boy of seven was acquitted on the same grounds in 1292,[69] and by the end of the reign of Edward I the dividing line between accountability and freedom of responsibility seems to have been established as the age of seven.[70] From his comments on clemency in court cases we may feel sure that John would have approved of this development.

Legal evidence also contributes to our appreciation of John's attitude to the discipline of children. We have said that he favoured moderation, and that this appears quite unusual for his time. A thirteenth-century German law stated that if one beat a child until it bled, then it would remember, but that if it dies, then the law must apply.[71] Harsh punishment may therefore have been generally accepted, and there must have been some cases where chastisement went too far. John's mild attitude to childhood is therefore no mere commonplace.

On boyhood, the period between the ages of seven and fourteen, John warns boys that they should specially beware of the sins which

---

[66] Steiner, ed., 1938.   [67] Book 6.   [68] N. D. Hurnard, 1969, p. 155.
[69] *Ibid.*, p. 156.   [70] *Ibid.*, p. 157.   [71] Lloyd de Mause, 1976, p. 42.

arise during this period: namely, lust and covetousness.[72] They should strive hard towards sobriety and chastity. As Chrysostom says in his *Commentary on Matthew*, youth is unfruitful ground which produces many thorns if neglected. John then refers again to Cicero's discussion of the laws of the Spartan Lycurgus, as an example of an effort to train boys effectively. Other examples come from Seneca and Sallust, and confirm our earlier impression that John favours discipline of body and of mind.

John now tells us about the *adolescentes*, the fourteen to twenty-eight year olds.[73] He says that they should beware of all the things previously mentioned, and agrees with Jerome that as one's physical condition improves, so may one's state of virtue. There is an implied recommendation to fitness here. John goes on to say that *adolescentes* should be warned even more strongly than children that they should beware of sins and avoid them by their own efforts, adorn themselves with honest habits and behave in a mature fashion. A silent mouth and a continent body are to be commended in the young. Even more important, the young should be respectful and obedient. For as a tree will not fruit without first having flowered, so it is with old age and youth. Those who do not strive towards any discipline in youth will not deserve honour or consequence in later life.

The next stage is *virilitas* or manhood, the stage between the ages of twenty-eight and forty.[74] John tells the reader that he has already dealt with the ideal behaviour of a man. Here he simply emphasises that man should serve his creator and place faith in him.

The elderly are warned that as their bodily condition decreases, so their state of virtue should increase, that at this stage they should abjure all the passions of youth, and that they should make solitary study their occupation. John quotes Avicenna for the view that the intellect is strengthened after the age of forty, and Cicero for the claim that memory, industry and capacity flourish in the elderly. People of this age are better able to give advice and to exercise authority, by virtue of their experience. This is something which John has already remarked upon in his discussion of the need for good counsellors.[75]

Finally, John deals with the phase of life which he characterises as decrepitude.[76] What has been said of the first class of elderly people

---

[72] *Communiloq.* 3.2.2.   [73] *Communiloq.* 3.2.3.   [74] *Communiloq.* 3.2.4.
[75] See *Communiloq.* 1.1.7., 1.6.1., and 1.6.4. All these chapters are discussed in chap. 4.
[76] *Communiloq.* 3.2.6.

should apply much more to this second class, says John. *Senectus* leads to death. The elderly should beware of excessive eating and drinking, because of the possible ill effects on the body. It ought to be the task of the elderly to live well through this phase of life, and then to die well. They should confess and abjure all previous sins, and behave appropriately for their age. John also suggests that they should die leaving a good example for the young people coming after them. He ends by turning to Valerius for examples of virtuous old men, their deeds and their longevity.

Having completed his round-up of instructive remarks on the different stages of life, John turns his attention to the proper instruction of the nobility. He recommends that they should not boast of or glory in their nobility, nor despise others nor hold them cheaply, for all are equally noble with respect to their origin.[77] He quotes from Gregory's *Moralia* that all men are equal by nature but achieve different ranks. There is no particular glory in nobility which is of flesh and blood, for neither the vices nor the virtues of the parents are imposed on the children, unless they are imitating their parents. In other words, unless one is good and noble in one's own behaviour, pedigree counts for nothing. John uses Jerome, Chrysostom, Boethius and Apuleius to support the contention that there is no such thing as inherited virtue, and then warns that nobles should be told that nobility often degenerates. John cites Valerius as a source of examples of the degenerate offspring of worthy parents. Nobility of birth is vain and fruitless and noxious unless it is accompanied by the true nobility which virtue creates. This true nobility is spiritual and should be sought, acquired and retained. Therefore he is fortunate who is well adapted to virtue by nature. John's message appears to be threefold: first, there should be no pride in nobility of birth; secondly, nobility of birth does not guarantee true nobility and counts for little; and, thirdly, true nobility, being a spiritual virtue, must and should be acquired by the efforts of the individual. As those who are born of noble parents may not deserve to be considered noble, so by implication ordinary folk may also earn true nobility by their behaviour. This latter point is implicit in the chapter, rather than explicit.

What kind of behaviour is required is indicated in the next chapter, which bears the heading *De vera nobilitate*.[78] John quotes Seneca to the effect that philosophy creates a noble spirit, and Chrysostom for

<hr>

[77] *Communiloq.* 3.3.1.   [78] *Communiloq.* 3.3.2.

the opinion that being accustomed to perform the wishes of God is a form of nobility. Through Bernard's *De Consideratione*, John reminds us that none of the apostles was of noble birth and repeats that nobles should not take pride in their fleshly nobility but should concentrate on keeping themselves from sin. A quotation from Cicero's *De Officiis* reminds us that the desire for honour, power and glory is in itself a source of sin. Some men of noble birth yield to ignobility of mind and make themselves as a fortress for sin, defending themselves in their sins with their nobility.

The *ignobiles* should strive to become noble through the virtues, although they may lack nobility of blood, because those born in humble places may achieve much renown.[79] John's examples indicate that he is thinking of genuine advancement in the world as much as the achievement of a noble spirit. Again he mentions Valerius as a good source, and himself tells the story of Servius Tullius, adopted by a Roman king and later ruler of Rome in his own right, despite his servile origins. On a slightly more realistic level, John also mentions the fact that Euripides' mother reputedly kept a market-stall, and ends by quoting Juvenal's belief that it is better to be born of a humble father than a noble one of poor habits.

The impression created by these chapters is very strong. We can see that hereditary nobility is not very highly valued by John. We can also see that he is presenting and apparently approving a concept of social mobility, for he not only states that the virtues of nobility may be achieved by those born base, but also positively advocates that they seek such nobility, and suggests that they may achieve real success and advancement through it. This appears to be a somewhat unusual attitude for the period.

It was during the early to mid-thirteenth century that the French aristocracy fused to form a single noble class.[80] This fusion and tightening of the ranks is seen by some historians as the reaction to infiltration from below of a group whose status and privileges had been largely established by heredity.[81] The implication is that the French nobles at least would have been opposed to upward mobility, though we cannot be sure that they were entirely successful in stopping it.

Many works were written in France in the mid- to late thirteenth century for the purpose of describing the appropriate behaviour of a noble. Such works place emphasis not only on birth, but also on

---

[79] *Communiloq.* 3.3.3. [80] G. Duby, 1977, pp. 97, 178–9.
[81] *Ibid.*, pp. 182–5.

possession of the correct virtues and values, these being instilled by proper education. So a noble was expected to behave in a special, virtuous, educated fashion if he was really to qualify for his status. This much is consistent with what John writes. The difference is that, for John, if you possess the appropriate virtues you also possess true nobility, whatever your origins. We can see that John was no more impressed by hereditary nobility than he was by hereditary princehood: in both cases an individual was expected to earn through virtue the right to a status conferred by other means, and the achievement of the individual was seen as the true measure of his stature.

In England, on the other hand, there is considerable evidence that there was substantial social movement in the thirteenth and fourteenth centuries. For example, we know that until 1300 it was not uncommon for the daughters of the nobility to marry outside their class, so that entry to the nobility through marriage was certainly a possibility.[82] We know also that of 357 families whose head had been summoned to parliament at least once by Edward I prior to 1301, or by Edward's successors in the first half of the fourteenth century, only 61 had unbroken male descent to 1500.[83] Between 1350 and 1500 there were 200 failures in the male line in this group and 114 replacements. Three-quarters of these replacements were genuinely new to the ranks of the nobility, and only a quarter were summoned because they had married noble women and thus acquired estates. In the same period, more than 80% of replacement earls were genuinely new, that is 49 out of 61.[84] So mobility seems to have extended from the lowest ranks of the nobility to the highest, and to have been a genuine option from the thirteenth century until the end of the fifteenth at least. John's comments on nobility and ignobility are not as far-fetched as they might seem at first glance, although a rise from servile status to the nobility in one generation would be very rare.

Having expressed himself on the subject of nobility, John turns to the question of natural gifts.[85] The reader is told that, just as one should not glory in nobility of birth or nobility through virtue, neither should one glory in the excellence of one's natural gifts, whether spiritual (for example, intelligence and memory) or physical (such as health, beauty or agility). Indeed, those who are well endowed should be all the more humble. John mentions the parable

[82] K. B. McFarlane, 1973, p. 152.   [83] *Ibid.*, p. 144.
[84] *Ibid.*, 1973, p. 151.   [85] *Communiloq.* 3.3.4.

of the talents, then uses quotations from Augustine, Gregory and Jerome to emphasise that such natural endowments are gifts from God and not for the individual to take pride in. He should not spend his time admiring his gifts, nor should he use them to influence others.

In the next distinction John tackles the first of the categories which develop through circumstance: the rich and the poor. The preacher, says John, should say something to men according to the differences in their possessions.[86] Because Gregory the Great covers this subject in sufficient detail, he himself will only discuss the matter briefly. The rich should take care not to obtain wealth through theft, usury or fraudulent trade. Men are warned not to desire wealth, for such desires lead one into temptation. John further warns against hoarding riches for oneself, quoting from the Gospels that if a wealthy man sees his brother in need and closes his heart to him, so will the love of God be closed off from that wealthy man. The rich should not rely too heavily on their wealth, as it will provide no protection on the Day of Judgement. John adds that it is praiseworthy to spend one's wealth on good works. He also tells the reader that love of temporal things is a source of spiritual punishment, and that because it is difficult to have riches without loving them, they are a danger to their possessors. For this and many other reasons, the ancients despised wealth – lords and kings, scholars and wise men quite as much as saints. John winds up with a reminder that the rich should distribute their excess among the indigent. Although he claimed at the outset to be covering the topic only briefly, this is in fact a fairly lengthy chapter, which clearly sets out a standard attitude to wealth.

John distinguishes two types of poverty: necessary and voluntary.[87] He is a true pauper who wishes to be rich, having few possessions but not through his own choice. John recommends the reader to turn to part 6, on the religious, for admonitions to those who have chosen poverty. The poor, he continues, should be instructed to endure their poverty patiently so that it may sustain them like a medicine and purge them of their imperfections and afflictions. Again Gregory and Chrysostom provide his main sources. John goes on to quote Seneca's observation that if one is satisfied with one's lot, one is not really poor. It is only the desire for more that makes one truly a pauper. John therefore warns the poor to beware of true poverty: namely, the desire for wealth. He

---

[86] *Communiloq.* 3.4.1.   [87] *Communiloq.* 3.4.2.

mentions the possibility of possessing riches in the form of health
and wisdom, and quotes Gregory's *Moralia* to the effect that God
hates a proud pauper. The poor are recommended to acquire
spiritual riches and to alleviate their poverty by contemplating the
perils of wealth and the conveniences of poverty, and to remember
that Jesus himself was poor and that poverty was commended by
him. John's vaguely sympathetic attitude to the genuine poor is
characteristic of the thirteenth century, although this century also
saw the emergence of a number of writers who showed vigorous
hostility to the poor as a group.[88]

The next distinction deals with classes of sinners and of
penitents.[89] Sinners appropriately come first, as the sin must precede
the repentance. John tells the preacher that he should persuade
sinners to lay sin aside, lest Satan lead them into hell.[90] As a source of
further reading on sins and transgressions, their accompanying
misery and their consequences, he recommends a *Breviloquium de
Viciis et Virtutibus*, which states how much sins were detested even
by the Gentiles.[91] Having used Cicero's *De Officiis* to establish here
that the Gentiles did indeed hate sin, because of its ugliness, John
points out that the faithful ought to hate it also, because it is
transgression of the divine law and the commands of heaven. John
quotes Anselm's *Meditations* for the comment that as a putrefying
dog smells to man, so does the soul of a sinner smell to God. Again
he mentions the *Breviloquium de Viciis* as a source of the reasons why
the faithful should hate sin. For a general discussion of the vices and
their hatefulness John recommends Hugh of Saint-Victor's *De
Sacramentis*, from which he takes a list of the seven *peccata criminalia*.
He defines each, lists their effects on the soul and repeats that the
work already mentioned will give much more detail.

John opens his chapter on penitents by telling the preacher that he
must persuade men to fight against the vices and encourage them to
repent, thereby wiping out the sin. John recommends Jerome's
Letters as a source of *exempla* on the great efficacy of true repentance,
before recommending a *Breviloquium de Penitentia*[92] as a source of
what penance should be, and on its parts and its usefulness.

[88] Jean Batany, 1974, pp. 469–86.   [89] *Communiloq.* 3.5.   [90] *Communiloq.* 3.5.1.
[91] There were many works on the vices available in John's day; I have been unable to
trace the one to which John refers. It is possible, from the title and from John's
claim that it told how much the Gentiles hated vice, that it was John's own *De
Poenitentia*.
[92] Again, possibly one of John's own works, although this is almost impossible to
check, as he does not include any direct quotation.

Distinction 6 discusses the appropriate admonitions for the three classes of women: wives, widows and virgins. John brushes off the married rapidly, pointing out that he has already dealt with this category earlier, and recommending Augustine's *De Bono Coniugali* in its entirety as a source of further material.[93] He then turns to the admonition of widows, which again he has already mentioned, though in less detail than is provided in this chapter.[94] He observes that, although St Paul allowed second marriages, we know from Valerius that the ancients gave a special honour – the *corona pudicicie* – to those who were content with only one man. Jerome is mentioned as a source of examples of such women. Indeed, Jerome's opinions form a major part of the chapter (as always when John is discussing women and their behaviour), supplemented by some biblical references and a couple of examples from Valerius. From this it would appear that John's attitude to widowhood was very old-fashioned: all his material is at least 900 years old, and he was not, as elsewhere, using his extracts to flesh out any new or different ideas.

The chapter on virgins is again lengthy, and it is similarly based mainly on very old material, with the main sources being Jerome, Augustine's *De Bono Virginali*[95] as a source and quotes it fairly extensively himself. He opens his chapter by establishing that there extensively himself. He opens his chapter by establishing that there is virtue in virginity, before going on to discuss the behaviour appropriate to those in this happy state.[96] They should, he says, be immaculate without and within, and should study hard to please God. He mentions the wise and the foolish virgins in Matthew 25, and extracts from Jerome the observation that the virgins are as the angels on earth, and from Ambrose the comment that virginity is the natural condition by which mankind is assimilated to the angels. The ideal virgin should be frugal with food and drink, humble in behaviour, taciturn, modest and prudent and occupied with virtuous works – in fact much like the ideal members of any class which John has discussed so far. The virgins are warned to guard their virginity, because it is a priceless and irreplaceable treasure. As encouragement, John gives a number of examples of beautiful women who had

---

93 *Communiloq.* 3.6.1.
94 *Communiloq.* 3.6.2.
95 Modern lists of Augustine's works do not include the *De Bono Virginali*. The title appears in Grosseteste's Index to patristic writers, although Hunt was unable to identify the work (R. W. Hunt, 1955, p. 142). The work was presumably in the library of the Oxford Franciscans, and John would have used it there.
96 *Communiloq.* 3.6.3.

difficulty defending their chastity but succeeded with the help of God. He then turns to the dreadful crime of violating a virgin, and particularly one dedicated to God. He also has harsh words for those who dedicate themselves to God and then change their minds, and gives the example of the Vestal Virgins in Rome, telling how they were buried alive if they lost the right to their title and status. Finally John recommends the lives of the saints as a source of examples of the perfection of virginity. The distinction as a whole is elementary but functional.

A rather different theme is dealt with in distinction 7, on differing degrees of fortune. John begins with those who are prospering.[97] He tells them not to be boastful of their condition or to despise the less fortunate. Indeed, they should try to share their benefits with others, and to remember that nothing is stable in this life and that their own prosperity may fade away and adversity replace it. John emphasises at length that both misery and happiness are transitory and prone to fluctuation.

In his comments to those in adversity, John advises that they should not be too weighed down by misfortune.[98] He quotes from Seneca that adversity is not a bad thing, and that nothing really bad can happen to a good man. Great men rejoice in adversity as brave soldiers in battle. Those in adversity should suffer it patiently and consider that it brings good, drives away evil and purges sin.

Finally, John offers comments suitable for the healthy and the sick. The healthy are advised not to misuse their health, but to expend it in fruitful work and thus store up merit and enrich themselves in heaven.[99] Moreover, a healthy body should lead to a healthy mind, and so they should not think of evil. Nor should they destroy their bodily health through passion, indulgent appetite and drunkenness. John repeats a comment he made earlier about ancient medicine involving only the knowledge of a few herbs.

The last chapter, on the sick, warns them that they should endure their condition patiently.[100] As strong medicine cures bodily ills, so bodily sickness wipes out the spiritual vices, and this is its great virtue. The sick should give thanks to God and will be honoured by him in exchange. John ends by recommending Gregory's *Pastoralia* as a source of further information.

Throughout this third part of *Communiloquium*, John has expressed recognisable Christian doctrine with the help and support of

---

[97] *Communiloq.* 3.7.1. [98] *Communiloq.* 3.7.2. [99] *Communiloq.* 3.8.1.
[100] *Communiloq.* 3.8.2.

a great many references to sources. Many still derive from classical works. This is true not only of the *exempla* cited, but also of the quotations which John uses to couch his attitudes to behaviour and morality, of his divisions of humanity and of his views on the various groups within society. The balance between classical and medieval works is clear from a brief numerical analysis of the references which appear during the section. John cites biblical books on 138 occasions, sometimes with an added comment by one of the church fathers, but frequently giving only the book name and the chapter number. There are several cross-references to other parts of *Communiloquium*, both preceding and following this third part, suggesting that the plan of the work was established before writing commenced. There are some 267 references to other non-biblical sources, varying from brief quotations or mere recommendations to lengthy extracts and *exempla*. Of these references, 205 come from works written before AD 450, although a significant number of these are patristic in content. John quotes 50 works from this earlier period, written by 20 authors. He shows three clear favourites – Augustine (47 references), Jerome (41 references) and Seneca (37 references). The 62 references which he makes to writers from after AD 450 come from 19 works by 12 authors. The lion's share of these references goes to Gregory the Great, who is responsible for 40 of the 62. The proportion of quotations from the earlier and the later periods closely matches that for the two earlier parts of *Communiloquium*, the three parts together totalling some two-thirds of the whole volume. John therefore seems to have an intrinsic consistency of proportion, whatever aspect of the secular world is under discussion. A detailed analysis of the non-biblical sources for parts 2 and 3 appears at the end of this chapter.

Throughout the second and third parts of *Communiloquium*, which contain John's advice to the different groups in society, we see John as a very humane man, aware of human nature and human problems as much as of church doctrine, and anxious that the latter be successfully applied to the former, for the benefit of individual and community alike. *Communiloquium* was intended as a tool to help the preacher advise the people, in conversation as in preaching. W. A. Pantin wrote: 'One can imagine the conscientious friar, about to dine out, getting up his table talk from the *Communiloquium* or *Breviloquium*, so as to be able to come out with "That reminds me of what Aulus Gellius (or it might be St Augustine) tells us . . . ".'[101]

[101] W. A. Pantin, 1961, pp. 299–300.

This is an attractive possibility. But friars in particular also spent much time on the move, on short journeys or long. They would meet people not only on overnight stops, but by the wayside, and many hours must have been whiled away in constructive conversation. Study of the *Communiloquium* would enable a preacher to have positive and telling advice for any man, whatever his problem. Whether he was a judge, about to become a juror, anxious about his role as a witness, sick, troubled by an ill-tempered wife or a fractious child, down on his luck or blessed with unexpected good fortune, in difficulties over an inheritance or a feud with a neighbour, considering marriage or committed and having problems in consequence, there were things which he ought to know, steps he could take, consolations which he could hug to himself. *Communiloquium* contained them all, together with *exempla* and recommendations to help those in dozens of other situations – each carefully supported by venerable authorities. The potential value of such a book was enormous, and all the evidence indicates that its value was recognised, for *Communiloquium* attained extraordinary popularity.[102] As we shall see, it did not confine itself to the secular world, but dealt also with all manner of scholars and churchmen. It thus provides a fairly complete picture of secular society, quite apart from its panoramic selection of sources. The advice it contained must have been applicable to millions of people all across Europe: John's efforts to provide a useful volume for preachers must be rated as highly successful.

SOURCE LIST FOR *COMMUNILOQUIUM* PARTS 2 AND 3

1. SOURCES FROM BEFORE AD 450

Ambrose	*De Officiis*	4
	De Paradiso	1
	De Virginitate	7
	Hexameron	8
Apuleius	*De Deo Socratis*	1
Aristotle	*Ethics*	5
Augustine	*Confessions*	11
	Contra Faustum	2
	Contra Iulianum	2
	De Bono Coniugali	1

[102] For details see the end of chap. 6, and chap. 8 *passim*.

	De Bono Virginali	4
	De Civitate Dei	26
	De Continentia Viduali	I
	De Decore Cordis	I
	De Ecclesiasticis Dogmatibus	I
	De Genesi contra Manicheos	I
	De Mendacio	I
	De Moribus Ecclesie	I
	De Patientia	I
	De Virginitate	I
	Epistolae	10
	Sermones	9
	Super Iohannem	4
	Super Psalmos	I
Aulus Gellius	*Noctes Atticae*	I
Chrysostom	*Super Iohannem*	9
	Super Matthaeum[103]	8
Cicero	*De Amicitia*	9
	De Officiis	7
	De Rhetorica	I
	De Senectute	5
	Tusculanae Quaestiones	5
pseudo-Cyprian	*De Duodecim Abusionibus*	4
Ennius *poeta*[104]		I
Eusebius	*Historia Ecclesiastica*	I
Herodotus[105]		2
Jerome	*Contra Iovinianum*	10
	De Coniugio	I
	Epistolae	37
	Super Isaias	I
Juvenal	*Satires*	3
Origen[106]		I
Sallust		2
Seneca	*De Beneficiis*	5
	De Clementia	2
	De Constantia Sapientis	2
	De Ira	4

---

[103] The genuine Chrysostom commentary rather than the *Opus Imperfectum*.
[104] Through Augustine.
[105] Cited as Erodocus.
[106] No title given. I have not managed to trace the quotation.

	De Naturalibus Quaestionibus	2
	De Providentia	4
	Epistulae[107]	37
Solinus	*Collectanea Rerum Memorabilium*	4
Suetonius	*De Vita Caesarum*	1
Terence[108]		1
Theophrastus	*Liber de Nupciis*[109]	1
Trogus Pompeius	*Historia*	6
Valerius Maximus	*Factorum ac Dictorum Memorabilium Libri ix*	44
Varro	*Satires*	1
Virgil	*Aeneid*	2
	Georgics	1

2. SOURCES FROM AFTER AD 450

Alexander Nequam,	*De Naturis Rerum*	1
Anselm of Canterbury	*De Similitudinibus*	1
	Meditationes	2
Avicenna	*Philosophia*[110]	2
Bernard of Clairvaux	*De Consideratione*	2
	Meditationes	1
Boethius	*De Consolatione Philosophiae*	4
pseudo-Boethius	*De Disciplina Scholarium*	1
Cassiodorus	*Historia Tripartita*	2
	Super Psalmos	1
Gregory the Great	*Dialogues*	3
	Moralia	26
	Registrum	2
	Regula Pastoralis	7
	Super Evangelia	3
	Super Ezechielem	8
Henry de Suza	*Summa Aurea*	1
Hugh of Saint-Victor	*De Sacramentis*	6
John of Salisbury	*Policraticus*	2
Papias	*Vocabularium*	2
Peter Lombard	*Sentences*	3
Robert Grosseteste	*Commentary on Ethics*	2

---

[107] John uses both the earlier and the later groups of these letters.
[108] Through Cicero.
[109] Through Jerome's *Contra Iovinianum 2*.
[110] John's title.

William of Auvergne	*Tractatus de Universo*	I

Also the following anonymous works:

Vitae Patrum	4
Paradisus Patrum	2
Vita Sancti Kinderini	I
Extravagantes de Ius Iurandum	I

Also the following unidentifiable works (perhaps by John of Wales):

Breviloquium de Viciis	3
Breviloquium de Penitentia	I
Summa de Viciis	I

Chapter 6

COMMUNILOQUIUM, PARTS 4–7: JOHN OF WALES ON SCHOLARS AND CHURCHMEN

John's discussion of non-secular groups begins with the fourth part of *Communiloquium*, which bears the heading *De republica ecclesiastica*. It deals with the various ranks of the clergy, their duties and appropriate behaviour, and supplies recommendations for further reading for those who are interested. There are five distinctions in this part of the work, their main topics being the ranks of the clergy, the proper behaviour of priests and of bishops, the various ecclesiastical offices and the appropriate behaviour of ecclesiastical judges.

John opens with a brief statement of purpose. He tells us that he has previously produced authoritative tales and *exempla* from which the preacher can instruct illiterate men, according to their different ranks and conditions. In this part, however, are gathered together the tales and *exempla* with which the preacher may more usefully instruct literate churchmen.[1] He confirms that the *respublica ecclesiastica* is composed of such (literate) persons, the head being the *summus pontifex* or the pope.[2] John recommends part 1 of *Communiloquium*, where he discussed the head of the civil republic. All this, he says, can be adapted to the pope, who is the head of everything. What has been said of the eyes and ears, heart, hands and feet can also be adapted to the limbs of the *respublica ecclesiastica*. This is an indication that John saw senior ecclesiastics in the role of administrators and rulers. It was quite natural that he should do so, for the church controlled much property and many men.

It would have been valuable to have had some detailed information on John's attitude to the pope, but he slides around this by observing that it is not for the ignorant or the inexpert to presume to describe how either the pope or the highest prelates next to him ought to be. How such men ought to be is well described in

---

[1] *Communiloq.* 4.1, Introduction.   [2] *Communiloq.* 4.1.1.

Bernard's *De Consideratione*. This attitude is one of the minor curiosities of *Communiloquium*. John may have been genuinely humble on this score, and truly convinced that he could not contribute anything to a description of the pope's proper function, but he seems happy to discuss everything and everyone else with freedom, and to quote others at length when he feels that they have already done the job adequately. This was an appropriate line to take in a work such as *Communiloquium*; indeed it was one of the main functions of the work. So it was perhaps a little hard to leave the eager preacher unable to comment on the pope unless he had access to the *De Consideratione*. We are left wondering whether John had views about the pope which he felt it wiser to keep to himself.

John presents a simile between the body and the ecclesiastical republic, the higher ranks taking the parts of the organs and the parish priests of the feet. All these gather together to form a body, as was said of the civil republic in part 1, because they are themselves more spiritual and more perfect. And, just as in general the prince is considered more noble than the people, so in the church it works in reverse, from the limbs to the head, because whoever is first a cleric and an ecclesiastic may later be elected bishop. Therefore, concludes John, all the ranks deserve their separate admonitions. He advises that each rank should understand its function and the origins of its name. This he explains for each rank in the subsequent chapters. The definitions and explanations are extremely basic. This probably indicates that many of the lowest ranks of churchmen barely knew their own duties, let alone why they should be performed.

John devotes one chapter to clerics in general.[3] They should beware, he says, lest they turn themselves from the sign of the Lord and profit through the divine ministry. Their tonsure bears witness that they are contemplators of the divine secrets and do not serve sin, or become involved in secular business and affairs. He briefly discusses the origins of the tonsure and repeats that it is very important that clerics should guard their status, because it is very improper that the crown of the Lord should become the crown of pride.

The first group to be admonished individually is the *ostiarii*, the lowest of the seven ranks which the clergy may ascend.[4] They have the duty of opening and closing the church doors, guarding the faithful who enter and throwing out excommunicates. Because of

---

[3] *Communiloq.* 4.1.2. [4] *Communiloq.* 4.1.3.

this, says John, the office is worthy of the Lord, who ejected the buyers and sellers from the Temple.

Each of the subsequent ranks is treated in much the same way, with Hugh of Saint-Victor almost the only non-biblical source. We learn that the lectors, the second rank, who announce the word of God, should be instructed so as to understand the sense of what they read, to accent the correct places and to read distinctly without confusion over pronunciation.[5] This office too is a worthy one, for the bishop hands over his codex to the lector, for him to read from, and hence this office too should be well performed. The exorcists, who have power over spirits not of this world, next receive their meed of praise, and are warned to beware of evil spirits in their own hearts.[6] John has little to say about the acolytes, who handle lamps and other vessels, except to draw a parallel with the Lord, who said 'ego sum lux mundi'.[7] The subdeacons get slightly more space. The worth of their task is said to lie in the fact that the Lord brought a basin and washed the feet of his disciples.[8] Because the subdeacons handle the sacraments they should be pure and observe the laws of chastity. The sixth rank discussed by John is that of the deacon, and John says this deserves to be ranked sixth because six is a perfect number.[9] The office of the deacon is to deal with everything concerning the sacraments: bringing and removing the offerings from the altar, bearing the cross of Christ, preaching to the listening people, telling them to genuflect, and so on. Because Christ himself encouraged the disciples to pray, this too is a worthy office. John then quotes I Timothy on the proper behaviour of deacons.

We now come to the priest.[10] John discusses his office and the way in which Jesus made it worthy (the transformation of bread and wine at the Last Supper). The priest's functions are listed as consecrating and dispensing the host, giving sermons in church, baptising and catechising, calling sinners to repent and encouraging them to purge themselves through their prayers. Again priests are warned to be worthy of their office through correct behaviour, and again I Timothy forms the basis for the discussion.

John's second distinction is devoted to the nature of the perfect priest. The priest should be knowledgeable about the secrets of God, because he is God's messenger to the people.[11] His habits should be serious and mature, rather than of worldly levity, and he should be

---

[5] *Communiloq.* 4.1.4. [6] *Communiloq.* 4.1.5. [7] *Communiloq.* 4.1.6.
[8] *Communiloq.* 4.1.7. [9] *Communiloq.* 4.1.8. [10] *Communiloq.* 4.1.9.
[11] *Communiloq.* 4.2.1.

wary of drunkenness.[12] John tells us that a priest should be chaste and stand aloof from women,[13] that he should be free from avarice and, indeed, generous in his behaviour.[14] Jerome's *Epistolae* join Hugh of Saint-Victor as one of the main sources for this entire section. Jerome is mentioned as advocating generosity and hospitality, and John observes that these topics are dealt with at greater length in the section on bishops. He then tells the reader that clerics should abstain from secular business and concentrate on church affairs, with a suggestion that the reader turn to the *Decretals* for further information.

John now justifies the space allotted to the priests.[15] As eminent as they are on account of their rank, says John, so much more should they be eminent in virtue. He connects the word *sacerdos* with sacrifice, and comments on the fact that ancient priests were more honest than other men, and hence were greatly honoured by the Gentiles. The priests of the Gentiles led a life of great austerity, as Plato observed in the *Timaeus*. John tells us that in Athens the priests lived apart from ordinary people, lest anything should pollute their chastity. He speaks of abstention from flesh and wine and states that Euripides, as a priest of Jove, abstained even from cooked food. John then mentions the three Jewish sects (the Pharisees, Sadducees and Essenes) and their abstentions, and also dietary traditions in Persia and India. If, says he, Gentile priests, serving superstitious cults and the arts of Satan, could abstain from these things, how much more should priests of the highest God do so, that they may serve him worthily. John takes his admiration of the ancients very seriously – recommending them as a model even to Christian priests.

In the last chapter of this distinction, John observes that the priests should be united in their concern for the church.[16] Such concern has been adequately described by Bernard in his *Sermons on the Canticle*, where he likens the ecclesiastics to good watchmen, vigilant while we sleep, watching over the soul, praying through the night, examining the enemy and anticipating evil counsel. John produces a selection of suitable texts on the theme of shepherds and watchmen, then returns to Bernard for authoritative comments on the wrong of those who cannot truly love Christ because they are given over to Mammon, rejoicing in fine things, costly vestments and gold and silver plate. John also mentions the role of the priest in teaching, and

---

[12] *Communiloq.* 4.2.2.
[13] *Communiloq.* 4.2.3.
[14] *Communiloq.* 4.2.4–5.
[15] *Communiloq.* 4.2.6.
[16] *Communiloq.* 4.2.7.

repeats that the preacher should urge clerks to perform their proper duties.

This is followed by a distinction on the admonition of bishops. John divides the distinction into four main parts. First, because bishops are chosen from among the clergy, all clerics are warned against ambition. Secondly, John discusses canonical and legitimate election and, thirdly, the dignity of the church and the proper humility with which one should undertake the prelacy. Finally we are told of the correct dignity of the bishop, his virtues and his duties.

The first chapter echoes the opening sections on the prince and on the other magistracies. As in the secular sphere, says John, one should not aspire to high office. A prelate, even if he possesses rank, should not desire it or seek it wishfully nor undertake it presumptuously. (Part 1 above discussed the many reasons for this.) Thus John seems to apply his arguments about secular rulers to the ecclesiastical sphere. He quotes from Jerome that a prelacy is hard work and effort, not dignity and pleasure. Because it is rare and difficult to desire such work, it is dangerous to want a church prelacy. Augustine is adduced here for the point that because men are by nature equal, no one should wish to rule any more than to be ruled, and so no one should seek high rank in the church. It is hard, says John, to tread a slippery path without falling, and similarly hard to live well in a position of rank. He closes his chapter with an attractive simile from the *De Similitudinibus* of Anselm of Canterbury, about how a boy who is chasing butterflies will fall into snares and pitfalls through disregarding the placing of his feet.

In support of the principle that ecclesiastical rank is not to be desired, John produces a number of examples of saints who shunned ecclesiastical rank.[17] Ambrose and Gregory are mentioned as examples, and Gregory and Bernard of Clairvaux recommended as sources of further detail. John repeats firmly that ambition is depraved and unsuitable, and then turns to a description of the proper way to carry out elections.[18] He states that people ought to be elevated to prelacies not through improper ambition but through canonical election. The choice should be correctly made, not from temporal convenience or hope of reward, from human intervention or persuasion or threatening, from undue affection or from carnal knowledge: the only criterion should be usefulness to the church of God. John says that he is going into the matter only briefly, because

---

[17] *Communiloq.* 4.3.2.   [18] *Communiloq.* 4.3.3–4.

the decretals give a full explanation, but he has said enough for us to see that he must have been opposed to all forms of intervention, which was still on issue in his day.

The next topic is that of the reasons for which a prelate should consent to be chosen, and of what he ought to feel about being chosen.[19] Those elected to the prelacy ought to take up the position in humility, fear and trembling. No one should praise himself because of such an appointment, but should be much more humble, thinking of the burdens which he undertakes and the dangers with which he surrounds himself. There is nothing more difficult, laborious and dangerous than the various church offices, but also nothing more blessed with God than to perform the duties as they should be done. Throughout this chapter, we again see John mirroring what he has already said with regard to the secular sphere: it is wrong to want office for the power and glory attached, but it is right to undertake it if it is offered, and humbly to do the duty to the best of one's ability.

John now tells us how a bishop ought to be after consecration.[20] He recommends the reader to see I Timothy and Jerome's 44th Epistle for full details, and adds the relevant chapter numbers and headings from Gregory's *Decretals*. He recommends the bishop to contemplate the meaning of his name, which derives from *scopos*, a rock, and adds that *pontifex*, derived from *pons*, is the title given to priests because they act as a bridge between man and God. A good mediator, says John, brings to God the prayers of the people, reporting them to God kindly and asking his forgiveness for sin. The mediator should not require gifts from the people or usurp the glory of God. John ends by saying that a bishop should be remembered not for his great dignity, but for his virtues and the excellence of his life.

John proceeds to explain in some detail exactly what is desirable and undesirable in a bishop. First, the bishop should beware of the vices. One sin leads to another, and in particular this applies to drunkenness.[21] Secondly, the bishop ought to beware of all kinds of luxury and indulgence. Because a bishop is so eminent, he requires the highest purity and chastity, and there ought to be no women in his household.[22] He should beware not only of extravagance but also of avarice, for a bishop should be generous in giving alms and offering hospitality.[23] A generous bishop is much more acceptable to God, says John, and he tells how Gregory's future as pope was

---

[19] *Communiloq.* 4.3.5.   [20] *Communiloq.* 4.3.6.   [21] *Communiloq.* 4.3.7.
[22] *Communiloq.* 4.3.8.   [23] *Communiloq.* 4.3.9.

sealed by his generosity to a passing traveller. He continues with the
theme of generosity, pointing out that bishops should be generous
not only in giving to the poor, but also in offering hospitality.[24]
Cicero, Ambrose and Seneca are quoted alongside Hugh of Saint-
Victor in praise of hospitality. John mentions the examples of
Abraham and Lot and of the disciples, then turns to the *Policraticus*
for proof that even infidels show hospitality. As usual, the ancients
are praised for the way in which they practised this virtue, and we are
also told that they despised ungracious hosts. The examples in this
paragraph come from Valerius Maximus and from Seneca's *De
Beneficiis*.

John elaborates on the form which hospitality should take in the
case of a bishop.[25] There is no hospitality unless it is given freely and
in a pleasant spirit, with generosity in providing necessities and a
desire for a modest amount of good humour. A bishop or other
churchman should be able to joke and be generous with guests, but
he should avoid superfluous conviviality and improper stories. From
Jerome John takes the comment that the proper sort of conversation
– what might be generally described as edifying – is a better
ornament to the table than gold or silver vessels. A bishop ought to
be convivial with his guests, not in a common way, but in a
philosophical and holy fashion.[26] There are three types of conviviality or feasting: common or vulgar, in which pleasure and
vanity rule; modest and courteous, in which stability and honesty
rule; and, finally, philosophical, in which truth reigns among the
philosophers and *caritas* and *veritas* among the saints.

Having enumerated some biblical texts on feasting and rejoicing,
John turns to Valerius for examples of how the ancients organised
feasts. He then returns to the bishop, whom he recommends to
follow the example of the pope in holding feasts and inviting people
to them, causing the distinguished deeds of the ancients to be read
out at his table, and excluding secular and scurrilous songs.[27] This
ends John's comments on bishops. The section shows careful
orchestration of authorities to describe precisely what John clearly
sees as a difficult behavioural balance. He indicates an awareness of
the difficulties faced by bishops in their many public and official

---

[24] *Communiloq.* 4.3.10.   [25] *Communiloq.* 4.3.11.

[26] *Communiloq.* 4.3.12. Cheerfulness at table was a characteristic often described in
vitae of bishops.

[27] An account of intellectual conversation at the papal dinner table appears in the
poem which Henry of Würzburg wrote at the request of Urban IV (1261–4): see H.
Grauert, 1912.

engagements, and strives to present a plausible solution to the question of appropriate behaviour.

Distinction 4 bears the heading *De officiis ecclesiasticorum*. Having seen how churchmen should be, says John, we now examine their offices, and particularly the triad composed of dispensing the sacraments, expounding the sacred lessons and divine precepts and sending prayers to God on behalf of the people.[28] John refers to St Matthew and St John for the origins of these functions before discussing them separately and in more detail.

He begins with the obligation to preach, and the nature of true preaching.[29] He gathers together biblical texts on preaching, and refers the reader to various parts of Gregory's works for further details on the matter. His purpose is simply to establish that a preacher ought to preach. In the next chapter he discusses the kind of life that a preacher ought to lead.[30] For preaching to be fruitful, says John, there must be holiness and perfection on the part of the preacher, for preachers are the organs of truth, and if they are holy and perfect their words will be irresistible. He tells a long story from Eusebius' *Historia Ecclesiastica* of how there was much dialectic and clever speaking at the Council of Nicaea, but finally all listened to a simple man not learned in rhetoric, because God spoke through him. This is followed by a similar story from Cassiodorus' *Historia Tripartita* of a dispute staged before Constantine at Byzantium. John concludes that if a preacher wishes his words to be effective, he should love God and give thanks to him.

We now learn which form preaching should take.[31] The preacher should carefully consider the quality and capacity of his listeners and offer appropriate sermons. He should strike the minds of his listeners like a musician plucking a lyre, and he should always be certain that what he preaches is the truth. The preacher ought to be a virtuous example in order to confirm his preaching.[32] Gregory's *Moralia* is cited as the source of a law of preachers – that they should practise what they preach – and Bernard's *De Consideratione* is the source of the comment that actions speak louder than words. Similar remarks from other authors are also gathered here. We would expect to learn more of John's views on preaching from his *Ars Praedicandi* and his *Moniloquium*, but we can already see that he is a 'no frills' man, who has more faith in teaching by example than in high-flown speeches.[33]

---

[28] *Communiloq.* 4.4.1.   [29] *Communiloq.* 4.4.2.   [30] *Communiloq.* 4.4.3.
[31] *Communiloq.* 4.4.4.   [32] *Communiloq.* 4.4.5.
[33] For an excellent study of thirteenth-century preaching, see D. L. d'Avray, 1985.

John next tells us that men of the church ought to nourish the people of God with the fruits of prayer.[34] They should receive from the people the tenth, and oblations and sustenance, so that they may pray for these same people in quiet and tranquillity, and plead for them with God. And therefore the priests ought to know the laws with respect to heaven, in order to plead for the people efficiently before the supreme judge. John ends with a condemnation of the many today who postpone all spiritual duties.

We now turn to the virtues which should belong to those having the cure of souls.[35] Because the performance of the aforementioned duties is not for boys, fools or the unskilled, the prelates or bishops ought to see that they do not bring into the church such people, who are not fitted for these offices. Rather, they should seek knowledgeable and industrious men. John includes a selection of biblical texts on the need for strength, before adding that, alas, on the contrary there are many today, puerile, weak and ignorant of the law of God, undertaking the redemption of souls and the supervision of the blood of the Saviour, like a pack of wolves rushing in on all sides. He likens the bishop to a builder, who should set up strong and upright columns to support the church, these columns being equivalent to the pastors and prelates. It is dangerous to put the ignorant in charge of souls, because they will spread ignorance. Moreover, says John with considerable force, one would not choose an unskilled man as a doctor or a warrior or a teacher, or an inexperienced man to captain a ship in a storm. So it should be with the ship of the church in the storms of this world. We can see that John is aware of a number of unsuitable people abusing pastoral posts, and lays the blame both on the unqualified candidate and on those in authority who pass such people through. He is also much opposed to those who slacken in their duties and use a benefice purely for their own financial benefit.

The fifth and final distinction of this section covers a wide range of topics. It opens with a chapter on how ecclesiastical judges ought to behave.[36] John says that this is shown in what was said earlier about secular judges, for if they should exercise justice diligently, how much more should the judges of the church. The next chapter tells us that a bishop's household ought to be modest, honest and disciplined.[37] We then learn of the significance of the bishop's vestments, through an analysis derived mainly from Hugh of Saint-Victor's *De Sacramentis*.[38] Finally John tells us of the need for the

---

[34] *Communiloq.* 4.4.6.   [35] *Communiloq.* 4.4.7.   [36] *Communiloq.* 4.5.1.
[37] *Communiloq.* 4.5.2.   [38] *Communiloq.* 4.5.3.

pastor to live among his flock.[39] John says that this is necessary if he
is to guard them adequately, and therefore it is wrong to leave one's
responsibility without legitimate excuse.

The entire section on the church is plainly an elementary run-
through of the kinds of things every preacher ought to know about
church personnel and their duties, with plentiful reference to the
works where more detailed or authoritative statements will be
found. John mentions the fact that in his own time many unsuitable
persons were being appointed to the cure of souls, and he speaks out
against interference with appointments and against the practice of
leaving a parish without good reason. He therefore identifies what
were probably some of the most common abuses of his period. In the
main, he discusses what should happen rather than what should not.
This fits with his central purpose, which we can see was to help the
very ignorant to understand how the church should function. The
very simple level of many of his comments indicates that he felt that
there were many most ignorant people about.

The fifth part of *Communiloquium*, which deals with scholars,
relates quite closely to what precedes it. John tells the reader that he
has gathered together the appropriate examples for the preacher to
confer usefully with ecclesiastics or philosophical men, so that they
may be greatly stimulated to desire knowledge. John quotes from
Policraticus the story that the ancient philosophers caused a picture of
Wisdom to be painted before all the temples. He uses Hugh of Saint-
Victor's *Didascalion* to explain that *philosophia* signifies the love of
wisdom, and discusses its nature and its relation to the liberal arts.[40]
In support of the *Didascalion* he adduces Al-Farabi and pseudo-
Boethius' *De Disciplina Scholarium*.

John tells us that honour and reverence are due to those who teach
the liberal arts and philosophy, and that those who study such
subjects should be of sound mind and pleasing disposition, lest they
bring the subject into disrepute.[41] Would-be scholars should have an
industrious and clear mind, whether they are of natural discretion or
of a lively spirit. As an example he tells us of the youth of Protagoras,
as described by Aulus Gellius in the *Noctes Atticae*.[42] Those having
charge of boys are warned to beware lest those of lively spirit
consume too much food or drink, when they should eat sparingly.

Now follow two chapters which remind us of something which
we have already observed – that John was aware of the nature of

[39] *Communiloq.* 4.5.4.
[41] *Communiloq.* 5.1.2.
[40] *Communiloq.* 5.1.1.
[42] *Communiloq.* 5.1.3.

infants and young children. Using as sources Jerome, the pseudo-
Boethian *De Disciplina Scholarium*, Quintilian, and Augustine's
Confessions, he tells us how boys should be instructed initially.[43]
They should be taught according to their capacity, beginning with
the elements of literacy. Boys should learn these thoroughly,
because nothing learnt thus in the beginning can be learnt so well
after, and it is a more serious and difficult thing to reinstruct badly
taught boys than those who have had no teaching. It is easier to put in
good information than to strike out bad, particularly when boys
cling so hard to their first instruction, whatever its quality. Therefore boys are to be instructed with great diligence, lest through
negligence the time of boyhood should pass them by. The boys
themselves are recommended to pay attention to their teachers and
not to deceive them. It is important that boys should be instructed
correctly in the elements, and first in *grammatica* and how to read
correctly and with the accents in the right places. The tenor of John's
comments shows that he has a real awareness of boys and their
habits, and of the tenacious nature of a very young mind. As a
Franciscan lector he would have had considerable teaching experience, and he would seem to have spent some of his time in accurate
observation. The section confirms our impression from earlier
chapters, that John was aware of a difference between the young and
the adult, and was able to identify the nature of the difference.

The following chapter continues the discussion of the correct
mode of instructing boys.[44] Care should be taken, says John, lest
boys should be much steeped in fabulous tales and become drawn to
their delights.[45] John tells a story from Valerius about a Spartan king
who operated a form of book censorship. Remember, John says,
how the minds of boys cling to the things which they first come into
contact with. Because of this it was the custom of the Hebrews to
teach all the scriptures to the boys, saving the most difficult portion
to the end. Note too how Augustine claimed to have imbibed
Christianity with his mother's milk. The point here seems to be that
the earliest influences will ultimately triumph, whatever happens in
between. John says that boys should be taught true and useful things,
not tales and stories. So first should come grammar, and then logic.
He mentions the *trivium* and the *quadrivium* as a sevenfold group of

---

[43] *Communiloq.* 5.1.4.
[44] *Communiloq.* 5.1.5.
[45] Plainly a case of the pot calling the kettle black. John himself could not resist tales of
this type.

studies inherited from the ancients, very useful and for this reason selected from among the others, as they prepare the spirit for the full understanding of philosophy.

John now turns to the necessary requirements for students.[46] He gives a triad – *natura* (natural capacity), *exercitium* (effort) and *disciplina* (discipline). *Natura* includes ease in perceiving and retaining what is heard, *exercitium* involves working assiduously and cultivating natural capacity, and *disciplina* is needed so that the student may live in a praiseworthy fashion. And people ought to study in all the arts as much as is required. All this is derived from the *Didascalion*, which John recommends as a good source on how scholars ought to apply themselves.

In his chapter on how pupils ought to be, John's main source is the *De Disciplina Scholarium*.[47] Pupils should listen intently, understand and retain what they have heard. They should beware of the vices, of taverns and public spectacles, processions and feasts. These things, like drunkenness and gluttony, impair the intellect in a variety of ways, and the scholar should replace them with humble and diligent study. The need for industry is then rammed home, as John tells the student that he must study hard to acquire knowledge.[48] As the Bible says, whoever ploughs and sows a field shall harvest it. There are many students, but few *sapientes*. John mentions the many years of industry and effort put in by the scholars of old, and their lack of interest in possessions or leisure, their purity and their involvement with the things of the mind. The pupil ought to lead an honest life, as described already.[49] Because of this, ancient philosophers used to lecture their pupils on morality. And therefore it is a great shame if a scholar, hearing daily the rules and precepts of philosophy, is not of more mature and honest habits than a layman, who hears nothing of such things. John closes his distinction by reminding the scholar that he should feel affection for his teachers.

John's comments on students are followed by a short distinction for the information of *doctores*. The doctor, says John, should rise to that rank honourably, being knowledgeable and virtuous as previously described.[50] John adds that there is a great art in teaching each according to his capacity. On the question of how many books a scholar ought to have, John quotes from Seneca that many books are a distraction when one is not able to read them all.[51] It is sufficient to have as many as one can read, for as the stomach turns squeamish

[46] *Communiloq.* 5.1.6.   [47] *Communiloq.* 5.1.7.   [48] *Communiloq.* 5.1.8.
[49] *Communiloq.* 5.1.9.   [50] *Communiloq.* 5.2.1.   [51] *Communiloq.* 5.2.2.

if it is fed too many and too varied things, so it is with books, and a
few authorities are better than many errors. Scholars should beware
of *noxia scientia* (hurtful knowledge), which is useless and unfruitful
and leads to the devil.[52] Scholars should study with the right
intentions and in the right way, not being elevated by knowledge,
but remaining humble. They should note that too much knowledge
causes indigestion in the spiritual stomach, the memory. Lastly, on
the subject of the study of the sacred writings, we should note that
they contain all knowledge.[53] John recommends the *Didascalion* as a
source on this and gives some extracts, along with appropriate
biblical quotations.[54] We can see that John shares the view put
forward in ancient Greece, that study and knowledge give one a basis
for better behaviour.

John has shown considerable sympathy with the scholars, at all
stages of their career, and given the reader some sound advice. By
essentially abstracting the pseudo-Boethian *De Disciplina Scholarium*
and the *Didascalion* of Hugh of Saint-Victor, he has also given his
readers access to two of the books on education which were most
popular during his period.

He now proceeds to devote a distinction to the members of
religious orders. He points out that the life and virtues of the
religious are covered by the *Dialogues* of Gregory, the *Vitae Patrum,
De Collationibus Patrum* and the *Paradisus Patrum*, and that because of
this he is going to be brief and general. He lists his topics: first, the
original institution of the religious life; secondly, the eminence of
this life; thirdly, the three necessary virtues – poverty, chastity and
obedience; fourthly, he will deal with the other necessary virtues;
fifthly, with the usefulness of such a life; sixthly, with the greatness
of the first religious; seventhly, with those who live badly in holy
religion and, finally, with the serious punishment which the latter
incur.

First, the origins of the religious life, and of how religious have
that name because they bind themselves to God.[55] John establishes
the eminence and dignity of the religious life such as was chosen by
Christ, assigned to the disciples and preached to others.[56] He quotes
Matthew 9: if you wish to be perfect, go and sell all that you have,
give it to the poor and come and follow me. The apostles followed
such a lifestyle after the ascension of the Saviour, when no one

---

[52] *Communiloq.* 5.2.3.   [53] *Communiloq.* 5.2.4.
[54] For the *Didascalion* see Jerome Taylor, 1961.
[55] *Communiloq.* 6.1–2.   [56] *Communiloq.* 6.2.1.

claimed anything as his, but all was held in common. John then mentions the faithful of Alexandria who left the city under the evangelist Mark, and the many who 'are kept busy in our monasteries'. He elaborates the eminence of the religious life and the value of voluntary poverty, which the Son of God made precious by descending to earth and choosing it for himself.[57] It is much more valuable than founding monasteries and sustaining the poor, and one will be rewarded for it in the kingdom of heaven. John points out that in many places Jerome calls men to the religious life, but that he also asks the rhetorical question 'Who will celebrate in the churches and help the secular clergy if everyone takes refuge in solitude?' The answer is that, though many are called, few are truly chosen, and that there is still a place for those who worship in church. We then get a whole chapter on the eminence of ancient religious.[58] John tells us how the ancient saints served God first in Egypt and then elsewhere. He lists the three types of Egyptian monk – cenobites, who lived communally, anchorites, who lived alone in the desert, and those who lived in twos and threes. Their dietary restraints are listed, and John discusses a vision of monasticism experienced by Anselm. He closes by telling the religious to think their life worthy and live it in a good and honourable manner. John had a particular interest in the monks of Egypt, for his *Breviloquium de Sapientia Sanctorum*, written after the *Communiloquium*, is devoted to their lives and experiences.[59]

John tells the reader that the religious life consists of three principal things – voluntary poverty, chastity and obedience, and he discusses each separately.[60] Poverty receives two whole chapters to itself. We learn first that the religious vow themselves to poverty and lack of possessions, excepting those held in common.[61] The religious ought to beware lest they betray their vows, and should follow the example of holy fathers such as Benedict and Francis. Voluntary poverty is the treasure of a monk, and he should guard it appropriately. John gives examples from the *Vitae Patrum*, and follows these up with examples from Valerius and Seneca, of ancient rulers who abandoned wealth. He also mentions the philosopher Diogenes, who lived in a barrel and drank from the palm of his hand rather than own a cup. If such people, ignorant of the divine law and without the hope of the eternal kingdom, could wish for poverty and show its value so well, the faithful should indeed wish to be contemptuous of

---

[57] *Communiloq.* 6.2.2. [58] *Communiloq.* 6.2.3. [59] See below, chap. 7.
[60] *Communiloq.* 6.2.4. [61] *Communiloq.* 6.2.5.

wealth. Poverty should be undertaken freely and on account of God.[62] The religious ought to love poverty as a bride, and should be good-tempered and cheerful, for he who accepts poverty well is not truly a pauper. It is a great abuse for those in religion to have wealth. John makes an association between voluntary poverty and the martyrs, and observes that the pauper should be able to endure hunger, thirst and other inconveniences and still serve God. Poverty should be regulated by knowledge and ordered by humility, which is the guardian of poverty. God hates a proud pauper, and therefore paupers should be wary of arrogance. John repeats that the religious should not break their vows with respect to poverty, and exhorts the preacher to persuade them of this. Throughout this section, John writes with the powerful conviction one would expect of someone in his position.

Chastity is the subject of John's third distinction. He reminds us that he has already discussed the topic in parts 3 and 4, and comments that if women and ecclesiastics (the groups previously admonished) ought to be chaste, how much more should religious.[63] He gives a number of complementary definitions of chastity and says that they all apply to the man in religion (*vir religiosus*). In order to preserve chastity, one should avoid a superfluity of food and leisure and set aside all carnal love.[64] To be perfectly chaste, one ought also to avoid all opportunities for familiarity with women. John tells a story from the *Vitae Patrum* of a woman who asked an abbot to remember her in his prayers, and received the reply that he would rather pray to God to make him forget her. John includes a number of other tales to the same effect, along with examples of the temptation of monks by the devil. He closes with a couple of quotations on the beauty of chastity.

For his fourth distinction, John concentrates on obedience. He begins by establishing its place in the triad, then goes on to discuss its true nature and the seven grades of obedience which exist.[65] These involve obeying freely, without question, cheerfully, rapidly, forcefully, humbly and perseveringly.[66] John takes all the details from Bernard of Clairvaux's *Sermons* and *Meditations*. They are followed by a chapter on the difficulty of obedience, and its subsequent excellence.[67] Through obedience, man conquers himself and his wishes and submits to others, and therefore obedience should be

---

[62] *Communiloq.* 6.2.6.
[63] *Communiloq.* 6.3.1.
[64] *Communiloq.* 6.3.2.
[65] *Communiloq.* 6.4.1.
[66] *Communiloq.* 6.4.2.
[67] *Communiloq.* 6.4.3.

praised. John returns to antiquity as a source of examples.[68] One
man watered dry wood for three years on the orders of his abbot,
until it finally bore fruit, another walked through fire when commanded to do so, and so on. Not only were the ancient religious
obedient to their superiors, says John, but also Gentile soldiers to
their leaders, as was shown by the examples in part I of
Communiloquium.

On the other hand, there are many, even among religious, who
are disobedient when their own wishes are opposed.[69] Again we are
given a selection of appropriate examples. Lastly, John covers the
dangers of disobedience.[70] The religious should beware disobedience as he bewares damnation. Even ancient princes caused
disobedient soldiers to be punished.

We learn from the fifth distinction that seven other characteristics
are necessary for the perfect life. John devotes a chapter to each:
abstention from secular business and worldly tumult; self-denial;
cultivation of the soul; minute internal scrutiny; self-knowledge;
true humility resulting from the latter; and fervent and devoted
prayer.[71] And if prayer is to be effective it also requires seven
things.[72] John tells us that these are charity in the heart; a blameless
conscience; freedom from sin; reconciliation to the offences of one's
brothers; seeking only what is necessary; perfection in deed; and
perseverance in prayer. Our information on religious life is rounded
off in the next distinction, which points out the greatness of the
earliest religious, criticises those who live badly in religion, and
discusses the significance of the religious habit.[73]

The whole section on the religious and their life is simple and
thorough, and could quite appropriately be used to preach to the
laity about the nature of religious life and religious vows. Indeed,
although John claims that it is intended for the admonishment of
religious, it is almost too elementary to be of real benefit to them. We
would expect all but the newest of novices to be already acquainted
with the information which this section contains. John was perhaps
aware of this, for he later wrote his *Ordinarium Vitae Religiosae*, a
detailed treatise on the religious life which enjoyed considerable
success: at least 41 MS copies survive, and the work was printed on
several occasions.[74] The *Ordinarium* puts together authoritative
comments and *exempla* in the characteristic John of Wales style, and

[68] *Communiloq.* 6.4.4. [69] *Communiloq.* 6.4.5. [70] *Communiloq.* 6.4.6.
[71] *Communiloq.* 6.5.1–7. [72] *Communiloq.* 6.5.8. [73] *Communiloq.* 6.6.1–3.
[74] For MSS, see Appendices 2 and 3. For printed editions, see Appendix 5.

gives detailed discussion of such topics as the dangers of laziness, the value of useful work, the significance of the various hours of prayer, proper behaviour before, during and after meals, how to behave in church and in every other part of a monastery including the dormitory and refectory, the dangers of going out into the world, grounds for doing so, how to behave in the outside world, what to beware of there, and the need to return to a place of quiet. The sixth part of *Communiloquium* may have been of particular interest to literate laymen anxious to model their lives upon a firmly religious basis.

Because this sixth section is so simple in its contents, and yet so thorough in achieving its aims, it provides a particularly clear example of the importance of structure in *Communiloquium*. John uses a complex set of groupings and divisions as the framework of his developing themes. The construction of this framework must have been an integral part of his technique.[75]

That John's aim was to provide sound basic instruction is confirmed by his refusal to discuss such controversial points as the problem of Franciscan poverty. We may be confident that he had views on this, so he must have decided that *Communiloquium* was not the place to air them. The value of *Communiloquium*, and its usefulness, were probably extended by centuries as a result of its basis in sound commonsense rather than controversy, for controversy sometimes dates and becomes irrelevant. It is noticeable that where John's views on an issue differ from those which seem to have been current in his time, the view which he supports often becomes current in later decades, as for example his attitude to child-rearing. The circulation of *Communiloquium* was so large that it may sometimes have contributed to such developments.

We come now to the final section of John's *Communiloquium*, which deals appropriately with the dying. Here laity and ecclesiastics come together, for both must eventually find themselves in this category. John begins by establishing that the preacher ought to be able to advise those approaching death.[76] People ought to be warned not to trust in the durability of this life, which is short and transient. They should use their short lives to accumulate merit rather than indulging in evil.[77] Death is inevitable, and all should be admonished to be

[75] For the development of divisions in preaching literature, see A. Forni, 1980.
[76] *Communiloq.* 7.1.1.
[77] *Communiloq.* 7.1.2.

continually aware of it, that they may be kept from sin and be humble in heart, stimulated to work well and desirous of immortal life.[78] Men should always be prepared for death, because it comes unexpectedly.[79] John ends his first distinction with a chapter on the errors of those who commit suicide.[80] John has already told the reader that women who have been or fear to be raped should not commit suicide, because as long as they are unwilling it is not they who have lost their honour and modesty.[81] In this chapter he expressly condemns the ancients, who were able to see virtue in suicide. Their view was vehemently opposed by St Augustine in his *De Civitate Dei*, and John quotes him at some length here.[82] He discusses the example of Plato's pupil who threw himself from a wall in his haste to reach a better life, of Cato, of Lucretia and of the Jews of Masada. He concludes, not unexpectedly, that it is always wrong for a Christian to take his own life.[83]

In his second distinction, John concentrates on the principle that death is something to be feared. He claims that there are several different types of death, involving various combinations of the body and the spirit, and states that the sinner should fear them all as the end of delight and the beginning of punishment.[84] Some lively descriptions of hell are included to encourage the proper state of fearfulness. John states that the deaths of the saints are precious in the eyes of God, but adds that everyone ought to fear death and to make proper preparation for it, even the saints.[85] Anything that a person has done wrongly or omitted will go before the eternal judge, and if a saint should try and prepare for death, then how much more should an ordinary person. John tells us of the visions of heaven which came to saints on their death-beds, and adds that sinners sometimes see frightful visions of what awaits them in purgatory.[86] He closes the section by emphasising the helpfulness of prayer to the dying.[87]

Distinction 3 concentrates primarily on the rites that follow death. John reminds the reader that man should prepare for death all his life, and particularly when it becomes imminent.[88] After death, he says, the manner of burying and the ceremony of the funeral are much more a solace to the living than an aid to the dead.[89] It is impious to

---

[78] *Communiloq.* 7.1.3–4.   [79] *Communiloq.* 7.1.5.   [80] *Communiloq.* 7.1.6.

[81] *Communiloq.* 3.1.3.

[82] F. Bourquelot, 1842–4, provides a useful summary.

[83] For other views on suicide, see J.-C. Schmitt, 1976; R. F. Hunnisett, 1961; E. Bigi, 1976; H. Baechtold-Staübli, 1936; Donat de Chapeaurouge, 1960.

[84] *Communiloq.* 7.2.1–3.   [85] *Communiloq.* 7.2.4.   [86] *Communiloq.* 7.2.5–7.

[87] *Communiloq.* 7.2.8.   [88] *Communiloq.* 7.3.1–2.   [89] *Communiloq.* 7.3.1–2.

place too much emphasis on great tombs, but permissible to bury someone in a church if they have been truly faithful in life. He observes that the saints were not greatly concerned with tombs, and nor were the philosophers, who did not care whether they were buried at all, let alone how.[90] John uses Jerome as a source on various curious Gentile customs with bodies, such as feeding them to the dogs, then tells us that the faithful really ought to be properly buried.

We also get a chapter on the subject of wills.[91] The rich should be particular to make their wills properly, to satisfy everyone and to return anything which they have acquired unjustly. They should be sure to acquire faithful executors, and they should remember that leaving offerings in the right places – that is, to a church or to the poor – can help greatly in freeing the soul from purgatory. People should also remember that they are able to alleviate the sufferings of the living after they themselves are dead.

In the first part of *Communiloquium*, John discussed the state and its true nature, and analysed the roles which should properly be played in it by the prince, by other rulers and administrators and by the humbler classes. Next he divided and redivided humanity in ways which cut across class, to advise the young and the old, parents and children, the sick and the healthy. In the final sections he discussed clerics, scholars, religious and the dying in terms which could be used to address ordinary people quite as well as the members of these specific groups. Throughout the sections, John remained true to the views which he expressed earlier in the work, with an emphasis on the vulnerability of the young, the need for properly qualified churchmen, and the need for all to strive after virtues and heed the example of the ancient world. The same techniques of authoritative comment backed by relevant *exempla* were used throughout, indicating that they were adaptable to all kinds of topics.

John found time in these sections to discuss the role of the various ranks of the clergy, and to speak out against some contemporary abuses. He told of the role and the proper behaviour of a bishop, and highlighted some of the particular difficulties which such men face. He told us why preaching is necessary, and how it should be done, who should have the cure of souls and who should not. We learn of the importance of education, the correct approach to teaching and learning, the best way to use books. We hear all about the religious orders, their origins and nature and the restraints which bind their members. Finally, we discover how to prepare for and face death, its

[90] *Communiloq.* 7.3.3–4. [91] *Communiloq.* 7.3.5.

rituals and its significance. Such material was potentially of great use to the preacher. Indeed, any medieval preacher armed with a Bible and a copy of *Communiloquium* was supremely well equipped to face the world and to provide advice, conversation and preaching relevant to anyone, whatever their circumstances, status and personal difficulties. The production of the work should be seen as a great achievement on John's part.

The nature of John's subject matter in these sections – primarily ecclesiastical – made it necessary for him to draw much more heavily on patristic works and later medieval authors, and less upon the writers of classical times. Authors from before AD 450 therefore lose their earlier ascendancy. They total 20, with 53 works to their credit, and John takes 218 quotations from these works. Thirty-two authors come from the later period: John gives 309 quotations from 50 of their works. He therefore uses a total of 527 quotations from 103 works by 52 authors. This does not include 234 biblical references.[92]

We should remember that John is really addressing two audiences in *Communiloquium*: first, the preachers, through the whole work and specifically the *exempla* and references; and, secondly, through the preachers, the population at large. The message for this latter audience lies in the outlines and themes of the various chapters. It therefore seems justified to separate this basic message from the padding of references and *exempla*, which was provided primarily as a tool for the preacher.

We see in *Communiloquium* an elementary but thorough analysis of the world, as an eminent scholar felt it ought to be presented to the general population. It represents the kind of message which any medieval person might hear from a parish pulpit or in the speeches of a wandering preacher. And this message was heard, because *Communiloquium* was widely copied, owned and used. It was one of the most popular books of the Middle Ages, being used by all sorts of people for a variety of purposes, including that originally intended by John. More than 450 MSS survive, each containing up to eight works written by him.[93] More than 140 MS copies of *Communiloquium* survive, dating from the late thirteenth century to the late fifteenth.[94] *Communiloquium* was printed on the continent in 1472: the edition was such a success that it was 'pirated' in the same year – a rival press obtained a copy of the printed text and reproduced

[92] A full list of John's sources appears at the end of this chapter.
[93] See Appendix 2.   [94] See Appendix 3.

it exactly (faults included) rather than preparing another text from an original MS.[95] *Communiloquium* was printed a further five or six times before 1518. Two Spanish translations survive from the late fourteenth or early fifteenth century, indicating particular popularity in Spain.[96]

These many copies of *Communiloquium* were not written, printed and translated for nothing. They were owned, and they were used. I have been able to trace over 120 owners of *Communiloquium*, ranging from the thirteenth century to the early sixteenth.[97] These owners include itinerant friars, individual monks, monasteries and convents of almost every religious order, from Austria, Bavaria, Belgium, Czechoslovakia, England, France, Germany, Italy, the Netherlands, Spain and Switzerland. Similarly, individual vicars, parish churches, Oxford colleges of the fourteenth and fifteenth centuries, cathedrals, the humanistic libraries of Italy and individual scholars from all over Europe had copies. Men from the Italian communes owned and used the work, as did Spanish kings and queens.

Communiloquium's success was both prompt and sustained. St Augustine's, Canterbury already possessed at least one copy in the 1290s, and five by the 1360s.[98] Around the end of the thirteenth century, a friar in Northern Italy was using the work for its intended purpose – as a source of ideas and *exempla* for sermons.[99] His sermon *On the Republic* is derived largely from John's *Communiloquium*. Scholars in Oxford and Paris were using *Communiloquium* as a source at about the same time.

We are therefore in a position to see *Communiloquium* from two different angles: as material which must have been widely used in popular preaching, and as one man's view of the world. It is clear throughout the work that John had, and held to, the intention of being both authoritative and elementary, so we must accept that this knowledgeable and judicious view of the world cannot be highly analytical, subtle and intellectual, and that it was not the last word of John's personal opinion on certain matters. *Communiloquium* was not the place for this, and we should commend John for recognising it, rather than condemn him as boring or intellectually incompetent. Such accusations are needless and untrue, as is amply shown both by John's other works and by *Communiloquium* itself.

Communiloquium was a success, and while it fits neatly into the developing trends in thirteenth-century preaching handbooks, it

---

[95] See Appendix 5.   [96] See below, pp. 201–26.   [7] See Appendix 4.
[98] See Appendix 4.   [99] J. H. Swanson, 1983.

offers much of interest in its own right. It raises a number of intriguing issues, and in particular it tells us a great deal about John himself, and about how and what he thought. He is no longer the shadowy figure that he was at the outset: we see a man deeply appreciative of the achievements of the ancients and deeply admiring of the early philosophers, a man who has developed and cherished a positive concept of the 'state', and who expresses sympathy and concern for ordinary people and less than complete satisfaction with the behaviour of kings and nobles. John is interested in politics, in justice and the law, in the classical world, in the problems of family life and of urban communities. He is a firm believer in self-achievement, and shows an unusual and genuine awareness of the characteristics of youth and a considerable sympathy with this group. There is much to admire in all this, and it confirms the view that John's *Communiloquium* is not a mere hotchpotch of platitudes. Rather, it is a highly organised and very coherent text, designed for a specific purpose which it admirably meets. The conspicuous lack of contradiction in the work shows that John has coherent opinions and is expressing them with deliberation. If the *exempla* with which he illustrates his beliefs are sometimes platitudinous, this is for a sound and openly admitted reason, being due to the nature and aims of the work. John wanted to provide a useful and wide-ranging basic tool for preachers, and we can see that he succeeded.

One final point may be made. *Communiloquium* contains a total of 796 biblical citations, 1020 citations from writers earlier than AD 450 and 573 citations from writers later than AD 450. In other words, John openly refers to the authority of other books a minimum of 2,389 times. This was a startling feat, but it would be all too easy to assume that many of the *exempla* used, and indeed some of John's paragraphs and chapters, are there only for literary completeness, rather than because John saw them as relevant or important. Today it is tempting to see certain types of advice by medieval writers as mere theorising derived from earlier writings, and of no serious intent. Thus, we might describe advice on the avoidance of overlaying or miscarriage, or on the approved severity of beatings, as practical, but classifying remarks on the need for scholars to be unblemished in body as mere rhetoric. But to make this kind of distinction is wrong. To the medieval reader and writer alike it probably did not exist, and these types of advice would be given, and taken, with equal seriousness. We have a concrete example of this in the setting-up of Ave Maria College in Paris, between 1339 and 1349. The founder, John

of Hubant, actually followed the recommendations laid down in the
Didascalion by Hugh of Saint-Victor, and later repeated by John of
Wales and Vincent of Beauvais, that the students should be free from
physical deformities, of good and pleasant voice, and so on.[100] John
of Wales intended the whole of *Communiloquium* to help preachers
act as a channel for practical advice, and we should bear this in mind
when we consider its contents.

SOURCE LIST FOR *COMMUNILOQUIUM*, PARTS 4–7

I. SOURCES FROM BEFORE AD 450

Ambrose	De Officiis	2
	Hexameron	1
Apuleius	De Deo Socratis	1
Aristotle	Ethics	2
Augustine	Ad Orosium	1
	Confessions	8
	Contra Faustum	1
	Contra Iulianum	1
	De Beata Vita	1
	De Civitate Dei	22
	De Cura pro Mortuis Agenda	3
	De Doctrina Christiana	2
	De Mendacio	1
	De Penitentia[101]	1
	De Perfectione Iusticie	1
	De Quantitate Animae	1
	De Sermone Domini in Monte	6
	De Trinitate	1
	De Vera Religione	2
	Enchiridion	1
	Epistolae	6
	Sermones	1
	Super Iohannem	6
	Super Psalmos	1
Aulus Gellius	Noctes Atticae	4
Cassian	Collationes	6
Cassiodorus	Super Psalmos	1

[100] A. L. Gabriel, 1955, p. 105. [101] Now regarded as spurious.

Chrysostom	Sermones	1
	Super Mattheum[102]	5
	Super Psalmos	1
Cicero	De Officiis	3
	De Rhetorica	2
	Tusculanae Quaestiones	4
ps. – Cyprian	De Duodecim Abusionibus	3
Eusebius	Historia Ecclesiastica	4
Hegesippus	On the Jewish War	4
Jerome	Contra Iovinianum	3
	Epistolae	49
Macrobius	Saturnalia	2
Origen	Glosa	1
	Super Cantica	1
Plato	Timaeus[103]	1
Quintilian	De Institutionibus Oratorum	2
Seneca	De Beneficiis	6
	De Brevitate Vitae	1
	De Ira	1
	De Naturalibus Quaestionibus	2
	De Providentia	1
	De Tranquillitate Animi	3
	Epistulae	23
	Liber Declamationum	1
Sulpicius Severus	Dialogus de Obedientia Antiquorum Religiosorum[104]	3
Valerius Maximus	Factorum ac Dictorum Memorabilium Libri ix	11
Varro	Historia de Liberis Educandis	1

2. SOURCES FROM AFTER AD 450

Alphorabius (Al-Farabi)	De Divisione Philosophie	2
Anselm of Canterbury	De Similitudinibus	8
	Proslogion	1
Bernard of Clairvaux	De Consideratione	11
	De Gradibus Humilitatis	1
	De Preceptis	1
	Epistolae	3
	Meditationes	1

[102] Not the *Opus Imperfectum*.   [103] In the version of Chalcidius.
[104] This is the supplement to the *Life of St Martin of Tours*.

	Sermones	8
	Sermons on the Canticle	10
pseudo–Boethius	*De Disciplina Scholarium*	15
Cassiodorus	*De Institutione*	1
	Historia Tripartita	2
Dionysius	*De Divinis Nominibus*	1
Glosa		2
Gratian	*Decretum*	6
Gregory the Great	*Dialogues*	17
	Epistolae	2
	Moralia	55
	Regula Pastoralis	13
	Registrum	12
	Super Evangelia	11
	Super Ezechielem	13
Gregory IX	*Decretals*	5
Haimo of Auxerre	*Super Primo ad Corinthios*	2
Hugh of Fouilloy	*De Claustro Animae*	1
Hugh of Saint-Victor	*De Sacramentis*	22
	Didascalion	14
	Super Angelicam Hierarchiam	2
Hugo	*De Studio Orandi*[105]	1
Isaac Israeli	*De Difinitionibus*	1
Isidore	*Etymologiae*	1
John of Damascus		2
John of Salisbury	*Policraticus*	9
John of Wales	*Breviloquium de Virtutibus*	1
Papias	*Vocabularium*	2

Anon.

De Collationibus Patrum	2
Paradisus Patrum	2
Tractatus de Vita Philosophorum	2
Tractatus de Penitentia	1
Vita de Beato Augustino	1
Vita Beati Bernhardi	1
Vita Iohannis Elemosinarii	2
Vitae Patrum	30

[105] I have been unable to identify the Hugh in question.

Chapter 7

PHILOSOPHERS AND SAINTS: THE *COMPENDILOQUIUM* AND *BREVILOQUIUM DE SAPIENTIA SANCTORUM* OF JOHN OF WALES

Internal cross-references tell us that John's *Compendiloquium de Vitis Illustrium Philosophorum et de Dictis Moralibus Eorundem* was written between the *Communiloquium* and the *Breviloquium de Sapientia Sanctorum*; and it almost certainly dates from the Paris period of John's life – more specifically from the early 1270s.[1] A number of copies of the work survive: we know of at least 27 MSS.[2] The work was also printed four times, in combination with others of John's works,[3] and an edition was prepared in 1655 by Luke Wadding, together with an edition of the *Breviloquium de Sapientia Sanctorum*.[4]

The key to the work lies in its title: the lives and moral sayings of illustrious philosophers. The reader who is already acquainted with John's work, and opens this treatise, will find himself in an easily recognisable world. It is noteworthy that John's interest lies in *philosophers* rather than in *philosophy*. That he produced this work at all indicates that he had a personal fascination with philosophers, and as one progresses through the work it is easy to see why. W. A. Pantin once remarked that John's philosophers emerged as curiously similar to the ideal friar.[5] Beryl Smalley later suggested that the likeness was the other way about.[6] Whichever way it went, the likeness is strong. John's choice of subject represents both its appeal to his personal taste and his belief that the lives of the philosophers offered a lesson to the medieval Christian.

[1] See above, p. 6.
[2] See Appendices 2 and 3.
[3] J. V. Scholderer, 1941.
[4] *Florilegium Iohannis Guallensis*, ed. Luke Wadding (Rome, 1655).
[5] W. A. Pantin, 1961, p. 301.
[6] B. Smalley, 1963, p. 66.

Study of the *Communiloquium* contributes to knowledge of the breadth of materials available to John and his capacity to use them, and helps with the attempt to date his sequence of works.[7] A short study of the work was published over a century ago, by A. Charma of Paris.[8] Charma did not think highly of John, for he observed: 'We have here a striking example of the intellectual sterility of the age from which *Communiloquium* dates.' Times have changed, and modern scholars are far less ready to dismiss the latter part of the thirteenth century as intellectually sterile.[9]

Compendiloquium opens with a description of how bees make honey by gathering nectar from flowers. In imitation of the bees, says John, we gather here flowers, namely the sayings and doings of philosophers, distinguishing between them and being wary of the noxious. Because of this it is not incongruous that the work be called the *Florilegium de Vitis et Dictis Illustrium Philosophorum*. John then explains the reasons for his choice of topic:

Because by the life of the Gentiles the life of those under the law is rebuked, and by the deeds of secular men the deeds of religious are confounded, since the latter promise but do not carry out what they receive as precepts, and the former in their lives keep even those things to which they are by no means bound by legal obligation . . . therefore I have thought fit to collect here the notable sayings of the philosophers and imitable examples of virtuous men, although I am ignorant of philosophy, lacking in philosophical perfection and unskilled in speech, in order to stimulate and incite the young, to instruct them, to induce among those who wish to imitate the said philosophers a salutary shame that leads to glory, to repress the elation of an arrogant heart, and to encourage humility in perfect men, so that although they do great and difficult things for God, they be not puffed up, when they hear and read of the Gentiles doing perfect things (in so far as these can be perfect without faith working through love) and bearing much for honour and human glory.[10]

John then quotes approving comments by St Augustine on the trials sustained by the Roman people on behalf of the Republic, and by Chrysostom upon the good that the Greek philosophers did for humanity, before repeating that these words and sayings are gathered not from presumption or mere curiosity, but for spiritual edification and avoiding of noxious errors and useless opinions.

[7] See in particular pp. 7–10, 24–36.
[8] A. Charma, 1866, pp. 119–34.
[9] An edition of parts of *Compendiloquium* is being prepared by Frau Monika Rappenecker of Tübingen University.
[10] W. A. Pantin, 1961, p. 309, provides the translation.

Thus there is censorship at work: John is only giving us what he thinks is useful or good. John further defends his right to use philosophy at all, by telling us of other sacred doctors who have used secular philosophy on behalf of the church. There are, says John, truths in the books of the Gentiles, which God revealed to them out of his great goodness. Therefore they can be used to illuminate the spirit and to express and testify to and confirm the truths contained in holy scripture. This is the main line of his argument in the prologue, supported by comments from Cicero and Seneca, Augustine and Jerome. We can clearly see that John is aware of the argument against the use by Christians of pagan writings, but he has prepared a coherent defence, and gives no indication that he has any personal doubts about what he is doing. This is in keeping with his abundant use of pagan and ancient works in his own writings.

We now turn to the main section of the book. The first part is concerned with definitions of philosophy and its general usefulness. John begins by telling us that philosophy has been described in a variety of ways, giving examples drawn from Seneca, Augustine, Boethius, Peter Damian, Hugh of Saint-Victor, Alphorabius (Al-Farabi) and Gundisalvus.[11] He then picks out the 'true' definition – *philosophia* is *amor sapientie*, love of wisdom – and lists a number of authorities who share this definition. Next he tells us about the divisions of philosophy.[12] As differing definitions of philosophy may be accepted in various ways, so may differing schemes of division, for example *moralis, naturalis* and *rationalis*, or *mathematica, physica* and *theologia*. John describes various sets of divisions and then uses parallel definitions to show that the two groups mentioned here are in fact equivalent. He goes on to establish that philosophy is more notable than other *scientiae*, and observes that philosophers call philosophy the study of virtue.

His third chapter deals with the symbolic description of philosophy as a woman, and explains that the *vir scholasticus* ought to pledge himself to her, because she is worthy.[13] This is supported by the next chapter, which tells of the worth and honour of philosophy among the ancients.[14] The reader should note, says John (referring to the *Policraticus* of John of Salisbury), that ancient philosophers were accustomed to paint the image of Wisdom before all the

[11] *Compendiloq.* I.I.
[12] *Compendiloq.* I.2.
[13] John takes this from Boethius, *De Consolatione Philosophiae*.
[14] *Compendiloq.* I.4.

temples. Seneca tells us that philosophy was held sacred and that those in search of it set aside worldly wealth and abandoned all carnal pleasures. And Alexander the Great, having conquered the whole world, still preferred to excel in philosophy. Philosophy is worthy of all respect, because without it and its leadership, men would have no temporal good.[15] Therefore it is worthy to acquire or desire philosophy.

We learn more about the uses and advantages of philosophy in the following chapters. First we hear of its spiritual advantages: it invigorates the languid mind, acts as a medication for the sick mind and prepares the mind for the virtues.[16] Next we hear that it is particularly useful in regulating human life.[17] It is as valuable in directing an entire republic as in regulating a family or in guiding an individual life. John mentions ancient statesmen who were philosophers – Solon and Themistocles – and ancient rulers who followed the custom of keeping a philosopher by them – Alexander and Aristotle, Nero and Seneca, Trajan and Pliny. He then quotes various sources on how philosophy helps to govern the three units of state, family and individual.

John's seventh chapter covers the acquisition of philosophy, how it ought to be used, and how taught. He tells us that it is acquired by earnest study, the setting aside of leisure, exclusive occupation in subtle investigation, and so on. The requirements of philosophy teachers are also discussed, and John cites the fourfold grouping of *amor* and *labor*, *cura* and *vigilia*.[18] Only a few, he says, can acquire true philosophy. Finally he recommends pseudo-Boethius' *De Disciplina Scholarium* and his own *Communiloquium* as sources for the proper behaviour of pupils.

This leads John to the ancient belief that philosophy could be used to correct *mores*.[19] He gives the opinions of various philosophers on the ultimate good and points out that different sects of philosophers held different views. He then tells us in detail of the proper use of philosophy.[20] As we might deduce from his previous chapters, this is indeed the correction of morals and the acquisition of blessedness. It is not enough to understand or to discourse in philosophy – one ought also to do, so that one may become a true philosopher. John quotes Matthew 5: 'he who does as he teaches, will stand high'. A

---

[15] This is interesting because it indicates that John felt that philosophy could have a practical function.
[16] *Compendiloq.* 1.5. [17] *Compendiloq.* 1.6. [18] From Hugh of Saint-Victor.
[19] *Compendiloq.* 1.8. [20] *Compendiloq.* 1.9.

counterbalance to this detailing of the correct use of philosophy is then provided, as John goes on to discuss the wrongful applications to which philosophy may be put.[21] He lists the use of philosophy merely to find things out rather than to acquire virtue, or to please others rather than to improve their *mores*. He mentions failure to love philosophy, its use to seek the high opinions of others, to seem wise to oneself and to please oneself alone.

This, says John, is enough about philosophy in general. He turns at once to the second part of his work, and becomes more specific about the philosophers as a group. He begins by confirming the definition of ancient philosophers as lovers of wisdom, telling the reader that from the time of Pythagoras the term *sapientes* had been applied to these wise men.[22] Then he turns to Augustine and tells us that there is no real virtue unless it is shaped by charity, no real philosophy unless it is operated by faith and directed by love, and no real philosopher unless he is a lover of the true God. In a sense this is an idle observation, for although it is doctrinally correct, it is clear that the philosophers, philosophy and virtue to be found in the ancient and pagan world were real enough to have fired John's enthusiasm and commanded his respect. John provides a form of escape for himself by observing at the end of the chapter that Plato wished a philosopher to be a lover of God. The idea that Plato and his followers were virtually Christian in outlook was first formulated in Augustine's *De Civitate Dei*, and further propagated when Boethius' *De Consolatione Philosophiae* presented the *Timaeus* in a manner which reminded medieval Christian readers of the book of Genesis.[23]

The profession of philosophy, John claims, lies in contempt for and setting aside of the worldly, in desire for and diligent study of wisdom, in honest life and conversation, and in bending philosophy to the correction of *mores*.[24] John quotes from Cicero and Seneca that it was not in their virtue or in their faith but in their mode of living that philosophers were recognised to be noble. Who, he says, takes on even the shadow of those virtues which we see to have flourished amongst the Gentiles, although they, without Christ, were not able to pluck the true fruit of blessedness? Who imitates the diligence of Themistocles, the gravity of Fronto, the continence of Socrates, the faith of Fabritius, the innocence of Numa, the modesty of Scipio, the longanimity of Ulysses, the economy of Cato, the piety of Titus?

[21] *Compendiloq.* 1.10.
[22] *Compendiloq.* 2.1.
[23] See R. Klibansky, 1939.
[24] *Compendiloq.* 2.2.

These, and other similarly great and praiseworthy men, shone like stars in their ages, and illuminated their times. And they were thus although they did not know the Lord Jesus Christ.

John goes on to tell us of the costume of philosophers and of the insignia of their profession.[25] He describes four things which are a distinctive part of the philosopher's dress – a cloak, a staff, a ring and an abundance of hair. These are signs of honour, rulership, magistracy and mature strength respectively. (This description of the archetypal wise man has retained its force into the twentieth century, as we can see from Tolkien's Gandalf.) John, having described the 'habit' of a philosopher, says that there were many who wore it without living the true philosophical life. He gives some examples from Aulus Gellius, and adds that false philosophers were detested among the true philosophers because they sullied their good name, just as false Christians and clerics, religious and doctors are hated by holy men because they defile a most illustrious name. John does indeed seem to have formed a parallel between philosophy as a lifestyle and some of the religious orders of his own day. One thinks particularly of his own order, the Franciscans. Others besides John had observed the resemblance: we know that the future Archbishop Pecham, in his young days, was first attracted to the Franciscan friars by their resemblance to the ancient philosophers.[26] The perception of such resemblances was perhaps inevitable, even if we disregard such points as the supposedly simple clothing and ascetic lifestyle of the ancient philosophers. To John and his fellows, it seemed that ancient philosophers not only practised virtue, but also proselytised on its behalf. In their own, medieval, period these were two activities which were particularly the province of those religious orders which were not confined within monastery walls.

The first two parts of *Compendiloquium* are carefully structured, and clear chapter headings follow one another in a rational and linked sequence, as in the *Breviloquium de Virtutibus* and the *Communiloquium*. John's urge to educate is clearly discernible: it is entirely characteristic of his style that, before we approach the illustrious philosophers who are his main topic, we must have thoroughly explained to us the meaning and nature of philosophy, its high status and the reasons for this, the good that philosophy can achieve and the harm that it can lead to if improperly approached. Similarly this must be followed by careful definition of philosophers, their general approach to philosophy and their distinguish-

[25] *Compendiloq.* 2.3.   [26] D. L. Douie, 1952, pp. 5–6.

ing features. Only then does John deem us ready to approach individual examples of the class and to appreciate their importance. In no place are we expected to take John's opinion for granted, for he consistently cites a large range of sources and is quite prepared to note differing attitudes and to help his reader to correlate and comprehend them. This thoroughness must have been of great value to many of John's readers. Even a man whose study of philosophy was non-existent or long in the past would be able to follow the argument and feel that he approached the core of the work with some understanding of the background.

So what could John's medieval reader learn from the third part of *Compendiloquium*? John begins by explaining that there were two races of philosophers: Italians from Magna Graecia and Ionians from what is now called Greece.[27] Among the Ionians the chief was Thales Milesius, one of the seven known as the *sapientes*, who were distinguished by their excellent mode of life, and were the most spoken of and the most illustrious of their times. As a source of information John recommends Augustine's *De Civitate Dei*, book 8. He discusses the significance of the number seven, the ancient respect for the term 'wisdom' (*sapientia*), and the humility of the ancient *sapientes*. He comments briefly on the succession of early philosophers, and then turns to his biographies of noteworthy individuals.

The first of these is the Athenian Solon, giver of laws. John uses stories from five ancient authors to illustrate how studious Solon was, how he used his wisdom for the benefit of others by establishing laws, and how modest he was in putting forward the laws among discord.[28] Wise Christians, says John, ought to imitate him in these things.

Next John deals with Anaxagoras, pupil of 'Aneximes'.[29] He is described as contemptuous of worldly things, patient in adversity, aware of the mortality of man and untroubled by the death either of his son or of himself. Again John commends him as a model for the Christian philosopher. These biographies are brief, but they set a pattern by indicating the kinds of virtue which John sees as typified by philosophers, and indeed the kinds of virtue which he hopes to commend to his audience. John gives a much more detailed description of these in the life of Diogenes, which occupies the next fourteen chapters of the work.

[27] *Compendiloq.* 3.1.1. [28] *Compendiloq.* 3.1.2.
[29] *Compendiloq.* 3.1.3. John must mean Aneximines here.

He begins by telling us that Diogenes was a pupil of Aneximes at the same time as Anaxagoras, and by claiming for Diogenes the belief that air was the stuff of all matter, and that things were formed from it by divine reason. John quotes from Jerome on how philosophers despised wealth and retained only wisdom and virtue.[30] Diogenes was inspired by his teacher to abandon all his possessions, with great benefit to himself.[31] John describes Diogenes' physical austerity: he lived in a barrel, and at one time possessed a cup. Then he saw a boy drinking from his hands, and threw the cup away in favour of this more natural method. John also describes how Diogenes patiently underwent death. He explains how Diogenes was more powerful than Alexander, the conqueror of all nations, because Alexander could give him nothing.[32] Because of this, Diogenes gave many thanks to his teacher, who made him poor.

John elaborates upon this point in a special chapter.[33] According to Seneca it is pleasanter and easier not to acquire money than to give it away, therefore those who look back on a fortune are more blessed because they have worked harder for their poor status. If anyone doubts the happiness of Diogenes, he must be able to doubt the existence of the immortal gods. Diogenes, with a single servant, was happier than Pompey, who had many. John further tells us that when this single servant ran away Diogenes refused to seek him out.[34] He praises Diogenes' generosity in refusing to seek out one who did not wish to live with him. He also tells us that Diogenes used to dispute as to whether the life of the king of Persia was more fortunate than his own, and would conclude that he himself was the better-off, because he lacked the desire for pleasure which the king was unable to satisfy in himself.

The emphasis changes somewhat in the next chapters, for John proceeds to tell us of Diogenes' patience in suffering insults and pain.[35] He was steadfast in opposing the vices, industrious in teaching others; he remained constant to his own way and refused adulation.[36] He also had compassion for the suffering of others.[37] Later chapters provide a selection of his sayings, and discuss his deserved fame and honour.[38] These were deserved on account of his many virtues (as far as he could possess these virtues without divine

[30] *Compendiloq.* 3.2.1.
[31] *Compendiloq.* 3.2.2.
[32] *Compendiloq.* 3.2.3.
[33] *Compendiloq.* 3.2.4.
[34] *Compendiloq.* 3.2.5.
[35] *Compendiloq.* 3.2.6–8.
[36] *Compendiloq.* 3.2.9–10.
[37] *Compendiloq.* 3.2.11.
[38] *Compendiloq.* 3.2.12–14.

grace). Not everything which commends him is gathered here, says John, yet, despite his lack of divine grace, faithful philosophers ought to be stimulated to imitate him in the deeds described.

Socrates, so the first chapter of distinction 3 tells us, was wondrous in philosophy and in the philosophic virtues, and was known as the Prince of Philosophy and judged the wisest by the Apolline oracle. John discusses the nature of that spirit which associated with Socrates and helped him – his daemon. This had been with him since boyhood, not to urge him on to do things, but to forbid him to do things which were not advantageous. John also gives information from Valerius Maximus on Socrates' parents and origins.

Socrates was most industrious, and strove to acquire wisdom even in old age.[39] And although he was so wise, he always believed himself ignorant. Note, says John, that continual study, internal humility and long life produce wisdom. Socrates is further described as a miracle of chastity, justice and other virtues.[40] For this heroic eminence he was honoured and declared to be greater than a man. From Aulus Gellius John draws illustrations of Socrates' virtues, describing his sobriety and how he would stand rooted to the spot day and night, lost in thought. His amazing patience is illustrated by his calm acceptance of a death sentence from the Thirty Tyrants, and by his earlier endurance of persecution from his wife and family, without losing his temper with them.[41] Although he occasionally felt anger, he strove hard to subdue it, and overcame it by the use of reason.[42] And, just as he was unbowed by the injuries caused by man, so he was unbowed by the inconveniences of poverty, because he was contemptuous of all worldly things, like other philosophers.[43] And indeed he was much more so, being the first among philosophers. He refused gold and silver when they were offered, and did not even particularly seek necessities. He was also contemptuous of secular pomp.[44]

We next read of the usefulness of Socrates' doctrine.[45] He was kind and generous in remitting debts and charged the poor nothing to hear him, for he desired not money but the perfect pupil. All this shows that he was well suited to teach others. Seneca tells us that men believe their eyes more than their ears, and indeed Plato and Aristotle and others gained more from the habits of Socrates than

[39] *Compendiloq.* 3.3.2.
[40] *Compendiloq.* 3.3.3.
[41] *Compendiloq.* 3.3.4–5.
[42] *Compendiloq.* 3.3.6.
[43] *Compendiloq.* 3.3.7.
[44] *Compendiloq.* 3.3.8.
[45] *Compendiloq.* 3.3.9.

from his words. Socrates showed particular correctness in judge-ment.[46] He felt that men should be preferred not for the prominence of outward goodness but for the presence of inward good qualities, such as wisdom and virtue. He judged the gods unworthy of honour and suffered death as a consequence of this opinion.[47] He spoke out against oracles and against appeals to the gods; he refused to advise a young man against matrimony; and when his wife complained that he was about to perish although innocent, he replied that it was better to die innocent than guilty.[48] John gives the reader these and other examples to illustrate the wisdom of Socrates' advice. He closes the section by telling of Socrates' bearing through imprison-ment and death, of a dream he had before death, of the honour shown to him after his death and of the punishment of his accusers.[49] He tells us that Socrates reached the age of 94, that he had no fondness for tombs, and that he was born in the age of Xerxes.[50] Finally John distinguishes him from two other eminent men named Socrates, who were an orator and a historian respectively.[51] These later chapters seem inconsequential, and perhaps reflect the degree of John's fascination with details of the lives of his philosophers.

A specific set of characteristics emerges as an integral part of John's views on ancient philosophers. The philosophers possess great learning and great humility. They are enthusiastic about teaching, and share John of Wales' own view that teaching by example is the best method, and that it is more useful to hear something explained than to read about it in a book. They exhibit great sobriety and patience, they favour poverty in a very positive way, and they have no fears where death is concerned. There is much here for a friar to find admirable, and John was not the only one to feel the attraction. Nor were Diogenes and Socrates the only examples which John was able to describe in detail in this mould, as we can easily see if we continue our analysis of *Compendiloquium*.

In *Compendiloquium*, the twenty chapters on Socrates are followed by seventeen on Plato. He emerges as another great man, but somehow a more fallible one. John begins with some intriguing biographical details, including the suggestions that Plato's mother had been impregnated by Apollo, or that he had been a virgin birth.[52] His father was descended from Solon, and his mother gave birth to him after a divine vision. He was named Aristocles, but

---

[46] *Compendiloq.* 3.3.10.   [47] *Compendiloq.* 3.3.11.   [48] *Compendiloq.* 3.3.12.
[49] *Compendiloq.* 3.3.14–16.   [50] *Compendiloq.* 3.3.17–19.   [51] *Compendiloq.* 3.3.20.
[52] *Compendiloq.* 3.4.1.

became known as Plato because of the breadth of his chest.[53] He studied philosophy in Egypt and in Italy, and once wrote plays, before Socrates humbled him out of it.[54] He made three trips to Sicily at the request of the tyrant Dionysius, and at one point was sold into slavery as a result of quarrelling with this ruler.[55]

After giving us this information, John turns to Plato's virtues. He tells us of Plato's abstinence and his mortification of carnal lusts, his labours, his long life and his diligence into old age.[56] He claimed that philosophers should desire death because it freed the soul from the body, and John observes that this shows how Plato's ideas agreed with apostolic and evangelical doctrine. He states that Plato was perfect in his contempt of all wordly things, adding the usual proviso 'as far as he could be'.[57] John also tells of Plato's struggle to conquer his internal passions, particularly anger.[58] He was modest in his conversation and acts, thus setting an example of virtue to his pupils.[59] He also showed proper gratitude for benefits given to him.[60]

John's tenth chapter tells how true Plato was in his doctrine – as far as he could be – and how close he was to the truth of holy scripture in his teaching. He said that the fate of man was to live in pursuit of virtue, and he believed in a single god who made the heavens and the earth. John now uses calculation and commonsense to refute the claim that Plato could have heard the prophet Jeremiah or read the prophetic writings of the Septuagint, on the grounds that the dates do not correspond.[61] John mentions Augustine's claim to have found parts of the Gospel in works by Plato, and observes that the words and deeds of the philosophers did have much in common with the Gospel.[62] This leads naturally into a chapter on Plato's sayings and eloquence. John tells the reader that the true worth of Plato's words and works shows in those who praise him.[63] He then gives a number of examples of Plato's 'moral and preachable sayings', including comments on the need to guard and preserve the state, on self-control, on the role of God in promoting good, and so on. John further observes that Plato's books contained certain irregularities – for example, the idea that women should be held in common,[64] or

[53] *Compendiloq.* 3.4.2.   [54] *Compendiloq.* 3.4.3.   [55] *Compendiloq.* 3.4.4.
[56] *Compendiloq.* 3.4.5.   [57] *Compendiloq.* 3.4.6.   [58] *Compendiloq.* 3.4.7.
[59] *Compendiloq.* 3.4.8.   [60] *Compendiloq.* 3.4.9.   [61] *Compendiloq.* 3.4.11.
[62] *Compendiloq.* 3.4.12.   [63] *Compendiloq.* 3.4.13.
[64] For discussion of how medieval writers coped with this idea, see S. Kuttner, 1976, pp. 93–118.

that the first among the men in strength, and the best warriors, should have the best sons and daughters. John tells us that Plato was most anxious to possess the books of others, although he was so wise, but that he still thought it better to hear teachers than to read books.[65] John tells us that Plato lived to be 81, and that he was so respected that it was disputed whether he was a god.[66] He closes this section by advising the reader to note how worthy of imitation Plato's words and deeds were.[67]

So Plato also could be made to fit John's pattern for the worthy philosopher, despite the irregularity of some of his ideas. John's mention of these irregularities shows that he is capable of expressing a negative opinion, though in all fairness we should note that he rarely does so, but prefers simply to ignore those things which do not meet with his approval.

The next of John's individual philosophers is Aristotle. This is the last of the lengthy biographies in *Compendiloquium*. It begins with a summary of Aristotle's life. We are told that he came from Stagira in Thrace and traced his descent back to Aesculapius. He was introduced to medicine and philosophy by his father, and was a young man already skilled in the arts and eloquence, and the author of several works, when he came to Athens and became attached to Plato. He remained with Plato until the latter died, after twenty years, and flourished for a further 34 years, partly teaching Alexander and travelling with him, partly writing books and partly teaching others. Alexander's parents held him in such honour that they had a statue made of him. He was most powerful in their kingdom and did much for the king. He was able to obtain benefits from Alexander for both Stagira and Athens, and the citizens of both places were grateful.

John rejects the view that Aristotle contradicted or opposed Plato, claiming that this view is due to a misunderstanding.[68] In fact Aristotle had a great affection for Plato and even consecrated an altar to him. John tells us that Aristotle was moderate in all his opinions, and believed that one ought to consider before making pronounce-

---

[65] *Compendiloq.* 3.4.14–15.
[66] *Compendiloq.* 3.4.16.
[67] John has not taken this life wholesale from any previous author, but has compiled it using extracts from more than twenty writers, including Augustine, Jerome, Cicero, Valerius Maximus, John of Salisbury, Pliny, Macrobius, Seneca, Origen, Boethius, Aulus Gellius, Isaac ben Miram and Plato himself. John also used the *Suda* here.
[68] *Compendiloq.* 3.5.4.

ments.[69] He claims that Aristotle lived for 63 years, studying under both Socrates and Plato, and that he died in Chalcidice, leaving a son, various notable pupils and a thousand written works.[70] We can see that not all John's information was entirely correct, but we must remember that he was at the mercy of his sources.

Following the pattern already established in the work, John now discusses Aristotle's distinctive qualities. He was a man of singular spirit, also studious, moderate and temperate.[71] He was a pre-eminent philosopher, who knew all the parts of philosophy and gave precepts to each.[72] Some thought him a son of the devil because of his accomplishments, and he delighted in having a familiar spirit. He was skilful and industrious in teaching his pupils, teaching them according to their capacity and at different times.[73] He gave two forms of teaching: *exotericae*, dealing with rhetoric, argument and civic affairs, and *acromaticae*, where those more eminent in philosophy considered the things pertaining to dialectic. The latter group worked in the mornings and the former in the evenings, and the teaching technique was very effective.

John tells us that Aristotle was also studious in his approach to the natural world.[74] He understood many things thoroughly and described them in books.[75] And, although he was so great a philosopher, he did not despise the work of others.[76] John quotes Alexander Nequam's claim that many of Aristotle's most subtle books had been entombed with him, and that the tomb was protected by some magical art, but he seems a trifle dubious about it.[77] John also says that Aristotle had some desire for fame and glory, before going on to discuss his moral sayings and his discretion in counsel and in teaching Alexander.[78] His devotion to his pupil Alexander is illustrated by an exciting tale of how he saved Alexander from a girl steeped in snake venom, in whose embrace he would surely have died.[79]

Aristotle is also praised for his concern towards the state, as shown in his books, which dealt with politics, government, and examples of how people were to live in the *respublica*.[80] John claims that

[69] *Compendiloq.* 3.5.5.
[70] *Compendiloq.* 3.5.7.
[71] *Compendiloq.* 3.5.8.
[72] *Compendiloq.* 3.5.9.
[73] *Compendiloq.* 3.5.10. John seems to mean that separate classes, based on ability, were taught at different hours.
[74] *Compendiloq.* 3.5.11.
[75] *Compendiloq.* 3.5.12.
[76] *Compendiloq.* 3.5.13.
[77] *Compendiloq.* 3.5.14.
[78] *Compendiloq.* 3.5.15–16.
[79] *Compendiloq.* 3.5.17.
[80] *Compendiloq.* 3.5.18.

Aristotle found poverty inconvenient because it prevented him from helping others, and commends him for his wise judgement in selecting Theophrastus as his successor.[81] Finally he comes to Aristotle's death, in a chapter which tells some of the more far-fetched versions of this and claims disbelief in them.[82]

This, says John, is enough of Aristotle.[83] He proceeds to give a number of short chapters, mainly on other pupils of Plato, before leaving the Ionian philosophers and turning to Pythagoras. He commends Apuleius for the many beautiful *sententiae* to be found in his *De Deo Socratis*, and tells us that Speusippos succeeded Plato.[84] Xenocrates is praised for his 'philosophic virtues' – despising wealth, mortifying the flesh, being modest and tranquil and reluctant to believe that anyone would speak ill of him – and also praised for his efficiency in teaching.[85] Phaedo's transition from slave to philosopher is mentioned, with appropriate comment on how he was always free in spirit.[86] Theophrastus, successor to Aristotle, is described as a distinguished and eloquent philosopher.[87]

Now John discusses Pythagoras, whom he describes as the founder of the Italian philosophers, and the first to call himself a philosopher rather than a *sapiens*.[88] John tells us that this man was born in Samos, the son of a rich merchant, and that he refused to go into business, but instead travelled widely and learned much.[89] His authority is shown by such things as his founding of Italian philosophy and his great reputation after his death.[90] He was so famed for justice that Cicero tells us that some people believed him to be King Numa. We learn from Aulus Gellius of the honesty of his life with his pupils, and of how they held everything in common.[91] He was wise and industrious in selecting his pupils and in teaching those he accepted. These latter he ordered to be silent for a certain time, according to his estimate of their ingenuity, but never for less than two years. During this period they listened to what was said by the others. John also tells us of Pythagoras' zeal and concern in correcting others, as when he tackled the problems of the town of Croton.[92]

---

[81] *Compendiloq.* 3.5.19. [82] *Compendiloq.* 3.5.20.

[83] Again John has used a number of sources, including works by John of Salisbury, Peter Comestor, Cicero, Valerius Maximus, Avicenna, Rabbi Moyses, Aulus Gellius, Pliny, Papias, Alexander Nequam, Jerome, Macrobius and Vincent of Beauvais. He also refers to the *Secreta Secretorum*. [84] *Compendiloq.* 3.5.21.

[85] *Compendiloq.* 3.5.22. [86] *Compendiloq.* 3.5.23.

[87] *Compendiloq.* 3.5.25. [88] *Compendiloq.* 3.6.1.

[89] *Compendiloq.* 3.6.2. [90] *Compendiloq.* 3.6.3.

[91] *Compendiloq.* 3.6.4. [92] *Compendiloq.* 3.6.5.

He was also experienced in calming troubled men, as when he pacified some drunken youths who had attacked women.[93]

We learn in chapter 7 of how Pythagoras discovered music when the ringing sounds of a smith's hammer blows caught his attention during a disputation, and that after this the Pythagoreans used singing to induce tranquillity. John describes some of Pythagoras' beliefs and quotes the praise given him by Cicero and Seneca.[94] He tells us how his pupils deservedly advanced under him, in wisdom and habits and philosophical lifestyle, and of how the single habitation and the shared possessions and doctrinal beliefs caused the Pythagoreans to love each other so much that one was prepared to die for another.[95] He also discusses Pythagorean error: due to Pythagoras' lack of the grace of faith, he believed that the soul transferred from body to body and was immortal.[96] John debates whether Pythagoras was contemptuous of the gods, and concludes that he probably was, in that he was opposed to sacrifice.[97] Finally we hear of the philosopher's death and of his home's subsequent conversion into a temple, where he was worshipped.[98]

This marks the end of the third part of *Compendiloquium*. The fourth part comprises brief chapters on sixteen other philosophers whom John found noteworthy, for the following reasons.

Carneades, fellow-ambassador with Diogenes, is commended for great age and continuing devotion to philosophy, and for his habit of purging himself with hellebore before tackling his opponents.[99] Demosthenes was greatly opposed to fleshly lusts and to the idea that money defended sins.[100] Of Isocrates, John can only cite a cool response to a jest by friends, and he is further forced to admit that some attribute this reply to Isocrates the orator rather than Isocrates the philosopher.[101] Democritus receives praise for having inherited enormous wealth but given most of it to his *patria*, seeking for himself anonymity in which to study.[102] Hippocrates, again, was opposed to passion and required his pupils to take an oath of silence before teaching them.[103] Demetrius of Phaleron wrote most learnedly on the Republic but was expelled by an ungrateful citizenry, taking refuge in Alexandria.[104] He also despised the

[93] *Compendiloq.* 3.6.6.
[94] *Compendiloq.* 3.6.8.
[95] *Compendiloq.* 3.6.9.
[96] *Compendiloq.* 3.6.10.
[97] *Compendiloq.* 3.6.11.
[98] *Compendiloq.* 3.6.12.
[99] *Compendiloq.* 4.1.
[100] *Compendiloq.* 4.2.
[101] *Compendiloq.* 4.3.
[102] *Compendiloq.* 4.4.
[103] *Compendiloq.* 4.5.
[104] *Compendiloq.* 4.6.

worldly and was steady in his labours and in sustaining insults. Zeno greatly despised worldly things and was very constant: he went through all tortures before giving evidence against fellow-conspirators in a plot to kill a tyrant.[105] His life was moderate and honest, but he erred in believing *voluptas* to be unimportant.

Of Taurus we are told that he became a Stoic, who underwent pain patiently and without complaint.[106] The Stoics, John explains, had no fear of death, although without the help of divine grace their understanding was imperfect. Publius Mimus was a charming and learned man who wrote sentences most useful for addressing the community.[107] Favorinus is said to have strongly opposed the practice of women sending their children out to be fostered, and to have had success in persuading them that a baby should be fed on its mother's own milk.[108] Favorinus was also able to explain the workings of the stomach and the reasons for loss of appetite, and helped Virgil to polish up and edit his verses.[109]

John then discusses Chilon, who debated to the end of his life whether at any time something could be done against justice or custom, on behalf of a friend.[110] In reply John quoted Cicero on conflicting loyalty to a friend and to the state, and his conclusion that arms should not be taken up against the state on behalf of a friend. Theophrastus is also quoted on this topic of conflicting loyalties. The chapter confirms the impression given by John's *Breviloquium de Virtutibus* and part one of his *Communiloquium*, that the state must take priority in any conflict of loyalties.

John also speaks highly of Cicero, of his studiousness and dutifulness, of how distinguished his knowledge was, of how many works he wrote.[111] He is described as most anxious for the health of the state, as cautious and discreet, as useful in warnings and correct in judgement, as fluent in speechmaking. Similar praise is awarded to Seneca, and, again, John cites that author's own works as proof.[112] John observes that some condemned him for vulgarity of speech, but that he was a faithful guardian of virtue and therefore highly regarded. The last of these individual philosophers is Boethius, Consul of Rome during the invasion of the Goths.[113] Again, his own

[105] *Compendiloq.* 4.7.
[106] *Compendiloq.* 4.8.
[107] *Compendiloq.* 4.10.
[108] *Compendiloq.* 4.11. John wrote in opposition to fostering in his *Communiloquium*.
[109] *Compendiloq.* 4.12–13.
[110] *Compendiloq.* 4.15.
[111] *Compendiloq.* 4.16.
[112] *Compendiloq.* 4.17.
[113] *Compendiloq.* 4.18. For other medieval writers on Boethius, see P. Courcelle, 1967.

works are described as proof of his wisdom, especially in theology. We are also told that he opposed Theodoric's plan to make Rome a tyranny, and was imprisoned as a consequence.

These lives do indeed confirm W. A. Pantin's and Miss Smalley's observation of an implicit parallel between the friars and the philosophers, the latter group possessing between them all the requisite virtues and characteristics, with the exception of faith. John's admiration of, and probable identification with, the philosophers may be highly significant, and may help explain some of his attitudes, in particular to political involvement and to tyranny. The first part of his *Communiloquium*, which discusses the state and kingship, showed that he thought highly of the state and felt it necessary and right that wise men should put their knowledge at the disposal of the state.[114] He also deemed it appropriate that a tyrant should be punished by death, defining as a tyrant any king who failed in his duty to the state and the people. John goes so far as to say that there is no blame in committing such a killing, thus going a little further than John of Salisbury's *Policraticus*, which was his own source, at least in part.[115]

Beryl Smalley has speculated as to how the medieval moralists reconciled the detachment of ancient sages with the Christian doctrine of involvement, and how they could admire the life the sages led.[116] The philosophers' lives quoted by John answer the question for us, at least as far as he is concerned. He did not have to reconcile the philosophy of detachment with his own Christian ideals, because he did not perceive a conflict. He does not see his philosophers as withdrawn from their obligations to state and society, but only as withdrawn from the trappings of honour and wealth and display and from irrelevant bustle and festivities. This is established from the outset of the biographical sections of *Compendiloquium*, where John tells us how Solon used his wisdom to bring good law to Athens in a time of trouble. Diogenes went on an embassy to Rome on behalf of his city; Socrates was killed by tyrants for his beliefs; Plato was sold into slavery after quarrelling with the Sicilian tyrant Dionysius; and Aristotle was active in Macedonia and showed concern for the state by negotiating with Alexander on behalf of Athens. Both these latter also wrote on the state and on politics. Pythagoras tackled the difficulties of the town of Croton and would not stand by while women were being molested. Car-

[114] See above, p. 63–106.   [115] See above, pp. 63–106.
[116] B. Smalley, 1963, pp. 66–7.

neades was also an ambassador; Zeno conspired against a tyrant, albeit unsuccessfully; and Cicero was active in the state and anxious for its health and safety. Finally, Boethius was a Roman consul and was imprisoned for opposing tyranny.

The men we are shown in these lives are frequently represented as men of action and responsibility, not only politically but also in a social sense. For example, John represents several of them as using their powers of persuasion to sway others from a life of vice. The philosophers are also represented as favouring the state and as coming off worst as a consequence of their individual oppositions to tyranny. This latter must have made a major contribution to John's acceptance of active opposition to tyranny.

In this respect, John's image of philosophers contrasts strongly with that of men like Peter Abelard, who believed that the perfect philosophic existence required the withdrawn, contemplative life of an anchorite, and who drew a parallel between the virtues of monks and those of philosophers, including withdrawal from the world.[117] Abelard, who became a monk himself, equated philosophers with the monastic ideal. Perhaps it is not surprising that John of Wales, as a friar, compared his philosopher heroes to a different model and interpreted their lives in a different light. His vision of the philosophers as politically and socially aware and active fits well with our impression of him as someone personally interested in these themes. He would probably have expected the good friar, like his philosophers, to have opinions about political and social ills, and to be prepared to oppose what was seen as wrong. All the evidence indicates that John lived up to this ideal. He wrote about the limitations on kingly power, and upon the desirability of a more flexible social structure. He went on an embassy to Wales on behalf of Archbishop Pecham – showing practical involvement in political affairs. There are clear parallels here with many of the philosophers whose lives he summarised in *Compendiloquium*. As far as we know, he did not achieve imprisonment for his political beliefs, but his transfer to Paris soon after the height of the baronial controversy may represent a prudent withdrawal from England.

The impressions produced by these philosophers' lives are only confirmed when we study part 5 of John's *Compendiloquium*. Here John re-groups and discusses the perfections of philosophers, using the philosophers to illustrate the virtues, rather than the other way

[117] J. Jolivet, 1980.

about. The following topics are covered by the various chapters: detestation of vice, mortification of carnal desire, dismissal of riches and the worldly, contempt for high positions and dignities, subjugation of the internal passions, mature dignity in their sayings and doings, industrious application and fervour for study, moderation in their comments, discretion at parties, perfection in the political virtues, patience in sustaining exile, patience in sustaining injuries and insults, virtuous and praiseworthy use of leisure. Throughout this section, John emphasises how active the philosophers were in these virtues – as far as they could be when ignorant of God – and recommends the Christian philosopher to be likewise. He includes numerous illustrative examples in each chapter, presumably for the benefit of those who wish to preach on the topic.

The chapter on the perfection of the philosophers in the *virtutes politicae* confirms John's belief in their involvement in political life. He tells his readers that the philosophers were good and prudent magistrates, gave wise counsel and ruled peoples well.[118] They were moderate and temperate and just, courageous in danger and patient with criticism.

The remaining five sections of the *Compendiloquium* deal respectively with the various philosophical sects, with the liberal arts, with fables and poetry, with abuses of philosophy and with the places where the study of philosophy flourished.

In part 6, the Peripatetics, Stoics and Epicureans are named as three very famous sects of philosophers, and John gives the origins of their names and lists their most basic principles. For example, we are told that little is written about the Peripatetics in ancient books, but that they were founded by Aristotle, and named for their habit of disputing while walking around. We also read that they praised anger. When John comes to the Epicureans, he tells us that they believed *voluptas* to be the greatest good, and that, although some have claimed that Epicurus was really referring to *voluptas* of the mind, his sayings indicate that he was indeed referring to *voluptas* of the flesh.

In part 7, appropriately, John discusses the seven liberal arts and their usefulness. He begins by quoting from Seneca that reason and natural philosophy lead to moral philosophy, and comments that the liberal arts do not in themselves give virtue, but that they prepare the mind for the reception of virtue.[119] He then draws on Alexander

118 *Compendiloq.* 5.11.
119 *Compendiloq.* 7.1.

Nequam's *De Naturis Rerum* for a parallel with the planets: as the
seven planets illuminate the world, so the seven arts aid all knowledge and philosophy.[120] Each planet is paired with a liberal art: the
moon with grammar, the sun with dialectic, Mercury with rhetoric,
Venus with arithmetic, Mars with music, Jupiter with geometry,
and Saturn with astronomy. John speaks of each art in turn,
explaining how it may be used to promote virtue. For example,
rhetoric is the art of speaking aptly for the purpose of persuasion, and
he is a good rhetor who, by showing examples of virtue and good
deeds to men, persuades them to believe the truth. Again, geometry
is the discipline of measuring sizes and their differences, and he is a
good geometer who knows his own measure. In the tenth chapter of
the section, John explains that in these ways the philosopher can use
the arts to correct *mores,* and that consideration of the speculative arts
ought to lead us to consider eternity and to desire perfection. He
concludes that all arts and all speculation can be adapted for the
benefit of one's neighbour. If Gentile philosophers used their philosophy for the correction of *mores,* what punishment are Christian
philosophers worthy of who abuse sacred scripture for ambition and
ostentation.

In part 8, *De apologis sive poetis,* John explains that, having dealt
with the principal sects of philosophers, he now looks briefly at the
lesser ones. First he comments on the gymnosophists.[121] They
philosophised naked, apart from a loincloth, and in many ways
should rather be called abusers of philosophy than a sect. Therefore,
says John, he will not discuss them.[122] Next John looks at illustrious
philosophers among the poets.[123] He chooses Virgil as an example,
and praises his descriptions of horses, men and bees. Virgil's three
works are listed as the *Aeneid,* the *Eclogues* and the *Georgics,* dealing
respectively with military, pastoral and communal lives.

John goes on to discuss the art of poetry more generally, telling us
that it is less highly regarded than philosophy, but still contains
much that is good and useful.[124] He mentions the three types of poet
listed by Papias (the eleventh-century dictionarist) – satirists, comic
poets and writers of farce – and adds that there was another kind of
poet, who composed fables, the better to express the truth.[125] John
gives Aesop as an example. He tells one of Aesop's fables and
recommends Aesop's book as a source of others. He then raises the

[120] *Compendiloq.* 7.2–9.   [121] *Compendiloq.* 8.1.
[122] *Compendiloq.* 8.1.   [123] *Compendiloq.* 8.2.
[124] *Compendiloq.* 8.3.   [125] *Compendiloq.* 8.4–5.

question of whether such fables may properly be used without lying.[126] He takes a passage from Augustine's *Contra Mendacium* to show that they may, and quotes examples of the use and approval of fables from a dozen different authors, including Cicero, Macrobius, Livy, Horace, Apuleius and Isidore, and also his own *Communiloquium*. Fables, he concludes, can be used to the good if one is wary of errors.

John now rounds off his discussion of philosophy by giving a section on the abuses of philosophy.[127] This begins with a list of types of abuse: errors, false opinions, seduction by fallacies, becoming puffed up with knowledge. John observes that philosophers did not seek to profit from the philosophical life, and condemns the abuse of those who pretend to be philosophers.[128] Philosophy is the study of virtue, and it is an abuse to subordinate that to anything.[129] Idle curiosity and the seeking of useless knowledge are likewise abuses.[130] John also issues a warning about books: it is an abuse if, rather than remembering precepts, one simply gathers books and puts faith in them.[131] A philosopher ought not to be content with the words of others, or to trust in books, but rather he should seek to increase discoveries. Also it is better to have a few precepts, if they come easily to hand, and are useful, than to have been taught many and have none to hand. Lastly, John warns professors of divine philosophy to be wary of the abuse of adopting philosophy superficially, without the correct life, customs and deeds.[132]

The tenth and last part of *Compendiloquium* comments upon those places where philosophy flourished: Athens, Rome, the France of Charlemagne, Paris, Oxford and Ireland. John attempts to explain why each particular place was so suitable and why the study flourished there. The inclusion of Ireland at the end is due to a prophecy attributed to Merlin, which John takes from Alexander Nequam. Having completed his journey from Athens to Oxford, John closes the work with a brief epilogue which reminds the reader of his original, instructive purpose.

The *Compendiloquium* is characteristic of John of Wales' work in several ways. Like many other writers of the thirteenth century, he appreciated definitions, good order and a balance of topics. The work is characteristically his in that it comprises hundreds of selected

[126] *Compendiloq.* 8.6.
[128] *Compendiloq.* 9.1–4.
[130] *Compendiloq.* 9.6.
[132] *Compendiloq.* 9.8.

[127] *Compendiloq.* 9.
[129] *Compendiloq.* 9.5.
[131] *Compendiloq.* 9.7.

extracts and comments from other writers, skilfully bound together to form a coherent and instructive narrative. It *is* a coherent narrative, and one extract or topic leads very naturally into another, so that what is actually a highly synthetic product retains a feeling of naturalness and reflects the development of a single train of thought. John has an extraordinary capacity to develop a sequence of extracts on the basis of a firm structure. This requires a wide acquaintance with the sources and a substantial capacity for the organisation of material. This technique of correlating and welding together information from a variety of sources led Charma mistakenly to condemn the *Compendiloquium* as a characteristic example of thirteenth-century intellectual sterility.[133] Certainly the *Compendiloquium* is not an original philosophical work, but it was not meant to be one. The more one studies John's works, the clearer it becomes that they were designed to help those less fortunate than himself, and to help those at different levels of understanding in different ways. It is an achievement to create an original thesis. It is also both satisfactory and praiseworthy to construct a good general textbook, well founded in the sources, which can help many less accomplished students to a better understanding of the subject, its depths and its limitations. If it encourages them to read further, and constructively direct that reading, so much the better. It seems clear that this is, at least in part, what John was trying to do in many of his works, and particularly in the *Compendiloquium*. This work has most of the characteristics of the better textbooks: clear articulation, a logical sequence of ideas and information, judicious repetition to confirm understanding and to link sections, good, accurate and copious references to the sources. It is true that, as both Charma and Pantin have pointed out,[134] there are a number of historical errors in the work, particularly in the sequence and dating of the philosophers. However, John's errors are mainly due to flaws in his sources, and to the depth of his faith in them.

John, then, was trying to produce a volume offering information and direction, with the purpose also of stimulating the reader into admiration and emulation of the virtuous lifestyle which he was portraying. There is something hagiographical in the longer lives in this book, but this is not unexpected, for hagiography was a very common form of biography at the time, and the method would thus be acceptable to writer and reader alike. The success of the volume

---

[133] See pp. 15–24 above.
[134] A. Charma, 1866, p. 119; W. A. Pantin, 1961, pp. 307–8.

indicates that he was filling a genuine gap and meeting a genuine need. He clearly had a special talent for this type of work, and would seem to have used it well.

In the course of this chapter, *Compendiloquium* has been inspected with some closeness, and some assessment made of its nature, contents and purpose. But where does it fit into the tradition of writing about philosophers, in so far as there was one? Can one see what inspired John to tackle this particular topic in this particular way? Does *Compendiloquium* reflect the style of any individual forerunner?

The last question may profitably be considered first. It relates to the issue of John's sources for the *Compendiloquium*. If we classify his sources according to date, we find, not unexpectedly, that quotations from ancient sources substantially exceed those of later date. The *Compendiloquium* contains 482 references to 82 works by 38 authors preceding AD 450, and 132 references to 37 works by 32 writers of later date than AD 450. There are also 54 references to the Bible. John's particular favourites among his sources can clearly be seen if we examine the twelve authors whom he quotes most frequently.

Seneca	102
Cicero	83
Augustine	70
Aulus Gellius	54
Jerome	38
John of Salisbury	34
Valerius Maximus	33
Boethius	12
Aristotle	11
John of Wales	11
Alphorabius (Al-Farabi)	10
Macrobius	10

John's own *Communiloquium* is cited on eleven occasions. His works tend to be very well cross-referenced: if he refers to a point or a story which he has already written about, then he usually tells the reader where to look for the details, rather than repeating them all. The quotations in *Compendiloquium* are given in John's characteristic manner, with references to the originals added in as accurate a manner as possible, and particular mention made when a quotation has been obtained at second hand. For example, John quotes Livy through the *Policraticus*, Quintilian through Aulus Gellius, Satyrus through Jerome and Helinand of Froidmont through Vincent of Beauvais, and tells the reader so. This is some indication of how highly he regarded detailed and accurate references.

What of possible forerunners to John's *Compendiloquium*? All his favourite sources are from the ancient period, with the exception of Al-Farabi, John of Salisbury and earlier works by John of Wales himself. Study of *Communiloquium* has shown that John of Salisbury influenced John of Wales considerably, but should we hold him entirely responsible for our John's absorption with the moral excellence of the ancient philosophers? Probably not. Nor should we attribute too much influence to Al-Farabi, who was much more concerned with the intricacies of philosophy itself than with its superior moral models.

Naturally John uses and mentions other works on philosophy and philosophers, some of them medieval. In particular, he makes one reference to Avicenna's *Metaphysics*, three to the *De Ortu Scientiarum* of Gundissalinus, two to works by Isaac Israeli. He also refers six times to an anonymous *Tractatus de Dictis Philosophorum* which is probably the *Moralium Dogma Philosophorum*. While these references to medieval works on philosophy amount to a dozen or so, none of them is sufficiently substantial to be considered the key to John's interest in the topic. In any case, John's interest began long before he wrote *Compendiloquium*, indeed in the days of his first surviving literary works.

John's peculiarly moral fascination with the philosophers, and his concern with their virtuous examples and lifestyle rather than with the details of their philosophy, is surely associated with his position as a Franciscan. We cannot say whether he, like his friend Pecham, was drawn to the Franciscans by an apparent likeness between them and the ancient philosophers whom he already admired, or whether his admiration of ancient philosophers grew after he had adopted the Franciscan habit and outlook. We can say that promoting an appreciation of the virtues of ancient philosophers was one of John's great passions, that he showed this even in his earliest works, that it endured throughout his literary career (and presumably to the end of his life), and that he expressed it to its fullest extent in the *Compendiloquium*. The power and breadth of his convictions are quite outstanding in the thirteenth century: it is difficult to think of many other scholars who so zealously promoted the value of pagan and philosophical examples, although both Albertus Magnus and Roger Bacon spring to mind.

Oxford, and the legacy of classical interest left by Robert Grosseteste (to the Franciscans in particular), must be accorded some importance in fuelling John's belief in the value and interest of the classics. So must John of Salisbury, whose works John of Wales may well have discovered in Oxford, and certainly took very much to heart. But John's interest in the classics may have been stimulated somewhat earlier in his life. He seems to have spent his early years near the Welsh borders,[135] and presumably went to school not far off – perhaps in Worcester. Both Worcester and the Severn area in general have some reputation for interest in the classics in the late twelfth and early thirteenth centuries. Such an interest might well have lingered among some of the local teachers, to fire the enthusiasm of a boy such as John of Wales must have been.

This is speculation, but not, I think, idle speculation. And whether or not John's interest was already excited before his arrival in Oxford, he certainly found the intellectual fuel and atmosphere to develop his interest during his studies in that city in the 1250s. The earlier involvement of Grosseteste, the interest maintained by other later friars,[136] the survival and availability of a selection of classical texts, the pioneering work of John of Salisbury and Alexander Nequam: all these could have contributed to an interest such as John's, pointing to the value of classical *exempla* in moralising and in education. Although John's interest was perhaps unusually strong for his period, it is not difficult to see possible roots or to trace a possible development for this interest. It is perhaps more curious that others had not already observed and followed the same path. It did become a very popular path later, particularly among Oxford friars such as Robert Holcot,[137] and this would seem to have been due primarily to the influence of John of Wales.[138]

There is no immediate, direct source to be seen for John's concern with the importance of ancient philosophers as examples, and it must be concluded that this was something which he developed for himself, in a favourable intellectual climate. Oxford University, and in particular the Franciscan portion of it, must be credited with the provision of this climate. Nonetheless, the *Compendiloquium* seems to have been written in Paris, *c.* 1270–2 or a little later.[139]

---

[135] See p. 4.
[137] B. Smalley, 1960.
[139] See above, pp. 24–34.

[136] One thinks particularly of Roger Bacon.
[138] For discussion of John's influence, see chapter 8.

Did Paris provide any particular stimulus towards the subject of the *Compendiloquium*? It was earlier argued that, among the friar scholars at least, ancient examples were not highly valued in the Paris of the 1260s and 1270s.[140] Men like Bonaventure and Aquinas had other fish to fry. It is therefore unlikely that they stimulated John to concern himself with the moral virtues of philosophers. Classical interest in this period was stronger among friars such as Vincent of Beauvais, who used many classical sources in compiling his encyclopaedic works.[141]

In one respect the *Compendiloquium* arises very naturally from its predecessors the *Breviloquium de Virtutibus* and the *Communiloquium*, the one dealing with the virtues of princes and philosophers, but with primary emphasis on the princes, the other discussing ideals of virtuous behaviour for all classes of society and all kinds of situations, again with considerable emphasis on princes. Having completed these volumes, John might well have felt the urge to return to the particular examples of the philosophers. And the mass of accompanying research for these earlier volumes might well have produced abundant material on the subject, ready for use.

I believe that this issue of material provides the key to *Compendiloquium*'s birth. Analysis of the sources of *Communiloquium* and *Compendiloquium* has shown that each reflected some use of new material not available in Oxford in the 1260s.[142] A distinct difference in the sources used in the two works appears to indicate that a specific change in availability of material took place between their respective appearances. This change was probably associated with the opening of the Sorbonne library and the fresh availability of a number of rare texts.[143] Some of these texts are first-class sources of moral tales about philosophers – for example, the *Noctes Atticae* of Aulus Gellius – and we can see that John of Wales used such sources to the full. The *Noctes Atticae* in particular ranks high on his list of favourite sources for *Compendiloquium*, although it was at that time a rare and little-used work.

Some discussion of the virtues of philosophers appeared in the earlier *Breviloquium de Virtutibus*, but this work had a much more limited compass and used a fairly restricted range of material: 246

---

[140] See above, pp. 56–7.
[141] See W. J. Aerts, E. R. Smits & J. B. Voorbÿ, 1986.
[142] See above, pp. 24–34.
[143] For discussion of the early development and contents of the Sorbonne Library, see R. Rouse, 1967.

quotations from 54 works by 36 authors, of which all but 32 came from a dozen favourite authors. *Compendiloquium* has a much wider compass, and covers its topics in much greater detail. It contains 614 quotations from 119 works by 70 authors. Although again the bulk of the quotations come from a 'Top Twelve' of favourites (472 out of the 614), yet we can see that the span of the work has increased considerably. Many of the sources brought within the span were only recently available, and we might well conclude that they provided an irresistible stimulus to John's strong interest in his particular subject. As his fascination with ancient virtue was coupled to an ardent desire to spread information, it was natural that he should turn at once to production of a work like *Compendiloquium*, which extolled the moral virtue of ancient philosophers and argued their value as an example to the contemporary faithful.

Compendiloquium was not as highly popular as the *Breviloquium de Virtutibus* or the *Communiloquium*, but it did enjoy considerable success, being copied across Europe during the thirteenth, fourteenth and fifteenth centuries, and then printed in combination with others of John's works. It was also the subject of a vernacular translation on at least one occasion.[144]

Compendiloquium may have been a considerable success, but no one could say the same of John's *Breviloquium de Sapientia Sanctorum*. This tract is the fourth of John's *loquia* sequence, the last of a quartet which was often copied together and eventually printed as a group. It is difficult to know what to say about the work, which is in quite a different class from its predecessors. A. G. Little preferred to pass it by without discussion, and W. A. Pantin was almost equally unenthusiastic.[145] One cannot blame them. While hesitating to describe this *Breviloquium* as dull, one must in all fairness admit that it lacks the fascination of the earlier trio.

There are eight sections to this *Breviloquium*. The basic theme is the virtuous example provided by the saints, as illustrated by the lives of the desert fathers. We are therefore still in the ancient world, though in a rather different part of it. John tells his readers that in a previous tract he brought together the lives, sayings and examples of Gentile philosophers.[146] However, these lacked knowledge of God, and so, although they believed themselves wise, they were in fact foolish. 'Stultus enim factus est omnis homo a scientia sua', writes

---

[144] See below, p. 207.   [145] A. G. Little, 1917, p. 185.
[146] *Brev. de Sap.*, Prologue.

John; 'and therefore I believe it to be expedient to collect something of the philosophy or wisdom of the saints, who were true philosophers and illuminated by true wisdom'.[147]

The structure of the book bears marked similarity to that of the *Compendiloquium*. John begins with progressive definitions of *sapientia*.[148] He proceeds to possible dangers and how they should be avoided, and to possible advantages and how they should be sought.[149] He then goes on to the particular *sapientia* of the saints, dealing primarily with a variety of definitions. For example, 'sapientia est modus anime', and 'sapientia est regimen vitae humanae'.[150] John deals with the ways in which saints exhibited wisdom, through true faith, sincere charity, piety, and so on. He lists nine of these modes and gives instances of how they should operate. He comments on the divine source of such wisdom, and on its great superiority.[151]

The work is brief, and follows John's familiar pattern in relying on accurate references to authoritative sources for the bulk of the text. However, the work shows none of John's characteristic flair. There are no interesting classical references, no lively *exempla*. There seems to be a basic lack of enthusiasm: the flavour is of duty rather than enjoyment, the structure is competent but the content uninspiring. We learnt much about John's interests and enthusiasms from his approach to the material in his earlier works, for he made no attempt to hide his admiration and affection for his subjects. The implication of the neutral tone of the *Breviloquium de Sapientia* is that, though John doubtless had a genuine respect for the desert fathers, as a literary subject they did not greatly attract or inspire him.

Why did John write this *Breviloquium*? We seem able to rule out personal enthusiasm. The *Breviloquium de Sapientia* gives the impression that it is something of an afterthought, an attempt to redress the balance of virtue which John has so far represented as coming down heavily on the side of the pagans. We wonder what led John to this afterthought. Not simply the realisation that the desert fathers were also a source of useful *exempla*, for relatively few *exempla* are given, and these not particularly inspiring. An attack of conscience, perhaps? This is a possibility, but John has already argued coherently and competently in favour of pagan *exempla,* and he returned happily to their use in works post-dating the *Breviloquium de Sapientia*.

---

[147] *Brev. de Sap.*, Prologue. [148] *Brev. de Sap.* 1. [149] *Brev. de Sap.* 2–3.
[150] *Brev. de Sap.* 4. [151] *Brev. de Sap.* 7–8.

The work has a dutiful flavour, and duty provides an adequate explanation for its production, and for John's odd observation that the Gentiles were in fact not wise but rather stupid, and that he *believes it to be expedient* to write about the saints. This seems almost to contradict all that John has said in his earlier works, on the wisdom of the ancients, and is a very non-committal explanation of motive from a man who spoke of his previous literary topics with substantial enthusiasm. Moreover John earlier claimed that 'the example of the saints shows sufficiently in their deeds and the tales of sacred writers'.[152] Something must surely have happened to make him change his mind about this.

We might well suspect that, if *Breviloquium de Sapientia* arose from a dutiful impulse, then that impulse was born of external pressure. Some people may well have thought that John had gone too far in his admiration of the ancients, and comments may have been passed upon his neglect of Christian sages. There may even have been some reprimand, or hint of it, from men in higher authority. Whatever the truth of the matter, the work was duly written. Its briefness and dryness suggest strongly that John did not enjoy its creation and would not particularly have admired the finished product.

If so, then John should be credited with an excellent appreciation of the interests and requirements of his designated audience. The reception of the *Breviloquium de Sapientia* was far from enthusiastic. Measured in terms of the numbers of surviving MSS, this *Breviloquium* ranks only ninth among John's works.[153] Although it was brief, and plainly belonged with the sequence of *Breviloquium de Virtutibus, Communiloquium* and *Compendiloquium*, these three works were very often copied without it, alone, or with the addition of other works by John. One cannot escape the conclusion that copyists and would-be users found it, for the most part, too dull or irrelevant to be worth even the short time that copying would take. In so far as the book did survive, it probably slipped through on the grounds of its association with the earlier and more successful trio. There is very little evidence of its use, or of ownership of copies now lost, so one cannot even argue that it was so well loved that copies simply fell to pieces and thus vanished.

The lack of popularity of the *Breviloquium de Sapientia* may partly reflect the absence of classical quotations and *exempla*. There are 57 biblical quotations in the text, and only 69 from other sources. These

---

[152] *Brev. de Virt.*, Prologue.
[153] Appendix 3.

69 derive from only 17 authors, the vast majority being patristic in both origin and content.[154] *Breviloquium de Sapientia* was of little use to a preacher, who could create a stronger impression among his audience by the use of some lively hagiography, if he was to use holy examples at all. It was also of little interest to most readers. Holy virtue was already well treated in a number of larger, more authoritative and more interesting volumes. John's dutiful little essay could not hope to compete with works like the *Legenda Aurea* or the *Vitae Patrum*. He may well have recognised this: the work was his first and only attempt to restrict himself entirely to Christian virtue. His *Legiloquium*, or discussion of the Ten Commandments, for example, comments again on the virtue of the Gentiles, as far as is possible when dealing with such a subject.

When John claimed, in the prologue of the *Breviloquium de Virtutibus*, that the deeds of the saints had already been adequately dealt with, it seems that he wrote truly. And whatever event or influence caused him to withdraw this comment and tackle the subject, the conversion was not lasting. John continued to make good use of classical and philosophical material for the remainder of his career.

SOURCE LIST FOR THE *COMPENDILOQUIUM*

I.   SOURCES FROM BEFORE AD 450

Aesop	*Fables*	1
Ambrose	*Commentary on Luke*	1
	De Officiis	3
	De Virginitate	1
Apuleius	*De Deo Socratis*	4
Aristotle	*De Anima*	1
	De Meteoris	1
	Ethics	4
	Metaphysics	1
	Physics	1
	Politics	1
pseudo-Aristotle	*De Vegetabilibus*	1
Arrian	*Anabasis*[155]	2
Augustine	*Confessions*	10
	Contra Academicos	2

[154] See list on p. 200.
[155] John names this as the *Alexandreidae*.

	Contra Iulianum	2
	Contra Mendacium	1
	De Civitate Dei	39
	De Doctrina Christiana	2
	De Libero Arbitrio	1
	De Patientia	1
	De Trinitate	1
	De Utilitate Credendi	1
	De Vera Religione	2
	Epistolae	6
	Sermones	2
Aulus Gellius	*Noctes Atticae*	54
Chalcidius	*Commentary on Timaeus*	3
Chrysostom	*Super Matthaeum*[156]	1
Cicero	*Academica Posteriora*	1
	De Amicitia	1
	De Divinatione	5
	De Natura Deorum	4
	De Officiis	14
	De Oratore ad Marcum Brutum	1
	De Senectute	10
	Rhetorica	2
	Tusculanae Quaestiones	45
Eusebius	*Historia Ecclesiastica*	1
Gregory of Nazianzen	*Tractatus*	2
Horace	*Epistulae*	1
Jerome	*Chronica Historiae*	1
	Contra Iovinianum	15
	Contra Rufinum	3
	Epistolae	16
	De Viris Illustribus	1
	Super Ecclesiastes	1
	Super Matthaeum	1
Juvenal	*Satires*	2
Expositor on Juvenal's *Satires*[157]		2
Livy[158]		1
Macrobius	*In Somnium Scipionis*	3
	Saturnalia	8

[156] Not the *Opus Imperfectum.*   [157] Unidentified.
[158] Through *Policraticus.*

Ovid	*Ars Amatoria*	1
Plato	*Phaedo*	2
Pliny	*Natural History*	3
Ptolemy	*Almagest*	1
Quintilian[159]		2
Satyrus[160]	*Bioi*	1
Seneca	*De Beata Vita*	1
	De Beneficiis	11
	De Brevitate Vitae	2
	De Consolatione ad Helviam Matrem	4
	De Constantia Sapientis	3
	De Ira	7
	De Providentia	1
	De Tranquillitate Animi	5
	Epistulae[161]	68
Solinus	*Collectanea Rerum Memorabilium*	4
Tertullian	*Apology*	5
Theophrastus	*Liber de Nupciis*[162]	1
Trogus Pompeius[163]		3
Valerius Maximus	*Factorum ac Dictorum Memorabilium*	33
Varro[164]		2
Virgil	*Aeneid*[165]	3

2. SOURCES FROM AFTER AD 450

Alexander Nequam	*De Naturis Rerum*	7
Alphorabius (Al-Farabi)	*De Divisione Philosophiae*	10
Anselm of Canterbury	*De Similitudinibus*	1
	De Veritate	1
Avicenna	*Metaphysics*	1
Bernard of Clairvaux	*Super Cantica Canticorum*	2
Boethius	*Arithmetica*	1

[159] Through Aulus Gellius.
[160] Through Jerome.
[161] John uses both the earlier and the later letters.
[162] Through Jerome.
[163] Justin's *Epitome*.
[164] Through Aulus Gellius and Augustine.
[165] On one occasion through Seneca.

	De Consolatione	11
Antiquus expositor super *De Consolatione*[166]		3
Pseudo–Boethius	*De Disciplina Scholarium*	4
Expositor super *De Disciplina Scholarium*[167]		1
Cassiodorus	*Historia Tripartita*	2
Fulgentius	*Mithologiarum*	1
Grosseteste	*Commentary on Ethics*	4
Gregory the Great	*Moralia*	5
	Regula Pastoralis	1
Gundissalinus	*De Ortu Scientiarum*	3
Helinand[168]	*Gesta Romanorum*	2
Hugh of Saint-Victor	*Didascalion*	4
	Super Angelicam Hierarchiam	1
	Super Ecclesiastem	1
pseudo-Hugh of Saint-Victor[169]	*Eruditione Theologicis ex Miscellanea*	1
Huguccio	*Magnae Derivationes*	3
Innocent III	*De Conditione Humanae Miserae*	1
Isaac	*De Definitionibus*	1
	De Elementis	1
Isidore	*De Summo Bono*	1
	Etymologiae	1
John Damascenus	*Logica*	1
John of Salisbury	*Policraticus*	34
John of Wales	*Communiloquium*	11
Papias	*Vocabularium*	4
Peter Comestor	*Historia Scholastica*	7
Rabbi Moyses		1
Vincent of Beauvais	*Speculum*	5

Anon.

Chronica Metropolis Arelatensis	1
De Collationibus Patrum	1
Quidam Sapiens in suo Tractatu	1
Secreta Secretorum	1
Suda	4
Tractatus de Dictis Philosophorum[170]	6

[166] Probably William of Conches.   [167] Unidentified.
[168] Probably through Vincent of Beauvais.   [169] Perhaps Richard of Saint-Victor.
[170] Probably the *Moralium Dogma Philosophorum*.

Vitae Patrum		I
Vita Sancti Athanasii		I
Vita Sancti Dionysii		2

SOURCE LIST FOR THE *BREVILOQUIUM DE SAPIENTIA SANCTORUM*

I. SOURCES FROM BEFORE AD 450

Aristotle	*Ethics*	I
Augustine	*De Beata Vita*	I
	De Civitate Dei	6
	De Libero Arbitrio	3
	De Spiritu et Anima	2
	De Trinitate	I
	De Utilitate Credendi	2
	De Vera Religione	I
	Epistolae	I
Cassian	*Collationes*	3
Chrysostom	*Super Matthaeum*[171]	3
Cicero	*Tusculanae Quaestiones*	I
Eusebius	*Historia Ecclesiastica*	2
Macrobius	*Saturnalia*	I
Seneca	*Epistulae*	4
Tertullian	*Apology*	I

2. SOURCES FROM AFTER AD 450

Bernard of Clairvaux	*Super Cantica*	9
Boethius	*Arithmetica*	I
Cassiodorus	*Historia Tripartita*	I
Gundissalinus	*De Anima*	I
	De Ortu Scientiarum	I
Gregory the Great	*Moralia*	14
	Regula Pastoralis	I
Hugh of Saint-Victor	*De Arca Noe*	I
	Didascalion	I
	Super Angelicam Hierarchiam	I
John of Wales	*Communiloquium*	3
Vitae Patrum		2

[171] Not the *Opus Imperfectum*.

Chapter 8

THE WORKS OF JOHN OF WALES: SPREAD AND INFLUENCE

READERS AND TRANSLATIONS

John of Wales was a prolific writer. Although many of the works once attributed to him are now very properly discounted, some twenty works are still accepted as genuine. These range from homiletic works such as the *Communiloquium*, through biblical commentaries, to sermon series and single sermons. The range of surviving works is impressive, and so is the number of MSS which have survived. A. G. Little wrote that he had found between 150 and 200 MSS of John's works in European libraries.[1] On the assumption that book production and possession were not matters to be taken lightly in medieval times, this alone would indicate a substantial and lasting popularity.

Modern library catalogues enable us to update the figures given by Little. I have found records of 453 surviving Latin MSS, each containing between one and eight of John's works. The survival figures for individual texts vary considerably, from 151 and 144 copies for the *Breviloquium de Virtutibus* and *Communiloquium* respectively to only 2 for certain of the sermon collections.[2] In addition to MSS of these Latin works, a number of printed editions appeared between 1472 and 1550.[3] The earliest was an edition of the *Communiloquium*, printed in 1472. This edition was such a success that it was pirated in that same year.[4] *Communiloquium* was printed on another six occasions before 1518, sometimes in association with others of John's works, so John still had an audience as late as the sixteenth century.

It is clear, from the evidence of surviving MSS and early printed editions, that very many copies of John's works existed. We wonder who owned them, when and where. Did they use them? If so, in what ways and for what purposes? Some form of answer to these

---

[1] A. G. Little, 1917, p. 175.   [2] For details, see Appendix 2.
[3] For details, see Appendix 5.   [4] J. V. Scholderer, 1944.

questions is an important part of any assessment of the spread, popularity and influence of John's works. My own conclusion is that John's works spread rapidly and widely across Europe, and that they were owned and used consistently for the best part of three centuries. Different groups used them in different ways, many but not all using them for the purposes originally designed by the author. The evidence for this takes the following forms:

1 The survival of large numbers of MSS and of early printed editions, and the certain existence of many more copies which did not survive.

2 The widespread ownership of copies of the texts – widespread chronologically, geographically and socially.

3 The use of surviving texts, as indicated by the texts themselves.

4 The use of John's works, as indicated in the written work of others.

5 The production of translations and imitations of certain of John's works, and the success of these offshoots.

First, specific instances of the use of John's works. I have so far traced seventeen specific examples of references to and use of John of Wales in other literary texts. These examples range in date from the late thirteenth century to the mid-fifteenth. Clearly they represent the tip of the iceberg, but they give a useful idea of the range of uses made of John's works.

We begin, appropriately enough, in Oxford, where John Wester-field OP (d. 1293) used the *Compendiloquium* of John of Wales in sermons given in the early 1290s.[5] We would expect the work of John of Wales to be noticed by the friars of Oxford, where he began both his scholarly career and his activities as a Franciscan. Nor should we be surprised that in this early example the *Compendiloquium* is seen to fulfil its purpose as a source of homiletic *exempla*.

Early instances of use are not confined to England. We have examples of use in Paris which cannot date from long after 1293. The *Manipulus Florum* of Thomas of Ireland, which was completed *c.* 1306,[6] appears to have relied on John's *Communiloquium* for at least one of its quotations.[7] Another writer who knew and used John of Wales was the Italian theologian Remigio Girolami (d. 1319), who annotated one of John's works with verses of his own.[8] Girolami

[5] B. Smalley, 1981, p. 199.   [6] R. H. & M. A. Rouse, 1979, p. 95.
[7] See above, p. 27–8.   [8] B. Smalley, 1960, p. 74.

studied in Paris and later wrote in Italy. His annotations were probably made in Paris in the late thirteenth century.

Neither of these two cases constitutes use of John's works as a preaching aid: Thomas of Ireland seems to have used the *Communiloquium* as a classical quarry, while Girolami used John for his own instruction. We return to the preaching theme with our fourth example, which takes us south to Italy. In the MS collection of Birmingham University lies a series of *collationes* of the late thirteenth or early fourteenth century, by an anonymous Franciscan who was Italian and/or living in Italy, and who had spent a period studying in Paris.[9] Study of one of these *collationes*, on the subject of the *Respublica*, shows that here at least the anonymous friar drew heavily on the *Breviloquium de Virtutibus* and *Communiloquium* of John of Wales, while referring not to these works but to the classical and patristic authors whose *exempla* on this topic had been collected by John.[10] In this single brief *collatio* there are eighteen places at least, where an *exemplum*, comment or other element has been drawn from John of Wales. The evidence for the friar's use of John is striking and conclusive.

The friar had studied in Paris, so he may have been able to take copies of John's works back to Italy with him. He uses not only John's *exempla* and some of his comments, but also his references to the sources. And there are clear indications that he has noticed and followed up cross-references between John's individual works. This is a distinctive example of a preacher using John's works for their intended purpose, and taking advantage of the different aids provided by John within his texts.

John's works were also used by Philippe dé Ferrare OP (d. 1350?). His *Manuel de Conversation* tells a story about Diogenes which is taken from *Compendiloquium*.[11]

Back in Oxford, both Thomas Ringstead and Robert Holcot made use of John of Wales in the early part of the fourteenth century. Holcot named the *Communiloquium* as a source on two occasions, and the *Breviloquium de Virtutibus* on one, and probably drew on John many more times than he admitted.[12] Ringstead also refers to the *Communiloquium*.[13]

[9] Birmingham University MS 6/iii/19: see D. L. d'Avray, 1981, p. 51.

[10] J. H. Swanson, 1983, pp. 342–9.

[11] *Manuel de Conversation* 1.17 quotes *Compendiloq*. 3.2.2 (Raymond de Creytiens, OP, 1946, p. 117).

[12] B. Smalley, 1960, pp. 54, 139n, 151.

[13] *Ibid*., pp. 54, 218.

When Ranulf Higden completed the earliest version of his popular *Universal Chronicle* in the 1320s, he made much use of John of Wales' *Compendiloquium*. Like a number of other medieval writers, he used John's careful source references to make himself appear more widely read than he actually was. A number of the *exempla* which he ascribes to Cicero, Aulus Gellius, the *De Naturis Rerum* of Alexander Nequam and the *Policraticus* of John of Salisbury, have all been shown to come from John of Wales' *Compendiloquium*.[14] Indeed, Higden liked John of Wales' work so much that when he produced an expanded version of his *Chronicle* in the 1340s, he took the opportunity of including further extracts from the *Compendiloquium*.[15] In all, two dozen or more passages in the expanded version of the *Universal Chronicle* were taken from the *Compendiloquium*.

A number of other fourteenth-century writers drew on John of Wales. They include Walter Burley,[16] John Bromyard in his *Summa Predicantium*,[17] Jean de Hesdin O.Hosp.S.Ioh. (Regent Master of Theol., Paris 1364),[18] and Master Robert Rypon of Durham, who used John in preparing his sermons.[19] A fifteenth-century copy of Ridevall's commentary on *De Civitate Dei* has some marginal notations which derive from John of Wales' *Breviloquium de Virtutibus*.[20]

The range of works in which John appears as a source widens during the course of the fourteenth century. Book 7 of Gower's *Confessio Amantis* relied heavily on the *Breviloquium de Virtutibus* as a source of examples,[21] and Chaucer's close acquaintance with the *Communiloquium* is shown by his use of it as a source of parts of the General Prologue, Tale of the Wife of Bath, Summoner's Tale and Pardoner's Tale in *The Canterbury Tales*.[22]

Francesc Eiximenis, Patriarch of Alexandria (d. 1409), possessed copies of John of Wales' works in Spain, and recommended them in his encyclopaedia *Del Cristia*.[23] In the 1430s, John's works appear as a source in an English political tract: the *Tractatus ad Regem Henricum Sextum* contains ten extracts from the *Communiloquium*, which is its main source of classical quotations.[24]

Finally, a concrete example of the continuation into the fifteenth

[14] John Taylor, 1966, pp. 74–80.
[15] *Ibid.*, p. 172.
[16] B. Smalley, 1960, p. 74.
[17] G. R. Owst, 1961, p. 573.
[18] B. Smalley, 1981, p. 368.
[19] G. R. Owst, 1961, p. 573.
[20] B. Smalley, 1960, p. 122.
[21] M. A. Manzalaoui, 1954, p. 8.
[22] R. A. Pratt, 1966, pp. 619–42.
[23] C. J. Wittlin, 1971, p. 199.
[24] J-P. Genet, 1977, p. 43.

century of John's influence in Italy. The Public Library in Florence was founded in 1445, on the basis of the book collection of the deceased humanist Niccolò Niccoli. Cosimo de' Medici took responsibility for filling gaps in the collection, using as a guide his own written list of the ideal contents of a library.[25] This list included the *Breviloquium de Virtutibus* and *Communiloquium* of John of Wales, which were duly donated between 1445 and 1463.[26]

Use of John's works begins by the late thirteenth century and continues at least into the mid-fifteenth. They are used in England, France, Italy and Spain. They are seen to fulfil their function as preaching aids, but they are also used as a guide to the classics for literary and scholastic purposes. Extracts appear in sermons, other preaching aids, a patristic commentrary, an encyclopaedia, a chronicle, classical commentaries, Walter Burley's *Lives of the Philosophers,* Latin and English verse of the fourteenth century, an English political tract and an Italian humanist's ideal booklist. All this provides a good beginning to our investigation of the influence of John of Wales. We can see that he is used by different sorts of authors in different ways. Some draw on him for *exempla*, some for classical references, some for political comments and statements.

We have looked at one type of literary use: specific citations by individuals. There is another important kind of use: that leading to the production of abridgements and vernacular translations. The existence of these presupposes that other medieval writers recognised John's works as interesting and useful, and likely to prove so even to people who lacked the capacity to deal with the Latin text. A number of abridgements and translations of John's works exist. Most are versions of the *Breviloquium de Virtutibus*, which survives in ten forms other than the Latin original (see figure 2). For example, a French version was produced in the late thirteenth century, by Jofroi de Waterford, together with the *Secreta Secretorum*. This version was then translated into English by James Yonge in 1422, at the request of the Earl of Ormonde.[27]

Two other French versions survive. The earlier appears in a MS dated 1450, together with the *Othéa* of Christine de Pisan.[28] The

---

[25] The list was compiled at his request by Tommaso de Sarzana, who was later Pope Nicolaos V: see B. L. Ullman and P. A. Stadter, 1972, p. 16.
[26] *Ibid.*, p. 179.
[27] M. A. Manzalaoui, 1954, p. 7.
[28] Oxford, Bodleian, MS Laud Misc. 570.

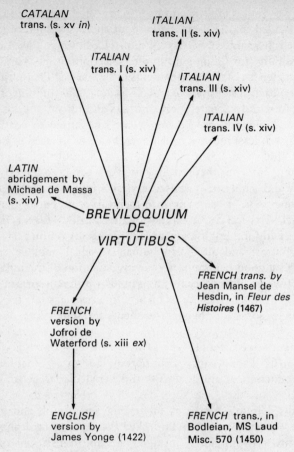

Fig. 2. Versions of the *Breviloquium de Virtutibus*.

translation is anonymous, but may possibly also be by Christine de Pisan, for the subject fits with her interests and her other works.[29]

Another, independent, translation into French of the *Breviloquium de Virtutibus* appeared in 1467, as part of the second recension of Jean Mansel's *Fleur des Histoires*.[30] Again this was a selective translation, though fuller than the earlier one. It appears in the later portion of the second volume of Mansel's work, and is often separately titled *Histoires Rommaines*. Rosemond Tuve has found that both these French translations of the *Breviloquium de Virtutibus* echo the Latin

[29] R. Tuve, 1963, pp. 265, 274.
[30] *Ibid.*, p. 265.

verbally and follow the order of the *exempla* in the Latin original. Mansel and Christine de Pisan were both associated with the French nobility: Mansel was connected with the court of the Dukes of Burgundy, while Christine de Pisan wrote at least one work for the young Duc de Berri. Whether or not Christine de Pisan was responsible for the French *Breviloquium de Virtutibus* in Oxford, Bodleian Library, MS Laud Misc. 570, the implication is that, although John's original began as part of a group of homiletic aids, it was reaching a wider and more secular audience in France by the mid-fifteenth century. If we look elsewhere in Europe, we can see signs of a similar trend in other countries, and rather earlier.

Abridgements and translations of the *Breviloquium de Virtutibus* were not confined to England and France. Four separate Italian translations were made during the fourteenth and early fifteenth centuries. These were briefly discussed by M. Barbi in the late nineteenth century, and referred to by A. G. Little somewhat later.[31] All four comprise fairly full versions of John's Latin text, although version A, the most common today, is shorter than the rest. All are fuller than the French version in Laud. Misc. 570.[32] Two of the versions survive in MSS belonging to the later half of the fourteenth century,[33] so they predate the versions by Mansel and Christine de Pisan. Twenty-four surviving MS copies have been listed. All but two are in Florence, one is in the Vatican and one is in London.[34]

Breviloquium de Virtutibus was not the only work by John to be translated into Italian. The Wellcome Historical Medical Library, MS 226 (s. xv) contains both the *Breviloquium de Virtutibus* and the *Compendiloquium* in Italian, and names a translator for the latter. It is not yet clear whether this copy of the *Breviloquium* is a fifth version, or an additional copy of one of the four translations already mentioned.

From Italy we turn to Spain, where John's works also seem to have made their mark. A number of Latin MSS of John's works survive in Spanish libraries, and the Spanish writer Michael de Massa pillaged the *Breviloquium de Virtutibus* in his search for *exempla* for his *Liber Communiloquiorum*, produced in the early fourteenth century.[35]

---

[31] M. Barbi, 1895; also A. G. Little, 1917, p. 175.

[32] R. Tuve, 1963, p. 273.   [33] A. G. Little, 1917, p. 175.

[34] See M. Barbi, 1895, Preface; also A. G. Little, 1917, p. 175. Neither of these mentions the London MS, listed in the catalogue of the Wellcome Historical Medical Library. There were several printings of the various Italian versions of the *Breviloquium de Virtutibus*: see A. Zawart, 1927, p. 358.

[35] C. J. Wittlin, 1971, p. 191.

Spanish translations of John's works were also made in the fourteenth century. We have three surviving fifteenth-century copies of a Catalan translation of the *Breviloquium de Virtutibus*,[36] and three copies of a Catalan version of the *Communiloquium*, the earliest dating from the mid-fourteenth century.[37] Contemporary library catalogues also refer to an Aragonese version of the *Communiloquium*, but no MS of this is known to survive. Royal correspondence of the fourteenth century makes several references to John's works, to their copying and possible translation.[38] The Catalan translation of the *Breviloquium de Virtutibus* can be ascribed to the reign of Martin I, el Humano, as a reference to the translation survives in his correspondence of 1404.[39]

There are a number of other references to John of Wales' works in the published correspondence of Spanish royalty. In an undated letter of the early fourteenth century, a notary of Saragoça informs King Jaime II (1291–1327) that he has written a copy of *Communiloquium* for him at the request of the prior of the city, and apologises for not having sent it to him.[40] The letter sheds interesting light on attitudes to the work at that time: 'Know then, my lord,' writes the notary, 'that some years ago the honourable Don Pascual de Gozman, prior of the seat of Saragoça, begged me . . . that I should make for him a book named *Communiloquium*, in a good hand and delicate material, and that he did this to be able to present it to you . . .' The notary explains that he made the book as beautifully and as delicately as he could. But on several occasions in the recent session of the Aragonese parliament, held in Saragoça, he has heard the king speak about this book, and how it deals with the public weal, with the virtues and conditions which the king shall have in himself, with all dealings with his vassals, with how the king should be ruled in himself, and with other good qualities that a lord should have. Moreover, he has heard that the king has not yet received the copy which this notary has written for him. The notary suggests that the king contact the prior, 'for I know well that if you had it you would enjoy it, but I believe that the prior covets the adornment of the book. And lord, let it be your wish that this should be a secret and that the prior should not learn that you had this from me.'[41]

---

[36] P. N. D'Ordal, ed., 1930, Preface.
[37] C. J. Wittlin, 1971, pp. 197–8.
[38] Published in A. Rubio y Lluch, 1908.
[39] *Ibid*., p. 430.
[40] *Ibid*., pp. 79–80.
[41] I am grateful to Dr Robert Pring-Mill of St Catherine's College, Oxford, for providing me with more reliable translations of these letters than I could produce myself.

So Jaime II was interested in the *Communiloquium* and its political aspects. Indeed, it almost seems that he had been using it as a source for his parliamentary speeches. We do not know whether he eventually extracted the fine copy from the clutches of the prior, but we know that he was not the last Spanish ruler to express an interest in John of Wales. We saw earlier that the translation of the *Breviloquium de Virtutibus* belonged to the reign of Martin I, el Humano. Between him and the earlier Jaime II, Peter IV (reigned 1336–87) also expressed considerable interest in John. On 7 April 1367 he wrote to a protonotary of Saragoça, ordering him to make a copy of the *Communiloquium* 'at the behest of the queen, similar to the one which was made for us, but in somewhat larger letters, on good parchment and in two volumes'. [42] So not only had Peter obtained a copy for his use, but the queen wanted a copy of her own, for her own purposes.

At the end of October 1372, this same king sent a letter which indicated further concern for and interest in the *Communiloquium*. He wrote to his cousin, the bishop of Valencia: 'several times have we written to you that you should hand over a book of ours [*Communiloquium*] which we lent to you, and that it should be delivered to the *batle general* of Valencia. We have had no reply from you, at which we marvel greatly. And since we have need of the same book, we wish you . . . to hand it over immediately to the said *batle general*, who is to hand it over to our faithful secretary Bernat de Bonastre, who will bring it to us.' [43]

Communiloquium was therefore no mere ornament on the king's bookshelf – he says himself that he has need of it, and he plainly noticed its absence. The above letter seems to have had little effect on the erring bishop, for on 6 June 1373, the king wrote to an aide, Francesch Marrades, commanding him to obtain from this bishop that copy of *Communiloquium* which was lent to him to be copied and had not yet been returned. It was to be carefully packed and sent to the king, so that it should not be damaged. [44]

Curt J. Wittlin suggested that this bishop of Valencia, Jaime of Aragón, may actually have been working on a translation of the *Communiloquium*. [45] Some scholars date the surviving translation to the reign of Peter IV, but others believe it was written after 1386, when the cultural atmosphere of Valencia favoured the translation of such classicising works. Wittlin himself proposes the existence of a literary circle including men like the book-loving bishop Gil Sanchez

[42] A. Rubio y Lluch, 1908, pp. 215–16.   [43] *Ibid.*, p. 243.
[44] *Ibid.*, 1908, p. 246.   [45] C. J. Wittlin, 1971, p. 192.

Muñoz, the future Pope Clement VIII, and Francesc Eiximenis. Their involvement with the translation of the *Communiloquium* has not been proved, but the oldest surviving copy of the Catalan version (a copy from the late fourteenth century) comes from the family of Gil Sanchez Muñoz, and Wittlin believes that this supports his suggestion.[46]

During the fourteenth century *Communiloquium* was becoming popular in high places in Spain. The aristocratic connections of the work, associated as it was with secular rulers and eminent churchmen, are borne out by our knowledge of lost copies. According to Villaneuva,[47] the library of the Capuchins at Barcelona contained until early this century a copy of *Communiloquium* ordered by the juggler and fool Borra, at the request of the King of Navarre, as a present for Martin I, el Humano. Medieval library catalogues also mention copies: in 1458 Queen Maria of Aragón possessed one which is described as an Aragonese version of the Catalan translation.[48] The inventory of Alfonso V also refers to the Aragonese version,[49] while a copy of the Catalan version is listed in the 1503 catalogue of Queen Isabel de Católica. The Catalan version of the *Breviloquium de Virtutibus* also appears in the royal library catalogues. The Spanish evidence seems to indicate that John's works were valued by rulers on account of their teaching on government as well as for their general counsel and learning.

It is clear that the works of John of Wales had a significant international success, in terms of translations and abridgements. We have been able to list twelve different vernacular versions of the works – nine of the *Breviloquium de Virtutibus*, two of the *Communiloquium* and one of the *Compendiloquium*. As has already been observed, surviving Latin MSS containing works by John number at least 453. MS numbers for the vernacular versions are more difficult to assess. We have 6 MSS in Spanish and know of several lost this century. We also have 25 Italian copies of the *Breviloquium de Virtutibus* and at least one of the *Compendiloquium*. The French version contained in MS Laud. Misc. 570 exists in at least one other copy. Mansel's *Fleur des Histoires* survives in a number of copies, but we cannot claim that this is particularly due to its incorporation of the *Breviloquium de Virtutibus*. Similarly, figures for Jofroi de Waterford's French version of the *Breviloquium de Virtutibus* and *Secreta Secretorum* need not be significant, as the *Secreta Secretorum* may have been the main attraction.

[46] *Ibid.*, pp. 193–4.   [47] *Ibid.*, p. 196.   [48] *Ibid.*   [49] *Ibid.*

What we can say is that we have over thirty surviving vernacular MSS of John's works, and many more MSS in which a vernacular version of John's work was incorporated. There are also a few MSS of Michael de Massa's Latin work, which depended so heavily on John's *Breviloquium de Virtutibus*.[50] If we remember that John's work was demonstrably a source for productions like *The Canterbury Tales* and Gower's *Confessio Amantis*, and take into account the many cases of reference to, or dependence upon, one of John's treatises, we must conclude that John's influence in Europe was very substantial in the later Middle Ages.

The works of John which seem to have been most used in the vernacular were all designed as homiletic aids for churchmen. Our information shows that they appealed to a much wider audience than John intended. When Pantin discussed the existence of the Italian versions of the *Breviloquium de Virtutibus*, he plausibly attributed their success to the appeal of John's ancient stories to educated professionals such as lawyers.[51] However, the French translators had firm links with the ducal courts, while the Spanish translations seem to have been instigated at least partly by royalty, and certainly appeared on royal bookshelves afterwards. Volumes of John's work figure as gifts from king to king, from churchman to king, from king to spouse. At least one letter concerning an order for *Communiloquium* described it as a work on government and public affairs, as to some extent it was. But was it really used as such? Whether read by Spanish rulers or Italian men from the communes, did John's appeal lie in his political or religious instructiveness, or in the interest of his *exempla* and classical references? Most probably, all these elements played a part in John's popularity, their relative importance varing with the individual reader. Peter IV of Spain ordered a copy of *Communiloquium* for his queen: it would be particularly interesting if we could know what she saw in it. Whatever the original function of John's works, their potential as manuals of government, and their fund of classical information, seem to lie behind much of their success.

CIRCULATION OF THE WORKS

At least 453 Latin MSS of John's works, containing between them some 604 individual texts, survive. I have traced the medieval owners of 198 of these MSS, and therefore the owners of 248

[50] M. W. Bloomfield, 1979.   [51] W. A. Pantin, 1961, p. 314.

individual texts. The main source of information is surviving marks of ownership in the texts themselves. A second source of information in the search for owners of John's works is surviving inventories of medieval libraries, many of whose contents are now untraceable.

By using these inventories it has been possible to increase the numbers of known owners of John's works to 339, possessing between them at least 570 copies of individual works by John. Doubtless, some of the surviving MSS whose medieval owners are not known, would, if we could only trace them, match some of the inventory entries which survive. However, this cannot always be the case. Many inventoried copies must have been destroyed, and many surviving copies can never have been listed on inventories, let alone on that selection of inventories which we still have. We can therefore use the two sets of figures given above, to extend our knowledge of the numbers of copies of John's works which circulated during the Middle Ages.

Of the 604 surviving Latin MS texts, 248 have known owners. Simple subtraction yields the following information:

	339 known owners	had	570 known copies
	198 known owners	had	248 surviving copies
so	141 known owners	had	322 known but untraced copies

If we add the 322 untraced copies to the 604 copies which survive, we have a total of 926 known Latin MS copies of individual works in existence in the Middle Ages. Since some of the untraced inventory copies must be among the copies which survive, this figure is a maximum for *known* Latin MS copies. We cannot estimate accurately the proportion of medieval books which have survived, although we can be sure that there were once many more copies of John's works than we now know of. So our total of 926 known Latin MS copies was certainly exceeded.

Our knowledge is extended when we add the figures for vernacular MSS and also for printed editions of the Latin texts. Surviving vernacular MSS number 35, and I know of at least 76 surviving copies of various printed editions, many of which contained more than one text. Many more copies of the printed texts must have existed, but if we confine ourselves to extant copies, we can claim to know of over 1,100 copies of John's works circulating in the later

Middle Ages. Substantially more than this number must actually have circulated between *c.* 1270 and *c.* 1550.

How do John's works compare with each other in popularity? The most popular appears to have been the *Breviloquium de Virtutibus* (151 surviving Latin MSS), and the *Communiloquium* (144). These were also the most popular works where printed editions are concerned, with *Communiloquium* outstripping the *Breviloquium de Virtutibus* by a considerable margin in this respect.[52] The most obvious reason for their widespread success is simply that they were much more 'popular' in content than some of John's other works: that is to say, they were written in a clear style, were not too technical, dealt with a wide range of topics of interest to many medieval readers, and included plenty of lively illustrative stories, both classical and medieval in origin. Analysis of their owners shows just how wide-ranging their appeal was.[53]

The next most popular work, the *Ordinarium Vitae Religiosae*, is far behind these first two, with 100 fewer copies than even the *Communiloquium*. Its topic – the religious life – was plainly popular with members of religious orders, but it seems also to have been used by seculars, particularly in the late fourteenth and the fifteenth centuries. It may have served as a useful introduction for those considering a religious life, or as a guidebook for those wishing to lead a pure lifestyle within secular society.

The fourth most popular work, the *Postilla in Apocalypsim*, had a considerable success in eastern Europe at the time of the Hussites. Nearly all the surviving MSS originated there and then, and the evidence of ownership by at least one prominent anti-Hussite in Czechoslovakia makes plain which side found the work so useful.[54]

John's *Ars Praedicandi*, with only thirty surviving copies, seems at first glance to be much less of a success than these others. But *Artes Praedicandi* do not seem to have been as popular as some kinds of preaching aid . . . 'for this genre ten manuscripts represents relative popularity'.[55] When we take this into consideration, we can see that the thirty surviving copies of John's *Ars Praedicandi* represent a considerable success in this particular field.

A number of John's texts survive in over twenty MS copies. Those which are rarer than that largely survive because of the interest shown in them by particular religious orders. For example,

[52] See Appendix 5.   [53] See Appendix 4.
[54] See Appendix 4.   [55] D. L. d'Avray, 1985, p. 79.

fifteen copies of single sermons by John of Wales survive today. Of these, ownership of twelve copies can be traced. Seven come from the Abbey of Saint-Victor in Paris, which preserved for us the only copies of sermons 1, 2, 3, 4 and 5. Numbers 6 and 7 were uniquely preserved by the Benedictines of St Emmeran in Regensburg, while number 9, which survives in five copies, managed to spread from France to both Germany and Italy.

John's *Expositio super Orationem Dominicam*, which survives in twelve copies, also had a patchy survival. It was apparently of particular interest to French Carthusians: one copy was owned by the Carthusians at Dijon, and three by those at Mont-Dieu, near Charleville. The Carthusians also preserved at least one copy of John's *Tractatus Exemplorum*, while the Dominicans of Frankfurt had another.

Some of John's works were plainly of limited interest. His biblical commentaries survive in only a few copies, and it is clear that John did not excel in this area of literature. His *Commentary and Collations on John*[56] survives in six copies (four of each part), and all six of the known owners are Franciscans. They include the Franciscans at Assisi, who seem to have had the nearest thing to a complete library of John's works, including texts which now survive in only a couple of copies.[57] John's high reputation among his own Order seems to have contributed largely to the preservation of a number of texts which would otherwise be lost to us.

The popularity of John's respective works varied widely, according to their nature and content. The preaching handbooks, with their impressive arrays of useful examples, were immensely popular. John successfully got in on the ground floor of this expanding literary field. With the exception of his *Postilla in Apocalypsim*, which was particularly appreciated by the anti-Hussites, his biblical commentaries did not attract much attention, and, without the support of his fellow-Franciscans, many would have sunk without trace.

The survival of volumes in pristine condition is not necessarily evidence that these volumes were not used: there is no medieval equivalent of the uncut book, and a volume in good condition may have been greatly treasured and carefully cared for. However, the existence of marginal notes and underlinings, and the addition of eye-catching signs by individuals other than the scribe or printer, are sure indications that a volume *has* been read and used. In both MSS

[56] For an assessment of this work, see B. Smalley, 1985, pp. 213–27.
[57] For details, see Appendix 4.

and incunabula of John's works, such signs of use are very common. For example, the Bodleian Library in Oxford possesses 8 incunabula containing works by John of Wales, of which 5 are abundantly annotated, and the British Library has 6, of which 3 are annotated. Munich Staatsbibliothek has 13 MSS and 25 incunabula, of which 10 and 7 respectively are annotated.

The annotations take a variety of forms, including underlinings and marginal comments in the text and in the indices, and marks such as the pointing-hand symbol so popular in the Middle Ages. I have taken a sample from libraries in Oxford, London, Paris, Munich, Vienna and Salzburg. In a total of 93 volumes, marginal annotations have been found in 59 (68% of the sample). This would seem to be a fairly normal proportion: at least 50% of the texts by John in each library had substantial annotations, sometimes in several different hands.

The fact that a text is annotated at all, shows that it was read and used. This is as we would expect: during the medieval period, books were in general too valuable to be bought or manufactured simply as shelf-fillers.[58] Of the 59 annotated texts mentioned above, some 20 are liberally annotated throughout. Although this satisfactorily proves the point about usage, we therefore cannot easily use them to learn much about which *particular* sections of a text were of interest. In the remaining three dozen texts, the annotators have either been more sparing or more specific in their approach, and we are able to ascertain which particular portions or aspects of a text appealed to particular individuals.

At least eight of the texts have abundant annotations throughout, referring mainly to sources quoted by John – particularly unusual or classical sources. Most annotations take the form of symbols or Latin comments, although two of the sample had comments in Greek, and one in French.[59] Notes on the classics or on ancient history often appear in the margins – for example, one MS of the *Communiloquium* contains an explanation of the nature of the hydra and a definition of the Epicureans,[60] while another has a note on the great war between Sparta and Athens in the fifth century BC.[61] Quotations from other texts also appear: one from book 2 of Ovid's *Metamorphoses* appears in the margin of a copy of John's *Moniloquium*,[62] and a piece from

[58] Except perhaps for a few aristocratic families.
[59] Munich, Bayerische Staatsbibliothek, 4° Inc. s.a.839 and 8° Inc. c.a.247e.
[60] Vienna, MS Nat. lat. 4572, ff. 305v and 324v.
[61] Paris, BN, MS lat. 14549, f. 11v.
[62] Paris, BN, MS lat. 6776, f. 161r.

John of Salisbury's *Policraticus*, book 4 chapter 4, in the margin of a copy of *Communiloquium*.[63]

Another particular interest of John's annotators was his *exempla*. Many copies were annotated primarily with these in mind, for example Vienna, Nat. Lat. MSS 2241 and 1658, which are both copies of ·*Communiloquium*. Many annotators were interested in classical or patristic sources also, so that certain copies are smothered in marginal markings – up to a dozen on every page, sometimes in a variety of hands.[64]

Some annotators were much more selective in marking their texts. They either marked only certain portions, or helpfully wrote comments indicating which topics they found most useful. Twenty-one copies from the sample fall into this category. All but one of the texts were copies of the *Communiloquium*. The exception, a copy of the *Breviloquium de Virtutibus* and *Compendiloquium*, has annotations throughout the text, followed by an unattributed extract from the *Communiloquium*, headed *An expediat homini sapienti philosophorum recipere uxorem*.[65]

Among the twenty copies of *Communiloquium* which are under consideration, the first part of the text, on the *respublica* and the *princeps*, attracted most attention. Twelve of the twenty annotators either paid most attention or all of their attention to these topics. It might be suggested that they had simply begun at the beginning, and become tired of making annotations before they reached the end of the first section, but we can see that this was probably not the case. For example, in the text in Munich, Bayerische Staatsbibliothek MS Clm 2° Inc. c.a. 2281ª, one hand has marked 29 sections, including those on the *Princeps, Iudices* and *Oratores*, while another hand has marked more contemplative and 'religious' topics such as *Patientia* and *Pastor Bonus*. Four texts only have annotations in the first part, but not *all* the first part is marked – only those sections on the *respublica* and the *princeps*. The other parts of the communal body do not seem to have attracted so much attention. Two texts are marked only at section 1.3.3., *Princeps non debet esse maculatus a sordidante culpa*, and at one other place.[66]

The text of Vienna Nat. Lat. MS 2241 is annotated throughout by

---

[63] Munich, Bayerische Staatsbibliothek, Clm 22374.
[64] Paris, Bibliothèque de l'Arsenal, MS 529 (*Moniloquium*) is an example of this.
[65] Paris, BN, MS nouv. acq. lat. 284.
[66] In one case (3.5.1) on vice in general, in the other case, (6.5.4) on the need for minute internal scrutiny if one is to lead a perfect life as a religious.

several hands, but the most heavily annotated section is part 1, on the
princeps and the *respublica*. That considerable time was spent in
contemplation of this portion of text is confirmed by the large
number of topical doodles (crowns and swords) which decorate its
margins. Other texts also show selective interest in annotation, for
instance marking the first section and one or two other sections. It
therefore seems fair to say that the first part of *Communiloquium*, and
particularly those portions of it which deal with the *princeps* and with
the *respublica* in general, were topics of particular interest among a
significant proportion of readers.

Another popular aspect of *Communiloquium* was the later sections,
on the church (5), the religious life (6) and death (7) respectively.
This is what we would expect from our sample, which contains a
substantial number of volumes owned by monasteries, but it does
serve to refute possible criticism that John's observations on these
topics were too superficial to be of interest or value. Of our sample of
twenty texts which were not evenly annotated throughout, six had
particular attention paid to these later parts of the work. In one text,
Communiloquium 6.5, *De oratione devotione*, was the only section to
rate any kind of comment, and the comment is a long one.[67] In
another, where most of the text is marked to some extent (excluding
section 11, on the bonds of society), sections 6 and 7 are heavily
marked, and the front of the volume bears an inscription stating
that part 6 is very useful for religious, and should be read
frequently in leisure time and at meals.[68] Two other texts show
careful attention to parts 6 and 7, one to 7 only and one to all of
sections 5–7.

A small number of the annotators examined revealed more
individual tastes through their markings of *Communiloquium*. One of
the readers of Munich Clm 12281 had a particular interest in material
on the subject of women, as is shown by his annotation of the section
De uxori male morigerate on f. 283r, and by his compilation (f. 371v) of
his own little subject-index – a series of notes as to which sections
and pages contained information on the subject of women. Another
reader, whose main interest seems to have been John's sources,
found time to make a marginal comment on the role of law in the
appropriate section of *Communiloquium*, while a third, having appreciated the chapter *Qualiter princeps debet esse humilis ecclesia*, wrote in

[67] Munich, Bayerische Staatsbibliothek, 2° Inc. c.a. 375a.
[68] Munich, Bayerische Staatsbibliothek, 2° Inc. c.a. 375. This belonged to the
Benedictines at Tegernsee.

its margin: 'Hic vide de reverentia.' Only one of the twenty annotators under discussion showed any special interest in part 2 of the
Communiloquium, on the bonds in society. All the others ignored it,
although it did receive a fair quota of annotations in the many texts
which were annotated throughout.

Finally, several annotators make clear their intention to use the
Communiloquium as a serious reference tool, either by adding their
own alphabetical list of contents, or by attaching folio numbers to a
list of contents provided by the original scribe.

To summarise: 68% of the texts sampled had annotations of some
sort, and of these roughly 65%, or 40% of the total, were fairly
generally annotated throughout, by between one and four hands,
indicating that the texts involved were of general use and interest. 21
of the sample texts (35% of the marked texts, 22% of the total
sample) had more specific annotations. Most of these texts were
copies of the *Communiloquium*, and two subjects within this proved
to be of particular interest: the *respublica* and *princeps*; and the church,
religious orders and death. Most of the twenty copies of *Communiloquium* revealed particular interest in one or both of these topics
on the part of the annotators, although both for these topics and for
others there were clear differences of individual taste. We also saw
samples of readers either using the indices provided or creating their
own.

From all this we can conclude that most of the topics which John
covered in his works, and particularly in the wide-ranging *Communiloquium*, appealed to at least some people, although some topics
were evidently much more popular than others. The evidence from
the annotations tends to support the belief that the wide-ranging
subject-matter of the *Communiloquium* was one of the main reasons
for its outstanding success. It could be, and was, used not only for its
primary, pastoral purpose, but also as a guide to the classics, as a
manual of government, as a volume of private devotional reading,
and as a volume of general information.

Marginal annotations provide valuable evidence for the nature of
use of John's works, and act as a guide to the degree of interest
attracted by specific sections of the work. There is another possible
source of information on these topics: the survival of partial copies of
several of John's works. An analysis of the particular pieces which
were extracted provides a counterpoint to the evidence derived from
annotations.

Of the 604 surviving Latin MS copies of John's works, 43 are

known to be abbreviated in some way. Seventeen of these abbreviated texts contain portions of *Communiloquium*, and an examination of their contents clearly shows that individuals found certain
portions of the text particularly worthy of attention. I mentioned
earlier that the first part of John's *Communiloquium* included an
unusual *capitulum* on hunting and fishing.[69] One reader at least found
this particularly interesting: we have a volume of theological extracts
written in the fifteenth century by one Frater Galterus le Blond, a
Celestine of Rouen, who included all of John's *Breviloquium de
Virtutibus*, and also the *Communiloquium* chapter on hunting and
fishing.

The section of *Communiloquium* which gave a moralisation of the
game of chess[70] escaped from the main text on more than one
occasion. Four MSS survive which contain only this section of
John's work among their other contents.[71] All are of the fifteenth
century and appear to be English in origin. One belonged to the vicar
Edward Wreche,[72] but we know nothing of the ownership of the
others, except for London, British Library, MS Royal 12. E.XX1,
which eventually belonged to the library of Archbishop Cranmer.

The section on confession, from the later part of *Communiloquium*,
was extracted into a fifteenth-century volume which belonged to the
Franciscans of Bamberg,[73] and the section *De sex aetatibus hominum*
appears in a volume of extracts written in 1462–3 by one Leonhart
Radawer, who was a *medicus* in Augsburg in 1470.[74] He also included
the complete *Breviloquium de Virtutibus* in his collection. The whole
of *Communiloquium* 5, on scholars and churchmen, and some of
Communiloquium 6, on religious, were written out in Erfurt,
Amplon. MS F.68, together with all *Breviloquium de Virtutibus* 3, on
temperance, and some of *Breviloquium de Virtutibus* 4, on fortitude.
Unfortunately we do not know the writer of the volume, but we can
clearly see that the principles of selection were in use. Again, it is
worth noting that those later parts of *Communiloquium* which deal
with the religious world in very simple terms, and have sometimes
been criticised by modern historians for their 'banality', were clearly
valued by at least some of the intended audience.

[69] See above, pp. 95–6.   [70] See A. G. Little, 1917.
[71] London, BL, MSS Harley 2253, Royal 8.D.X., Royal 12.E.XX1; Oxford,
Bodleian, MS Rawl. A 423.
[72] London, BL, MS Royal 8.D.X.
[73] Bamberg, MS 195 = Q.V.29b.
[74] Budapest, Orsz. Széch. Kön, MS 276. This section was also printed separately in
the sixteenth century.

In fact study of the extracted portions of *Communiloquium* shows that all of the seven parts appealed particularly to some individuals. These extracts are mostly taken from the later and more religious parts of the work (5–7), but we also have an example where the purely secular portion has been preferred: Madrid, Escorial, MS L.111.7 is a fifteenth-century text which includes all of *Communiloquium* 1 and 2, and some of 3.

Communiloquium was not the only work of John's which merited extraction. I have already mentioned the use of *Breviloquium de Virtutibus* 3 and 4 in Erfurt, Amplon. MS F.68. Seven other incomplete copies survive (I exclude Paris, Bibliothèque Nationale, MS lat. 6776, where the first page of an otherwise complete text has vanished). Some of the extracts are very brief. Oxford, Corpus Christi College, MS 183, has the prologue and first four-and-a-half capitula of *Breviloquium de Virtutibus*. In this case we cannot really assess what happened to the rest of the text, or why the scribe stopped.

Bern, Bürgerbibliothek, MS 527, a volume containing 43 excerpts from various works, includes the first section of *Breviloquium de Virtutibus*, on *iustitia*. This must have been a topic of special interest to the writer. The text is fifteenth century and apparently belonged to a Dr Barbatus, who wrote it while studying in Rome and Padua. The book of extracts was presumably one product of his period of study.

The Dominican Konrad Textoris of Worms seems to have had similar tastes to the unknown compiler of Erfurt, Amplon. MS F.68. The MS Frankfurt am Main, Praed. MS 123 (later fifteenth century) also contains most of *Breviloquium de Virtutibus* 3 and some of *Breviloquium de Virtutibus* 4, as a part of a general collection of preaching material. Temperance and fortitude would seem to have been more popular virtues among preachers than were justice and prudence. It is also possible that some readers preferred John's expositions of the classical virtues to his chapters on virtue in general. We have a copy of the *Breviloquium de Virtutibus* which seems to have been written without the fifth and final part, although all the other sections are included.[75]

We also have one set of extracts from the *Postilla in Apocalypsim*,[76] two sets of extracts from the *Ordinarium Vitae Religiosae* (one only a

---

[75] Chapel Hill, North Carolina Univ. MS 515.
[76] Breslau, Univ., MS 828, ff. 14–26.

fragment,[77] the other all of part 1),[78] and one incomplete copy of the *Legiloquium*.[79] This latter piece may originally have been complete, as only the end is missing. As with the selective annotations which were examined earlier, it can be seen that the tastes of individual extractors varied widely. In general, the context of the extracts (that is, the other works and portions of works with which they were copied and/or bound), shows clearly that these extracts represent the tastes of individuals who were compiling their own selections of preaching material. They chose sections of John's works which they thought would be generally useful, or which covered topics not dealt with elsewhere, or which appealed to their own private tastes. Again we see the flexibility of John's works as a source, particularly when used by their intended audience of preachers.

It is profitable to assess the surviving texts from one other point of view: that of their actual physical nature. The materials, penmanship, decoration and binding of a text can tell us much of its intended and actual owners and uses. Such copies of John's works as I have been able to examine confirm that the audience which gained access to his works was wide. Large numbers of good, plain, well-written copies survive, mostly of monastic origin. There are also some very scrappy copies, written on relatively poor-quality paper in unruly hands, mostly by individual scholars for their own use. Some copies are completely unadorned, while others are beautifully decorated, with ornate or illuminated capitals, or other drawings, or both. The Paris libraries in particular have some very attractive copies. Most copies of John's works lack any but the most simple type of decoration, indicating that they were generally intended to be functional. The few particularly fine copies belonged to royalty and to nobles of classical or humanistic bent, particularly in Italy and Spain.

MEDIEVAL OWNERSHIP OF JOHN'S WORKS

The hundreds of surviving MS copies range in date from the late thirteenth century to the late fifteenth, when printed editions became available and reduced the need for manual copying. They survive in libraries all over Europe, from England west to Spain, south to Italy,

[77] Klosterneuburg, MS 84, ff. 73v–75v.
[78] Oxford, Bodleian, MS 867, ff. 307v–317v.
[79] London, BL, MS Harley 632, ff. 307–317v.

east to Poland and Czechoslovakia. This distribution reflects a wide geographical spread in the medieval period.

With so many copies surviving, and with many containing marks of ownership, it has been possible to make some kind of analysis of those who owned works by John. Surviving MSS are not the only source of information about ownership, as large numbers of medieval library catalogues also survive, and many are edited, if not indexed. They provide further evidence of the wide spread of John's works, beyond that indicated by surviving copies. Of course some of the copies mentioned in the medieval lists survive today and provide a certain overlap, but very many have vanished.

I have identified 338 individuals or institutions who owned works by John of Wales during the period from the late thirteenth century to the later sixteenth. In many cases identification comes from a library catalogue, while in others book inscriptions provide the key. The works and copies listed in Appendix 4 below represent a minimum holding only. Medieval catalogues frequently listed volumes by their first work only, or by a general title. Many volumes contained a number of works, and so large numbers of works went unlisted. In the case of John of Wales, where we know that his works were frequently copied in groups, we may be sure that very many more texts existed in catalogued libraries than those which we have been able to trace. Nor should we place too much weight on apparent proportional numbers of copies for individual works. Many medieval catalogues did not name authors. John's *Communiloquium* and *Breviloquium de Virtutibus* have distinctive titles which are easy to recognise in a catalogue, but in general there is no way to distinguish John's works on, say, vices or the Ten Commandments from other works on the same subjects. In such cases, it is highly likely that a false impression of scarcity is created by the list of owners.

Catalogues and inscriptions do not tell us everything about book-ownership, but they do tell us a great deal. We know that copies of John's works were owned in many areas which today include Austria, Belgium, Bavaria, Czechoslovakia, England, France, Germany, Italy, the Netherlands, Poland, Sardinia, Spain and Switzerland. Owners of the works included itinerant friars, individual monks, monasteries and convents of almost every order. Similarly, individual vicars, parish churches, Oxford colleges in the fourteenth and fifteenth centuries, cathedrals, the humanistic libraries of Italy and individual scholars from all over Europe had copies. Men from the Italian communes owned and used the works, as did Spanish kings and queens.

As so many copies of John's works can be traced, they can almost be used to produce a history of book-owning and use from the late thirteenth century until the sixteenth. Austrian owners included Benedictines, Cistercians, Dominicans and Augustinian canons. The chaplain of Henry V de Rosenberg had a copy of *Communiloquium* which he indexed himself because he found the contents confusing.[80] A number of Viennese scholars also had copies, including Wolfgang de Egenburg, Professor of Theology and Canon of St Stephens, who died in 1470. He was one of a number of scholars who bequeathed their copies of John's works to the Vienna Arts Faculty Library.

A similar spread of ownership existed in Czechoslovakia, where we know that copies were owned by monks, canons, friars, a church and a number of individual scholars. John's *Postilla in Apocalypsim* was particularly popular in this part of eastern Europe, and was owned by men like Andreas de Broda, magister in the University of Prague and an ardent opponent of the Hussites.

We have a great deal of evidence for ownership in England, partly because a large number of medieval catalogues are readily available. Examination of these catalogues suggests that ownership of John's works was the rule rather than the exception, taking the period as a whole. I have been able to list 97 English owners. Monasteries figure largely, as do Oxford and Cambridge colleges. We also know of ownership by a substantial number of individuals, some fellows of colleges, others scholars or churchmen of various degree. The fifteenth-century scholar John Warkeworth, of Cambridge, owned several works, and so did the fourteenth-century Bishop of Chichester, William Reede. Thomas Sprot, historian, who was a Benedictine monk of St Augustine's Canterbury, had a copy by the late thirteenth century, and several other Canterbury monks had copies by the early fourteenth century. Most of these copies passed eventually to the monastery library, which had over twenty copies of various of John's works by the end of the fifteenth century.

Archbishop Thomas Cranmer owned a volume containing five of John's works,[81] and William Neel, vicar of Blokley in the early sixteenth century, owned copies of the *Breviloquia*.

---

[80] This copy survives as Prague, MS 68 Cpl (452.a) 101. See the inscription for an explanation of how the index came to be written. [81] The printed edition of 1518.

We have a good example of joint ownership in a volume inscribed Robert Jones 'et amicorum'.[82] Jones was at Oxford in 1520, and was later rector at Lower Heyford in Oxfordshire and at Eaton Bishop in Hertfordshire.[83] His copy is well annotated and was presumably used as a sermon aid.

More illustrious owners include the humanistic scholar Robert Flemyng (1417–83), who studied in Oxford, Cologne, Padua and Ferrara, and showed considerable enthusiasm for Greek.[84] Flemyng owned a copy of the *Summa Iustitiae*. A later scholar, the sixteenth-century writer Thomas Browne, owned a copy of John's *Ars Praedicandi*, in addition to one of the *Summa Iustitiae*. Other owners of John's works were a fifteenth-century chaplain of St Paul's, a fifteenth-century Chancellor of Oxford University and William Gray, Bishop of Ely (d. 1478). Friar William Woodford also owned works by John.[85]

A number of vicars also appear on our list of owners. In some cases we know that they bequeathed copies of John's works to individual successors, or to their parish. We also have evidence of several secular owners, particularly in the sixteenth century. One copy of John's *Legiloquium* bears the name of a certain Margaret Wright.[86]

The inscriptions contained in many of the surviving copies are particularly fascinating, as they reflect some of the ways in which books were obtained and transferred. Some tell the price of a volume, or of its transfer through inheritance or in payment of debt. Some volumes bear indications that they were used as pledges, and we may be sure that not all were redeemed. One volume, a copy of the *Summa Iustitia*, bears the following inscription on the flyleaf: 'Once the book of Magister Nicholas Kempston A.D. 1477. Never to be sold, according to the wishes of the deceased, but to be used freely by priests under instruction in preaching, and passed from one to another without charge for as long as it lasts. Therefore pray for his soul.' Six successive owners' names appear on a separate leaf, suggesting that the request was carried out. Nicholas Kempston is another example of someone who believed that John's works were of use to preachers – presumably he based his opinion on personal experience.[87]

---

[82] Oxford, Bodleian, MS Auct.2.Q.V.20.
[83] A. B. Emden, 1974, I.320.
[84] A. B. Emden, 1959, I.69.
[85] Woodford appears in the list of owners made by A. G. Little, 1917, p. 176.
[86] Now Cambridge, St John's College, MS A.15.
[87] For information about Kempston, see A. B. Emden, 1959, I.1034.

Another inscription appears in Oxford, Bodleian Library, MS Bodley 630, on a copy of John's *Ars Praedicandi*. It reads: 'Johanna Buklonde, widow of Richard Buklonde, citizen and fish-monger of London, gave this book to brother Roger Twiforde and the other brothers of Syon to pray for her and for the soul of the said Richard.' The inscription seems to be late fifteenth century. It is unlikely that Richard Buklonde, citizen and fishmonger of London, would have had any personal use for a copy of the *Ars Praedicandi*. But, however the volume came to be selected as suitable, it is fascinating to see his wife making the gift of the book on his behalf.

If we now return over the channel to France, we see that such examples of ownership as have so far been collected do not include much evidence of thirteenth-century ownership. Most of the known owners are churchmen, ranging from friars to an abbot and a cardinal. A possible secular owner is Jehan Chastellier, who possessed copies of the *Breviloquia* in the fifteenth century.

Germany is particularly rich in evidence of fifteenth-century ownership. We know that many religious foundations owned copies of the works during this century. Inscriptions, and watermarks in paper, make clear that many new copies of the works were still being written at the beginning of the sixteeenth century, particularly by friars of various orders. As elsewhere, many scholars and vicars owned copies, and these often went to parish or college libraries when their owners died.

Italy is also rich in evidence of ownership, owing largely to the survival of many catalogues of friary libraries. Italian Franciscans owned many copies of John's works, and so did a range of other types of library, particularly in Florence. John's works also appealed to humanistic scholars like Pico della Mirandola and Oliviero Forzetta, and appeared in the famous library of the Visconti–Sforza. At least six Italian bishops owned one or more of John's works. So did Franciscus Rufulus, Doctor Decretorum of Naples (before 1340), Jacobus de Susato, Dominican and Professor of Theology, and Pietro de Regio, 'medico in fisico', to whom is attributed an Italian translation of the *Compendiloquium*.

In Spain, as I have already shown, prominent churchmen and royalty shared a taste for John's works, while more usual types of owner have been traced in the Netherlands, Sardinia and Switzerland.

All the information gathered above is strong evidence for widespread and persistent copying, ownership and use of John's works across Europe. We have good evidence for quick spread in England, France and Italy – that is, by the end of the thirteenth century. The works were certainly in Spain not much later, and reached central, northern and eastern Europe by the end of the fourteenth century, if not well before. We can see that many different types of person owned John's works. Presumably they found somewhat different reasons for using them. The *Breviloquium de Virtutibus*, for example, was very popular in mid- to late fourteenth-century Italy, its four separate vernacular translations indicating a strong secular audience. The *Postilla in Apocalypsim* was a success in Czechoslovakia at the time of the Hussites: nearly all surviving MSS originated there and then. The evidence of ownership by at least one prominent anti-Hussite makes plain which side found the work useful. *Communiloquium*'s popularity in Spain seems to be due partly to its classical sources, partly to its advice on the topics of kingship and government.

Beyond these more specific instances of popularity with particular groups, in particular times and places, lies a broader, more consistent popularity with preachers, scholars and churchmen at all levels. Owners range through monasteries, convents and friaries of all types to vicars, itinerant friars, professors of theology, abbots, bishops, archbishops and a cardinal. Humanistic scholars, as well as family, individual, college and public libraries, also feature. Very many of these known owners, and probably the majority of those as yet unidentified, must have been using the works as preaching aids, their original intended function. By any standards John's works as a group must be considered a success. They flourished on their own terms and were used by their intended audience for their intended purposes, over a period of three centuries. That they also reached a wider circle in no way detracts from John's achievement.

CONCLUSION

We have considered John of Wales' four earliest preaching aids. How
does John himself emerge from this study? Perhaps the strongest
characteristic to appear is his depth of commitment and consistency
of purpose. Although the four texts are his earliest preaching aids,
and seem to predate most of his other surviving work, they are in no
sense juvenilia: the first, the *Breviloquium de Virtutibus*, was written
some years after John held the position of lector to the Oxford
Franciscans. They are therefore the work of a mature mind,
although the first bears signs that the author was feeling his way –
coming to terms with an unfamiliar medium.

This coming to terms was accomplished successfully. *Communiloquium*, on a grander scale in every respect and showing signs of
greatly increased confidence, is remarkably faithful to the distinctive
characteristics which can be isolated in its predecessor. The stated
aim of helping preachers, the faith in the value of classical lore and
exempla, the rigorous citation of a wide range of sources (some most
uncommon), the enthusiasm for organisation, the clear interest in
political systems – all these appear in the *Breviloquium de Virtutibus*,
but blossom and expand in the *Communiloquium*. Having established
a technique in the *Breviloquium de Virtutibus*, John used it with ease in
the *Communiloquium*, developing and expressing more fully his
views on society in general and rulers in particular.

In the *Compendiloquium* he followed a slightly different path, but
his passionate interest in ancient philosophers, and his sincere belief
that they were politically and socially involved, committed and
aware, had again been foreshadowed in the earlier works. The
Breviloquium de Sapientia Sanctorum, last of the quartet, attempted to
apply John's characteristic techniques to a subject which plainly did
not excite him. A brief work, it must have been soon written and no
doubt soon and joyfully left behind him. In his *Legiloquium*,
Moniloquium and *Summa Iustitiae*, and in his *De Poenitentia* in particular, John of Wales returned to his consuming interests. These four

227

preachers' handbooks, like the earlier quartet, are based around complex divisions, and they are illustrated with selections of extracts from an even wider range of works and authors than were the first quartet. John's commitment to the hypothetical young preachers of his intended audience was never-failing.

If preaching aids were cakes, John of Wales' works would represent the archetypal wedding-cake, so stuffed with fruit and nuts that the flavour of the original cake mixture is difficult to detect. Difficult, but not impossible – and the reward is well worth the effort. The very wide range of John's medieval readership indicates that the flavours were more than welcome in that period. He was not alone in preparing such popular aids to preaching. They will repay further study.

APPENDIX 1: THE WORKS OF JOHN OF WALES

I here list the surviving works which modern scholars have attributed to John of Wales, as a complete list is not readily available.

1 *Breviloquium de Virtutibus Antiquorum Principum et Philosophorum.*
   Inc: *Quoniam misericordia et veritas custodiunt regem* . . .
   A number of alternative incipits are listed by Bloomfield.[1]
2 *Communiloquium sive Summa Collationum.*
   Inc: *Cum doctor sive praedicator* . . .
3 *Compendiloquium de Vitis Illustrium Philosophorum et de Dictis Moralibus Eorundem.*
   Inc: *Cum enim debeamus apes imitari* . . .
4 *Breviloquium de Sapientia sive Philosophia Sanctorum.*
   Inc: *Cum vani sint* . . .
5 *Legiloquium* or *Tractatus de Decem Preceptis.*
   Inc: *Scribam eis multiplices leges meas* . . .
6 *Moniloquium*
   Inc: *Cum almus Christi confessor Beatus Franciscus* . . .
   This work was known by a variety of titles. Charland gives *Collectiloquium* as an alternative,[2] and Baldwinus of Amsterdam mentions *Tractatus de Arte Praedicandi* and *Summa de Vitiis et Virtutibus* as other alternatives.[3]
7 *Summa Iustitiae* or *Tractatus de Septem Viciis.*
   Inc: *Summa iustitiae christifidelium est declinare iustitia que est via ad regnum, ut supra dictum est* . . .
   This work survives in two recensions, one substantially longer than the other.[4]
8 *De Poenitentia.*
   Inc: *Quoniam provida sollertia est jugiter meditari necessaria ad salutem* . . .
9 *Ars Praedicandi.*
   Inc: *In libro isto quatuor capitula continentur* . . .
   or *Ad petitionem cuiusdam praedilecti mei satisfaciens* . . .
   The two alternative incipits are given by Caplan.[5] It is important to

---

[1] M. W. Bloomfield, 1979.
[2] T. M. Charland, 1936, p. 55.
[3] Baldwinus ab Amsterdam, 1970, p. 90 n. 93.
[4] M. W. Bloomfield, 1979, p. 249, ref. 2881.
[5] H. Caplan, 1934 and 1936.

distinguish between this and John's *Moniloquium*, sometimes also referred to as an *Ars Praedicandi*. This particular work is a treatise on the technical art of preaching, while the *Moniloquium* is much more wide-ranging.

10 *Ordinarium seu Alphabetum Vitae Religiosae.*
   Inc: *Numquid nostri ordinem celi et rationem eius . . .*

11 *Expositio in Evangelium Iohannis.*
   Inc: *Numquid ad praeceptum tuum elevabitur aquila, et in arduis ponet nidum suum (Iob. 39,27). Cum inter quattuor sancta animalia, mystica significatione quattuor evangelistas designantia . . .*
   This work was mistakenly ascribed to Bonaventure, and published under his name. For proof of John's authorship, see Baldwinus ab Amsterdam.

12 *Collationes in Evangelium Iohannis.*
   Inc: *In principio erat verbum . . .*
   These were edited along with the previous work, under the same mistaken circumstances. They are in fact an extension of John of Wales' *Commentary on John*.

13 *Collationes super Matthaeum.*
   Inc: *Liber generationis – Tria insinuantur dignitationis filii Dei generandi . . .*

14 *Expositio super Orationem Dominicam.*
   Inc: *Pater noster . . .*
   It is not agreed whether this should be attributed to John of Wales. Glorieux expressed doubts[6] and, though Stegmüller accepted John's authorship,[7] the editor of his *Supplementum* was uncertain.[8]

15 *Expositio Regulae Ordinis Fratrum Minorum.*
   Inc: *Quoniam, ut scriptum est Eccles.* 3 . . .
   Both Doucet[9] and Baldwin[10] accept John's authorship of this work.

16 *Tractatus Exemplorum.*
   Inc: *Tractatus exemplorum de abundantia adaptionum ad omnem materiam in sermonibus secundum ordinem alphabeti. Accidia: nota, accidiosus est sicut canis fameticus etc . . .*
   Both Glorieux and Stegmüller accept that this work is by John. It was attributed to him as early as the thirteenth century.[11]

17 *Postilla in Apocalypsim.*
   Inc: *Spiritu magno vidit . . .*

18 *Sermones.*
   These are described by Schneyer, who lists a total of 413 sermons.[12] They are divided as follows:
   a. *Sermones Singuli*
   b. *Sermones de Tempore*

---

[6] P. Glorieux, 1971, p. 210.
[7] F. Stegmüller, 1951, p. 339.
[8] *Ibid.*, p. 196.
[9] V. Doucet, 1934, pp. 550ff.
[10] Baldwinus ab Amsterdam, 1970, p. 92.
[11] P. Glorieux, 1933, lists under the entry Jean de Galles a thirteenth-century MS which contains this work under John's name.
[12] J. B. Schneyer, 1969, vol. I–J, pp. 480–510.

c. *Sermones de Evangeliis Dominicalibus et Quadragesimales*
d. *Collationes in Evangelium S. Iohannis*
     For this group see entry 12 above.

Finally, four works which have been attributed to John in the past, but of which his authorship is now seen as doubtful. Few MSS survive, and I have been unable to inspect any of them for myself. For further details see the works of Glorieux and Stegmüller:

1 *Tractatus de Poenis Inferni.*
2 *Legimus apud Eusebium.*
3 *Postillae in Epistolas Pauli.*
4 *De Factis Mahumetis.*

APPENDIX 2: MSS CONTAINING WORKS BY JOHN OF WALES

No full list of Latin MSS containing works by John of Wales has previously been made. Partial lists were provided by Bloomfield, Caplan, Charland, Doucet, Glorieux, Schneyer and Stegmüller. These have proved valuable. As far as possible I have checked their information with the available catalogues, but a further catalogue search turned up dozens of additional MSS. A startling total emerges, although I feel sure that there are still a number of MSS surviving which have not been noticed yet.

The MSS are listed alphabetically according to their current home. As far as possible, the appropriate foliation has been given, and also the date of the copy.

In the course of the list I have used a number of superscript symbols. For works like the *Summa Iustitiae*, where two distinct recensions have been established, the superscript ^{a} indicates the longer recension, while ^{b} indicates the shorter. If the superscript is missing, then I have not been able to establish the recension. I have also tried to indicate where a text is incomplete. Those copies marked * are to some extent abbreviated, while those marked ** are only small portions of the complete text.

MS no.	The manuscripts	Folio ref.	Work	Date of copy
1.	Amiens, Bibl. mun. 303		Communiloq.	s. xv
2.	Arezzo, Bibl. della Città 367		Brev. de Virt.	
3.	Arezzo, Bibl. della Città 373		Ord. Vit. R.	
4.	Arezzo, Bibl. della Fraternità dei Laici 325	ff. 42ᵛ–51	Ars Praed.	s. xv
5.	Arras 584		Communiloq.	s. xiv
			Ord. Vit. R.	
			Brev. de Virt.	
6.	Arras 759	f. 112ra	Sermon 9.	1347
7.	Arras 1018		Brev. de Virt.	s. xv
8.	Assisi 46	ff. 129–73	Post. in Apoc.	s. xiv
9.	Assisi 50	ff. 1–113	Post. in Apoc.	s. xiv
10.	Assisi 66	ff. 1–154	Post. in Apoc.	s. xv
11.	Assisi 71	ff. 1–62	Post. in Apoc.	s. xiv
12.	Assisi Com. 167	ff. 105–66	Moniloq.	s. xiv
		ff. 166–90	Ord. Vit. R.	
		ff. 190–201	Legiloq.	
		ff. 201–25	De Poenit.	
		ff. 225–60	Communiloq.	
		f. 260	Brev. de Sap.	
		ff. 266–76	Brev. de Virt.	
13.	Assisi 358	ff. 1–167	Post. in Apoc.	s. xiv
14.	Assisi 397	ff. 1a–112d	Communiloq.	s. xiv
		ff. 168a–181d	Brev. de Virt.	
		ff. 181d–216b	Ord. Vit. R.	
		ff. 216b–221a	Brev. de Sap.	

MS no.	The manuscripts	Folio ref.	Work	Date of copy
15.	Assisi 410	ff. 221a–295d	Moniloq.	s. xiii/xiv
		ff. 295d–310c	Legiloq.	
		ff. 311a–358a	Compendiloq.	
16.	Assisi 433	ff. 1–104	De Poenit.	s. xiv
17.	Assisi 446	ff. 105–50	Legiloq.	s. xiv
18.	Assisi 462		Super Orat. Dom.	s. xiv
			Tract. Exemp.	
			Serm. de Temp.	
			Serm. de Evang.	
19.	Assisi 466		Serm. de Temp.	s. xiv.
20.	Assisi 511		Serm. de Evang.	s. xiv
21.	Assisi 669	ff. 1–145	Moniloq.	s. xiv
		ff. 146–212	Ord. Vit. R.	
		ff. 213–74	De Poenit.	
		ff. 274–300	Brev. de Virt.	
22.	Avignon 331	ff. 110–41	Brev. de Virt.	s. xv
		f. 144r	Communiloq. **	
23.	Bamberg Q. III.26 (Theol 120)	ff. 1–161	Communiloq.	s. xv
24.	Bamberg Q.IV.33 (Theol 58)	ff. 343–373v	Brev. de Virt.	s. xv
25.	Bamberg Q.V.29b (Theol 195)	ff. 1–6	Communiloq. **	s. xv
26.	Bamberg Q.V.34 (Theol 194)	ff. 1–159	Communiloq.	s. xv
27.	Bamberg Q.V.53 (Theol 235)	ff. 343–373v	Brev. de Virt.	s. xv
28.	Barcelona, Archiv. de la Corona de Aragon, proc. de Ripoll. 228		Communiloq.	
29.	Barcelona, Bibl. Cent. 659		Super Orat. Dom.	1424

No.	Shelfmark	Folios	Work	Date
30.	Barcelona, cap 73		*Brev. de Virt.*	
31.	Barcelona, Inst. Stud. Cat. 248	ff. 1–156	*Communiloq.*	
32.	Barcelona, Inst. Stud. Cat. 648	ff. 1–155	*Communiloq.*	s. xv
		ff. 157–95	*Ord. Vit. R.*	
33.	Barcelona, Inst. Stud. Cat. 649	ff. 1 et seq.	*Ord. Vit. R.*	s. xv
34.	Barcelona, Inst. Stud. Cat. 650	ff. 137 et seq.	*Summa Iust.*[a]	s. xv
		ff. 183 et seq.	*De Poenit.*	s. xv
		ff. 190 et seq.	*Brev. de Sap.*	
		ff. 214 et seq.	*Brev. de Virt.*	
			Legiloq.	
35.	Basel, Univ. A. VIII.1.	ff. 147–56v	*Ars Praed.*	
36.	Basel, Univ. A.x.132.	ff. 88–101	*Brev. de Virt.*	1465
37.	Basel, Univ.B.VI.6.	ff. 1ra–96vb	*Communiloq.*	s. xiv
38.	Basel, Univ.F.III.16.		*Communiloq.*	
39.	Berlin, Staatsbibliothek, Preussischer Kulturbesitz, 412 (theol lat fol 90)	ff. 14–112a	*Post. in Apoc.*	s. xiv
40.	Berlin, Staatsbibliothek, Preussischer Kulturbesitz, 447 (theol lat fol 237)	ff. 1–68	*Communiloq.*	1465
41.	Berlin, Staatsbibliothek, Preussischer Kulturbesitz, 448 (theol lat fol 147)	ff. 1–127	*Moniloq.*	s. xv
42.	Berlin, Staatsbibliothek, Preussischer Kulturbesitz, 840 (lat fol 173)	ff. 222–37	*Brev. de Virt.*	1424
43.	Berlin, Staatsbibliothek, Preussischer Kulturbesitz, 947 (theol lat qu 10)	ff. 39–59	*Brev. de Virt.*	1445
44.	Berlin, Staatsbibliothek, Preussischer Kulturbesitz, theol lat qu 152	ff. 2–90	*Moniloq.*	1408

MS no.	The manuscripts	Folio ref.	Work	Date of copy
45.	Berlin, Staatsbibliothek, Preussischer Kulturbesitz, theol lat qu 159	ff. 35r-45	*Brev. de Virt.*	s. xv
46.	Berlin, Staatsbibliothek, Preussischer Kulturbesitz, theol lat qu 186		*Communiloq.*	
47.	Berlin, Staatsbibliothek, Preussischer Kulturbesitz, theol lat qu 298	ff. 9-17	*Ars Praed.*	
48.	Berlin, Staatsbibliothek, Preussischer Kulturbesitz, Hamilton 630	ff. 53v-73r	*Brev. de Virt.*	s. xiv
49.	Bern 213		*Compendiloq.*	s. xiv
50.	Bern 260	ff. 47v-61	*Brev. de Virt.*	s. xiii/xiv
51.	Bern 527		*Brev. de Virt.* ★	s. xv
52.	Bologna, Univ. 1567		*Brev. de Virt.*	
53.	Bologna, Univ. 2249	ff. 88v-104	*Brev. de Virt.*	
54.	Bordeaux 118	ff. 51-104	*Brev. de Virt.*	s. xv
55.	Bordeaux 311	ff. 1-148	*Communiloq.*	s. xiv
56.	Brescia, Sanctuario delle Grazie 2	ff. 1-22	*Brev. de Virt.*	
57.	Breslau, Univ. I.F.78 (=83)	ff. 1-178	*Post. in Apoc.*	
		ff. 178-256	*Communiloq.*	
58.	Breslau, Univ. I.F.118	ff. 15 et seq.	*Brev. de Virt.*	
59.	Breslau, Univ. 828	ff. 14-26	*Post. in Apoc.* ★★	
60.	Brugge, Stadsbibl. 126	ff. 84-145	*Post. in Apoc.*	
61.	Brugge, Stadsbibl. 217	ff. 53r-68r	*Brev. de Virt.*	s. xv
62.	Brugge, Stadsbibl. 239	ff. 155-67	*Legiloq.*	
63.	Brugge, Stadsbibl. 244	f. 2 and back leaf	*Communiloq.* ★★	s. xiv
64.	Brunswick LXVI	ff. 1-16	*Brev. de Virt.*	

65.	Brunswick XCIX	ff. 247a–290b	*Ord. Vit. R.*	1451
66.	Budapest, Orsz. Széch. Kön. 274	ff. 1–17v	*Brev. de Virt.*	s. xv
67.	Budapest, Orsz. Széch. Kön. 276	f. 193	*Communiloq.***	1462–3
		ff. 198–214	*Brev. de Virt.*	
68.	Cambridge, Fitzwilliam Museum, Add. 50 (MS CFM 23)		*Communiloq.**	s. xv[2]
69.	Cambridge, Corpus Christi 177	ff. 146–7	*Brev. de Virt.**	s. xv
70.	Cambridge, Corpus Christi 307.II	ff. 1–42	*Compendiloq.*	s. xv
		ff. 43–7	*Brev. de Sap.*	
		ff. 48–62	*Legiloq.*	
		ff. 64–95	*De Poenit.*	
71.	Cambridge, Gonville and Caius 437	ff. 1–64	*Ord. Vit. R.*	s. xiv (1st ¼)
72.	Cambridge, Jesus Q.B.19 (36)	ff. 1 seq.	*Summa Iust.*[a]	s. xv
73.	Cambridge, Jesus Q.G.6. (54)	ff. 16–33	*Brev. de Virt.*	s. xiv
74.	Cambridge, Jesus Q.G.19. (67)		*Communiloq.*	s. xiv
75.	Cambridge, Pembroke 123		*Moniloq.*	s. xiv
76.	Cambridge, Pembroke 229	ff. 1–118	*Communiloq.*	s. xiv
77.	Cambridge, Pembroke 265	ff. 121–68	*Ord. Vit. R.*	s. xiii
78	Cambridge, Peterhouse 89 (=151)		*Moniloq.*	s. xiv
79.	Cambridge, Peterhouse 200	ff. 1–62	*Moniloq.*	s. xiv
80.	Cambridge, Peterhouse 237	ff. 1–69	*Communiloq.*	s. xiv
81.	Cambridge, Peterhouse 238	ff. 3–116	*Summa Iust.*[a]	s. xiv
82.	Cambridge, Peterhouse 252	ff. 1–79	*Communiloq.*	s. xv[1]
83.	Cambridge, Queens' 10	ff. 118 et seq.	*Brev. de Virt.*	s. xiii/xiv
84.	Cambridge, St John's A.15 (=15)	ff. 3–70	*Summa Iust.*[b]	s. xiv
85.	Cambridge, St John's G.7 (=175)	ff. 1–12v	*Ars Praed.*	s. xiv
86.	Cambridge, Trinity B.15.35 (=370)	ff. 86–158	*Communiloq.*	s. xiv

MS no.	The manuscripts	Folio ref.	Work	Date of copy
87.	Cambridge, Trinity B.15.38	ff. 204b–208	Sermon 9	s. xiii
88.	Cambridge, University Library Ff.3.24	ff. 1–116	Summa Iust.[a]	
89.	Cambridge, University Library Ii.6.15	ff. 140–1	Ars Praed.	s. xv
90.	Cambridge, University Library Kk.2.11	ff. 195–214r	Communiloq.★	s. xv
91.	Cambridge, University Library Add. 3470		Communiloq.	
			Moniloq.	
92.	Cardiff Public Library		Brev. de Virt.	
93.	Charleville 47		Super Orat. Dom.	s. xiv
94.	Charleville 113		Ord. Vit. R.	s. xiii/xiv
			Serm. de Temp.	
95.	Charleville 120		Super Orat. Dom.	s. xiv
96.	Charleville 136		Tract. Exempl.	s. xiv
97.	Charleville 272		Ord. Vit. R.	s. xiv
			Super Orat. Dom.	
98.	Chicago, Univ. 791	ff. 1–125	Communiloq.	1430
99.	Coblenz, Staatsarch. 702		Communiloq.	
100.	Colmar 290	f. 116ra	Sermon 8	
101.	Cordoba, Cath. 126	ff. 1r–8r	Ars Praed.	s. xv
102.	Cortona 45	ff. 2–56	Ord. Vit. R.	s. xv
103.	Cortona 53		Moniloq.	s. xv
104.	Cortona 58	ff. 9–56	De Poenit.	s. xv
		ff. 56–154	Summa Iust.[a]	
		ff. 165–87	Brev. de Virt.	
		ff. 187 et seq.	Legiloq.	
105.	Cues 91	ff. 1–91	Communiloq.	s. xv

No.	Shelfmark	Folios	Work	Date
106.	Dijon 223	ff. 92–108	Brev. de Virt.	s. xv
107.	Dresden A.103	ff. 108–44	Compendiloq.	s. xv
108.	Dresden P.32	ff. 155–67	Legiloq.	s. xv
		ff. 4–111	Super Orat. Dom.	
		ff. 1–12	Brev. de Virt.	
		ff. 1–415	Communiloq.	
109.	Dublin, Trinity Coll. 115 (A.5.3.)	ff. 392–415	Brev. de Virt.	1375
110.	Dublin, Trinity Coll. 138 (278)		Ord. Vit. R.	
111.	Dublin, Trinity Coll. 331		Communiloq.	s.xv
112.	Durham, Cath. B.IV.38	ff. 1–74	Moniloq.	
		ff. 75–85	Legiloq.	
			Brev. de Virt.	
113.	Durham, Cath. V.II.5	ff. 217–76	Communiloq.*	1456
114.	Einsiedeln 213	ff. 49–52	Brev. de Virt.**	
115.	Erfurt, Amplon. F.68	ff. 52–96	Communiloq.	
116.	Erfurt, Amplon. F.398	ff. 1–108	Communiloq.	1403
117.	Erfurt, Amplon. Q.117	ff. 44–80v	Compendiloq.	s. xv[1]
		ff. 80v–84	Brev. de Sap.	
		ff. 95v–109v	Legiloq.	
118.	Erfurt, Amplon Q.151	ff. 164–93	Brev. de Virt.	s. xiv/xv
119.	Erlangen 221	ff. 99–138	De Poenit.	s. xiv in
120.	Erlangen 276	ff. 26–65	Ord. Vit. R.	s. xiii ex
		ff. 124–57	De Poenit.	
121.	Erlangen 300	ff. 1–60	Ord. Vit. R.	s. xiv
122.	Erlangen 322	f. 126v	Sermon 9	s. xiii/xiv
123.	Evreux 11		Communiloq.	s. xiv
124.	Falaise 38	ff. 1–325	Communiloq.	

MS no.	The manuscripts	Folio ref.	Work	Date of copy
125.	Firenze, Laur. Plut 32.s.2.	ff. 325–72	Legiloq.	
		ff. 372–468	De Poenit.	
		ff. 468–723	Moniloq.	
			De Poenit.	
			Communiloq.	
			Compendiloq.	
			Brev. de Sap.	
126.	Firenze, Laur. Plut 32.s.3.	ff. 152 et seq.	Legiloq.	s. xiv/xv
		ff. 205 et seq.	Ord. Vit. R.	
			Communiloq.	
			Compendiloq.	
			Brev. de Virt.	
		ff. 241 et seq.	Brev. de Sap.	
			Exp. in Ioh.	
127.	Firenze, Laur. Conv. Sopp. 236	ff. 1–110	Post. in Apoc.	
128.	Firenze, Laur. Conv. Sopp. 239		Brev. de Virt.	
129.	Firenze, Laur. Strozzi 36	ff. 19–81	Post. in Apoc.	
130.	Firenze, Naz. Conv. Sopp. 547	ff. 67–86	Brev. de Virt.	
131.	Firenze, Naz. Conv. Sopp. D.2.1538		Communiloq.	
132.	Firenze, Naz. Conv. Sopp. D.8.1224	ff. 18v–24v	Ars Praed.	
133.	Firenze, Naz. Conv. Sopp. D.8.1412	ff. 1–62v	Moniloq.	
134.	Firenze, Naz. Conv. Sopp. F.8.1225	ff. 63–90	De Poenit.	
		ff. 90–117	Ord. Vit. R.	
		ff. 117–28	Brev. de Virt.	
		ff. 128–41	Legiloq.	

No.	Shelfmark	ff.	Work	Date
135.	Firenze, Naz. Conv. Sopp. G.5.1223	ff. 142–220	*Communiloq.*	
136.	Firenze, Naz. Conv. Sopp. I.II.26	ff. 221–44	*Compendiloq.*	
137.	Firenze, Naz. Conv. Sopp. I.V.7		*Communiloq.*	
138.	Firenze, Naz. Conv. Sopp. I.VI.I	ff. 183–98	*Ord. Vit. R.* *Brev. de Virt.*	
139.	Firenze, Naz. Conv. Sopp. I.VI.I.	ff. 1–84 ff. 85–139 ff. 139–91	*Communiloq.* *Brev. de Virt.* *Moniloq.*	s. xiii
140.	Firenze, Naz. Conv. Sopp. II.VI.I.	ff. 191–256 ff. 252–97	*Moniloq.* *Legiloq.* *De Poenit.* *Communiloq.* *Ord. Vit. R.*	
141.	Firenze, Riccard. 1030	ff. 249–56	*Brev. de Virt.*	s. xiv
142.	Firenze, Riccard. 1230 (M.II.7.)	ff. 1v–77v	*Compendiloq.*	s. xiv
143.	Frankfurt am Main, Barth.62	ff. 123ra–135vb	*Brev. de Virt.*	1459
144.	Frankfurt am Main, Barth.69	ff. 298ra–312ra	*Brev. de Virt.*	1460
145.	Frankfurt am Main, Oct. 67	ff. 156r–166r	*Ars Praed.*	1420–30
146.	Frankfurt am Main, Praed 59	ff. 1r–40vb	*Tract. Exemp.*	1437
147.	Frankfurt am Main, Praed 86	ff. 75r–137r	*Communiloq.*	1444/5
148.	Frankfurt am Main, Praed 123	ff. 35–71	*Brev. de Virt.* ★	s. xv²
149.	Frankfurt am Main, Praed 142	ff. 35v–71v	*Brev. de Virt.*	s. xvi in
150.	Gdansk, Mar. F.274	ff. 43–57	*Brev. de Virt.*	s. xv¹
151.	Gdansk, Mar. F.283		*Communiloq.*	s. xv¹
152.	Gotha, Herzogl. Bibl. Chart A 12	ff. 1–164	*Post. in Apoc.*	
153.	Graz, Univ. 174	ff. 1–109	*Communiloq.*	s. xiv
154.	Graz, Univ. 592		*Communiloq.*	1453

MS no.	The manuscripts	Folio ref.	Work	Date of copy
155.	Graz. Univ. 667	ff. 147–300	Communiloq.	1441
156.	Graz. Univ. 2069	ff. 143v–174	Brev. de Virt.	s. xiv med
157.	Grenoble 346	ff. 1–146v	Super Orat. Dom.	
158.	Hamburg, Staatsbibl. S.Petri 22	ff. 1–126va	Super Orat. Dom.	
159.	Heidelberg, Univ. 729		Communiloq.	
160.	Heiligenkreuz, Cistercienser 170	ff. 242–52	Tract. Exemp.	
161.	Heiligenkreuz, Cistercienser 240		Communiloq.	
162.	Hereford, Cath. o.6.11	ff. 1–102	Communiloq.	s.xv
		ff. 103 et seq.	Brev. de Virt.	
163.	Herzogenburg, Bibl. Can. 16	ff. 1–101	Moniloq.	
164.	Huntington Library (San Marino, California) 1345	ff. 112r–184r	Brev. de Virt.	c. 1350
165.	Iena, Univ. E1.F.19		Post. in Apoc.	
166.	Innsbruck, Univ. 796	ff. 111–17	Ars Praed.	
167.	Innsbruck, Univ. 946	ff. 133–140v	Ars Praed.	
168.	Klagenfurt, Studienbibl. Pap 171	ff. 201–67r	Compendiloq.	s. xv
		ff. 267v–84v	Brev. de Virt.	
169.	Klosterneuburg 320	ff. 1–116v	Communiloq.	s. xiv
170.	Klosterneuburg 328	ff. 133–304	Communiloq.	1439
171.	Klosterneuburg 382	ff. 25–82	Compendiloq.	c. 1449–57
		ff. 82v–98	Brev. de Virt.	
172.	Klosterneuburg 748	ff. 129–43	Brev. de Virt.	s. xiv
173.	Klosterneuburg 823	ff. 25–48'	Brev. de Virt.	c. 1455–9
174.	Klosterneuburg 841	ff. 73'–75'	Ord. Vit. R.**	c. 1458–62
175.	Köln Wf 140	ff. 146–210	Communiloq.	
176.	Köln Wq 202	ff. 10–189	Communiloq.	

No.	Shelfmark	Folios	Work	Date
177.	Köln Wq 316		*Communiloq.*	1431
178.	Köln GB f° 195	ff. 1r–149r	*Communiloq.*	1470
179.	Köln GB 4° 164	ff. 1r–74r	*Ord. Vit. R.*	s. xv
180.	Krakow, BJ 693	ff. 419–520	*Compendiloq.*	1412
181.	Krakow, BJ 2211	ff. 185–247	*De Poenit.*	
		ff. 248–303	*Brev. de Virt.*	
182.	Laon 194		*Ars Praed.*	s. xiv
183.	Leipzig, Univ. 168	ff. 7–70	*Post. in Apoc.*	s. xiv
184.	Leipzig, Univ. 170	ff. 1–98	*Post. in Apoc.*	s. xv
185.	Leipzig, Univ. 457	ff. 210–26	*Brev. de Virt.*	s. xv med
186.	Leipzig, Univ. 499	ff. 134 et seq.	*Moniloq.*	1466–9
187.	Liège, Univ. 190	ff. 201–45	*Ord. Vit. R.*	s. xv[1]
188.	Lisbon, Nación 269		*Communiloq.*	
189.	Lisbon, Acad-Scien. 5.22.3	ff. 1–153	*Communiloq.*	
			Moniloq.	
			Brev. de Virt.	
			Legiloq.	
190.	London, BL Add. 14082	ff. 8r–141r	*Communiloq.*	
			Brev. de Virt.	
			Brev. de Sap.	
			Ord. Vit. R.	
191.	London, BL Add. 21202	ff. 71–73v	*Ars Praed.*	s. xv
192.	London, BL Add. 38005	ff. 1–46	*Brev. de Virt.*	s. xv
193.	London, BL Burney 360	ff. 1–35	*Brev. de Virt.*	
194.	London, BL Cotton Vitell. C.xiv	ff. 72–7	*Ars Praed.*	
195.	London, BL Harley 362		*Brev. de Virt.*	
196.	London, BL Harley 632	ff. 1–24	*Ord. Vit. R.*	

MS no.	The manuscripts	Folio ref.	Work	Date of copy
197.	London, BL Harley 1298	ff. 25r–36r	Brev. de Virt.	
198.	London, BL Harley 1615	ff. 36r–131v	Communiloq.	
199.	London, BL Harley 2253	ff. 168r–247v	Summa Iust.ᵃ	
200.	London, BL Harley 5369	ff. 248r–307v	Moniloq.	
201.	London, BL Harley 37681	ff. 307v–317v	Legiloq.★	
		ff. 49 et seq.	Summa Iust.ᵇ	
		ff. 1r–1v	Ars Praed.	
		f. 135b	Communiloq.★★	
		ff. 101 et seq.	Summa Iust.ᵇ	
			Communiloq.	
			Brev. de Virt.	
			Brev. de Sap.	
			Ord. Vit. R.	
202.	London, BL Lat. 37075	f. 38 Add.	Communiloq.★	
203.	London, BL Royal 5.A.xii	ff. 1–21	Brev. de Virt.	s. xv
		ff. 21b et seq.	Brev. de Sap.	
204.	London, BL Royal 10.A.ix	ff. 2–50b	De Poenit.	s. xiv
		ff. 71b et seq.	Brev. de Virt.	
205.	London, BL Royal 6.B.xi	ff. 126–52	Compendiloq.	s. xiv in
		ff. 152b–54	Brev. de Sap.	
		ff. 155 et seq.	Communiloq.	
206.	London, BL Royal 8.B.xvii		Summa Iust.ᵇ	s. xv¹
207.	London, BL Royal 5.C.iii	ff. 317r–317v	Ars Praed.	s. xv
208.	London, BL Royal 7.C.i	ff. 206b–213	Brev. de Virt.	s. xiv
209.	London, BL Royal 4.D.iv	ff. 226b–44a	Summa Iust.	s. xv

No.	Location	Work	Folios	Date
210.	London, BL Royal 8.D.x.	De Poenit.	ff. 244b et seq.	s. xv
211.	London, BL Royal 10.D.iv	Communiloq.**	f. 203	s. xiii ex
212.	London, BL Royal 8.E.xii	De Poenit.	ff. 244v–62r	s. xv med
213.	London, BL Royal 12.E.xxi	Ars Praed.	ff. 216v–17v	s. xiv[1]
		Brev. de Virt.	ff. 27–43	s. xv
		Communiloq.**	f. 103b	s. xiii/xiv
214.	London, BL Royal 12.E.xxv	Brev. de Virt.	ff. 133b–41	
215.	London, BL Sloane 985	Summa Iust.[a]	ff. 1–171	
216.	Lons–Le Saunier, Arch. de Jura 7	Super Orat. Dom.	ff. 1–200v	
217.	Lucerne, Bibl. Cant. 66	Communiloq.		
218.	Lucerne, Escorial L.iii.7.	Communiloq.		
219.	Lucerne, Centralbibliothek 36	Communiloq.		
220.	Lyon 479 (409)	Super Orat. Dom.	ff. 1–94	1466
221.	Madrid, Escorial I.iii.6	Compendiloq.	ff. 1–35	s. xiii ex
		Brev. de Sap.	ff. 36–40	
		Brev. de Virt.	ff. 41–56	
222.	Madrid, Escorial L.iii.7	Communiloq.**	ff. 1–87	s. xv
223.	Madrid, BN 1470	Communiloq.	ff. 1–201	s. xiv
		Brev. de Virt.	ff. 205–26	
224.	Madrid, BN 8848	Brev. de Virt.	ff. 1–15	s. xv
225.	Magdeburg, Domgymnasium 163	Post. in Apoc.	ff. 41–74	
226.	Melk 129 (Co 7)	Communiloq.	ff. 1–167	
227.	Metz 479	Legiloq.		1390
228.	Metz 634	Ord. Vit. R.		s. xiv[1]
229.	Milan, Ambr. A.23.Supp.	Brev. de Virt.		s. xv
230.	Milan, Ambr. A.93.Inf.	De Poen. Inf.	ff. 79c–91b	
231.	Milan, Ambr. C.24.Supp.	Tract. Exemp.	ff. 109–200	

MS no.	The manuscripts	Folio ref.	Work	Date of copy
232.	Milan, Ambr. I.92.Supp.		*Moniloq.*	
			Communiloq.	
233.	Milan, Ambr. N.148.Supp.		*Brev. de Virt.*	
234.	Milan, Ambr. P.26.Supp.		*Moniloq.*	
235.	Milan, Brera AD XIII.11		*Super Orat. Dom.*	
236.	Modena, Bibl. Estense, γ.ο.5.2		*Brev. de Virt.*	s. xiv
			Legiloq.	
237.	Mondée Abbey, Cod. 3		*Super Orat. Dom.*	
238.	Montecassino 207.k	ff. 11–62	*Brev. de Virt.*	
239.	Monteprandone, S. Giacomo della Marca 13	ff. 1r–34v	*Brev. de Virt.*★	
240.	Monteprandone 19		*Ars Praed.*	
			De Poenit.	
			Ord. Vit. R.	
			Brev. de Virt.	
			Brev. de Sap.	
			Legiloq.	
			Communiloq.	
241.	Munich, Bayerische Staatsbibliothek Clm 4784	ff. 155r–65v	*Ars Praed.*	s. xv
242.	Munich, Bayerische Staatsbibliothek Clm 7588	ff. 108r–244v	*Communiloq.*	s. xv
243.	Munich, Bayerische Staatsbibliothek Clm 11427	ff. 279r–432r	*Communiloq.*	1433
244.	Munich, Bayerische Staatsbibliothek Clm 12281	ff. 216–369	*Communiloq.*	1454
245.	Munich, Bayerische Staatsbibliothek Clm 14054	ff. 1–191v	*Communiloq.*	s. xv
246.	Munich, Bayerische Staatsbibliothek Clm 14241	ff. 1–182r	*Communiloq.*	s. xv
247.	Munich, Bayerische Staatsbibliothek Clm 14893	ff. 69–250	*Communiloq.*	s. xiv/xv
248.	Munich, Bayerische Staatsbibliothek Clm 16211	ff. 1–154	*Communiloq.*	s. xv

249.	Munich, Bayerische Staatsbibliothek Clm 17657	ff. 1–151	*Communiloq.*	s. xv
250.	Munich, Bayerische Staatsbibliothek Clm 18430	ff. 135–231	*Communiloq.*	s. xv
251.	Munich, Bayerische Staatsbibliothek Clm 22374	ff. 1–142	*Communiloq.*	s. xv
252.	Munich, Bayerische Staatsbibliothek Clm 23595	ff. 72 *et seq.*	*Collat. super Matt.* *Moniloq.*	s. xiv
253.	Munich, Bayerische Staatsbibliothek Clm 26941	ff. 198ra–202ra	Sermon 9	
254.	Naples, branc. I.F.7	ff. 1–68	*Moniloq.*	
255.	New York, Union Theol. Seminary	ff. 105–9	*Brev. de Virt.*	
256.	North Carolina, Univ. 515	ff. 39–107	*Post. in Apoc.*	s. xiv[1]
257.	Nürnberg. Cent. iv.74	ff. 3r–15v	*Brev. de Virt.*★	s. xv[1]
258.	Olomouc CO 240	ff. 1ra–132rb	*Communiloq.*	
259.	Olomouc CO 284		*Brev. de Virt.*	
260.	Olomouc CO 429		*Brev. de Virt.*	
261.	Oxford, Bodleian Auct.F.3.5 (=SC 2684)	ff. 108 *et seq.*	*Communiloq.*	s. xv
262.	Oxford, Bodleian Bodley 50	f. 305v	A sermon	
263.	Oxford, Bodleian Bodley 58 (= SC 2006)	ff. 1–50	*Brev. de Virt.*	c. 1400
264.	Oxford, Bodleian Bodley 402 (= SC 2235)	ff. 329–45	*De Poenit.*	s. xv
265.	Oxford, Bodleian Bodley 571 (= SC 2019)	ff. 161–169v	*Ars Praed.*	s. xv[1]
266.	Oxford, Bodleian Bodley 630 (= SC 1953)	ff. 273v–274	*Ars Praed.*	s. xv in
267.	Oxford, Bodleian Bodley 687 (= SC 2501)	ff. 150–72	*Legiloq.*	s. xv in
268.	Oxford, Bodleian Bodley 867 (= SC 2746)	ff. 132–65	*Ord. Vit. R.*★	s. xv in
269.	Oxford, Bodleian Bodley 881 (= SC 27707)	ff. 46–67r	*Brev. de Virt.*	c. 1458
270.	Oxford, Bodleian Hamilton 31 (= SC 24461)	ff. 1–179	*Post. in Apoc.*	s. xv
271.	Oxford, Bodleian Hatton 105 (= SC 4054)	ff. 109–52	*Brev. de Virt.*★	c. 1458
272.	Oxford, Bodleian Laud Misc. 402	ff. 71–90	*Brev. de Virt.*	s. xv
273.	Oxford, Bodleian Laud Misc. 497	ff. 1–66	*Ord. Vit. R.*	s. xv

MS no.	The manuscripts	Folio ref.	Work	Date of copy
274.	Oxford, Bodleian Laud Misc. 603	ff. 61–98	*Compendiloq.*	s. xiv
		ff. 99–103	*Brev. de Sap.*	
		ff. 103 *et seq.*	*Brev. de Virt.*	
275.	Oxford, Bodleian Rawlinson A.423	f. 46b	*Communiloq.* ★★	s. xv
276.	Oxford, Bodleian Rawlinson C.534	ff. 106 *et seq.*	*Legiloq.*	
277.	Oxford, Bodleian Tanner 110	ff. 124–55	*Ord. Vit. R.*	
278.	Oxford, Balliol 274	ff. 1–130	*Communiloq.*	1409
		ff. 130–45	*Brev. de Virt.*	
279.	Oxford, Balliol 320	ff. 57–150v	*Summa Iust.*[b]	s. xv[1]
280.	Oxford, Corpus Christi 18		*Brev. de Virt.*	
281.	Oxford, Corpus Christi 39	ff. 48–64	*Brev. de Virt.* ★	1475
282.	Oxford, Corpus Christi 183	ff. 21–2	*Brev. de Virt.* ★★	s. xv
283.	Oxford, Exeter 7	ff. 163 *et seq.*	*Summa Iust.*	s. xv
284.	Oxford, Exeter 39	ff. 1–257	*Collat. in Ioh.*	s. xiv
285.	Oxford, Jesus 18	ff. 1–23	*Brev. de Virt.*	s. xiii ex
286.	Oxford, Lincoln 67e	ff. 9–141	*Communiloq.*	s. xiv
		ff. 142–60	*Legiloq.*	
287.	Oxford, Lincoln 69		*Communiloq.* ★★	s. xv
288.	Oxford, Lincoln 105	ff. 1 *et seq.*	*Summa Iust.*	s. xv
289.	Oxford, Magdalen 27	ff. 1–90	*Collat. super Matt.*	s. xiv
290.	Oxford, Merton 47	ff. 49–67	*Brev. de Virt.*	
		ff. 68 *et seq.*	*Brev. de Sap.*	
291.	Oxford, Oriel 34	ff. 154–62	*Brev. de Virt.*	s. xiv
292.	Oxford, Oriel 183	ff. 161v *et seq.*	*Brev. de Virt.*	s. xiv
293.	Oxford, Univ. Coll. e.36	ff. 237–9	*Ars Praed.* ★★	s. xiv

294.	Oxford, Univ. Coll. d.109	ff. 247 et seq.	*Summa Iust.*[b]	s. xv
295.	Padua, Anton 325		*Post. in Apoc.*	
296.	Padua, Anton 326		*Exp. in Ioh.*	
			Collat. in Ioh.	
297.	Padua, Anton xx.463		*Ord. Vit. R.*	
298.	Padua, Anton 542		*Ord. Vit. R.*	
299.	Padua, Cap. A.56		*Brev. de Virt.*	
300.	Padua, Museo C.M.6		*Brev. de Virt.*	
301.	Padua, Univ. 1788		*Ord. Vit. R.*	
302.	Paris, BN lat. 3241	ff. 1–65	*Moniloq.*	s. xiii/xiv
		ff. 65–77v	*Brev. de Virt.*	
303.	Paris, BN lat. 3243	ff. 1 et seq.	*Moniloq.*★	s. xiii/xiv
304.	Paris, BN lat. 3488	ff. 7–172v	*Communiloq.*	s. xiv
305.	Paris, BN lat. 3588	ff. 1r–111	*Ord. Vit. R.*	s. xiv
306.	Paris, BN lat. 3706	ff. 89v–120r	*Brev. de Virt.*	s. xiii/xiv
307.	Paris, BN lat. 3935	ff. 1 et seq.	*Communiloq.*	
308.	Paris, BN lat. 6346	ff. 21r–30r	*Brev. de Virt.*	
309.	Paris, BN lat. 6776	ff. 1–54	*Brev. de Virt.*★	
		ff. 55 et seq.	*Moniloq.*	
310.	Paris, BN lat. 11135	ff. 45–79	*Brev. de Virt.*	
311.	Paris, BN lat. 12430	ff. 1–138	*Communiloq.*	
312.	Paris, BN lat. 13964	ff. 1r–76r	*Brev. de Virt.*	1473
313.	Paris, BN lat. 14549	ff. 4–133v	*Communiloq.*	s. xv[1]
314.	Paris, BN lat. 14909	f. 125r–v	*Ars Praed.*	
		f. 144c	Sermon 4	
315.	Paris, BN lat. 14947	f. 166b	Sermon 5	
		f. 187	Sermon 3	

MS no.	The manuscripts	Folio ref.	Work	Date of copy
316.	Paris, BN lat. 14976	f. 19-95v	*Ord. Vit. R.*	
317.	Paris, BN lat. 15005	ff. 79-86r	*Ars Praed.*	
		f. 92	Sermon 3	
		f. 144ra	Sermon 4	
		f. 166rb	Sermon 5	
318.	Paris, BN lat. 15034	ff. 127-129d	Sermon 2	
319.	Paris, BN lat. 15451	ff. 1-84	*Communiloq.*	
320.	Paris, BN lat. 15962	f. 35ra	Sermon 9	s. xiii/xiv
321.	Paris, BN lat. 17834	ff. 1-117	*Communiloq.*	
		ff. 124-39	*Brev. de Virt.*	
		ff. 144-87	*Compendiloq.*	
		ff. 188-192v	*Brev. de Sap.*	
		ff. 194-231	*Ord. Vit. R.*	
		ff. 231-249r	*Legiloq.*	
		ff. 249-86	*De Poenit.*	
		ff. 287-98	*Moniloq.*	
322.	Paris, BN lat. 18425	ff. 6r-311v	*Communiloq.*	
323.	Paris, BN nouv. acq. lat. 284	ff. 1r-26v	*Brev. de Virt.*	
		ff. 32-75r	*Compendiloq.*	
324.	Paris, Arsenal 529	ff. 135-208	*Moniloq.*	s. xiii
325.	Paris, Arsenal 1199	ff. 108-58	*Brev. de Virt.*	s. xv/xvi
326.	Paris, Mazar. 569=295	ff. 80-86v	*Ars Praed.*	s. xiv
		ff. 86v-112r	*De Poenit.*	
		ff. 112v-38v	*Ord. Vit. R.*	
		ff. 139v-51	*Legiloq.*	

327.	Paris, Mazar. 727=1255	ff. 77–108	*Compendiloq.*	s. xiv
		ff. 109 et seq.	*Brev. de Sap.*	
328.	Paris, Ste-Geneviève 251		*Communiloq.*	
329.	Pelpin, Semin. 283		*Moniloq.*	
330.	Prague, 68 Cpl (452a) 101	ff. 1–132	*Communiloq.*	1421
331.	Prague, Cap. 220 (A.119)	ff. 1–169	*Post. in Apoc.*	
332.	Prague, Cap. 222 (A.121)	ff. 1–108	*Post. in Apoc.*	
333.	Prague, Univ. 320 (I.G.4)	ff. 54–89	*Brev. de Virt.*	s. xiv
334.	Prague, Univ. 395 (III.A.10)	ff. 1–35	*Compendiloq.*	s. xiv (ante 1394)
		ff. 35–40	*Brev. de Sap.*	
335.	Prague, Univ. 591 (IV.A.15)	ff. 37–59	*Brev. de Virt.*	s. xv
336.	Prague, Univ. 760 (IV.G.281)	ff. 1a–312b	*Post. in Apoc.*	
337.	Prague, Univ. 821 (V.B.4)	ff. 1–137	*Communiloq.*	
338.	Prague, Univ. 975 (V.G.23)	ff. 1–300	*Post. in Apoc.*	s. xv
339.	Prague, Univ. 1052 (VI.B.18)	ff. 1a–159a	*Post. in Apoc.*	1389
340.	Prague, Univ. 1302 (VII.E.13)	ff. 93–131	*Brev. de Virt.*	1415
341.	Prague, Univ. 1426 (VIII.A.19)	ff. 174–91	*Brev. de Virt.*	s. xiv/xv
342.	Prague, Univ. 1433 (VIII.A.25)	ff. 40–64	*Brev. de Virt.*	s. xiv ex
343.	Prague, Univ. 1913 (X.E.12)	ff. 1–33	*Brev. de Virt.*	s. xv
344.	Prague, Univ. 1983 (X.H.5)	ff. 212–32	*Brev. de Virt.*	s. xiv
345.	Prague, Univ. 1985 (X.H.7)	ff. 63–94	*Brev. de Virt.*	s. xv (pars 1436)
346.	Prague, Univ. 2100 (XII.A.23)	ff. 1–15	*Brev. de Virt.*	1398
347.	Prague, Univ. 2116 (XII.B.11)	ff. 1–96	*Post. in Apoc.*	1408
348.	Prague, Univ. 2119 (XII.B.14)	ff. 122–39	*Brev. de Virt.*	s. xv
349.	Prague, Univ. 2125 (XII.B.20)	ff. 23–36	*Brev. de Virt.*	s. xiv/xv (pars 1410)
350.	Prague, Univ. 2543 (XIV.E.9)	ff. 128–30	*Brev. de Virt.*	s. xiv
351.	Prague, Nat. Mus. 3865 (XVI.D.9)	ff. 1–129	*Post. in Apoc.*	

MS no.	The manuscripts	Folio ref.	Work	Date of copy
352.	Ravenna, Classense 133(7)	ff. 2–17	Exp. Reg. OFM	s. xiv
353.	Reims 168	ff. 56–185	Collat. in Ioh.	s. xiii ex.
354.	Rome, Angelica 490	ff. 1–30	Communiloq.	
355.	Rome, Casanatense 16	ff. 2–18	Brev. de Virt.	
356.	Rouen A.156 (592)	ff. 26–151	Brev. de Virt.	s. xiv/xv
		ff. 151–93	Communiloq.	
		ff. 193–7	Compendiloq.	
			Brev. de Sap.	
357.	St-Florian XI.234	ff. 243–59	Communiloq.**	s. xv
358.	Saint-Omer 285		Post. in Apoc.	s. xiv
359.	Saint-Omer 400		Brev. de Virt.	s. xiv
360.	Saint-Omer 622		Brev. de Virt.	1346
			Compendiloq.	
			Brev. de Sap.	
			Communiloq.	
361.	S. Paul (Lavent) pap 48 (2)		Serm. de Temp.	
362.	Salzburg, St Peter a. v.14	ff. 74–80	Brev. de Virt.	1462
363.	Salzburg, St Peter a. ix.10	ff. 3–275	Post. in Apoc.	s. xiii ex
364.	Salzburg, St Peter b. I.37	ff. 84–137	Communiloq.*	s. xv²
365.	Salzburg, St Peter b. ix.1	ff. 68–85	Brev. de Virt.	s. xv
366.	Salzburg, St Peter b. ix.16	ff. 1–166	Communiloq	s. xv
367.	Salzburg, St Peter b. ix.20	ff. 192–243	Compendiloq.	1467
368.	Salzburg, St Peter b. ix.25	ff. 34–213	Communiloq.	s. xv ex
369.	Salzburg, Univ. M.II.345	ff. 1–90v	Communiloq.	s. xiv ex
370.	Salzburg, Univ. M.II.371 (IV.2.A.14)	ff. 1–11	Ars Praed.	

No.	Manuscript	Folios	Work	Date
371.	Sarnano 53 (E.127)			
372.	Seville, Colomb. Y.128.18	ff. 151 et seq.	*Brev. de Virt.*	
373.	Seville, Colomb. Y.130.40	ff. 157–204	*Post. in Apoc.*	
			Ord. Vit. R.	
374.	Seville, Colomb. Z.131.32		*Communiloq.*	
375.	Seville, Colomb. Z.136.8		*Post. in Apoc.*	
376.	Siena G.VII.7		*Communiloq.*	
377.	Siena L.XI.22		*Brev. de Virt.*	
378.	Solothurn S.369	ff. 1r–34v	*Brev. de Virt.*	1449
379.	Solothurn S1.250	ff. 216r–24r	*Ars Praed.*	1431–2
380.	Sydney NSW, Univ. Nicholson 23	ff. 165–95	*Brev. de Virt.*	s. xiv/xv
381.	Todi, Communale 68		*Post. in Apoc.*	
382.	Toledo Cap. 21.12	ff. 1–16	*Brev. de Virt.*	
383.	Tortosa Cap. 37	ff. 1–91	*Communiloq.*	s. xiv
		ff. 93–131	*Compendiloq.*	
384.	Tortosa Cap. 231	ff. 7–99v	*Compendiloq.*	s. xiv
		ff. 100r–250v	*Moniloq.*	
385.	Toulouse 340	ff. 279–414	*Compendiloq.*	s. xiii and s. xiv
		ff. 415–26	*Brev. de Sap.*	
		ff. 427–64	*Brev. de Virt.*	
		ff. 465–507	*Legiloq.*	
386.	Toulouse 540	ff. 103v–183	*Brev. de Virt.*	s. xiv
387.	Tours 44	ff. 1–56	*Communiloq.*	s. xv
388.	Tours 404		*Brev. de Virt.*	
389.	Turin E.IV.41	ff. 282v–293r	*Brev. de Sap.*	
			Brev. de Virt.	
			Moniloq.	
			Ord. Vit. R.	

MS no.	The manuscripts	Folio ref.	Work	Date of copy
390.	Troyes 1922		*Legiloq.*	
			De Poenit.	
391.	Utrecht, Univ. 237	ff. 87–95	*Ars Praed.*	s. xiv
392.	Uppsala, Univ. C.393	ff. 1–31	*Brev. de Virt.*	
393.	Uppsala, Univ. C.614	ff. 68–121	*Post. in Apoc.*	
394.	Valencia, Cath. 44	ff. 1r–106v	*Communiloq.*	
395.	Valencia, Cath. 135		*Communiloq.*	
		ff. 1–90	*Brev. de Virt.*	
			Communiloq.	
396.	Valencia, Cath. 186	ff. 1–197	*Serm. de Temp.*	
		ff. 198–262	*Collat. super Matt.*	
397.	Valencia, Cath. 286	ff. 1–40	*Compendiloq.*	s. xiv
398.	Valencia, Cath. 288	ff. 1–55	*Brev. de Virt.*	s. xv
399.	Vatican lat. 939	ff. 124–32	*Brev. de Sap.*	1433
400.	Vatican lat. 1018	ff. 1–142	*Communiloq.*	s. xv
401.	Vatican lat. 1266	ff. 404–6	Sermon 9	s. xv
402.	Vatican lat. 1860	ff. 92–101	*Brev. de Virt.*	1313
403.	Vatican lat. 4357	ff. 1–31	*Brev. de Virt.*	
404.	Vatican lat. 7613		*Communiloq.*	
405.	Vatican lat. 7723		*Comm. in Ioh.*	
406.	Vatican lat. 10289	ff. 24–84	*Ord. Vit. R.*	s. xiii/xiv
407.	Vatican Ottob. 396	ff. 51–59v	*Ars Praed.*	
408.	Vatican Rossian lat. 470	ff. 1–78	*Post. in Apoc.*	
409.	Vatican Urbin lat. 510	ff. 1–24	*Brev. de Virt.*	
410.	Venice, Marz. L.III.35	ff. 25–204	*Communiloq.*	1476

411.	Venice, Marz. L.III.36	ff. 1–23	*Brev. de Virt.*	s. xiv
412.	Venice, Marz. L.III.106	ff. 1–72	*Communiloq.*	s. xiv
413.	Venice, Marz. L.III.122	ff. 1–144	*Communiloq.*	s. xiv
414.	Venice, Marz. L.VII.24		*Ord. Vit. R.*	s. xv
415.	Venice, Marz. L.VII.25		*Communiloq.*	
416.	Venice, Marz. L.VII.26		*Communiloq.*	
417.	Venice, Marz. L.VII.27		*Brev. de Virt.*	
418.	Venice, Marz. L.XI.34		*Ord. Vit. R.*	
419.	Venice, Marz. L.XII.62	ff. 127–9	*Brev. de Virt.*	
420.	Vienna, Nat. Lat. 603		*Communiloq.*	s. xiv *med*
421.	Vienna, Nat. Lat. 1399	ff. 123b–166a	*De Poenit.*	s. xv *med*
422.	Vienna, Nat. Lat. 1533		*Exp. in Ioh.*	s. xiv *med*
423.	Vienna, Nat. Lat. 1658	ff. 132–67	*Collat. in Ioh.*	s. xiv *med*
424.	Vienna, Nat. Lat. 2241	ff. 305r–450v	*Communiloq.*	s. xiv *med*
425.	Vienna, Nat. Lat. 3420		*Communiloq.*	s. xv
426.	Vienna, Nat. Lat. 4211	ff. 1r–16v	*Brev. de Virt.*	s. xv
			Post. in Apoc.	
427.	Vienna, Nat. Lat. 4214	ff. 1r–165v	*Communiloq.*	s. xv
428.	Vienna, Nat. Lat. 4230	ff. 1r–160v	*Communiloq.*	s. xv
429.	Vienna, Nat. Lat. 4412	ff. 1a–80a	*Communiloq.*	s. xv
430.	Vienna, Nat. Lat. 4572	ff. 254–398	*Communiloq.*	1423
431.	Vienna, Nat. Lat. 5284	ff. 1r–154r	*Communiloq.*	s. xv
432.	Vienna, Nat. Lat. 5381	ff. 1r–163r	*Communiloq.*	s. xv
433.	Vienna, Scott. 171	ff. 193–210	*Communiloq.*	1462–3
434.	Vienna, Scott. 297	ff. 1–82	*Communiloq.*	s. xv
435.	Vienna, Scott. 308	ff. 1–127	*Communiloq.*	1429

MS no.	The manuscripts	Folio ref.	Work	Date of copy
436.	Vorau 133	ff. 152r–257r	Communiloq.	1454
437.	Vorau 289	ff. 12–170	Post. in Apoc.	
438.	Warsaw, Staatsbibl. Abtl.II.Chart.Lat.Fol.I.280	ff. 166–233	Post. in Apoc.	
439.	Wiesbaden, Landesbibl. 35	ff. 161–70	Ars Praed.	
440.	Windesheim, Reichstadt 93	ff. 1r–146v	Communiloq.	1469
441.	Wolfenbüttel 429	ff. 129–267	Post. in Apoc.	
442.	Wolfenbüttel 743	ff. 137r–147v	Exp. Reg. OFM	1440
443.	Wolfenbüttel 2687	ff. 80–155	Communiloq.	1431–2
444.	Wolfenbüttel 2861	ff. 23–169	Communiloq.	1461
445.	Worcester, Cath. F.114	ff. 101–60	Communiloq.	s. xv
446.	Worcester, Cath. F.115	ff. 227–34	Brev. de Virt.	s. xv
447.	Worcester, Cath. F.154	ff. 17–22v	Brev. de Virt.	s. xv
		ff. 204–7	Ars Praed.	
448.	Worcester, Cath. Q.27	ff. 8–135b	Communiloq.	s. xiv
449.	Worcester, Cath. Q.72	ff. 1–34	Compendiloq.	s. xv
		ff. 35–42	Brev. de Virt.	
450.	Würzburg, Univ. F.174		Communiloq.	
451.	Würzburg, Univ. F.208		Communiloq.	
452.	Yale, Univ. T. E. Marston Coll. 223	ff. 52v–78v	Brev. de Virt.	
453.	Zwettl 319	ff. 1–52v	Ord. Vit. R.	

APPENDIX 3: NUMBERS OF SURVIVING LATIN MS COPIES FOR INDIVIDUAL TEXTS BY JOHN OF WALES

Breviloquium de Virtutibus Antiquorum Principum et Philosophorum	151
Communiloquium sive Summa Collationum	144
Ordinarium seu Alphabetum Vitae Religiosae	44
Postilla in Apocalypsim	37
Moniloquium	31
Ars Praedicandi	30
Compendiloquium de Vitis Illustrium Philosophorum et de Dictis Moralibus Eorundem	27
Legiloquium or *Tractatus de Decem Preceptis*	26
Breviloquium de Sapientia sive Philosophia Sanctorum	23
De Poenitentia	22
Summa Iustitiae or *Tractatus de Septem Viciis*	16
Sermones Singuli (9 in total)	15[13]
Expositio super Orationem Dominicam	12
Sermones de Tempore	5
Tractatus Exemplorum	5
Expositio in Evangelium Iohannis	4
Collationes in Evangelium S. Iohannis	4[14]
Collationes super Matthaeum	3
Sermones de Evangeliis Dominicalibus et Quadragesimales	2
Expositio Regulae Ordinis Fratrum Minorum	2
De Poenis Inferni	1

[13] This figure refers to the number of individual copies of one or other of the single sermons.
[14] Not the same group of MSS as for the *Expositio in Evangelium Iohannis*.

APPENDIX 4: A LIST OF INSTITUTIONS AND INDIVIDUALS WHO OWNED COPIES OF JOHN OF WALES' WORKS UP TO THE MID-SIXTEENTH CENTURY

I here present a list of those institutions or individuals which can be shown to have possessed copies of works by John of Wales. The list is by no means full, even where catalogues and inventories of medieval libraries survive. It can be seen that only some of John's known works are represented on this list: they are those whose titles are easily distinguished in even a scanty inventory, and those which remained firmly associated with John's name. Some of his works were misattributed at an early date, or confused with other works of identical title. Others were often copied anonymously. Thus John's *De Poenitentia* and *De Septem Viciis*, for example, are hard to spot unless a catalogue contains incipits. Very many medieval catalogues did not. It is therefore reasonable to assume that, even in the libraries listed here, there will often have been more of John's works than we can tabulate. And many more copies must have existed which went unrecorded and are now lost to us.

I have used two main sources in compiling this list: first, surviving catalogues or parts of catalogues from the medieval period; and, secondly, marks of ownership in surviving MSS and early printed editions of John's works. I have personally examined as many as possible of these texts – primarily those in Oxford, Cambridge and London, Paris, Munich, Vienna and Salzburg – and have otherwise relied on the information given in modern catalogue descriptions.

Partial lists of owners of John's works were given by A. G. Little[15] and W. A. Pantin.[16] All the owners mentioned on their lists have been checked, and the information about them expanded to include the particular works which were in their possession and, where possible, the dates of ownership.

The basic structure of my list is as follows. Owners are grouped as far as possible by the modern state within whose boundaries they would have fallen. Within each group, owners are arranged alphabetically, with some minor deviations for the sake of clarity and continuity. I have tried to give some indication of the date of ownership. Sometimes this is an accurate date of purchase or production, but more often it is a *terminus ad quem* provided by a dated catalogue. I have also tried to indicate which works were owned by whom, and in how many copies. This list cannot be used directly to calculate the number

---

[15] A. G. Little, 1917.   [16] W. A. Pantin, 1961.

of known copies of John's works. Some of the copies here had as many as six
different owners. It has not always been possible to indicate such transfers of
ownership.

A full discussion of the significance of the contents of this list appears in
chapter 8.

Superscripts used in the list
Where listings of a work have the same numerical superscript attached, this
indicates that they are listings of a single copy which has had a change of owner.

Superscript [P] indicates an early printed edition.

Superscript [V] indicates a vernacular copy.

All other copies are Latin MSS. Works bracketed together are contained within
one volume. The MS number in the final column refers to the number which I
have given to the MS in Appendix 2.

	Date of ownership	Work	Reference
AUSTRIA			
Maria Laach, Benediktinerstift	s. xiv	*Brev. de Virt.*	MS 156
St Lambrecht, Benediktinerstift	after 1453	*Communiloq.*	MS 154
Heiligenkreuz, Cistercians	by 1374	*Communiloq.*	T. Gottlieb, 1915
Herzogenburg, Chorherrenstift		*Moniloq.*	MS 163
Klosterneuburg, Augustinian Canons	after 1330	*Communiloq.*	T. Gottlieb, 1915
Klosterneuburg	s. xiv/xv	*Brev. de Virt.*	MS 172
	s. xiv/xv	*Communiloq.*	MS 169
Johannes alias Hascone, capellanus Henrici (V) de Rosenberg in Krummau	1405	*Communiloq.*°	MS 330
Thomas, praedicator in Patavia near Krummau	1421	*Communiloq.*°	MS 330
Melk, Benedictines	by 1390	*Communiloq.*	MS 226
	by 1483	*Communiloq.*	T. Gottlieb, 1915
Neuburg, Cistercians	after 1441	*Communiloq.*	MS 155
	s. xiv	*Communiloq.*	MS 153
Salzburg, Augustinian Hermits	after 1467	*Compendiloq.*	MS 367
	by 1469	*Compendiloq.*[43]	MS 440
St Florian, Augustinian canons	s. xv	*Communiloq.* (extracts)	MS 357
Vienna, Schottenkloster, Benedictines	by 1513	*Communiloq.*	A. G. Little, 1917
Vienna, Dominicans	by 1513	*De Poenit.*	T. Gottlieb, 1915
	by 1513	*Legiloq.* / *Ord. Vit. R.*	T. Gottlieb, 1915
	by 1513	*Brev. de Virt.*	T. Gottlieb, 1915

Vienna, Monastery of St Dorothy	by 1513	*Brev. de Virt.*	T. Gottlieb, 1915
Vienna, St Stephen's	s. xiv/xv	*Communiloq.*	MS 424
Wolfgang de Egenburg, Magister, Prof. of	s. xv	*Communiloq.*	MS 427
Theology and Canon of St Stephen's in Vienna	until 1470	*Communiloq.*[1]	T. Gottlieb, 1915
Magister Georgius Sleithel of Linz, Master of Arts and Theology	1470–82	*Communiloq.*[2]	MS 429
Vienna Arts Faculty Library	after 1470	*Communiloq.*[1]	T. Gottlieb, 1915
	after 1482	*Communiloq.*[2]	MS 429

BELGIUM

Aulne, Cistercians	by 1632	*Brev. de Virt.*	BBM, p. 215
	by 1632	*Ord. Vit. R.*	BBM, p. 215
	by 1632	*Brev. de Sap.*	BBM, p. 215
Huy, Couvent des Croisiers	s. xv	*Ord. Vit. R.*	MS 187
Dunes, Cistercians	by 1638	*Legiloq.*	BBM, p. 171
	by 1638	*Brev. de Virt.*	BBM, p. 171
Louvain, Valle S. Martini, Augustinian Canons	by 1639	*Communiloq.*	BBM, p. 219
Abbey of Ter Doest, near Brugge	s. xiv	*Communiloq.*	MS 63
Tongerloo, Praemonstratensian	by 1640	Title unclear	BBM, p. 155
Tongres, Library of the Canons Reg.	by 1638	*Compendiloq.*	BBM, p. 193
Andreas Zeeburgensis	1434	*Brev. de Sap.*	MS 399

CZECHOSLOVAKIA

Borovanensis, Augustinian Canons	s. xiv	*Brev. de Virt.*	MS 333
Oywinensis, monastery	s. xv ex	*Brev. de Virt.*	MS 345

	Date of ownership	Work	Reference
Andreas de Broda, Magister, Prague Univ., and ardent anti-Hussite	after 1407, before 1427	*Post. in Apoc.*	MS 39
Rosenberg, Johannes Stropnicz, pronotharius	s. xv ex	*Brev. de Virt.*[3]	MS 350
Trzebon, Monastery	s. xv/xvi	*Brev. de Virt.*[3]	MS 350
Nicolaus Puschmann, prepositus Sliwensis	s. xv	*Communiloq.*	MS 108
Olomouc, Augustinian Hermits		*Brev. de Virt.*	MS 260
Monastery of St Corona	1408	*Post. in Apoc.*	MS 347
	after 1410	*Brev. de Virt.*	MS 349
Swin Church	s. xiv/xv	*Brev. de Virt.*	MS 341
Trzebon, Monastery of St Egidius	after 1398	*Brev. de Virt.*	MS 346
Magister Matthie de Janow	before 1394	{ *Compendiloq.* *Brev. de Sap.*	MS 334
Petrus Cremsirz	s. xiv/xv	*Post. in Apoc.*	MS 339
Frater Nycolai Lange de Ylgenburk	s. xv	*Communiloq.*[4]	MS 151
Dominus Johannes Piscatoris	s. xv	*Communiloq.*[4]	MS 151
ENGLAND			
Babwell, Franciscans		{ *Communiloq.* *Moniloq.*	MS 91
Burton-upon-Trent, Benedictines of BVM and St Modwenna	after 1511	*Communiloq.*[P] *Compendiloq.* *Brev. de Virt.* *Brev. de Sap.* *Ord. Vit. R.*	N. Ker, 1964
Bury St Edmunds, Benedictines			A. G. Little, 1917

David Lloyd of Llwydiarth, Anglesey	before 1597	Brev. de Virt.[5]	MS 271
Edward Hughes, fellow of Jesus Coll., Cambridge	1597	Brev. de Virt.[5]	MS 271
W. P. Norvicem	s. xv med	Communiloq.[6]	MS 82
John Warkeworth, Magister	1462	Communiloq.[6]	MS 82
	1462	Moniloq.[7]	MS 79
	s. xv med/ex	Summa Iust.[8]	MS 81
Pembroke Coll. Cambridge	s. xiv ex	Communiloq.	MS 76
	c. 1404	Moniloq.	MS 75
Peterhouse, Cambridge	s. xv ex	Communiloq.[6]	MS 82
	s. xv ex	Moniloq.[7]	MS 79
	s. xv ex	Summa Iust.[8]	MS 81
Richard Cleypoole	s. xv	Ars Praed.	MS 89
Robert Portlond, frater	s. xv med	Summa Iust.[9]	MS 84
Nicholas Kempston, Magister	before 1477	Summa Iust.[9]	MS 84
Robert Elyott, Magister	1477	Summa Iust.[9]	MS 84
John Thorp, Magister	after 1477	Summa Iust.[9]	MS 84
John Talbott, Magister	s. xv ex	Summa Iust.[9]	MS 84
Henry Murgetrode		Summa Iust.	MS 72
Thomas Sheldon	s. xvi	Brev. de Virt.	MS 69
Frater Thomas Wicford, Magister		Ord. Vit. R.	MS 77
Adam de Stockton, Cambridge	1375	Brev. de Virt.	MS 109
Thomas Sprot, St Augustine's Abbey, Canterbury. Historian of the abbey	s. xiii ex	Communiloq.[10]	A. B. Emden, 1968
Robert de Elmerston, St Augustine's Abbey, Canterbury	s. xiv in	Communiloq.[11] Brev. de Virt. Ord. Vit. R.	A. B. Emden, 1968

	Date of ownership	Work	Reference
Thomas de Wyvelsberghe, St Augustine's Abbey, Canterbury	s. xiv in	Communiloq.[12] / Brev. de Virt. / Ord. Vit. R.	A. B. Emden, 1968
William Reede, Bishop of Chichester	by 1360s	Compendiloq.[13] / Brev. de Sap. / Brev. de Virt. / + others	A. B. Emden, 1968
Michis de Northgate cum B., Canterbury	before s. xv ex	Communiloq.[14] / Ord. Vit. R. / Brev. de Virt. / + others	M. R. James, 1903
	before 1500	Communiloq.[15]	A. B. Emden, 1968
Georgius Penshurst, Abbot of St Augustine's Abbey, Canterbury, c. 1450	s. xv med	Summa Iust.[16]	MS 200
St Augustine's Abbey, Canterbury*	s. xiii ex/s. xiv in	Communiloq.[10]	A. B. Emden, 1968
	s. xiv med	Communiloq.[11] / Brev. de Virt.	A. B. Emden, 1968
	s. xiv in	Ord. Vit. R. / Ord. Vit. R.	A. B. Emden, 1968
	after 1324	Communiloq.[12] / Brev. de Virt. / Ord. Vit. R.	A. B. Emden, 1968

* The St Augustine's Abbey catalogue for the end of the fifteenth century lists a number of other volumes containing works by John of Wales, but it does not give sufficient detail for identification.

	Date	Works	Reference
	c. 1360	Compendiloq.[13] / Brev. de Sap. / Brev. de Virt. + others	A. B. Emden, 1968
	by 1500	Ord. Vit. R. / Communiloq. / Brev. de Virt.	M. R. James, 1903
	by 1500	Communiloq.[14] / Ord. Vit. R. / Brev. de Virt. + others	M. R. James, 1903
	by 1500	Communiloq.[15]	M. R. James, 1903
	after 1450	Summa Iust.[16]	MS 200
Cardiff (cell of Tewkesbury Abbey)	s. xiv/xv	Compendiloq. / Brev. de Sap. / Communiloq.	MS 205
Carlisle, Aug. Cathedral Priory of BVM	s. xv	Assorted works	MS 112
Chester, Benedictines of St Werburgh	1320s	Compendiloq.	J. Taylor, 1966
Dover, Library of the Prior of St Martin	by 1389	Ord. Vit. R.	M. R. James, 1903
	by 1389	Brev. de Virt.	M. R. James, 1903
	by 1389	Communiloq.	M. R. James, 1903
Robert Brakenbury	s. xv	Compendiloq.[17] / Brev. de Sap. / Brev. de Virt.	MS 274
Durham Monastery, Communal Library	s. xiv	Compendiloq.[17] / Brev. de Sap. / Brev. de Virt.	MS 274

	Date of ownership	Work	Reference
Durham, Benedictine Cathedral of St Cuthbert	s. xiii	*Summa Iust.*	MS 72
	s. xiv	*Communiloq.*	MS 74
	s. xv	*Brev. de Virt.*	MS 73
	s. xv	*Brev. de Virt.*	MS 272
	s. xiv	*Brev. de Virt.*	
T. Stevynson, Magister	after 1478	*Ars Praed.*[18]	MS 212
Glastonbury, Benedictine Abbey of BVM	s. xiv/xv	*Ord. Vit. R.*	MS 273
Hales, Shropshire, Cistercians		*Communiloq.*	MS 86
Hereford, Cathedral Chapter	after 1400	Sermon 9	MS 87
	s. xv	{ *Communiloq.* / *Brev. de Virt.*	MS 162
Heyles, Glos., Cistercians	Apr 1533	{ *Brev. de Virt.*[19] / *Brev. de Sap.*	MS 203
Magister William Neel, Vicar of Blokley	before 1533	{ *Brev. de Virt.*[19] / *Brev. de Sap.*	MS 203
Ipswich, Franciscans		*Ars Praed.*	A. G. Little, 1918
Lincoln Cathedral Chapter		{ *Communiloq.*[P] / *Compendiloq.*	A. G. Little, 1918
Thomas Cranmer, Archbishop	after 1518	{ *Brev. de Virt.* / *Brev. de Sap.* / *Ord. Vit. R.*	MS 207 / Jayne & Johnson, 1956

London, Franciscans		{ Brev. de Virt. / Communiloq. (extracts)	MS 213
	s. xv	{ Communiloq. / Summa Iust. / De Poenit.	J. Leland, 1715 / MS 209
London, St Paul's		Communiloq.	J. Leland, 1715
Oxford, Carmelites		Moniloq.	J. Leland, 1715
Robert Jones et amici. Jones was at Oxford in 1520, rector Lower Heyford before 1527, rector Eaton Bishop, Herts., 1527–9.	s. xvi in	Communiloq.P / Compendiloq. / Brev. de Virt. / Brev. de Sap. / Ord. Vit. R.	Oxford, Bodleian Auct. 2.Q.V.20.
Robert Flemyng, b. 1417, d. 1483. Humanistic scholar, studied in Oxford, Cologne, Padua, Ferrara	s. xv med	Summa Iust.[20]	MS 288
Oxford, Lincoln Coll.	s. xv ex	Summa Iust.[20]	MS 288
Thomas Browne	s. xvi ex	Ars Praed.[21]	MS 293
Thomas Walker	s. xvi ex	Ars Praed.[21]	MS 293
Oxford, Univ. Coll.	s. xvi ex	Ars Praed.[21]	MS 293
Thomas Raynes, fellow of New Coll., Oxford and Vicar of Basingstoke 1474–99	before 1499	Summa Iust.[20]	MS 294
Richard Gosmore, fellow of Magdalen Coll., Oxford, and Vicar of Basingstoke 1499–1541	from 1499	Summa Iust.[22]	MS 294
Thomas Browne	s. xvi	Summa Iust.[22]	MS 294
Oxford, Univ. Coll.	s. xvi	Summa Iust.[22]	MS 294

	Date of ownership	Work	Reference
William Romsey, fellow of Merton Coll., Oxford 1452–63, and Vicar of Collingbourne Kingston, 1465–77	s. xv *med*	Brev. de Virt.[23] / Brev. de Sap.	MS 290
Oxford, Merton Coll.	1493	Brev. de Virt.[23] / Brev. de Sap.	MS 290
Magister Thomas English, MA 1454, Canon, St Chads, Shrewsbury, 1465, Chaplain, St Paul's, London, 1475	s. xv *med*	One of John's sermons	MS 261
Robert Roke, MA 1426, Vicar, St Lawrence Jewry 1438–58, d. 1458	s. xv *med*	Collection of John's works[24]	N. R. Ker, 1978
Oxford, Balliol Coll.	after 1458	Collection of John's works,[24]	N. R. Ker, 1978
Robert Thwaites, Chancellor of Oxford Univ. 1466, Dean of Auckland, 1451–8	s. xv *med*	Summa Iust.[25]	MS 279
Oxford, Balliol Coll.	after 1458	Summa Iust.[25]	MS 279
William Gray, resident Balliol 1430s, Bishop of Ely later, d. 1478	s. xv *med*	Communiloq.[26] / Brev. de Virt.	MS 278
Oxford, Balliol Coll.	s. xv *med*	Ars Praed.[18]	MS 212
	c. 1478	Communiloq.[26] / Brev. de Virt.	MS 278
Peterborough, Benedictines	s. xiv	Ord. Vit. R.[27]	MS 71
	s. xiv	Ord. Vit. R.	M. R. James, 1909
Friar William Woodford	s. xiv	Ord. Vit. R.[27]	MS 71
Ramsey, Benedictines	s. xiv	Brev. de Virt.	MS 208

		De Poenit. / *Brev. de Virt.*	J. Leland, 1715
John Sheppey, Bishop of Rochester	s. xv ex	*Ord. Vit. R.*	A. G. Little, 1918
Romsey, Dane Rolande Sentynvys, monk			J. Leland, 1715
Syon Monastery	s. xv ex	*Ars Praed.*	M. Bateson, 1898
Syon Monastery	s. xv med/ex	*Ord. Vit. R.*[28] / *Brev. de Virt.* / *Communiloq.* / *Summa Iust.* / *Moniloq.* / *Legiloq.*	MS 196
	after 1489	*Communiloq.*[P]	London, BL, I.B.2012
	1512–26	*Communiloq.*[P][29]	M. Bateson, 1898
Syon, men's library	1504–26 catalogue	*Communiloq.*[P] / *Compendiloq.* / *Brev. de Virt.* / *Brev. de Sap.* / *Ord. Vit. R.*	M. Bateson, 1898
York, Austin Friars	1372 cat.	*Communiloq.* / *Compendiloq.* / *Brev. de Sap.*	M. R. James, 1909
	1372 cat.	*Communiloq.*	M. R. James, 1909
	1372 cat.	*Brev. de Sap.*	M. R. James, 1909
	after 1372	*Summa Iust.*	M. R. James, 1909
	after 1372	*Brev. de Virt.*	M. R. James, 1909

	Date of ownership	Work	Reference
Wells Cathedral		*Communiloq.*	T. W. Williams, 1897
Winchester, Benedictines	s. xiv/xv	*Brev. de Virt.*	MS 263
Windsor, Dean and Canons	s. xv/xvi	*Ord. Vit. R.*	MS 267
Worcester, Benedictine Cathedral Priory of BVM	s. xv	{ *Compendiloq.* / *Brev. de Virt.*	MS 449
Johannes Godeman, Westham, Sussex	s. xiv	*Communiloq.*	MS 448
Richard Norys, Sussex	s. xv	*Legiloq.*[30]	MS 267
Margaret Wright	s. xv	*Legiloq.*[30]	MS 267
Rauf Hassoll de Hankelow	s. xvi *in*	*Legiloq.*[30]	MS 267
Thomas Cardiff	s. xvi *med*	*Legiloq.*[30]	MS 267
Friar William Hotoft	s. xvi *ex*	*Legiloq.*[30]	MS 267
Anthony Maxton, Magister		*De Poenit.*[31]	A. G. Little, 1917
Daniel Birkhead		*De Poenit.*[31]	MS 272
Jacob Ware		*Legiloq.*[32]	MS 272
Henry, Earl of Clarendon		*Legiloq.*[32]	MS 276
Thomas Graunt, fellow of Oriel Coll., Oxford, 1425-?, d. 1475		{ *Ord. Vit. R.*[28] / *Brev. de Virt.*	MS 276 / MS 196
	s. xv *med*	{ *Communiloq.* / *Summa Iust.* / *Moniloq.* / *Legiloq.*	
Richard Terynden, priest	before 1512	*Communiloq.*[P29]	M. Bateson, 1898
Richard Midwinter	s. xvi *ex*	*Ars Praed.*	MS 212

Owner	Date	Work	Reference
Edward Wreche, Vicar	s. xv	Communiloq. (extracts)	MS 210
Johannes Peche	s. xvi	De Poenit.[33]	MS 211
Marcellus de St Aldegund	s. xv	Brev. de Virt.	MS 192
Dominus William Woddrest		Ars Praed.	MS 191
Magister Ricardus de D . . . . . sel		Brev. de Virt.	MS 214

FRANCE

Owner	Date	Work	Reference
Amiens, Celestines	before 1550	Sermon 9	MS 6
Arras, Benedictines of Saint-Vaast	after 1400	Communiloq. / Ord. Vit. R. / Brev. de Virt.	MS 5
Bordeaux, Augustinian Canons	s. xiv or later	Communiloq. / Brev. de Virt. / Ord. Vit. R. / Serm. de Temp.	MS 55 / MS 54 / MS 94
Bordeaux, Library of the Petits Carmes	s. xv		
Charleville, Carthusians of Mont-Dieu			
	s. xiv	Super Orat. Dom.	MS 95
	s. xiv	Super Orat. Dom.	MS 93
	s. xiv	Tract. Exemp.	MS 96
	s. xiv	Super Orat. Dom. / Ord. Vit. R.	MS 97
Clairvaux, Cistercians, Abbey Library	1472 cat.	Communiloq.	Vernet & Genest, 1979
	1521 cat.	Communiloq.	Vernet & Genest, 1979
	1521 cat.	Communiloq. / Brev. de Virt. / Ord. Vit. R.	Vernet & Genest, 1979
	1521 cat.	Ord. Vit. R. / Compendiloq.	Vernet & Genest, 1979

	Date of ownership	Work	Reference
	1521 cat.	Ord. Vit. R.	Vernet & Genest, 1979
	1521 cat.	Communiloq.	Vernet & Genest, 1979
	1521 cat.	{ Communiloq.P, Compendiloq.	Vernet & Genest, 1979
		{ Brev. de Virt., Brev. de Sap., Ord. Vit. R.	
Clairvaux, Bibl. du Dortoir	1520 cat.	{ Communiloq., Brev. de Virt.	Vernet & Genest, 1979
	1520 cat.	Communiloq.	Vernet & Genest, 1979
	1520 cat.	Ord. Vit. R.	Vernet & Genest, 1979
	1520 cat.	{ Communiloq.P, Compendiloq., Brev. de Virt., Brev. de Sap., Ord. Vit. R.	Vernet & Genest, 1979
Corbie, Benedictines.	s. xv	Super Orat. Dom.	A. G. Little, 1917
Dijon, Carthusians	s. xv	Brev. de Virt.[34]	MS 106
Frater Angerius de Furcho, OFM	s. xv/xvi	Brev. de Virt.[34]	MS 306
Cardinal Pierre de Foix			MS 306
Grenoble, Dominicans			A. G. Little, 1917
Jumièges, Abbot Simon du Bosc	before 1390	{ Brev. de Virt.[35], Communiloq., Compendiloq., Brev. de Sap.	MS 356

Jumièges, Benedictine Abbey	after 1390	*Brev. de Virt.*[35] *Communiloq.* *Compendiloq.* *Brev. de Sap.*	MS 356
Laon, Abbey of Cuissy	s. xiv	*Ars Praed.*	MS 182
Maguelonne, Bishop Berengar de Frédol (1263–90)	s. xiii ex	*Brev. de Virt.*	MS 292 W. A. Pantin, 1961
Marmoutier, Benedictine Abbey			
Metz, Cathedral	s. xiv	*Legiloq.*	MS 227
Metz, Celestines	s. xv	*Ord. Vit. R.*	MS 228
Paris, Austin Friars		*Communiloq.* *Brev. de Virt.* *Compendiloq.* *Brev. de Sap.* *Ord. Vit. R.* *Legiloq.* *De Poenit.* *Moniloq.*	A. G. Little, 1917
Paris, Carmelites		*Brev. de Virt.*	MS 321
Paris, Cathedral Chapter	s. xv/xvi	*Ars Praed.* *De Poenit.* *Ord. Vit. R.* *Legiloq.*	MS 325 A. G. Little, 1917
Paris, Grands Augustins	s. xiv or later		MS 326
Paris, Saint-Victor		Sermon 2 *Ars Praed.* Sermons 3, 4, 5	MS 318 MS 317

	Date of ownership	Work	Reference
		Ord. Vit. R.	MS 316
		Sermons 3, 4, 5	MS 315
		Ars Praed.	MS 314
	1448–68	Communiloq.	MS 313
		Moniloq.	MS 324
Paris, Sorbonne Library		Communiloq.	MS 319
Gerardus de Trajecto, Magister (=Utrecht or Maastricht)	after 1319	Sermon 9[36]	MS 320
	before 1319	Sermon 9[36]	MS 320
Paris, Abbey of Saint-Germain-des-Prés	after 1473	Brev. de Virt.	MS 312
Pontigny, Cistercians		Communiloq.	C. Talbot, 1954
Pruliaco, Abbot Humbertus de Gendreio	s. xiv or later	Ars Praed.	MS 390
Friars P. and R. Mercaderius, Conventus Fratrum Minorum Insule	s. xiv in	Collat. in Ioh.[37]	MS 353
Frater Adam, episcopus Eugubinus	s. xiv in/med	Collat. in Ioh.[37]	MS 353
Magister Johannes Sicardus, OFM, Avignon	s. xiv med/ex	Collat. in Ioh.[37]	MS 353
Reims, Guy de Roye, Archbishop	1407	Collat. in Ioh.[37]	MS 353
Reims Cathedral	after 1407	Collat. in Ioh.[37]	MS 353
Rouen, monastery of St Mary, Celestines	s. xv	Brev. de Virt. Communiloq. (extracts)	MS 22
Laurentius	s. xiv	Ord. Vit. R.[38]	MS 305
Toulouse, Frater Iohannes Garcie	1397	Ord. Vit. R.[38]	MS 305
Rouen, Abbey of Saint-Ouen	s. xv	Ord. Vit. R.	G. Nortier, 1966

Saint-Omer, Abbey of St Bertin	s. xv	*Brev. de Virt.* / *Compendiloq.* / *Brev. de Sap.* / *Communiloq.*	MS 360
	s. xiv/xv	*Post. in Apoc.*	MS 358
	s. xiv/xv	*Brev. de Sap.*	MS 359
Jehan Chastellier	s. xv	*Brev. de Virt.* / *Brev. de Sap.*	MS 388
Johannes Groulardius	s. xv	*Moniloq.*	MS 324
Bernhardus clericus dioc. carnotensis (Chartres)		*De Poenit.*[33]	MS 211

E. and W. GERMANY

Abensberg, Lower Bavaria, Carmelites	after 1475	*Communiloq.*[P]	Wellcome Historical Medical Library 3c7.44781
Augsburg, Carmelites of St Anna	1497 cat.	*Communiloq.*	T. Gottlieb, 1918
	1497 cat.	*Communiloq.*	T. Gottlieb, 1918
	1497 cat.	*Communiloq.*	T. Gottlieb, 1918
	1497 acquired	*Communiloq.*	T. Gottlieb, 1918
Augsburg, Leonhart Radawer, medicus	1462/3	*Communiloq.* (extracts) / *Brev. de Virt.*	MS 67
Bamberg, Benedictines of Michelsberg	1475–83 acq.	*Communiloq.*	T. Gottlieb, 1918
	1483	*Communiloq.*	T. Gottlieb, 1918
Bamberg, Carmelites	s. xv	*Brev. de Virt.*	MS 24
Bamberg, Dominicans	1427	*Communiloq.*	MS 26
	s. xv	*Brev. de Virt.*	MS 27
	s. xv	*Communiloq.* (extracts)	MS 25

	Date of ownership	Work	Reference
Bamberg, Franciscans	s. xv	Communiloq.[39]	MS 23
	s. xiv/xv	Communiloq. (extracts)	MS 25
Benediktbeuern, Benedictines	s. xv	Ars Praed.	MS 241
Brunswick, Frater Ludolfus Sunne OFM	1451–70	Ord. Vit. R.[40]	MS 65
Brunswick, Franciscan Convent	c. 1470	Ord. Vit. R.[40]	MS 65
Burghausen, Upper Bavaria, Jesuits	by 1500	Communiloq.[P]	Wellcome Historical Medical Library, 3e8.44788
Frater Emelricus de Carpena		Communiloq.	MS 116
Conradus Almans	after 1431/2	Communiloq.	MS 443
Cues, Augustinian Hermits	s. xv	Legiloq. / Communiloq. / Brev. de Virt. / Compendiloq.	MS 105
Dinckilspiel, Carmelites	after 1475	Communiloq.[P]	Oxford, Bodleian, Byw.D.3.12
Erfurt, Carthusians	s. xv	Post. in Apoc.	MS 271
Erfurt, Collegium Amplonianum (founded 1412)	1410–12 cat.	Brev. de Virt.	T. Gottlieb, 1918
	1410–12 cat	Communiloq.	T. Gottlieb, 1918
Erfurt, Collegium Universitatis, (formerly Coll. Amplon.)	1497 cat.	Communiloq. / Brev. de Virt.	MS 115
	1497 cat.	Communiloq. / Compendiloq. / Brev. de Sap.	T. Gottlieb, 1918
	s. xv	Legiloq.	MS 117

Institution	Date	Work	Reference
Erfurt, Augustinian Canons	s. xiv/xv	*Brev. de Virt.*	MS 118
		Sermon 9	MS 122
	s. xv	*De Poenit.*	MS 119
	s. xv	{ *Ord. Vit. R.*[41] / *De Poenit.*	MS 120
Frankfurt, Dominicans	s. xvi *in*	*Brev. de Virt.*[42]	MS 149
	by 1500	*Tract. Exemp.*	MS 146
	1445	*Communiloq.*	MS 147
	1561	*Brev. de Virt.*[42]	MS 149
Frater Nicolaus Bernardi Aquensis, Frankfurt Dominicans	after 1475	*Communiloq.*[P]	Munich, Bayerische Staatsbibliothek 2° Inc.c.a.375[a]
Freising, Franciscans	after 1475	*Communiloq.*[P]	London, BL 1B.5793
Gamundia, Dominicans	s. xv	*Ord. Vit. R.*	MS 121
Heilsbronn, Benedictines / Arnoldus de Herpibolim	s. xiv	{ *Ord. Vit. R.*[41] / *De Poenit.*	MS 120
Hildesh, monastery of St Michael	s. xv	*Brev. de Virt.*	MS 107
Indersdorf, monastery of the BVM	s. xv	{ *Communiloq.* / *Compendiloq.*	MS 242
Klagenfurt, Augustinian Hermits	s. xv	*Brev. de Virt.*	MS 168
Donatus Klug, Magister	after 1451	*Brev. de Virt.*	MS 185
Klus, near Gandersheim, Benedictines			A. G. Little, 1917
Köln, Kreuzherrenbibliothek	after 1470	*Ord. Vit. R.*	MS 179
Köln, Klosterbibliothek Gross St Martin	1431	*Communiloq.*	MS 178
Köln, Franciscans		*Exp. and Collat. in Ioh*	R. B. Marks, 1974
Köln, Charterhouse of St Barbara	s. xiv ex/xv *in*	*Communiloq.*	MS 175

	Date of ownership	Work	Reference
Matheus Prenne, Rector in Stendal 1448, Canon at Lebus 1478	after 1424	*Brev. de Virt.*[42]	MS 42
Magister Nicolaus Wolkensteyn, Leipzig	s. xv	*Post. in Apoc.*	MS 184
Leipzig, Johannes Pauli de Lorch, matriculated from Bavarian nation summer 1431	1432	*Ars Praed.*	MS 379
Leipzig, Barfüsskloster: Johannes Rotha, conventual. 1480 went to the university to study theology. 1485 went to rule convent at Erfurt.	before 1480	*Moniloq.*	MS 186
Nicolaus Sculteti, Magister of Arts, Frankfurt. 1424 Rector of Leipzig University	1424	*Brev. de Virt.*[42]	MS 42
Lippstat, Augustinian Hermits	after 1465	*Communiloq.*	MS 40
		Brev. de Virt.	MS 43
Magdeburg, Bertoldus, perpetuus vicarius of the ecclesia Magd.	1427–53	*Post. in Apoc.*[44]	MS 39
Magdeburg, ecclesia	1453	*Post. in Apoc.*[44]	MS 39
Meissen, Franciscans	s. xv	*Communiloq.*	MS 108
Munich, Augustinian Hermits	after 1479	*Communiloq.*[P]	Munich, Bayerische Staatsbibliothek 2° Inc. c.a.2281[a]
Nürnberg, Augustinian Hermits. Johannes Rup. Prior in 1450. Went to Bamberg in 1451. Wrote this copy in Salzburg	1469	*Communiloq.*[45]	MS 440
Nürnberg, Benedictine of St Egidius	s. xv ex	*Communiloq.*	T. Gottlieb, 1918
	s. xv ex	*Communiloq.*	T. Gottlieb, 1918
Nürnberg, Franciscans	1448 cat.	*Communiloq.*	T. Gottlieb, 1918
	1448 cat.	*Communiloq.*	T. Gottlieb, 1918

278

Nürnberg, frater Luitperdus Helffendorff		Communiloq.[39]	MS 23
St Nicholas Church, Passau	s. xv	Communiloq.	MS 248
Pollingana, Library of the Canons	after 1433	Communiloq.	MS 243
Raitenbuch, Monastery of the BVM, Canons Regular	c. 1454	Communiloq.	MS 244
Rebdorf, Augustinerchorherrenstift	1500 cat.	Communiloq.	T. Gottlieb, 1918
	1500 cat.	Communiloq.	T. Gottlieb, 1918
	1500 cat.	Communiloq.	T. Gottlieb, 1918
	1500 cat.	Communiloq.	T. Gottlieb, 1918
	1500 cat.	Communiloq.	T. Gottlieb, 1918
	1500 cat.	Communiloq.	T. Gottlieb, 1918
Regensburg, Benedictines of St Emmeran	after 1329	Sermon 9	MS 253
	1476 cat.	Communiloq.	B. & C. Bischoff et al., 1977 (=MS 245)
	1500 cat.	Brev. de Virt.	B. & C. Bischoff et al., 1977
	1501 cat.	Summa Inst.	B. & C. Bischoff et al., 1977
	1501 cat.	Communiloq.	B. & C. Bischoff et al., 1977 (=MS 246)
	1501 cat.	Compendiloq.	B. & C. Bischoff et al., 1977
	1501 cat.	Communiloq.	B. & C. Bischoff et al., 1977 (=MS 247)
	1501 cat.	Communiloq.[P]	B. & C. Bischoff et al., 1977
	1501 cat.	Communiloq.[P,46]	B. & C. Bischoff et al., 1977
Subprior Erasmus Davm Australis, Regensburg Benedictines	after 1472, before 1501	Communiloq.[P,46]	B. & C. Bischoff et al., 1977
Rottenbuech, Friars	after 1481	Communiloq.[P]	London, BL, 1B.9197
Salvatorberg, Carthusians	s. xv ex cat.	Communiloq.	T. Gottlieb, 1918
	s. xv ex cat.	Communiloq.	T. Gottlieb, 1918

	Date of ownership	Work	Reference
Schyrensis, monastery	after 1475	Communiloq.^P	Munich, Bayerische Staatsbibliothek 2° Inc. c.a. 375[b]
Semanshausen, Benedictines	s. xv	Communiloq.	MS 249
Jakob von Soest, Dominican and Professor of Theology	s. xv in	Brev. de Virt.[47]	MS 45
Soest, Dominicans	s. xv med	Brev. de Virt.[47]	MS 45
	1483 cat.	Brev. de Virt.	
Tegernsee, Benedictines	1483 cat.	Communiloq.^P	
	after 1475	Communiloq.^P	Munich, Bayerische Staatsbibliothek 2° Inc. c.a. 375
	before 1483	Ord. Vit. R.	MS 192
Trier, Sanctus Mar	s. xv	Brev. de Virt.	MS 44
Frater Nicolaus, lector Torgau (=Thorn) 1408, lector Dresden 1412	1412	Moniloq.[48]	MS 44
Johannes Polonus, Frater and lector, Thorn	after 1412	Moniloq.[48]	MS 44
Thorn, Franciscan Convent	after 1412	Moniloq.[48]	MS 44
Ulm, Franciscans	after 1496	{ Brev. de Virt.^P / Communiloq. / Compendiloq. / Brev. de Sap. / Ord. Vit. R.	Munich, Bayerische Staatsbibliothek 8° Inc. c.a. 247[d]
Ulm, Neihartschen Familienbibliothek	1465 cat.	Communiloq.	T. Gottlieb, 1918
Westdeutschland, vicar of Bartholomaeusstift, Jakob Rudesheim	1459	Brev. de Virt.[49]	MS 143

Library of the church of St Bartholomaeus Westdeutschland	after 1459	*Brev. de Virt.*[49]	MS 143
Johannes of Widimstadius	after 1479	*Brev. de Virt.* *Communiloq.*[P 50]	MS 144 Munich, Bayerische Staatsbibliothek 2° Inc. c.a.2281
Windberg, monastery	s. xv	*Communiloq.*	MS 251
Windesheim, Augustinian Hermits	after 1469	*Communiloq.*[45]	MS 440
Konrad Textoris, of the Convent of Worms	s. xv	*Brev. de Virt.*	MS 148
Monastery of St Zeno, Canons Regular	1498	*Brev. de Virt.*[P] *Communiloq.* *Compendiloq.* *Brev. de Sap.* *Ord. Vit. R.*	Munich, Bayerische Staatsbibliothek 8° Inc. c.a.247[c]
Dr George Hüsner	after 1479	*Communiloq.*[P 50]	Munich, Bayerische Staatsbibliothek 2° Inc. c.a.2281
Sigifrimundus Valtensdorff	s. xv	*Communiloq.*[51]	MS 246
Georgius Lembith	s. xv	*Communiloq.*[51]	MS 246
Oswaldus Romes	s. xv	*Communiloq.*[51]	MS 246

ITALY

Assisi, Franciscans, libraria publica	1381 cat.	*Brev. de Virt.* *Brev. de Sap.* *Communiloq.* *Moniloq.* *Ord. Vit. R.* *Legiloq.* *De Poenit.* *Compendiloq.*	MS 12

	Date of ownership	Work	Reference
Assisi, Franciscans, biblioteca segreta	1381 cat.	Communiloq. Brev. de Virt. Ord. Vit. R. Brev. de Sap. Moniloq. Legiloq. Compendiloq.	MS 14
	1381 cat.	Communiloq.	L. Alessandri, 1906
	1381 cat.	Serm. Quadrages.	MS 20
	1381 cat.	Collat. super Matt. Moniloq.	MS 252
	1381 cat.	Super. Orat. Dom.	MS 16
	1381 cat.	Tract. Exemp.	MS 19
	1381 cat.	Summa*	L. Alessandri, 1906
Assisi, Franciscans, books in Sacristy	1473 invent.	Communiloq.	L. Alessandri, 1906.
Beneventanus, Archbishop	C14 or later	Communiloq.	MS 8
Bologna, Franciscans, Convent library	by 1421	Post in Apoc.	
Camaldoli, Hermitage	by 1406	Communiloq.	MS 3
	by 1406	Ord. Vit. R.	MS 2
Candia, Franciscans	by 1417	Brev. de Virt. 'Summa'*	

*The term *Summa* in a catalogue may refer to John's *Communiloquium* alone, or to some other combination of his works. It is generally impossible to work out which is meant, so I leave the entry in its original form.

Cortona, Marchus Michael, Priest	s. xv	*De Poenit.* *Summa Inst.* *Brev. de Virt.* *Legiloq.*	MS 104
Cortona, Franciscans Fabriano, Franciscans	between 1348 and 1347 1348–1357 1348–1357	Titles unknown Titles unknown Titles unknown	A. G. Little, 1917
Firenze, Carmelites	by 1396 by 1396 by 1396 by 1396 by 1396 by 1396 by 1396	*De Poenit.* *Brev. de Virt.* *Moniloq.* *Brev. de Virt.* *Brev. de Virt.* *Moniloq.* ? *Moniloq.*	K. W. Humphreys, 1964 K. W. Humphreys, 1964 K. W. Humphreys, 1964 K. W. Humphreys, 1964 K. W. Humphreys, 1964 K. W. Humphreys, 1964 K. W. Humphreys, 1964
Firenze, Convent of S. Marco	after 1445	*Communiloq.* *Brev. de Virt.*	B. L. Ullman and P. A. Stadter, 1972
Firenze, Biblioteca di S. Maria Novella	by 1489	*Moniloq.* *Legiloq.* *De Poenit.*	MS 140
	after 1410, before 1489	*Communiloq.* *Legiloq.* *Compendiloq.* *Brev. de Virt.* *Ord. Vit. R.* *De Poenit.* *Moniloq.*	MS 134

	Date of ownership	Work	Reference
	by 1489	De Poenit. / Ord. Vit. R. / Brev. de Virt. / Legiloq. / Compendiloq.	S. Orlandi, 1952
	by 1489	'Summa'*	S. Orlandi, 1952
	by 1489	Communiloq.	MS 132
Franciscus Sylvestrus, Bishop of Firenze, 1323–41	before 1341	Brev. de Virt.[52]	M-H. J. de Pommerol, 1980
Firenze, Monastery of S. Maria	1342	Brev. de Virt.[52]	M-H. J. de Pommerol, 1980
Pico della Mirandola, humanistic scholar (1463–94)	before 1494	Communiloq.[P]	P. Kibre, 1936
	before 1494	Brev. de Virt.	P. Kibre, 1936
Forli, S. Giacomo, Dominicans	1512 cat.	Communiloq.	AFP, 36, p. 21
Guy d'Ibelin, Dominican bishop of Limassol, d. 1367	before 1367	'Summa'*	M-H. J. de Pommerol, 1980
Milan, Library of St Eustorgius (Dominicans)	by 1494	Ord. Vit. R. / Moniloq.	AFP, 25, p. 26
Milan, Library of the Visconti–Sforza	1426 listing	Brev. de Virt.	MS 302 and 303
	1426 listing	Ord. Vit. R.	E. Pellegrin, 1955
	1426 listing	Ord. Vit. R.	E. Pellegrin, 1955
	1426 listing	Communiloq.	E. Pellegrin, 1955
	1426 listing	Brev. de Virt.	MS 308
	1426 listing	Brev. de Virt.	E. Pellegrin, 1955
Monteprandone, S. Giacomo della Marca	s. xv	Brev. de Virt.	AFH, 48, p. 131

Monteripido, Biblioteca	after 1496	{ Brev. de Virt.^P, Communiloq., Compendiloq., Brev. de Sap., Ord. Vit. R.	M. Pecugi, 1976
Franciscus Rufulusa, doctor decretorum of Naples	before 1340	Communiloq.^53	M-H. J. de Pommerol, 1980
Nicolaus, Bishop of Bisagnano 1319–31, and of Nola 1331–40	s. xvi in	Communiloq.^53	M-H. J. de Pommerol, 1980
Odo, Doctor of Laws, former treasurer of Nicosia, Bishop of Paphos 1337–57	before 1357	Ord. Vit. R.	M-H. J. de Pommerol, 1980
Orzinuovi, Frater Rafaele, OFM	by 1523	Brev. de Virt.	MS 56
Padua, Franciscans of St Anthony	by 1396	Moniloq.	K. W. Humphreys, 1966
	by 1449	Exp. and Collat. Ioh.	MS 296
	by 1449	Ord. Vit. R.	MS 297
	by 1449	Ord. Vit. R.	MS 298
	by 1449	Communiloq.	K. W. Humphreys, 1966
	by 1449	Communiloq.	K. W. Humphreys, 1966
	by 1449	'Summa'*	K. W. Humphreys, 1966
	by 1449	'Summa'*	K. W. Humphreys, 1966
Padua, Dominicans of S. Agostino	after 1363, before 1390	Communiloq.	L. Gargan, 1971
S. Domenico di Perugia	by 1474–8	{ Communiloq., Brev. de Virt. + others	T. Kaepeli, 1962
Pisa, Library of the Franciscans Sardinia, Messer lo giudice de Ghallura	1355	'Postillae'	A. G. Little, 1917

	Date of ownership	Work	Reference
Frater Richardus, OFM, Rome	s. xiii	Moniloq. / Legiloq. / Communiloq. / Ord. Vit. R.	MS 140
Siena, Franciscans	by s. xv ex	Brev. de Virt.	K. W. Humphreys, 1966
	by s. xv ex	De Poenit.	K. W. Humphreys, 1966
	by s. xv ex	Brev. de Virt.	K. W. Humphreys, 1966
	by s. xv ex	De Poenit.	K. W. Humphreys, 1966
Bartolus Bardi, Bishop of Spoleto 1320–48		Communiloq.[54]	M-H. J. de Pommerol, 1980
Spoleto, Chapter	1348/9	Communiloq.[54]	M-H. J. de Pommerol, 1980
Oliviero Forzetta of Treviso	s. xiv med	Communiloq.[55]	L. Gargan, 1970
Treviso, Franciscans	1375	Communiloq.[55]	L. Gargan, 1970
Treviso, Library of the Convent of St. Margherita	1374–8	Communiloq.	L. Gargan, 1970
Udine, Dominicans	after 1440	Communiloq.[56]	
Cristoforo Fabiani da Uldine, provincial prior of the provence of S. Domenico	1440	Communiloq.[56]	
Franciscus di Silanis, OFM, Bishop of Valva 1350–68		Communiloq.	M-H. J. de Pommerol, 1980
Venice, Franciscans			A. G. Little, 1917
Venice, Frater Mattheus, OP	s. xv	Ord. Vit. R.	MS 413
Venice, SS Giovanni e Paolo	s. xiv or later	Brev. de Virt. / Legiloq.	MS 236

Frater Lucius de Masig[no]	after 1496	Brev. de Virt.[P] / Communiloq. / Compendiloq. / Brev. de Sap. / Ord. Vit. R.	London, Wellcome Historical Medical Library 2b22. 44789
Frater Baptista de Bino	1490	Brev. de Virt.	MS 452
Pietro de Regio, medico in fisico. Said to have translated Compendiloq. into Italian	s. xv	Compendiloq.	London, Wellcome Historical Medical Library MS 556
Frater Michael, of the Sancti Augustini	s. xiv or later	Compendiloq.	MS 327

NETHERLANDS

Onbekond Cloister	by 1390	Brev. de Virt.	K. O. Meinsma, 1903
Tongerlen, F. Arnaldo, Abbot of the Praemonstratensians	after 1472	Communiloq.[P]	Cambridge, University Library Inc. n° 327
Utrecht, Carthusians	by 1426	Brev. de Virt.	J. P. Gumbert, 1974
Utrecht, Bibliotheca Traiectana ad Rhenum	by 1608	Brev. de Virt.	BBM, p. 89
Bibliotheca Collegiate Ecclesie Zutphanensis (Zutphen)	by 1566	Communiloq.[P]	K. O. Meinsma, 1903

POLAND

Breslau, Dominicans	1480s	Post. in Apoc. / Communiloq.	MS 57
Gdansk, Augustinian Hermits	s. xv	Brev. de Virt.	MS 150
Magister Johannes de Dąbrówka, Krakow	s. xv	Compendiloq.	MS 180
Magister Cruczborg, Krakow	1412	De Poenit. / Brev. de Virt.	MS 181

	Date of ownership	Work	Reference
SPAIN			
Valencia, Franciscans	after 1409	Brev. de Virt.[57]	
Francesc. Eiximenis, OFM, Patriarch of Jerusalem	before 1409	Brev. de Virt.[57]	
	before 1409	Communiloq.	
Library of the widow of King Alfonso V, el Magnanimo		Brev. de Virt.	C. J. Wittlin, 1971
Queen Maria of Aragon		Moniloq.	C. J. Wittlin, 1971
		Legiloq.	C. J. Wittlin, 1971
Pedro IV		Communiloq.	C. J. Wittlin, 1971
Martin el humano, humanistic scholar, received volume as a gift from the King of Navarre	c. 1438	Communiloq.	C. J. Wittlin, 1971
Ruy Sanches, Archdeacon of Trevinnii	s. xv med	Communiloq.	MS 400
Frater Johannes de Pino	after 1424	Super Orat. Dom.	MS 29
Alfonso V, el Magnanimo		Communiloq.[V]	C. J. Wittlin, 1971
Queen Maria of Aragón	by 1458	Communiloq.[V]	C. J. Wittlin, 1971
Bishop Gil Sanchez Muñoz, later Pope Clement VIII	s. xv	Communiloq.[V]	C. J. Wittlin, 1971
Isabel de Catolica	1503 cat.	Communiloq.[V]	C. J. Wittlin, 1971
SWITZERLAND			
Bâle, Augustinian Hermits of St Leonards	after 1465	Brev. de Virt.	MS 36
Bâle, Dominicans	s. xv ex	Communiloq.[58]	MS 37
Bâle, Magister Theobald, quondam provincialis theutonie	after 1502	Communiloq.[58]	MS 37

Name	Date	Work	MS / Location
Nicholas Breschli de Chur	1449	*Brev. de Virt.*	MS 378
Metz, Celestines		*Brev. de Virt.*	MS 50
Frater Leonhardus de Ruetlingen	*c.* 1555	*Communiloq.*	
Johannes Stark of Solothurn	s. xv	*Brev. de Virt.*	MS 378
Zwifalten, Monastery		*Communiloq.*	MS 114

MISCELLANEOUS

Name	Date	Work	MS / Location
Doctor Barbatus. Studied in Rome and Padua	s. xv *med*	*Brev. de Virt.*	MS 51
Andreas Vock de Widerin, OP		*Brev. de Virt.*[P59]	Oxford, Bodleian, Byw. O.8.9.
	after 1511	{ *Communiloq.* *Compendiloq.* *Brev. de Sap.* *Ord. Vit. R.*	
J. Schraier	after 1481	*Communiloq.*[P]	Oxford, Bodleian, Auct. 5.Q.5.48
Leonard Hayde, Magister	after 1481	*Communiloq.*[P]	Oxford, Bodleian, Byw. F.2.13
Comensis Wimpinensis, OP		{ *Brev. de Virt.*[P]	Oxford, Bodleian, Byw. O.8.9
	after 1511	{ *Communiloq.* *Compendiloq.* *Brev. de Sap.* *Ord. Vit. R.*	

APPENDIX 5: A CHECKLIST OF EARLY PRINTED EDITIONS OF WORKS BY JOHN OF WALES

This is purely a checklist, for the aid of those who wish to know when John's works were printed, and to help them to find early printed editions of John's works in modern libraries. Most of the information in this list derives from the useful article by Julius V. Scholderer (see bibliography).

14 July 1472   *Communiloquium*. Cologne. Arnold Ther Hoernen. Shorter recension.

late 1472   *Communiloquium*. Cologne. Zel. Replication of above text.

c. 1472–5   *Brev. de Virt.* and *Brev. de Sap*. Cologne. Ther Hoernen. Printed with *Secreta Secretorum*.

1475   *Communiloquium*. Augsburg. A. Sorg. Longer recension.

c. 1480   *Brev. de Virt.* and *Brev. de Sap*. Reprint of Cologne edition of *Secreta Secretorum*, by John of Westphalia at Louvain.

1481   *Communiloquium*. Longer recension. Reprint of the Augsburg edition of 1475. Probably by Johann Zainer of Ulm.

25 May 1489   *Communiloquium*. Strasburg. Anonymous printer: the 'printer of Jordanus de Quedlinburg'. Shorter recension.

1493   *Communiloquium*. Perhaps a reprint by Zainer of his 1481 edition, but no copies ever known, so perhaps a ghost.

1494   *Expositio super Orationem Dominicam*. Paris (Incunabel H 8219).

20 July 1496   *Summa de Regimine*. Contained *Communiloquium, Compendiloquium, Breviloquium de Virtutibus, Breviloquium de Sapientia, Ordinarium Vitae Religiosae*. Venice, Georgius Arrivabenis. *Communiloquium* in longer recension.

1511   *Summa de Regimine*. Reprint of above. Lyons.

1513   *Expositio Regulae Ordinis Fratrum Minorum*. Venice. In *Firmamentum*, Paris III, ff. 98–106.

31 May 1518   *Summa de Regimine*. Revised and reprinted at Strasburg by Johann Knoblouch and Paul Getz.

c. 1550   *Communiloquium*. Shorter recension printed for the last time. Paris. Wolfgang Hopyl.

BIBLIOGRAPHY

The following list includes mainly works to which reference has been made in the footnotes. To make it easier to find the full references to works cited in abbreviated form in the footnotes, I have not separated printed primary sources from modern secondary works and unpublished theses.

Aerts, W. J., Hermans, Jos. M. M. and Visser, Elizabeth, eds., *Alexander the Great in the Middle Ages: Ten studies on the last days of Alexander in literary and historical writing*, Mediaevalia Groningana, 1 (Nÿmegen, 1978)

Aerts, W. J., Smits, E. R., and Voorbij, J. B., *Vincent of Beauvais and Alexander the Great: Studies on the 'Speculum Maius' and its translations into medieval vernaculars*, Mediaevalia Groningana, 7 (Groningen, 1986)

Alessandri, L., *Inventario dell'Antica Bibliotheca del S. Convento de S. Francesco in Assisi (1381)* (Assisi, 1906)

Alexander, J. J. G., and Gibson, M. T., eds., *Medieval Learning and Literature: Essays presented to Richard William Hunt* (Oxford, 1976)

Aquinas, Thomas, *Summa Theologiae* (Rome, 1948)

Bacon, Roger, *Compendium Studii Theologie*, ed. Hastings Rashdall, British Society of Franciscan Studies, 3 (Aberdeen, 1911)

Baechtold-Stäubli, H., *Handwörterbuch des deutschen Aberglaubens*, 7 (Berlin–Leipzig, 1935–6)

Baldwin, J. W., *Masters, Princes and Merchants* (Princeton NJ, 1970)

Baldwinus ab Amsterdam, OFM Cap., 'The Commentary on St John's Gospel edited in 1589 under the name of Bonaventure, an authentic work of John of Wales, O.Min.', *Collectanea Franciscana*, 40 (1970), 71–96

Ball, R. M., 'Thomas Cyrcetur, a fifteenth-century theologian and preacher', *Journal of Ecclesiastical History* 37:2 (1986), 205–39

Barbi, M., ed., *La leggenda de Traiano nei volgarizzamenti del Breviloquium de Virtutibus de Fra Giovanni Gallese* (Florence, 1895)

Batany, Jean, 'Les pauvres et la pauvreté dans les revues des "estats du monde"', *Etudes sur l'Histoire de la Pauvreté* 2 (1974), 469–86

Bateson, Mary, *Catalogue of the Library of Syon Monastery* (Cambridge, 1898)

Bell, Dora M., *L'Idéal éthique de la royauté en France au moyen âge* (Geneva–Paris, 1962)

Bennett, H. S., *English Books and Readers 1475–1557*, 2nd edn (Cambridge, 1969)

Berges, W., *Die Fürstenspiegel des hohen und späten Mittelalters* (Leipzig, 1938)

Bibliography

Bigi, Emilio, 'Suicidi', in *Enciclopedia Dantesca*, (Rome, 1976), pp. 477–8

Bischoff, B. and C., *et al.*, *Mittelalterliche Bibliothekskataloge*, I–IV (Graz, 1977)

Bloomfield, M. W., *Incipits of Latin Works on the Virtues and Vices* (Cambridge, Mass., 1979)

  The Seven Deadly Sins: An introduction to the history of a religious concept with special reference to medieval English literature (East Lansing, Mich., 1952)

Boese, H., *Bibliothek, Bibliothekar, Bibliothekswissenschaft: Festschrift Joris Vorstius* (1954), pp. 286–95

Bolgar, R. R., ed., *Classical Influence on European Culture AD 500–1500* (Cambridge, 1971)

Born, L. K., 'The perfect prince: a study in thirteenth and fourteenth century ideals', *Speculum*, III, 1928, pp. 470–504

Bougerol, Jacques Guy, OM, *Les Manuscrits franciscains de la Bibliothèque de Troyes*, Spicilegium Bonaventurianum, 23 (Rome, 1982)

Bourquelot, F., 'Recherches sur les opinions et la législation en matière de mort volontaire pendant le moyen âge', *Bibl. de l'Ecole des Chartes*, 3 (1842–4), 539–60; 4 (1844), 242–66

Boyle, L. E., 'A Study of the Works attributed to William of Pagula', D.Phil. thesis, Oxford, 1956

Braet, Herman, and Verbeke, Werner, eds., *Death in the Middle Ages*, Mediaevalia Lovaniensia, I:9 (Louvain, 1983)

Bremond, C., Le Goff, J., Schmitt, J-C., *L'Exemplum,* Typologie des sources du moyen age occidental, 40 (Turnhout, 1982)

Brewer, J. S., ed., *Monumenta Franciscana*, Rolls Series, 4 (London, 1858)

Bryce, W. M., *The Scottish Grey Friars*, 2 vols. (Edinburgh–London, 1909)

Burr, D., 'Petrus Iohannis Olivi and the philosophers', *Franciscan Studies*, 31 (1971), 41–71

Callus, D. A., ed., *Robert Grosseteste, Scholar and Bishop: Essays in commemoration of the seventh centenary of his death* (Oxford, 1963)

Caplan, H., *Mediaeval Artes Praedicandi*, Studies in Classical Philology, 24 (Ithaca, NY, 1934)

Cary, G., *The Medieval Alexander* (Cambridge, 1956)

Cataluccio, M. E. M., and Fossa, A. U., *Biblioteca e cultura a Camaldoli dal medioevo all'umanesimo* (Rome, 1979)

Catto, J. I., ed., *The History of the University of Oxford*, Vol. I: *The Early Oxford Schools* (Oxford, 1984)

Cenci, Cesare, OFM, *Bibliotheca Manuscripta ad Sacrum Conventum Assisiensum* (Assisi, 1981)

Charland, Th.-M., OP, *Artes Praedicandi* (Paris–Ottowa, 1936)

Charma, A., 'Etude sur le Compendiloquium de Vita, moribus et dictis illustrium philosophorum, de Jean de Galles', in *Mémoires lus à la Sorbonne* (Paris, 1866), pp. 119–34

  'Notice sur un manuscrit . . . [of John of Wales' *Summa de Preceptis*]', *Mémoires de la Société des Antiquaires de Normandie*, 60 (1851), 37–44

Chrysostom, John, *Address on Vainglory*, trans. in M. L. W. Laistner, *Christianity and Pagan Culture in the Later Roman Empire* (Ithaca, NY, 1951)

Bibliography

Coleman, Janet, *Medieval Readers and Writers: English literature in history 1350–1400* (London, 1981)

Congar, Y., *L'Ecclésiologie du haut moyen âge* (Paris, 1968)
L'Eglise: De Saint Augustin à l'epoque moderne (Paris, 1970)

Copleston, F., *A History of Medieval Philosophy* (London, 1972)

d'Alverny, M.-Th., *The Secret of Secrets* (London, Warburg Institute 1983)

Davis, Charles T., 'The early collection of Books of S. Croce in Florence', *Proceedings of the American Philosophical Society*, 107 (1963), 399–414

d'Avray, D. L., 'A Franciscan and history', *AFH*, 74 (1981), 456–82
'Another Friar and Antiquity', *Studies in Church History*, XVII, ed. Keith Robbins (Oxford, 1981)
'Sermons to the upper bourgeoisie by a thirteenth-century Franciscan', *Studies in Church History*, XVI, ed. D. Baker (Oxford, 1979)
The Preaching of the Friars (Oxford, 1985)

d'Avray, D. L., and Tausche, M., 'Marriage sermons in the *ad status* collections of the central Middle Ages', *AHDLMA*, 1980

De Creytiens, Raymond, 'Le manuel de conversation de Philippe de Ferrarre O.P. (1350?)', *AFP* 16 (1946), 117–35

de La Mare, A. C., Marshall, P. K., and Rouse, R. H., 'Pietro da Montagna and the text of Aulus Gellius', *Scriptorium*, 30 (1976), 219–25

Delcorno, C., *Giordiano da Pisa et l'antica predicazione volgare* (Florence, 1975)

Delhaye, Ph., 'Deux textes de Senatus de Worcester sur la pénitence', *Recherches de théologie ancienne et médiévale*, 19 (1952), 203–24

Delhaye, Ph. and Talbot, C., eds., *Florilegium Moralium Oxoniense, Analecta Mediaevalia Namurcensia*, 5–6 (Namur–Lille, 1955–6)

De Mause, L., ed., *The History of Childhood* (London, 1976)

De Pommerol, M-H. J., *Bibliothèques ecclésiastiques au temps de la papauté d'Avignon*, I (Paris, 1980)

Denholm-Young, N., 'Feudal society in the thirteenth century: the knights', in his *Collected Papers on Medieval Subjects* (Oxford, 1946)

Desideri, Salverio, *La 'Institutio Traiani'*, Università di Genova, Facoltà di Lettere, Pubblicaziono dell'istituto di filologia classica, 12 (Genoa 1958)

Dickinson, J. C., *The Later Middle Ages* (London, 1979)

Dod, Bernard G., 'Aristoteles Latinus', in *The Cambridge History of Later Medieval Philosophy*, ed. Norman Kretzmann *et al.* (Cambridge, 1982)

Donat De Chapeaurouge, 'Selbstmorddarstellungen des Mittelalters', *Zeitschrift für Kunstwissenschaft*, 14 (1960), 135–46

D'Ordal, P. Norbert, ed., *Breviloqui*, Els nostres classics colleccio A, 28 (Barcelona, 1930)

Douie, D. L., *Archbishop Pecham* (Oxford, 1952)

Duby, G., *The Chivalrous Society*, trans. Cynthia Postan (London, 1977)
The Three Orders: feudal society imagined, trans. Arthur Goldhammer (Chicago, 1980)

Dunbabin, J., 'Aristotle in the Schools', in *Trends in Medieval Political Thought*, ed. B. Smalley (Oxford, 1965)
'Robert Grosseteste as translator, transmitter and commentator: the Nichomachean Ethics', *Traditio*, 28 (1972), 460–72

Bibliography

'The reception and interpretation of Aristotle's Politics', in *The Cambridge History of Later Medieval Philosophy*, ed. Norman Kretzmann *et al.* (Cambridge, 1982)

Durkan, J., and Ross, A., *Early Scottish Libraries* (Glasgow, 1961)

Emden, A. B., *A Biographical Register of the University of Oxford to A.D. 1500* (Oxford 1959)

   A Biographical Register of the University of Oxford A.D. 1501–1540 (Oxford, 1974)

   Donors of Books to St Augustine's Abbey Canterbury (Oxford, 1968)

Forni, A., 'Giocomo da Vitry, predicatore e "sociologo"', *Estratto da 'Le cultura'*, 17 (1980) 34–89

   'Kerygma e adattamento: aspetti della predicazione cattolica nei secoli XII e XIV', *Bullettino dell'Istituto Storico Italiano per il Medio Evo e Archivio Muratoriano*, 89 (1980–1), 261–348

Forrest, W. G., *A History of Sparta 950–192 B.C.* (London, 1968)

Gabriel, A. L., *Student Life at Ave Maria College, Mediaeval Paris* (Notre Dame, Ind., 1955)

Gargan, L., *Cultura e arte nel Venete al tempo del Petrarca* (Padua, 1970)

   Lo studio teologico e la bibliotheca dei Domenicani a Padova nel tre a quattrocento (Padua 1971)

Gautier, F., 'Trois commentaires averroistes sur l'ethique Nicomaque', *AHDLMA*, 21 (1948), pp. 187–336

Gautier, R. A., *Translatio Grosseteste textus purus*, Aristoteles Latinus, 26: 1–3, fasc. 3. (Leiden 1972)

Genet, J-P., *Four English Political Tracts of the Later Middle Ages*, Camden Society, Society, 4th ser., 18 (London, 1977)

Gilchrist, John, *The Church and Economic Activity in the Middle Ages* (London, 1969)

Glorieux, P., 'D'Alexandre de Hales à Pierre Auriol: la suite des maîtres franciscains de Paris au XIIIe siècle', *AFH,* 26 (1933), 257–81

   La Faculté des Arts et ses maîtres au XIIIe siècle (Paris, 1971)

   Répertoire des maîtres en théologie de Paris au XIIIe siècle (Paris, 1933)

Goff, F. R., *Incunabula in American Libraries: 3rd Census* (New York, 1964)

Gordon, D. J., ed., *Fritz Saxl: a volume of memorial essays,* (London, 1957)

Gottlieb, T., *Mittelalterliche bibliothekskataloge Deutschlands und der Schweiz* (Munich, 1918)

   Mittelalterliche Bibliothekskatalage Österreichs (Vienna, 1915)

   Ueber Mittelterliche Bibliotheken (Leipzig, 1890)

Grabmann, M., *Guglielmo di Moerbeke O.P., il traduttore delle opere di Aristotle* (Rome, 1946)

Grauert, H., *Magister Heinrich der Poet in Wurzburg und die römische Kurie* (Munich, 1912)

Gumbert, J. P., *Die Utrechter Kartauser Und Ihre Bücher* (Leiden, 1974)

Harriss, G. L., *King, Parliament and Public Finance in Medieval England to 1369* (Oxford, 1975)

Highet, G., *Juvenal the Satirist* (Oxford, 1954)

Humbert De Romans, *De Eruditione Praedicatorum*, Maxima Bibliotheca Patrum, 25 (Lyons, 1677)

Bibliography

Humphreys, K. W., *The Book Provisions of the Medieval Friars 1215–1400* (Amsterdam, 1964)

The Library of the Carmelites of Florence (Amsterdam, 1964)

The Library of the Franciscans of St Anthony at Padua at the Beginning of the Fifteenth Century (Amsterdam, 1966)

The Library of the Franciscans of Siena (Amsterdam, 1978)

Hunniset, R. F., *The Medieval Coroner* (Cambridge, 1961)

Hunt, R. W., 'English learning in the late twelfth century', *TRHS*, 4th ser. 19 (1936), 29–42

'The library of Robert Grosseteste', in *Robert Grosseteste, Scholar and Bishop*, ed. D. A. Callus (Oxford, 1963)

Hurnard, N. D., *The King's Pardon for Homicide before AD 1307* (Oxford, 1969)

Hyams, P. R., *Kings, Lords and Peasants in Medieval England* (Oxford, 1980)

James, M. R., *The Ancient Libraries of Canterbury and Dover* (Cambridge, 1903).

'The Catalogue of the library of the Augustinian friars at York, now first edited from the MS at Trinity College Dublin', in *Fasciculus J. Willis Clark dicatus* (Cambridge, 1909), pp. 2–96

Jayne, Sears, and Johnson, Francis R., *Catalogue of the Library of John Lord Lumley* (London, 1956)

John of Salisbury, *Policraticus*, ed. C. C. J. Webb, 2 vols. (Oxford, 1909)

John of Wales, For early printed editions see Appendix 5.

Florilegium de Vita et Dictis Illustrium Philosophorum et Breviloquium de Sapientia Sanctorum, ed. Lucas Waddingus (Rome, 1655)

Kaepeli, T., *Inventario de libri de S. Domenic di Perugia 1430–1480* (Rome, 1962)

'La bibliothèque de Saint-Eustorge à Milan à la fin du XVe siècle', *AFP*, 25 (1955), 5–74

Ker, N. R., *Medieval Libraries of Great Britain*, 2nd edn, (London, 1964)

'Oxford college libraries before 1500', in *The Universities in the Later Middle Ages*, ed. J. IJsewijn and J. Paquet (Louvain, 1978), pp. 309–11

Kibre, P., 'The intellectual interests reflected in the libraries of the fourteenth and fifteenth centuries', *Journal of the History of Ideas*, 7 (1946), 257–91

The Library of Pico della Mirandola (New York, 1936)

Kingsford, C., ed., *The Song of Lewes* (Oxford, 1890)

Kirschner, J., and Pluss, J., 'Two fourteenth century opinions on dowries, paraphernalia and non-dotal goods', *Bulletin of Medieval Canon Law*, new ser., 9 (1979), 65–77

Kleineke, W., *Englische Fürstenspiegel vom Policraticus bis zum Basilikon Doron Königs Jacob I* (Halle, 1937)

Kuttner, Stephan, 'Gratian and Plato', in *Church and Government in the Later Middle Ages: Essays presented to C. R. Cheney*, ed. C. N. L. Brooke, D. E. Luscombe, G. H. Martin and Dorothy Owen (Cambridge, 1976), pp. 93–118

Laarhoven, Jan van, 'Thou shalt *not* slay a tyrant! The so-called theory of John of Salisbury', in *The World of John of Salisbury*, ed. Michael Wilks (Oxford, 1984), pp. 319–42.

Labarge, M. W., *A Baronial Household of the Thirteenth Century* (Brighton, 1980)

Bibliography

Laistner, M. L. W., *Christianity and Pagan Culture in the Later Roman Empire* (Ithaca, NY, 1951)

Lambert, M. D., *Franciscan Poverty: The doctrine of the absolute poverty of Christ and the apostles in the Franciscan Order 1210–1323* (London, 1961)

Leland, J., *Collectanea*, ed. T. Hearne (London, 1715)

De Scriptoribus Brittanicis, ed. T. Hearne (London, 1715)

Lemoine, Michel, 'L'œuvre encyclopédique de Vincent de Beauvais', *Cahiers d'histoire mondiale*, 9 (1966), 571–9

Lerner, Robert E., 'Poverty, preaching and eschatology in the Revelation commentaries of "Hugh of St Cher"', in *The Bible in the Medieval World: Essays in memory of Beryl Smalley*, ed. Katherine Walsh and Diana Wood (Oxford, 1985), pp. 157–89

Leyerle, John, ed., 'Marriage in the Middle Ages' [Symposium], *Viator*, 4 (1973), 413–501

Liebeschutz, H., *Mediaeval Humanism in the Life and Writings of John of Salisbury* (London, 1950)

Little, A. G., *Eccleston's De Adventu Fratrum minorum in Angliam*, 2nd. edn (Manchester, 1951)

Studies in English Franciscan History (Manchester, 1917)

'The Franciscan school at Oxford in the thirteenth century', *AFH*, 19 (1926), 803–74

The Grey Friars in Oxford, Oxford Historical Society, 20 (Oxford, 1892)

Little, L. K., 'Pride goes before Avarice: social change and the vices in Latin Christendom', *American Historical Review*, 76:1 (1971), 16–49

Lyman, R. B., 'Barbarism and religion: late Roman and early medieval childhood', in *The History of Childhood*, ed. L. de Mause (London, 1976), pp. 75–99

McEvoy, J., *The Philosophy of Robert Grosseteste* (Oxford, 1982)

McFarlane, K. B., *The Nobility of Later Medieval England* (Oxford, 1973)

Maddicott, J. R., 'The Misc of Lewes, 1264', *EHR*, 98: 388, July 1983, 558–603

Manwood, *Treatise of the Lawes of the Forrest* (1598)

Manzalaoui, M. A., 'The Secreta Secretorum in English thought and literature from the fourteenth to the seventeenth century, with a preliminary survey of the origins of the *Secreta*', D.Phil. thesis, Oxford, 1954

Marks, R. B., *The Medieval MS Library of the Charterhouse of St Barbara in Cologne*, 2 vols. (Salzburg, 1974)

Markus, R. A., *Saeculum: History and Society in the Theology of Augustine* (Cambridge, 1970)

Marshall, P. K., Martin, Janet, and Rouse, R. H., 'Clare College MS 26 and the Circulation of Aulus Gellius 1–7 in Medieval England and France', *Mediaeval Studies*, 42 (1980), 353–95

Martin, C., 'Some medieval commentaries on Aristotle's *Politics*', *History*, 326 (1951), 29–44

Meinsma, K. O., *Middeleeuwsche Bibliotheken* (Zutphen, 1903)

Mercken, H. P. F., *Books 1–11 of Grosseteste's Translation of the Ethics* (Brussels, 1964)

Bibliography

Grosseteste's Translation of Greek Commentaries on Aristotle's 'Nichomachean Ethics' (Brussels, 1973)

Metlitzki, Dorothee, *The Matter of Araby in Medieval England* (New Haven–London, 1977)

Mollat, Michel, ed., *Etudes sur l'histoire de la pauvreté*, 2 vols. (Paris, 1974)

Momigliano, A., 'Notes on Petrarch, John of Salisbury and the *Institutio Traiani*', *Contributo alla storia degli studi classici*, Edizioni di storia e letteratura, 47 (Rome, 1955), 377–9

Moorman, J., *A History of the Franciscan Order* (Oxford, 1968)

Morris, J. E., *The Welsh Wars of King Edward I* (Oxford, repr. 1969)

Murray, A., *Reason and Society in the Later Middle Ages* (Oxford, 1978)

  'Religion among the poor in thirteenth century France', *Traditio*, 30 (1974), 285–324

Mynors, R. A. B., 'The Latin classics known to Boston of Bury', in *Fritz Saxl. A Volume of Memorial Essays*, ed. D. J. Gordon (London, 1957)

Nelson, B., *The Idea of Usury: From tribal brotherhood to universal otherhood* (Chicago–London, 1969)

Noble, Peter, Polak, Lucie, and Isoz, Claire, eds., *The Medieval Alexander Legend and Romance Epic: Essays in Honour of David J. Ross* (Millwood, NY, 1982)

Noonan, John T., Jr, *The Scholastic Analysis of Usury* (Cambridge, Mass., 1957)

Nortier, G., *Bibliothèques médiévaux des abbayes de Normandie* (Caen, 1966)

Ogilvie, R. M., *Early Rome and the Etruscans* (London, 1976)

Opie, I. and P., *The Lore and Language of Schoolchildren* (London, 1982)

Orlandi, S., *La Biblioteca di S. Maria Novella in Firenze del sec XIV–XIX* (Florence, 1952)

Orme, Nicholas, *Early British Swimming 55BC–AD 1719* (Exeter, 1983)

Owst, G. R., *Literature and the Pulpit in Medieval England*, 2nd edn (Oxford, 1961)

Pantin, W. A., 'John of Wales and medieval humanism', in *Medieval Studies Presented to Aubrey Gwynn S.J.*, ed. J. A. Watt *et al.* (Dublin, 1961), pp. 297–319

  The English Church in the Fourteenth Century (Cambridge, 1955)

Parkes, M. B., 'The influence of the concepts of *ordinatio* and *compilatio* on the development of the book', in *Medieval Learning and Literature: Essays presented to Richard William Hunt*, ed. J. J. G. Alexander and M. T. Gibson (London, 1976)

Pecugi, M., *La biblioteca di Monteripido* (S. Maria degli Angeli, 1976)

Pellegrin, E., *La Bibliothèque des Visconti et des Sforza, ducs de Milan au XVᵉ siècle* (Paris, 1955)

Petit-Dutaillis, Ch., and Lefebvre, G., *Studies and Notes Supplementary to Stubbs' Constitutional History* (Manchester, 1930)

Pézard, André, *Dans le sillage de Dante* (Paris, 1979)

Post, Gaines, 'Bracton as jurist and theologian on kingship', in *Proceedings of the Third International Congress of Medieval Canon Law, 1968* (Vatican City, 1971)

  'Philosophy and citizenship in the 13th century – laicisation, the two laws and 'Aristotle', in *Order and Innovation in the Middle Ages*, ed. William C. Jordan, Bruce McNab and Teofilo F. Ruiz (Princeton, NJ, 1976)

Bibliography

Powicke, F. M., *King Henry III and the Lord Edward: The community of the realm in the thirteenth century*, 2 vols. (Oxford, 1947)

Pratt, R. A., 'Chaucer and the hand that fed him', *Speculum*, 41 (1966), 619–42

Prestwich, M., *War, Politics and Finance under Edward I* (London, 1976)

Rawson, E., *The Spartan Tradition in European Thought* (Oxford, 1969)

Read, E. A., *The Cathedral Libraries of England* (Oxford, 1970)

Reeve, M. D., and Rouse, R. H., 'New light on the transmission of Donatus' "Commentarium Terentii"', *Viator*, 9 (1978) 235–50

Reuter, J., 'Petrus Alphonsi: an examination of his works, their scientific content and their background', D.Phil. thesis, Oxford, 1975

Reynolds, L. D., *The Medieval Tradition of Seneca's Letters* (London, 1965)

Reynolds, L. D., and Wilson, N. G., *Scribes and Scholars: A guide to the transmission of Greek and Latin literature,* 2nd edn (Oxford, 1968)

Rhodes, D. E., *A Catalogue of Incunabula in all the Libraries of Oxford University outside the Bodleian* (Oxford, 1982)

Ross, D. J. A., *Studies in the Alexander Romance* (London, 1985)

Rouse, R. H., 'Florilegia and Latin classical authors in twelfth and thirteenth century Orleans', *Viator*, 10 (1979), 131–60

'The early library of the Sorbonne', *Scriptorium*, 42 (1967), 42–71, 227–51

Rouse, R. H. and M. A., 'John of Salisbury and the doctrine of tyrannicide', *Speculum*, 42 (1967), 693–709

Preachers, Florilegia and Sermons: Studies on the Manipulus Florum of Thomas of Ireland (Toronto, 1979)

'The *Florilegium Angelicum*, its origin, content and influence', in *Medieval Learning and Literature*, ed. J. J. G. Alexander and M. T. Gibson (Oxford, 1976), pp. 66–114

'The medieval circulation of Cicero's *Posterior Academics* and the *De Finibus Bonorum and Malorum*', in *Medieval Scribes, Manuscripts and Libraries: Essays presented to N. R. Ker*, ed. M. B. Parkes and A. G. Watson (London, 1978), pp. 333–70

'The verbal concordance to the Scripture', *AFP* 44 (1974), 5–30

Rowland, Beryl, 'Classical and medieval ideas on the "Ages of Man"', *Poetica* (Tokyo), 3 (1975), 17–29

Medieval Woman's Guide to Health (Kent, Ohio, 1981)

Rubio y Lluch, A., *Documentos de la cultura Cataluna mig-Eval*, 2 vols. (Barcelona, 1908)

Russell, F. H., *The Just War in the Middle Ages*, Cambridge Studies in Medieval Life and Thought, 3rd ser. 8 (Cambridge, 1975)

Sanderus, Antonius, *Bibliotheca Belgica Manuscripta*, 1641 (repr. Brussels, 1972)

Schmitt, J-C., 'Le suicide au moyen âge', *Annales ESC*, 31 (1976), 3–28.

Schneyer, J. B., *Repertorium der lateinischen Sermones des Mittelalters für die Zeit von 1150–1350* (Münster, 1969)

Scholderer, J. V., 'The early editions of Johannnes Vallensis', reprint. from the *National Library of Wales Journal* (Aberystwyth, 1944)

Schulz, F., 'Bracton on Kingship', *EHR*, 60 (1945), 136–76

Smalley, Beryl, *English Friars and Antiquity in the Early Fourteenth Century* (Oxford, 1960)

Bibliography

'Moralists and philosophers in the thirteenth and fourteenth centuries', *Miscellanea Mediaevalia*, 1963, pp. 66–72.

Studies in Medieval Thought and Learning (London, 1981)

The Gospels in the Schools c.1100–c.1280 (London, 1985)

The Study of the Bible in the Middle Ages, 2nd edn (Oxford, 1952)

Southern, R. W., ed., *The Life of Anselm, Archbishop of Canterbury, by Eadmer* (Oxford, 1972)

Robert Grosseteste: The growth of an English mind in medieval Europe (Oxford, 1986)

Stegmüller, F., *Repertorium Biblicum Medii Aevi* (Madrid 1951–)

Steiner, A., ed., *Vincent of Beauvais: De Eruditione Filiorum Nobiliorum* (Cambridge, Mass., 1938)

'Guillaume Perrault and Vincent of Beauvais', *Speculum*, 8 (1933), 51–8

Stenton, D. M., *English Society in the Early Middle Ages,* 4th edn (Harmondsworth, 1965)

Stinissen, W., *Grosseteste's Ethics VIII–IX: Aristoteles over de Vriendschap* (Brussels, 1963)

Swanson, J. H., 'John of Wales and the Birmingham University MS 6/iii/19', *AFH* 76 (1983), 342–9

Sweet, J., 'Some thirteenth century sermons and their authors', *Journal of Ecclesiastical History*, 4 (1953), 27–36

Talbot, C. H., 'Notes on the library of Pontigny', *Analecta Sacri Ordinis Cisterciensis*, 10 (1954), 106–68

Taylor, Jerome, trans., *The Didascalicon of Hugh of St Victor* (New York, 1961)

Taylor, John, *The Universal Chronicle of Ranulf Higden* (Oxford, 1966)

Thiébaux, M., 'The medieval chase', *Speculum*, 42 (1967), 260–74

Thompson, J. W., *The Medieval Library* (New York, 1957)

Thomson, S. Harrison, 'Grosseteste's topical concordance of the Bible and the Fathers', *Speculum*, 9 (1934), 139–44

The Writings of Robert Grosseteste (Cambridge, 1940)

Turner, G. J., *Select Pleas of the Forest*, Selden Society, 13 (London, 1901)

Tuve, R., 'Notes on the virtues and vices', *Journal of the Warburg and Courtauld Institutes*, 26 (1963), 264–303

'Notes on the virtues and vices, part two', *Journal of the Warburg and Courtauld Institutes*, 27 (1964), 42–72

Ullman, B. L., and Stadter, P. A., *The Public Library of Renaissance Florence* (Padua, 1972)

Ullmann, W., 'John of Salisbury's *Policraticus* in the later Middle Ages', in *Festschrift F. H. Lowe. Geschichtsschreibung und geistiges Leben im Mittelalter* (Cologne–Vienna, 1978), pp. 524–5

Principles of Government and Politics in the Middle Ages, 3rd edn. (London, 1974)

Verbruggen, J. F., *The Art of War in Western Europe during the Middle Ages* (Amsterdam, 1977)

Vernet, A., and Genest, J-F., *La Bibliothèque de l'Abbaye de Clairvaux du XIIIe au XVIIIe siècle* (Paris, 1979)

Von Moos, Peter, 'The use of *exempla* in the Policraticus of John of Salisbury', in

Bibliography

The World of John of Salisbury, Studies in Church History, Subsidia 3, ed. M. Wilks (Oxford, 1984), pp. 207–61

Walsh, Katherine, and Wood, Diana, *The Bible in the Medieval World: Essays in memory of Beryl Smalley* (Oxford, 1985)

Webb, C. C. J., ed., *John of Salisbury's 'Policraticus'*, 2 vols. (Oxford, 1909)

Weisheipl, J. A., *Friar Thomas d'Aquino* (New York, 1974)

Wenzel, S., 'The Seven Deadly Sins: some problems of research', *Speculum*, 43 (1968), 3–10

The Sin of Sloth (Chapel Hill, NC, 1967)

Williams, Thomas Webb, *Somerset Medieval Libraries* (Bristol, 1897)

Wittlin, C. J., 'La "Suma de Colaciones" de Juan de Gales en Cataluna', *Estudios Franciscanos*, 72 (1971), 189–203

Zawart, A., OFM Cap., *The History of Franciscan Preaching and of Franciscan Preachers*, The Franciscan Educational Conference 9, 1927 (repr. from microfilm, 1971)

INDEX

Index

Index

Index

princes (and rulers) 41–62, 72–84, 88–9
Protagoras, example of 151
Ptolemy, *Almagest* 21, 198
Ptolemy Philadelphus 50
Publius Mimus 182
Pythagoras 180–81, 183

Quintilian 21, 23, 152, 165, 190, 198
Quintus Curtius 21
   Historia Alexandri Magni 61
quotations at second hand 17

Rabanus Maurus 19, 103
Rabbi Moyses 180n, 199
Ralph of Diss (de Diceto), *Abbreviationes
   Chronicorum* 25–6
Ranulf Higden, *Universal Chronicle* 204
rape of Lucretia 125, 159
Raymond de Cretiens 203n
Raymond de Pennaforte 119
   Summa de Casibus 36
Registrum Librorum Angliae 15, 38
religious life 154–8
Remigio Girolami 202–3
respublica (=state) 10, 47, 58, 65–73
Richard of Bury, Bishop of
   Durham 1333–45 9, 24, 26
Richard Fournival 10, 27–8, 34
Richard of Saint-Victor 199n
Robert of Cricklade 29
Robert Grosseteste 18, 37–8, 60, 61n,
   191
   Lyons Index 15, 30
   Translation of Nicomachean Ethics 7, 9,
     46, 62, 69, 105, 121–3, 140, 199
   Translation of ps.-Dionysian corpus 36
   Translation of the Suda 36
Robert Holcot 30, 191, 203
Robert Rypon of Durham 204
Roger Bacon 1, 23, 30–34, 191
   Opus Maius 7, 33–5
Roman triumph, moralisation of 46,
   50–1

Sallust 21–3, 90, 93, 104, 129, 139
Satyrus 21, 23, 190, 198
scholars 151–4
Scipio 22–3, 171
Secreta Secretorum 62, 78, 180n, 199, 205
Seneca 18, 29–34, 50, 52, 54, 60, 68, 70,
   90, 97, 102, 111–12, 118, 129–30,

133, 136, 148, 153–5, 169, 174–5,
   178n, 185, 189
Ad Elbiam 33, 104
Bioi 21
De Beata Vita 21, 33, 104, 198
De Beneficiis 21, 29, 61, 104, 121,
   139, 148, 165, 198
De Brevitate Vitae 7, 21, 33, 165, 198
De Consolatione ad Helviam 7, 33, 198
De Clementia 21, 29, 61, 76, 104, 139
De Consolatione ad Marciam 7, 33
De Constantia Sapientis 7, 21, 33, 61,
   104, 139, 198
De Ira 7, 21, 33, 61, 104, 139, 165,
   198
De Naturalibus Quaestionibus 21, 29,
   62, 104, 139, 165
De Providentia 7, 21, 33, 62, 139, 165,
   198
De Remediis Fortuitorum 21, 29
De Tranquillitate Animi 21, 33, 104,
   165, 198
De Virtutibus 21, 29
Epistulae 21, 29–34, 62, 104, 109,
   122–3, 139, 165, 198, 200
ps.-Seneca
   Proverbiae 21, 29, 104
Servius Tullius, example of 131
Silius Italicus 21, 23, 104
sin 2
society, divisions of 3
Socrates, example of 53, 97, 171, 175–
   6, 183
soldiery 92–4, 100–2
Solinus, *Collectanea Rerum
   Memorabilium* 21, 49, 62, 74, 104,
   115, 126, 140, 198
Solon, lawgiver of Athens 68–9, 170,
   173, 176, 183
Song of Lewes 83–6
Sorbonne Library, Paris 10, 27–8, 34–5,
   192
Sozomen 62
Spartans, example of 111, 152
   see also Leonides, Lycurgus,
     Thermopylae
state, – see respublica
Stoics 54, 182, 185
Suda 21, 178n, 199
   see also Robert Grosseteste
suicide 48, 55, 159
Suetonius 21
   Liber de Vitae Caesarum 104, 140
Sulpicius Severus 21, 165

306

Index

Taurus 182
Temporal power, limits upon 74
Ten Commandments 3
Terence 21, 23, 140
Tertullian 19, 198, 200
Thales Milesius 173
Thaurus 21–23
  Commentarium super Gorgias 23, 104
Themistocles, example of 170–1
Theodosian Code 104
Theodosius, emperor 50
Theophrastus 21, 180, 182
  Liber de Nupciis 23, 114, 140, 198
Thermopylae, battle of 51, 53, 79
Thomas Aquinas 1, 2, 7, 33, 56, 84, 192
  Commentary on Aristotle's
    Politics 33, 63
  De Studio 97n
  Summa Theologiae 122
Thomas à Becket 26
Thomas Eccleston 4
Thomas of Ireland, *Manipulus Florum* 3,
  27–8, 202–3
Thomas Ringstead 203
Titus, example of 171
Trajan, Roman emperor 50, 170
Trogus Pompeius, *see* Justin
Trojan horse, the 52
tyrants and tyranny 68, 79–84, 99–100,
  183

Ulysses, example of 171
Universities 1–2, 41
Urban IV, Pope 148n
usury 119–20

Valerius Maximus 18, 21, 23–4, 60, 62,
  75, 88–90, 102, 104, 111–12, 114–
  16, 121, 125, 130, 135, 140, 148,

  152, 155, 165, 175, 178n, 180n,
  189, 198
Varro 21, 23, 198
  Historia de Liberis Educandis 165
  Satires 140
Vegetius 18, 21, 24, 60, 88, 102
  De Re Militari 62, 92, 104
Velleius 23, 69, 104
vices 2–3, 10, 52
  seven curial 89–92, 100
Vincent of Beauvais 56, 128, 164, 180n,
  190, 192
  Speculum Maius 2, 3, 35–6, 199
Virgil 21, 23, 32
  example of 182
  Aeneid 62, 76, 104, 110, 140, 186, 198
  Eclogues 186
  Georgics 111, 140, 186
virtues 2–3, 41–61
Vitae Patrum 18–19, 119, 141, 154–5,
  166, 196, 200

Wales 4
Walter Burley 204–5
wealth 155–7
William of Auxerre 119
William of Auvergne, *Tractatus de*
  Universo 141
William of Conches 18
William of Malmesbury 25, 29
William of Moerbeke 7
women 124–6
Worcester. Franciscan custody of 4, 30–
  31

Xenocrates 180
Xerxes, Persian king 51, 113

Zeno, philosopher 53, 182, 184